# Organization Design

# Organization Design

Jay R. Galbraith
*The Wharton School*
*University of Pennsylvania*

**Addison-Wesley Publishing Company**
Reading, Massachusetts • Menlo Park, California
London • Amsterdam • Don Mills, Ontario • Sydney

ISBN 0-201-02558-2
ABCDEFGHIJ-MA-7987

To James D. Thompson

# Preface

This book like my first one, *Designing Complex Organizations,* is focused on choices of organization forms. The audience is primarily those people who will make the choices by which organizations will be designed. These people are the managers and employees who work or will work in these social forms. My purpose is to present a framework to aid these people in recognizing the ways by which their organization can be designed. The framework is to give people a language for creating alternative organization forms and for assessing the likely consequences of that form. The ultimate organization designers are those who have to make the design work.

Another purpose I have is to convince people that organizations can be designed and that they are the ones who design them. There are many views on these points. Some people view reorganization as something that is done to them every two years. Others write off organization entirely and focus on selecting a few good people. I view the options as being much richer than focusing only on boxes on the organization chart or only on an inner circle of people. We can change structure and people, but we also have options of changing reward systems, jobs, information technology, physical location, and numerous communication and decision processes. We need to be aware of these options rather than focusing only on part of the design. I see the design process as a continuous one of adjustment of rewards, processes, structures, and tasks. Good organization designs, like good theories, are those that last long enough until you get a new one. The design should continuously change as people and tasks change. The design decision should be made as routinely and with as much seriousness as schedule and budget decisions.

I have yet another reason for stressing that organizations can be designed. I do not believe that there are imperatives or inviolable relations between technology and structure or computers and structure to name a few possibilities. Organizations are what we want them to be. Computers can be used to centralize decisions or to decentralize decisions. The choice is ours. As I write this preface, I am aware of Blau's recent study (Blau *et al., Administrative Science Quarterly,* March, 1976) in which he and his colleagues report results consistent with some of Woodward's original findings and which again raises the technological imperative argument. I interpret these findings as a reflection on the managers in these plants as well as an indication of the possible impact of technology. My interpretation is that the managers in the sample *chose* to increase role specialization, decrease spans of control of first-line supervisors, etc. In so doing, they probably have discovered a viable social form. But I am aware of other managers designing automated, process technology plants in which role specialization is decreased. In these plants the span of control of the first-line supervisor is not decreased but the role of supervisor has been eliminated entirely. These forms are also viable. The managers wanted to do something different and have designed and are designing a social system to do it.

I do not want to give the impression that organization design is easy and we can do anything we want. We cannot. The new plants mentioned above are the result of years of experimentation with structures, rewards, and people. The purpose of this book is to present a framework for guiding choice among structures, reward systems, decision processes, etc. There are some forms that will not be viable. Our task is to identify the conditions under which certain forms are or are not viable.

A third purpose of this book is to take a first step at integrating the topics of organization behavior and organization structure or what are sometimes called micro and macro approaches. It seems that professionals in the field have drawn a distinction between the social psychological questions like reward systems design and training and development processes and those of organization structure. In part, this state is a reflection of the importation of psychologists and sociologists into schools of management following criticisms of our curricula by the Ford Foundation. However, the division of labor used by behavioral scientists does not reflect the nature of organization design choices. That division of labor has retarded the applicability of organization theory. The organization designer must simultaneously consider structure, rewards, tasks, and processes in order to create a viable package. I hope this book can stimulate some research aimed at integrating micro and macro approaches.

The research suggested above is needed. I have tried to put together a number of phenomena which have been separately conceived and researched. Quite often the pieces do not fit. I have forced them to fit anyway.

There will be some round pegs in square holes. My intention this time was to fill as many holes as possible. I would like help in finding and filling more holes more adequately.

The book only partially satisfies another objective. Organization design consists of two choices. The first is what kind of structure, process, and reward system package should we adopt. That question is addressed in this book. The second is how do we get from where we are to where we want to be. This is the organization change question, and it is not directly addressed. Often these are inseparable questions. If there is a next time, I will try to add this material.

I have tried to reduce the private sector, manufacturing bias that characterized my first book. I have not been completely successful. Public sector readers must still make translations into their domain.

In addition to the inadequacies mentioned above, there are others such as a lack of a section on new forms of organization or one on organizational effectiveness, whatever that means. However, my publisher has convinced me that one never finishes a book. One only arrives at a time when he or she is willing to let it go. After five years of trying, they have wrenched it from me. I would like to thank them for their understanding and persistence.

To continue with acknowledgements, I want to do more than acknowledge an intellectual debt to James D. Thompson. He is the one responsible for my focusing on organizations rather than computers. I was extremely fortunate to be able to take his doctoral seminar as he was writing *Organizations in Action*. The class discussions of each new chapter gave me an appreciation of the man as well as the material. I was greatly impressed with both. After that experience I changed career orientations, and I am still grateful. For this reason, I would like to dedicate this book to him.

Several others deserve my thanks and appreciation. Michel Kilduff started the typing when I was at M.I.T. Winnie Baker, Cindy Kee, and Joann Cohen from Wharton finished the typing and duplicating and said that they cannot wait to see the movie. My special thanks to Simone Attalah who typed the entire manuscript while I was in Brussels and who, despite the fact that English was her third language, made numerous editorial improvements. (The last statement was intended as a reflection on Simone's language ability rather than on mine.)

I also want to thank my family for sacrificing that night out or that trip to the beach while Dad worked on his book. I hope the appreciation of one's family support has not lost meaning because every author does it. It should not. Every author appreciates it.

*Philadelphia*                                                                                   J.R.G.
*January 1977*

# Contents

|                  | CHAPTER |
|------------------|:-------:|
| **INTRODUCTION** | **1**   |

It is customary to begin a book on organizations by acknowledging their pervasiveness. That custom will be followed here largely because organizations *are* pervasive. We spend most of our lives in some form of transaction with them as an employee, a customer, a client, a patient, a student, or an owner. One effect of this pervasiveness is that in these many transactions one is struck by the differences among organizations. Some are small while some are extremely large. Some are dynamic and always changing while others are stable and predictable. But most of all we are struck by variations in effectiveness of these organizations. By whatever criteria one might choose, these organizations exhibit wide differences in the degree to which they seem to accomplish their objectives. For example, our society was successful in organizing to create and operationalize a technology to put a man on the moon by 1970. Conversely, hardly anyone is satisfied with our ability to organize to rehabilitate individuals who exhibit criminal behavior.

There are several factors which can limit the effectiveness of any large-scale endeavor.[1] One factor is a *theoretical bottleneck*. That is, we do not know enough about a phenomenon in order to effect the desired changes. The dissatisfaction with the prison system may be due to deficiencies in the theories of psychology and psychiatry. In contrast, the theories of physics underlying the space program are relatively well developed.

A second limiting factor is a *resource bottleneck*. That is, the knowledge may be available to change people's behavior but the funds necessary for implementation may be lacking.

The third limiting factor is an *organizational bottleneck*. That is, we may possess the knowledge to solve a problem and have the funds to finance the project but may not be able to organize the resources in order to carry

1

out the problem-solving effort. It is this limiting factor that is addressed in this book. While it is often difficult to attribute the ineffectiveness to a particular limiting factor (e.g., all three are probably present in the prison situation), there are many situations where ineffectiveness is directly attributable to the lack of cooperative system of behaviors. Many a business firm has introduced a new product whose technology they had mastered and which was adequately funded only to see the effort founder as it passed through multiple departments on the way to the marketplace. It is rare to find a successful program of interdisciplinary research carried out in a university. Adequate funding is not the cause. A presidential task force, the Ash Council, suggested that the failure of some federal grant programs was due to a lack of interagency cooperation and centralization of decision power in Washington far removed from the actual problems. Other examples could be given relating to problems in public schools, hospitals, or prisons. The point, however, is that the limiting factor in achieving society's goals is quite often the manner in which resources are organized. In order to remove the limiting factor, we must identify the design variables and learn how to change them.

The objective of this book is to bring modern organization theory to bear on the problem of designing organizations. Therefore we must (1) identify the design variables which are controllable by the organization, (2) review what is known about the relationship between design variables and contextual variables, and (3) show how to use this knowledge. But before getting into the theory, there are several very basic questions that one might ask. Specifically, what is this thing called organization which may limit performance? What is organization design? Can organizations be designed? Why design them? Who should design them?

## WHAT IS ORGANIZATION?

The term organization and organization structure are terms everyone understands until he or she is asked to define them. Since the entire book is about designing organizations, some time, however short, should be taken to clarify the concept. As a beginning, it can be said that organization is that "something" which distinguishes any collection of 50 individuals in Kennedy International Airport from the 50 individuals comprising a football team in the National Football League. In the first case, the aggregation is no more than fifty times one individual. The football team, on the other hand, is something more than just 50 individuals.

A good way of defining organization and of understanding the contribution of organization to effective performance is to analyze the synthetic organization.[2] Synthetic organizations are organizations that arise after a disaster, such as a hurricane, flood, or earthquake, has struck a community.

When a major disaster strikes a community, the resources which are designed for disaster recovery operations are inevitably in short supply. Very quickly resources which are designed for other purposes are disengaged from their intended use and are adapted for disaster recovery operations, thus creating a problem of allocation of these new resources for disaster recovery operations. Thompson[3] describes the genesis of the synthetic organization which performs this resource allocation:

> Initial efforts at disaster recovery occur whenever resources and an obvious need or use for them occur simultaneously so there is not at this point highly organized effort. Instead there are a series of efforts, each isolated from the others. In a relatively short time, usually, two things happen to change this situation—to bring about a synthetic organization: (1) uncommitted resources arrive, and those who possess them seek a place to use them, and (2) information regarding need for additional resources begins to circulate. When knowledge of need and knowledge of resources coincide at a point in space, the "headquarters" of the synthetic organization has been established. Such headquarters only occasionally emerged around previously designated offices, indicating their power rests not on authority in any formal sense but upon the scarce capacity to coordinate. Only occasionally does this power fall to previously designed officers; rather authority to coordinate the use of resources is attributed to—forced upon—the individual or group which by happenstance is at the crossroads of the two kinds of necessary information—resource availability and need.

Several points are suggested by this analysis. First, organization emerges whenever there is a shared set of beliefs about a state of affairs to be achieved and that state of affairs requires the efforts of more than a few people. That is, the relationships among the people involved become patterned. The behavior patterns or structure derive from a division of labor among the people and a need to coordinate the divided work. Thus, a primary contribution of organization structure is to coordinate the interdependent subtasks which result from the division of labor. Second, the analysis and the points just made above introduce the essential attributes of organization and allow us to define what we mean by the term organization. We can say that organizations are (1) composed of people and groups of people (2) in order to achieve some shared purpose (3) through a division of labor (4) integrated by information-based decision processes (5) continuously through time. In a summary of definitions of organizations, Porter, Lawler, and Hackman[4] expand on the idea that organizations are

> . . . first and foremost, social entities in which people take part and to which they react. The second fundamental feature stresses the pur-

poseful, goal-oriented characteristic of organizations. This focuses our attention on the instrumental nature of organizations; that is, they are social instruments set up to do something. The third and fourth features concern the means by which organizations go about the process of trying to accomplish objectives. . . . There are two major types of methods that are seen as essential for this: the differentiation of functions and positions, and the deliberate, conscious, intendedly rational planful attempts to coordinate and direct activities. . . . Finally . . . a fifth basic feature: the continuity through time of the activities and relationships within organizations.

A third point suggested by the analysis is a question about design. If organizations emerge naturally, why should we design them? The primary reason is that design efforts can result in organizations which perform better than those which arise naturally. If the synthetic organization is evaluated on its performance, it would be rated as effective but inefficient. It is effective in that it gets the job done. Recovery operations are carried out. However, by economic criteria, it is inefficient. It requires more resources to accomplish its task than a designed organization would. The recovery operations are characterized by underutilization of resources and activities which sometimes work at cross-purposes. To avoid such problems, the ad hoc synthetic organization eventually gives way to civil defense and other formally designed organizations. These forms of organization make more efficient use of their resources in carrying out the recovery operations.

Another reason can be cited for the superiority of a designed structure. Most organizations in which we earn our livelihood are regarded by sociologists to be unnatural social units.[5] In the process of growing up, we learn the behaviors that are appropriate for the family and community situations which we face. On the other hand, appropriate task behaviors are not necessarily learned in the process of growing up. This is because organizations are more complex in terms of size and division of labor. They are very concerned about performance. In order to perform well, individuals must undertake unnatural and sometimes unpleasant behaviors. The situation is well stated by Etzioni[6] as follows:

The artificial quality of organizations, their high concern with performance, their tendency to be far more complex than natural units, all make informal control inadequate and reliance on identification with the job impossible. Most organizations most of the time cannot rely on most of their participants to internalize their obligations, to carry out their assignments voluntarily, without additional incentives.

Structures are designed to provide these additional incentives.

## WHAT IS ORGANIZATION DESIGN?

The concept of organization design results from a combination of our definition of organization and the concept of strategic choice.[7] Organization design is conceived to be a decision process to bring about a coherence between the goals or purposes for which the organization exists, the patterns of division of labor and interunit coordination and the people who will do the work. The notion of strategic choice suggests that there are choices of goals and purposes, choices of different organizing modes, choices of processes for integrating individuals into the organization, and finally a choice as to whether goals, organizations, individuals, or some combination of them should be changed in order to adapt to changes in the environment. Organization design is concerned with maintaining the coherence of these intertwined choices over time. The concept is shown schematically in Fig. 1.1. Let us look at the blocks in a little more detail.

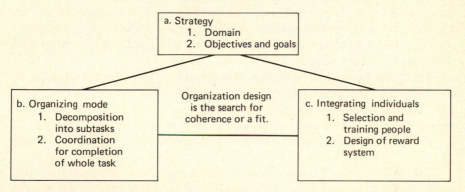

Fig. 1.1   Concept of organization design.

The first block (a) represents the choice of strategy. Strategy consists of two choices. The first is a choice of what will be the organization's distinctive competence or domain?[8] This choice determines which parts of the total environment are relevent for goal setting. The second is a choice of how to relate to the relevant elements in the environment and which specific goals will be pursued. Domain is determined by choices of (1) products/services to be offered (2) customers/clients to be served (3) technology to be utilized and (4) location at which work is to be performed. Collectively these four choices determine the boundaries of the organization or points at which the organization is dependent on others (investors, unions, customers, governments, clients, etc.) outside of the organization. The second part of strategy is the determination of how to relate to these others. These decisions result in the explicit or implicit objectives of the organization which are shared to varying degrees among the members who hold positions of influence. In the short run these objectives are translated into aspiration level goals.[9] Whether these goals are made explicit or not, it is assumed that there exists a level of goal attainment sufficiently low that the organization, or a part of it, is motivated to act. Collectively, these operational goals constitute the short-run task of the organization. Further discussion of domain, the choices about organization and domain, and the evidence concerning those choices will be discussed in Chapters 14 and 15.

The next choices concern the mode of organizing (b). The organizing mode consists first of choices as to how to decompose the overall task into subtasks which can be performed by individuals and groups of individuals. These subtasks can be centered around common client groups such as youth and adults in correctional organizations, around regions such as in state universities and the regional campus system, around technical specialties such as radiology and psychiatry in hospitals, etc. The other organizing choice concerns the means to reintegrate the subtasks into the completion of the whole task. Here there are choices of using the hierarchy of authority, rules, information systems, etc. A good portion of the book is concerned with the alternative organizing modes. These will be discussed along with cases in Chapters 3 through 13.

The third block (c) represents the choices of policies to integrate individuals into the organization. The task is to select people, design tasks, and arrange incentives so that individuals choose to perform those acts which produce the desired effect on the environment. These choices and the relevant empirical support are discussed in detail in Chapters 16 through 21.

The design problem is to bring about a coherence between these decision areas. This book presents a framework for identifying what are the alternatives in these choices, what are the policy variables, and what are the likely consequences of a change in that variable. The framework is based on an assumption that coherence is the primary determinant of success. Also coherence can be achieved in a multitude of ways. All the policy variables are both independent and dependent variables. It is assumed that there is no universally preferred form of organizing nor are there any organizing imperatives, such as a technological imperative, which directly determine the appropriate form. Instead there is a rich choice of actions to adjust strategies, structures, rewards, or some combination so as to create a viable form. However, not all combinations of strategy, structure, and reward systems are viable. Choice makes a difference. For example, a reward system that encourages competition between subordinates and a coordination mode that requires cooperation are not viable in combination. Thus, "It doesn't make any difference what you do, just so long as you do it well."

The task of organization design is to "do it well." Organization design is the continuous monitoring and assessing of the fit between goals, structures, and rewards; the creation and choice of alternative actions when there is no fit; and the implementation of the chosen design. This book concentrates mainly on the alternative creation process and the theories and empirical studies concerning these alternative forms. Subsequent chapters discuss these alternative organizing modes and reward systems.

### Is There a General Theory Relevant to a Specific Organization?

The problem for organizing design is whether there is a theory that has anything to say about a specific organization providing specific services at a specific point in time to specific clients in a specific location while employing a specific group of people. Is a general theory relevant to a specific organization? Every consultant who recommends a technique successfully used by General Motors, IBM, or TRW Systems invariably receives the reply, "Yes, but my problem is different." What if the client is correct? Let us address this question by using the diagram shown in Fig. 1.2.[10]

Fig. 1.2   Schematic of general and unique organizational aspects.

Assume that we can represent an organization by a circle. Figure 1.2 shows three organizations and also three different areas. The first, represented by the shaded area, is the intersection of all organizations. That means that on some dimensions every organization is like every other organization. For example, every organization has rules and procedures for handling recurrent activities. While some organizations have more rules and procedures than others, it is doubtful that there is an organization that has none. The second area, represented by parallel lines, contains dimensions in which an organization is like some organizations but unlike others. For example, some organizations have created the role of product manager while many others have no such role. Empirical studies show that this role emerges in industrial firms engaging in high levels of new product activity. Current theory development is concerned with constructing explanations about these similarities and differences through comparative studies.

The third area, represented by the unshaded, unlined portions, portrays those features that are unique to the specific organization. The unique personality of the leaders, the unique physical location, the unique history of development all create a combination of factors which are not found in any other organizations. These are the factors that cause managers to say "My problem is different." In many respects, their problems *are* different.

The critical question is, what is the relative importance of these three areas? If the unique third area is predominant, then organization theory has relatively little to say about organization design. Behavioral scientists should become process consultants to help managers who possess the unique information to design their own organizations. If areas one and two predominate, then the organization theorists have some expertise to bring to bear on organizational design questions. However, current theory cannot answer this question. It can be acknowledged that all three areas of Fig. 1.2 exist but their relative importance cannot be determined. Therefore it must be stated that the assumption on which this book is based is that the factors comprising areas one and two can account for about 50 to 75 percent of the variance in organizational form. This means that organization design efforts must combine the theoretical knowledge about organizations with the factors that are unique to the particular organization.

The assumption above needs some substantiation. Why does the author believe that a general theory can explain as much as 75 percent of the variance when organizations can be characterized by so many unique factors? First, some empirical studies report correlations explaining approximately 50 percent of the variance in some dimensions.[11] It is believed that the discovery of new contextual variables, of interaction effects, of new methodologies, and of dynamic theories will raise the proportion of explained variation on some issues. Second, not all of the unique features of organizations are relevant macrodesign choices. An analogous situation exists in chemistry. Much of the theory in chemistry rests on Dalton's atomic theory of matter which, among other things, proposed that atoms were indivisible. Currently physicists have discovered over 100 subatomic particles. However, this fact is not important to questions about how atoms combine to form elements and compounds. In similar fashion, it is hypothesized that unique locations, personalities, and histories are not as relevant to a question of whether product divisions or regional divisions are the most effective organizational forms as they are to questions of managerial style. Thus, even in the presence of apparent contradiction, generalizations can be valid. This is the reasoning that underlies the assumption.

## WHO SHOULD DESIGN THE STRUCTURE?

The question was partially answered in the preceding section. First, there is some abstract, theoretical knowledge that can be brought to bear on the issue. This expertise can be utilized in the form of internal staff or outside consultants. The remainder of this book is devoted to a presentation of the theory which underlies this expertise. However, the fact that the organization must also be designed around its unique features such as its people, its location, or its distinctive competence prevents the sole reliance on the outside expert. The people who perform the work are the ones who possess the information about the unique features of the organization. Design decisions require both outside and inside expertise. Recent advances in design technology make this combination feasible.[12]

In summary, it is assumed that a consciously designed structure based on the current theories of organization can improve the effectiveness of organizations because the best structure is not likely to evolve spontaneously out of human interactions over a reasonable time span. However, an organization cannot be designed without the people who are to operate within it. Participation of members is needed not only for acceptance of the new design but also to generate the new design which must take account of the many unique features of any specific organization.

## SUMMARY

This initial chapter has introduced the idea of organization design as a conscious, rational choice of the organization form to be used in the pursuit of specific objectives. It was conceived to be a continuous decision process to bring about coherence among people, organizing mode, and strategy. The assumptions underlying this approach were discussed. The remainder of the book is a presentation of a framework for creating and choosing among alternative actions for implementing this coherence.

In Chapter 2, previous research and points of view on organizing are reviewed with the purpose of articulating more completely the author's conception of designing organizations. Chapter 3 presents the framework on which the book rests. Subsequent chapters elaborate upon pieces of the framework, introduce empirical evidence where appropriate, and use case studies to illustrate how the approach can be used.

## NOTES

1. R. Walton 1969. Conflict management in interagency projects. Unpublished paper delivered at conference on Matrix Organizations and Project Management at M.I.T., May.
2. J. D. Thompson 1967. *Organizations in action.* New York: McGraw-Hill, pp. 52–54.
3. *Ibid.,* p. 52.
4. L. Porter, E. Lawler III, and R. Hackman 1975. *Behavior in organizations.* New York: McGraw-Hill, pp. 69–71.
5. A. Etzioni 1963. *Modern organizations.* Englewood Cliffs, N.J.: Prentice-Hall, Chapter 6.
6. *Ibid.,* p. 59.
7. J. Child 1972. Organization structure, environment and performance: the role of strategic choice. *Sociology,* January: 1–22.
8. Thompson, Chapter 3.
9. R. Cyert and J. March 1963. *A behavioral theory of the firm.* Englewood Cliffs, N.J.: Prentice-Hall, Chapter 3.
10. This scheme was suggested by John Dutton at the Kiev Seminar on Organization Design, Kiev, USSR, May 29–June 2, 1972.
11. D. S. Pugh, D. J. Hickson, C. R. Hinings, and C. Turner 1969. The context of organization structure. *Administrative Science Quarterly* 14: 91–114.
12. W. McKelvey and R. Kilman 1975. Organization design: a participative multivariate approach. *Administrative Science Quarterly,* March: 24–36.

## QUESTIONS

1. What are the differences between formal organizations and synthetic organizations?

2. What advantages do formal organizations, with designated roles and authority relations, have over spontaneous or synthetic organizations?

3. Explain the concept of strategic choice and how it applies to choices of organization structure and process.

4. What are the features of organizations that make them unique?

| APPROACHES TO ORGANIZATION DESIGN | CHAPTER 2 |
|---|---|

In this chapter we will review previous approaches to designing organizations with the purpose of more completely defining the one to be followed in this book. Our objective in the review will be to identify the dimensions of organization which require choice, i.e., the policy variables, the controllable variables or the knobs to be turned and the levers to be thrown. In other words, design requires that we first discover those things that we can do something about. By tracing the history of inquiry into organizations, we can discover those factors which require choice.

The design of organizations is not new. As a matter of fact, every organization is designed. It is the conscious, continuous planning of the organization that may be different. What is also new is the sustained interest in accumulating a body of public knowledge about organizations and organizing. This accumulation began at about the turn of the century. This is about the time that large organizations other than the church and the military began to appear. Most of the management theorists are referred to as belonging to the Classical School of Management. The early theorists tended to be practitioners who took the time to record what they did. Their prescriptions were collected to form the principles of management and eventually the process of management.[1] Most of their thinking was directed to questions of choosing an organizing mode.

A second stage of inquiry began in the 1930s and grew out of the Hawthorne studies.[2] The work of the theorists during this stage had a distinct empirical flavor in contrast to that of the management theorists. The theorists of the second stage are probably best known as belonging to the Human Relations School. They varied from earlier theorists in their focus of attention. These theorists were concerned more with motivation and integrating the individual and organizational interests than with organizing modes. They have contributed to our ability to design reward systems.

A third stage, consisting of several schools of thought, began in the 1940s. This stage is concerned with information and decision processes. It consists of at least two groups emphasizing different but complementary ideas. One group suggested that much of what takes place in organizations reflects people's limited ability to process information and make decisions while the other stressed the potential of rationalizing decision processes through operations research and the use of computers to expand our limited computational capacities.[3] These theorists contributed to our knowledge about coordinating the divided functions of work.

Finally there were some who said that the key to organization is people, not structure, computers, and planning processes. This last diverse group cannot be considered a school of thought nor a stage of inquiry. It probably has gone through several stages itself. It consists first of practitioners, aided by industrial psychologists, who believe the key problem is to sort through numbers of people to find the good ones and put them in positions of influence. Then there are others who are interested in changing the people themselves through a number of processes referred to as socialization processes.[4] The common thread is the focus on individuals and changing individuals, as a means of integrating the individual's and the organization's interests.

The most recent stage of inquiry is characterized by attempts to integrate these various approaches. There is no emphasis on any one factor but an emphasis on establishing a coherence between structure, decision process, reward systems, and people. Let us develop each of these policy areas more completely by reviewing the work of the theorists in each of the approaches outlined above.

## CLASSICAL MANAGEMENT THEORY

The classical school of management thinking arose from the scientific management movement of the early 1900s. It began with the contributions of practitioners who took the time to write about their experiences. This practitioner dominance was their strength and their weakness. It gave them an orientation to design, practical relevance, and operationality on the one hand accompanied by a lack of an empirical orientation with which to purge the error from their theories on the other. The review of the classical school will be more extensive here because of this design orientation. It is a good introduction to the design problem. Other theories will be more extensively reviewed in various chapters throughout the book.

## Division of Labor

The organization design problem as conceived by the classical theorists begins with the division of labor; that is, the task of the organization has to be divided into subtasks and each subtask has to be assigned to an individual. While there are several ways to divide a task, it was usually recommended to divide the work so that the portions be differentiated rather than similar, and that each individual have a small portion of the overall task. This scheme is contrasted in Fig. 2.1 with another scheme where each individual has the whole task. If the task is making shoes, Fig. 2.1a represents a work breakdown where each individual performs the whole task from cutting leather to final polishing and preparation. Alternatively the work breakdown in Fig. 2.1b assigns only one-fifth of the whole task to an individual. In this scheme each individual specializes in cutting, assembling, polishing, etc. This is referred to as the horizontal division of labor. The division of labor in Fig. 2.1b is hypothesized to be more productive because it overcomes physical limitations and the cognitive, knowledge limitations of people. Each individual could become more skillful at a smaller task. Thus with the same labor input, greater output was obtained with specialization.[5] Adam Smith's description of pin manufacturing is the classic illustration of the effects of the division of labor. He observed one factory where ten workers produced as many as 48,000 pins per day. This was accomplished by breaking the task into subtasks such as straightening the wire, cutting the wire, etc. If each worker had to make the whole pin alone, each could only produce around 20 pins a day. Thus division of the task into 10 subtasks increased the output 240 times.

After reading Adam Smith's description, one is usually led to ask the question, "Why stop at 10?" If a division of the task into 10 subtasks increased output 240 times, why not divide it into 20 subtasks? or 50? or 100? If a little division of labor is good, would not more be better? Thus one is led to ask if there is a limit to the division of labor. The answer is, yes, there is a limit. It was Adam Smith who stated that the division of

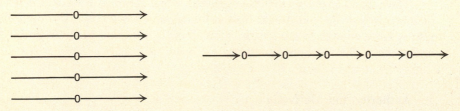

(a)  Each worker performs whole task.          (b)  Each worker performs one-fifth of task.

Fig. 2.1   Alternative bases for division of labor.

labor is limited by the extent of the market. Thus, if the volume of activity is not sufficiently high, among other things, fractional usages of specialized resources would offset the economies of greater skill. The trade-off has been analyzed more recently with identification of some other limiting factors.[6] But the analysis still assumes that the factors limiting productivity are physical, technological, and cognitive.

Another effect of the division of labor is to increase the interdependence among the subtasks. In the case of Fig. 2.1a, there is a minimum of interdependence. The output of the organization is little more than the sum of the outputs of each individual worker. If one of the workers should fail to show up, the output would be reduced by one-fifth. In the case of Fig. 2.1b, the interdependence is much greater. If a worker fails to show up or produces defective work, there is no output at all. The increased interdependence creates problems of coordination and a need for reliability.

The most common response to the need for coordination was the vertical division of labor. That is, a new role, a managerial role, was evolved to handle the problems of coordination. The work was divided between those who physically performed the work and those who coordinated the work flow between interdependent, specialized work roles. Thus the horizontal division of labor must meet the economic constraint of increasing output by an amount sufficient enough to pay for someone who does none of the work but must be present to coordinate the work.

The division of labor, and in particular the vertical division, created two new problems that the theory had to answer. The first problem was the possibility of motivational limitations on efficiency. Once the task has been divided into pieces and the planning and control decisions taken away, have we not created a situation which deprives individuals of any personal work satisfaction? What will motivate them to assume such roles and devote their time and energy to the subtask? If decisions are made by individuals who do not perform the work, why will the doers adopt behaviors selected for them by others? This is the problem that is created by separating the planning and the doing.

The second problem that is suggested when there is a vertical division of labor is how do you divide up the managerial work when the organization is large enough to have many managers? Let us turn to these problems and some of the suggested solutions.

## Authority and Motivation

Prior to the industrial revolution, individuals were motivated to work primarily by identification with the work itself. In some societies individuals took their surnames based upon their work. Names such as Baker, Carpenter, Cooper, Smith, Mason, and Weaver all come from this source. After the application of the division of labor, the individual performed only a piece of the work and was not responsible for major decisions. This state of affairs made it difficult to identify with the work and to be personally responsible for it. The classical approach to the motivational problem was the offering of financial incentives and the application of authority. If the division of labor resulted in greater output, then the organization should share the fruits with the employees by providing greater incomes for them. (The emergence of labor unions might suggest that this did not always happen.) In the case of piece-rate incentives, there was an attempt to directly link each individual's performance to the individual's output. The better the work performance, the greater the income for the individual and the organization. But quite often employees were expected to do their best in exchange for wages.

The other solution to the motivation problem was the application of authority. The managerial role which evolved was not simply another role equal to the other doing roles. The managerial role was given authority over the other roles. Authority was conceived to be "... the right to give orders and the power to exact obedience...."[7] This concept of authority views it as something to pass to the manager. The right to expect obedience inheres in the state or in the institution of private property. The owners or government merely pass on this right to the manager but hold him or her responsible for its use and accountable for results of the organization. The manager was also given the power to make promotions, grant raises, and dismiss inefficient or lax workers. The power of authority and power of reward and punishment was believed to be a solution to the problem of separation of the planning and doing.

## Hierarchy of Authority

It is almost impossible to find an organization that does not create separate and distinct managerial roles and which does not define a power difference between them and the roles of the workers. Thus, every large organization is faced with choices as to how to divide up the managerial work. This is the second issue created by the vertical division of labor.

One of the first theories as to how to divide managerial work was Frederick Taylor's functional foremanship.[8] His prescriptions were based on the same logic that he applied to the division of labor for workers. If specialization was good for the workers, then why not apply it to the task of management itself? He postulated that a single individual could not know enough about machine maintenance, quality control, inspection, materials, schedules and machine speed, product routings, etc., to make good decisions on all these issues. Therefore, for each of these functions there should be a foreman responsible for making these functional decisions. In this way the organization could maximize the expertise brought to bear on each decision area. His model is depicted schematically in Fig. 2.2.

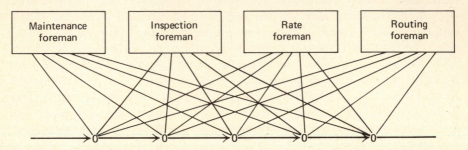

Fig. 2.2   Taylor's functional foremanship.

Few of Taylor's peers disagreed that specializing the management role would maximize the expertise that could be brought to bear on decisions facing the organization. However, virtually none of them agreed with the multiple authority relations which would necessarily follow if the decisions of the specialists were to be translated into the behavior of the workers. Since authority was so essential to the solution of the motivation problem, its exercise was recommended to be as clear and unambiguous as possible. The preferred clarity of authority relationships was stated in the form of two design principles of management theory. The first was the unity of command. In its original version the principle stated that no member of the organization should receive directives from more than one superior. As modern organizations have gotten more complex, theorists recognized that employees are always subject to multiple influences. However, if faced with conflicting pressures, the individual should have a single superior to whom he or she could go and have the conflict resolved.

If the principle of unity of command was applied to each role in the organization, a second principle, the scalar principle, necessarily followed. This principle stated that authority should flow in a clear, unbroken line from the role of chief executive to the lowest worker. Applied throughout the organization this principle led to a chain of command and the representation of the organization as a pyramid referred to as the hierarchy of authority. The hierarchy is shown in Fig. 2.3 with each position subject to superior-subordinate relationships. Each role except the top is obliged to follow the directives emanating from the role superior to it. Each role, except those of the workers, is obliged to issue directives to coordinate the work of the roles which are subordinate to it. In this way no role is left uncoordinated.

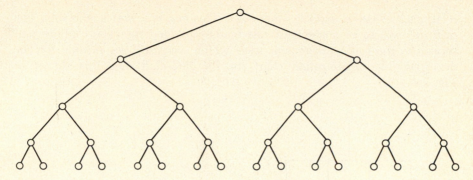

**Fig. 2.3 The hierarchy of authority.**

The conception of the organization as a hierarchy of authority relations created a new design choice. The question is how many subordinate roles can a supervisor coordinate. This is the question of span of control. On the one hand the cognitive limits of human beings would suggest that the number of subordinates should be kept to a minimum. There must be a limit to the number of employees whose work can be coordinated. On the other hand, the smaller the span, the greater the number of nonproductive roles that must be offset by the greater efficiency generated by the division of labor. There was a great deal of debate but very little empirical analysis on the question until very recently. This research will be reviewed later in another context.

The unity of command and scalar principles were fundamental to the classical theory. Their prominence underlies the importance of authority as the basis for coordination of interdependent work roles and for motivating the acceptance of managerial decisions by subordinates. Following the example of church and military organization structures, the classical theorists choose authority based on rank over authority based on expertise or age, to the extent that they differed. The choice of unity of command over managerial role specialization still left the question of how to bring expertise to bear on complicated managerial decisions. The solution recommended by the classical theorists was the line–staff model of organization.

### Line–Staff Organization

The choice facing the organization designer appeared to be one between an organization which maximized expertise and confusion and irresponsibility and one which maximized clarity, responsibility, and accountability, but made little use of expertise. But rather than choose between the alternatives of a dilemma, the solution was to evolve a new role and define authority relations between it and the other roles. This new role was a staff role. The staff role was to be a specialist role which provided the expert advice and service to the line management roles which were still responsible for the decisions. The organization chart for the line–staff model is shown in Fig. 2.4.

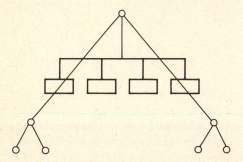

**Fig. 2.4 Line–staff model of organization.**

However clear the distinction between line and staff was to the theorists, it was never clear in practice.[9] The relations were continually redefined as was the concept of unity of command as indicated previously. There were many attempts to partition the decision domain into independent subparts. For example, the staff specialist was responsible for questions about how to do something and the line manager was responsible for questions of what and when to do something. If there was a conflict between the line and staff or between different staff directives, there was a line manager to resolve the conflict. More and more the hierarchy of authority became a route of appeal for conflict resolution. But the intent was always the same. It was felt that areas of responsibility and authority should be partitioned into independent subparts for which a single individual could subsequently be held accountable. Problems and conflicts were to be solved by greater clarity and definition of areas of authority. In trying to work out solutions to the partitioning of authority, the theorists encountered two more design decisions—centralization and departmentalization.

## Centralization

The line–staff model shown in Fig. 2.4 is not the only possible structure. Another is shown in Fig. 2.5. It depicts a line–staff structure with the staff units reporting to line managers at a lower level. The model in Fig. 2.4 was effective because it brought all experts together in a single place and

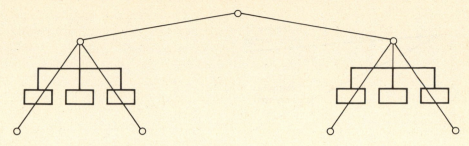

**Fig. 2.5   Decentralized line–staff model.**

they could apply their expertise with a global perspective and minimize the number of experts needed. But when there was variation in the nature of the subtasks, it was better to bring decision-making authority down to lower levels even though duplication resulted. Thus, organizations in which decisions were made at the top were called centralized. Those in which authority was distributed to lower levels were to exhibit varying degrees of decentralization. Thus centralization–decentralization refers to the vertical distribution of power associated with the vertical division of labor.

It was recognized by the classical theorists that centralization was not good or bad per se. Rather the degree of centralization depended on the situation.

> The question of centralization-decentralization is a simple question of proportion. It is a matter of finding the optimum degree for the particular concern.[10]

The basis for choosing the optimum degree of centralization was to identify those factors which were relevant, determine their importance in a particular situation, weigh the pros and cons, and make a judgmental decision. This approach to design questions was typical of the classical theorists. Various theorists developed lists of pros and cons and, through an adversary process of written debate, refined the knowledge that could be brought to bear on questions of centralization.

Currently attempts are being made to measure the degree of centralization in particular contexts. One of the measures is the slope of the line in Tannenbaum's control graph.[11] The graph for two hypothetical organizations is shown in Fig. 2.6.

While dealing with questions of centralization, the theorists found that design choices about the distribution of power and authority were not independent of design choices about how the managerial work was divided. If decision making was decentralized, the theorists faced the problem of fragmented, noncoordinated decisions. But if the work was divided into

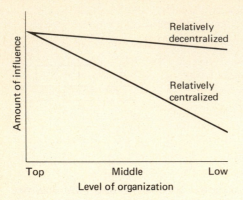

Fig. 2.6   The control graph.

self-contained units, decisions in one unit would not have a direct impact on another. Thus, design choices about centralization must be made with design choices about departmentalization.

### Departmentalization

Once the work has been divided, the problem is to aggregate work roles to form groups, units, departments, and divisions. The grouping decision is referred to as the departmentalization problem. The classical treatment of the design choice is usually credited to Luther Gulick.[12] He suggested that each role could be characterized by four attributes, any one of which could become the basis for aggregation into departments.

It will be found that each worker in each position must be characterized by:

1. The major *purpose* he is serving, such as furnishing water, controlling crime, or conducting education;

2. The *process* he is using, such as engineering, medicine, carpentry, stenography, statistics, accounting;

3. *The persons or things* dealt with or served, such as immigrants, veterans, Indians, forests, mines, parks, orphans, farmers, automobiles, or the poor;

4. The *place* where he renders his service, such as Hawaii, Boston, Washington, the Dust Bowl, Alabama, or Central High School.

Where two men are doing exactly the same work in the same way for the same people at the same place, then the specifications of their jobs will be the same under 1, 2, 3, and 4. All such workers may be easily combined in a single aggregate and supervised together. Their work is homogeneous. But when any of the four items differ, then there must be a selection among the items to determine which shall be given precedence in determining what is and what is not homogeneous and therefore combinable.

A few illustrations may serve to point the problem. Within the city of New York, what shall be done with the doctor who spends all of his time in the public schools examining and attending to children in the Bronx? Shall we (1) say that he is primarily working for the school system, and therefore place him under the department of education? (2) say that he is a medical man, and that we will have all physicians in the department of health? (3) say that he is working with children, and that he should therefore be in a youth administration? or (4) say that he is in the Bronx and must therefore be attached to the Bronx borough president's office? Whichever answer we give will ignore one or the other of the four elements characterizing his work.[13]

As with many other nonempirical classification schemes, subsequent theorists expand[14] and contract[15] the basic list to increase generality or reduce ambiguity. The preference in this book is for a three-way categorization around input resources, outputs, and physical location. The last one, that is, physical geographic location, is unambiguous but the input and output categories are not. There are many subcategories for each which vary with the particular context in which the organization exists. There can be several output categories of product (nylon), market (textiles), and clients or customer (government). Similarly work can be grouped around input resources such as type of function (accounting), technical specialty (electronics), or process (drilling). The input categories reflect the professional and occupational training structure in the larger society. While the categories are admittedly still ambiguous, there remains a choice of attributes for grouping. The attributes will change in a given situation but how does one choose? What is the difference between a project organization and one based on technical specialty?

The classical theorists handled the choice of attributes in the same manner as the choice of degree of centralization. The alternatives were identified as being function, product, geographical location, etc.; the pros and cons of each attribute were listed; the importance of each pro and con was determined in the particular situation; and a judgmental decision was made. However, the departmentalization choice was more complex because there were more alternatives, the alternatives may or may not conflict in any situation, and a choice had to be made at each level of the hierarchy. More discussion of this choice is postponed until Chapter 6.

### Summary: Classical Theorists

In summary, the classical theorists invented a language for talking about organization structure and identified the design choices which have to be made for any organization. They started with the *division of labor* which had been discussed for years by the economists. They noted that the division of labor had two effects. It increased the amount of production per worker, but it also increased interdependence necessitating a need for coordination among the interdependent work roles. The need for coordination was handled by inventing new roles, managerial roles, to handle these questions. The design issue was: How many managerial roles are needed for a given size work force? The answer to this question is determined by choices of span of control and the number of staff experts employed. Currently these issues are referred to as the shape or *configuration* of the organization. They are measured by average spans of control and the ratio of managers and staff to total personnel. Once a configuration is determined, there are questions of the *distribution of power* and authority. The vertical distribution was the question of centralization but there is also an issue of lateral influence which was dealt with in the line–staff authority definition. Finally, there is the choice at each level of the departmental structure. This was the *departmentalization* problem.

Finally, the classical theorists also recognized that the separation of planning and doing created motivational problems. Therefore, they did some thinking about the organization's human system or, more precisely, the reward system. Most attention was focused on authority as the basis for achieving compliance with directives. Thus, *leadership* was a primary variable to be determined by the designers. They also relied heavily on extrinsic rewards of monetary *compensation* and *promotion* based on performance to round out the reward system.

Thus, the classical theorists identified several key variables with which we can expand our design schematic as shown in Fig. 2.7. Recall that the task of the organization consisted of the short-run goals which are determined by the strategy choices. In order to meet these goals, the organization must choose an organizing mode consisting of a division of labor, a configuration, a distribution of power, and a departmental pattern. Further, in order that individuals choose to perform behaviors leading to the accomplishment of the goals, a reward system is chosen consisting of a compensation system, a promotion basis, and a leader style to implement the authority vested in the organization.

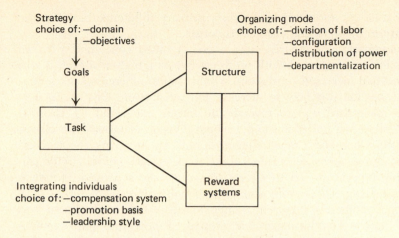

Fig. 2.7   Organization design choices of the classical school.

## THE HUMAN RELATIONS SCHOOL

The second stage of inquiry was triggered by the Hawthorne studies.[16] This stage is characterized by an interest in informal or humanistic organization, rather than in mechanistic organization, and by an empirical orientation as opposed to a conceptual one. In part, it was a reaction against the apparently rigid reliance upon the hierarchy and the unsystematic theory-building methods of the classical theorists. The substance of this approach will constitute a basis for the subsequent chapters on reward systems; therefore, this chapter will present enough content to be illustrative of the approach and to introduce the design variables used by organization designers identified with this approach.

The Hawthorne studies triggered the interest in what became known as the human-relations approach. In these studies, variations in performance could neither be explained by cognitive or physical factors nor could they be explained by wage incentives or authority. Instead the researchers suggested that the relations among group members and between the group members and the supervisor were the critical variables. After a vast amount of empirical research, Likert has elaborated upon and become a proponent of just that position.[17] The formation of cohesive groups led by considerate, supportive leaders who link the group with other groups lies at the heart of Likert's ideal organization. The key design variable is the behavior of the leader. However, instead of being the one who gives orders and exacts obedience, the leader in this approach is employee-oriented, supportive, and considerate. The leader allows employees themselves to exercise influence over what goes on in their groups. Thus, it was not the importance of, but the *style of,* leadership that was a primary difference between the human-relations theorists and classical theorists.

The human-relations theorists also were as much concerned with an individual's job satisfaction as with productivity. As a matter of fact, it was hypothesized that increased satisfaction would result in increased productivity. So the question was how to increase job satisfaction. One of the key policies in this regard was to reverse the trends advocated by classical theorists of increased horizontal and vertical division of labor. The classic experiment by Coch and French suggested that by involving the workers in planning the changes concerning their work, greater productivity can result.[18] This experiment led to efforts to reduce the separation between planning and doing. There were also calls for job enlargement rather than fractionation.[19] Thus, the research seemed to suggest that *job design* was a powerful motivator and a means for integrating individual and organizational interests. In addition it was the democratic, supportive leader that was to be the primary vehicle for implementing this approach by involving subordinates in their work.

In addition to looking in different places for explanations of organizational effectiveness, the researchers in this area continued to study the design variables of the classical school but from an empirical point of view. Large numbers of social psychologists and industrial psychologists have studied performance appraisal schemes, compensation practices, etc. The result has been a more balanced approach to these design variables.

In summary, the research that followed from the Hawthorne studies added to the list of design variables and both modified and reinforced some of those of the classical school. Our concept of organization design can be expanded to include these areas of choice.

## INFORMATION AND DECISION PROCESSES

Two separate lines of inquiry have focused on information and decision processes in organizations. One is the Barnard, Simon, March, and Cyert or Carnegie-Mellon School.[20] These theorists suggested that much of what goes on in organizations is decision making and information processes and that these processes are reflections of people's limited ability to process information. This approach is, on the one hand, crucial to the development of this book and, on the other, not very valuable to organization design. It is crucial because the information-processing approach is the foundation of this book's framework. So this point of view will prevail throughout the text. But at the same time, theorists of the Carnegie-Mellon School have had a limited impact on design choices because, with a few exceptions, they never attempted to be normative or make prescriptions based on their theories. This book is an attempt to do so.

The other line of inquiry is that associated with the new information technology. This group of researchers began working on management problems after their apparent success at tackling military problems via the scientific method during World War II. The line of inquiry was given impetus during the 1950s and 1960s by the widespread use of computers and an interest in using them fully. This combination led to a belief that there would be a "new science of management decision."[21]

Initially the thought was that decision making could be improved through the use of operations research/management science. Decision making had always been improved by selecting and promoting those who appeared to make better decisions than others and through the provision of staff specialists. The operations research/management science approach had such goals as improving decision making by rationalizing the process, formulating the decision problem as a mathematical problem, and testing alternatives on the model before real world implementation. This approach modified or provided new *mechanisms for decisions* such as computers and various man-computer configurations. The improved decisions were to result from greater knowledge of the decision problem and from a more comprehensive treatment of the problem by exploiting the information processing power of the combination of mathematics and computers.

Through the use of such tools as linear programming, it was discovered that operations researchers were not dealing with decision processes but rather with information and decision processes.[22] Most of the work in implementing any operations research technique was devoted to collecting data. Therefore an effort was made to collect decision information systematically. This collection usually led to a *formalization* of the information system by creating categories and coding schemes. The formalized data were then fed into the decision process.

The collections of data were called data bases. Once formalized data were collected in the form of a data base they could be transmitted almost anywhere, at a cost to be sure, to any decision maker. Thus, the *scope of the data base* used by decision makers became a design variable. If properly collected and transmitted, the data base could permit visibility of upstream and downstream effects of choices to be made.

The last design variable arose because even a computer-assisted decision scheme supported by a data base was of little use if the information in it was not current or if managers did not have access to the computer at the moment they felt a decision was required. This problem has led to an interest in time-shared computers and "on-line," "real-time" systems. The design variable is the *frequency* of data collection and decision making.

In summary, the information and decision process approach has produced four additional design variables. One has a choice of the *decision mechanism* to be used in choosing an alternative, of the *degree of formalization* of the data to be used in decision making, the *scope of the data base,* and finally the *frequency* with which the system produces decisions. All are design variables which exist to various degrees in all organizations. These have been added to our expanding concept of organization design which is shown in Fig. 2.8. The choices of information and decision processes are part of the choice of organizing mode. In addition, the lines between the other choices indicate that these choices are dependent on each other.


## THE PEOPLE APPROACH

This last approach brings together a disparate group who share a common focus in improving organizations—people. There are differences in the means for changing the people variable. One approach advocates moving people in and out of positions while the other focuses on changes to the individuals themselves.

The first group is usually led by practitioners who believe that the key to organizational effectiveness is to find the good people and get them into positions of power. These people consider *selection* as the key design variable. They are joined by industrial psychologists who have conducted a great deal of research on selection criteria. The entire career system or people movement system becomes a design decision. Through selection and self-selection, *promotion,* and *transfer,* a better match between job and individual can be attained. Thus, to the extent that people are mobile and the career system is controllable, these areas become design decisions.

Another group approaches the issue by looking at changes to individuals that occur as a result of organizational experiences such as the first job, indoctrination courses, training, and transfers.[23] To some extent these theorists have evolved out of the human-relations movement. When these theorists implemented new styles of leadership, they had to train most people to be participative and supportive. Other theorists focused on interpersonal relations since interpersonal competence was critical when not using an impersonal position or rank as the basis of influence. The members of these groups are interested in changes in attitudes and values of managers toward people. Theorists are interested in using *training and development* experiences to change managers and employees in order to integrate the individual and the organization.

This completes the identification of the design variables and the concept of organization design. The complete representation is shown in Fig. 2.8. It indicates that the organizing mode consists of choices of struc-

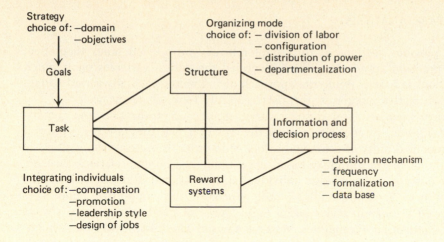

**Fig. 2.8  Partial concept of organization design.**

ture and information and decision processes and that the integration of individual and organizational interests can be accomplished through choices of reward systems and people.

Figure 2.8 indicates several points. First, if the designers want to improve task performance or increase job satisfaction, any of the policy dimensions can be changed so as to bring about the desired state. A particular variable may have more leverage in some situations while other variables may not be alterable in other situations, but in the abstract all variables can be changed.

A second point is that all the approaches are partial. A change in one of the variables often requires coordinated, compensating, or reinforcing changes in the others. An attempt to create decentralization through establishing product divisions (a structural change) requires an information system that reports profit by products, training or selection of general managers, and perhaps a bonus or profit-sharing compensation plan for completeness. Organization design is not simply a psychological, a sociological, an economic, or an information problem.

The third point, partly suggested above, is that the schematic boxes are causally connected in an interdependent system. A change in one can cause a change in the others for the better or for the worse. Organization design must, therefore, be a comprehensive effort.

The issue now is, "How does one choose among the policy variables in designing the organization?" In addition, "What are the dimensions for describing the task?" It will be these dimensions that will guide our thinking.

## TASK ANALYSIS

The previous sections of this chapter briefly introduced other theoretical and practical approaches which identified the design variables upon which this book is based. While the approach of individual theorists varied widely in each of the categories, theorists generally took advocacy positions. The classical theorists treated some variables, e.g., centralization and departmentalization, as contingent upon the situation, but they always employed the modified unity of command principle in order to preserve the legitimacy of a hierarchy of authority based upon rank. The human-relations theorists were quick to acknowledge individual and situational differences, but even when read sympathetically it still appeared that supportive, employee-centered leadership styles and a high degree of participation were always superior to other alternatives. Most meetings of The Institute of Management Sciences devoted a great deal of discussion to the implementation of models and information systems. Indeed, an entire issue of the institute's journal was devoted to the topic. It was noted that the ability of management scientists to model problems far exceeded their ability to fit the problems into the organization's decision processes. It was decided that the interactions among the information technology, reward system, and structure needed analysis and study. A dissatisfaction with existing theories was a necessary first step. What remained was the task of formulating other theories which could answer the questions being raised concerning the limitations of the current theories.

One of the promising formulations is contingency theory. This theory is based on two conclusions drawn from the large cross-sectional comparative studies of the past 15–20 years.

1. There is no one best way to organize.
2. Not all the ways to organize are equally effective.

The theory suggests that we can observe a wide range of differences in effective organizations but these differences are not random. The form of organization makes one difference. On what factors does the choice of organization form depend? What are the characteristics of organizational contexts which appear to make a difference? Research in the most recent stage of inquiry suggests several characteristics. One is the nature of the organization's task.

One of the first studies was performed by Burns and Stalker.[24] In observing 20 English and Scottish firms, they identified two types of organization—mechanistic and organic. More important, they suggested that each type was effective. The mechanistic form, the type suggested by the classical theorists, was effective in stable markets while the organic, the type suggested by human-relations theorists, was effective in the presence of rapidly changing markets and technologies.

In another study of 100 British firms, Woodward[25] found a relation only between structure and effectiveness when the production technology was controlled. Among other features, small-batch, custom-design technologies used flat organizations with relatively little staff personnel. Mass production, stable technologies were tall with a large indirect labor component.

Alfred Chandler, using the methodology of comparative historical analysis, studied over 70 of America's largest industrial firms.[26] He was interested in the creation and spread of the decentralized, multidivisional structure. He discovered that the multidivisional structure was not uniformly adopted throughout industry. The determining factor appeared to be the growth strategy of the firm. Those firms pursuing a growth strategy in a single industry utilized the centralized functional form while those pursuing growth through diversification assumed the decentralized division form or geographical division form. These results have been confirmed and extended to international diversification in a recent study of 170 American firms.[27]

A study by Richard Hall, a sociologist, has produced an interesting variation.[28] The previous studies accounted for variations in structure between organizations by analyzing task predictability and diversity. Hall pointed out that the same differences in task predictability occurred within as well as between organizations. Using categories conceptually equivalent to Burns and Stalker's mechanistic and organic types, Hall found the predicted internal structure variation. That is, the research and development departments approximated the organic form while the manufacturing department had a mechanistic form.

More recently Van de Ven and Delbecq[29] have replicated the Hall study and have elaborated the types of structures. But they still vary systematically with measures of task variability and task difficulty. These studies of within-organization structure variation add greatly to the generality of the findings.

In the area of leadership, Fiedler found that supportive leadership styles were not always effective and that, in some circumstances, a directive style was more effective. He has shown that the most effective style varies with the nature of the task, the relations between superior and subordinate, and the power of the leader.[30]

The next study to be described is one which combines the approaches of the previously mentioned studies.[31] Lawrence and Lorsch's proposition was that there are two considerations in the organization design problem. The first is to organize each subtask in a manner which facilitates the effective performance of that subtask. To the extent that subtasks vary in their predictability, different structures should be applied. It also follows that different cognitive and emotional orientations will arise in the different structures. This aspect of the design problem is called *differentiation.*

The other aspect of the design problem is to provide for the *integration* of the differentiated subtasks so as to achieve successful completion of the whole task. The appropriate way to achieve integration depends first upon the degree of differentiation, since the greater the differences between two subtasks, the more difficult it is to achieve effective collaboration. Also the integration problem varies with the rate at which new products are being introduced. This approach would account for task predictability differences which exist between and within organizations.

The results of the study, carried out with ten organizations in three industries, strongly supported the propositions. That is, the successful organizations had differentiated internal structures when the subtasks varied in predictability. They also adopted integrating mechanisms in proportion to the amount of differentiation and the amount of new product introduction. The study confirms again the proposition that the predictability of the task is a basic conditioning variable in the choice of organizational forms.[32]

Finally it appears that there is a match between the personality of individuals and the predictability of the task.[33] This work is just beginning

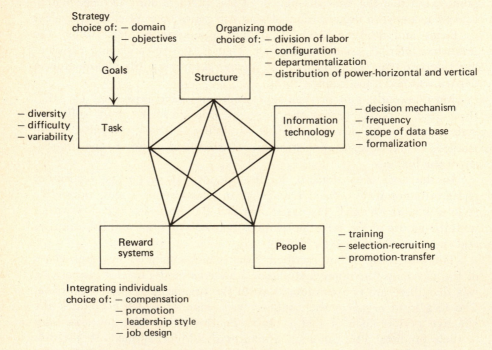

**Fig. 2.9   Organization design policy variables.**

but results suggest that certain personality types choose predictable tasks or make them predictable, are more satisfied with these tasks, and are more effective at them. Another type prefers uncertain, ambiguous tasks. But again it is task predictability which is associated with the systematic variation in personality type.

In summary, a number of theorists employing different labels for a similar attribute have discovered relationships between what we will call task uncertainty and the other design variables. These studies found that task variability, diversity, or difficulty were systematically related to structure, leadership style, personality, and decision processes. Our conceptual framework is shown in Fig. 2.9. It indicates all five areas of choice; task, structure, information and decision processes, reward systems, and people. All should be regarded as variable and controllable to various degrees by the organizations' decision makers. The choice of which variables to change is the strategic choice. It is assumed that there is no single relation between task attributes and any one dimension. Task diversity led American firms to abandon functional organization for the multidivisional form, while European firms maintained functional or holding company models and re-

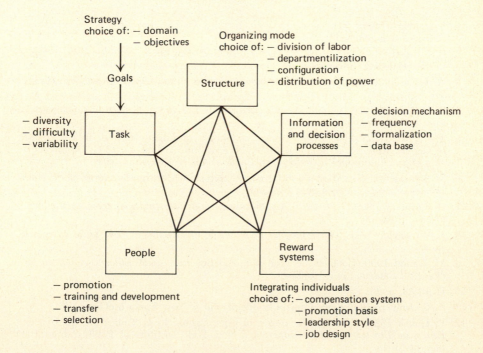

Fig. 2.10   Concept of organization design.

duced the implications of diversity by negotiating tariff barriers and keeping out competition. What is critical is the maintenance of coherence. How to maintain coherence and the alternatives to do so are spelled out in the next chapters.

## SUMMARY

In this chapter, a review of past approaches was used as a vehicle for elaborating on the design choices available. The classical and the decision theorists contributed primarily to choices of organizing modes. The human-relations theorists and the more recent behavioral science approaches deal mainly with the problem of integrating individual and organizational interests. More recent empirical research has shown that these approaches are not incorrect but all are partially correct. What is needed is a framework to combine them. A framework based on task uncertainty is presented in Chapter 3 for choices of organizing modes. Another framework, one for choices of integrating individuals, is presented in Chapter 16.

## NOTES

1. J. L. Massie 1965. Management theory. In J. G. March, *Handbook of organizations.* Chicago: Rand McNally.
2. F. J. Roethlisberger and W. J. Dickson 1939. *Management and the worker.* Cambridge: Harvard University Press.
3. H. Simon 1960. *The new science of management decision making.* New York: Harper & Row.
4. E. H. Schein 1968. Organizational socialization and the profession of management. *Industrial Management Review* 9: 1–6.
5. The classic description of the division of labor is in Adam Smith 1776, *The wealth of nations,* New York: Random House, 1937, and in C. Babbage 1832, *On the economy of machinery and manufactures.* London: Charles Knight, 1832.
6. M. Kilbridge and L. Wester 1966. An economic model for the division of labor. *Management Science,* (February): 255–269.
7. H. Fayol (C. Stours (trans.)) 1949. *General and industrial management.* London: Pitman, p. 21.
8. F. W. Taylor 1911. *The principles of scientific management.* New York: Harper & Row.
9. M. Dalton 1950. Conflicts between staff and line managerial officers. *American Sociological Review,* (June): 342–351.
10. H. Fayol, p. 33.
11. A. S. Tannenbaum 1968. *Control in organizations.* New York: McGraw-Hill.
12. L. Gulick 1937. Notes on the theory of organization. In L. Gulick and L. Urwick, *Papers on the science of administration.* New York: Institute of Public Administration, pp. 3–45.
13. *Ibid.,* p. 15.

14. W. H. Newman 1951. *Administrative action: the techniques of organization and management*. Englewood Cliffs, N.J.: Prentice-Hall, p. 125.

15. E. J. Miller 1959. Technology, territory, and time: the internal differentiation of complex production systems. *Human Relations* 12: 243–272.

16. Roethlisberger and Dickson.

17. The best summaries of this work are R. Likert 1961, *New patterns of management* and 1967, *The human organization*. McGraw-Hill.

18. L. Coch and J. R. P. French 1948. Overcoming resistance to change. *Human Relations:* 512–532.

19. M. S. Myers 1970. *Every employee a manager*. New York: McGraw-Hill.

20. J. G. March and H. Simon 1958. *Organization*. New York: Wiley, and R. Cyert and J. G. March 1963, *The behavioral theory of the firm*. Englewood Cliffs, N.J.: Prentice-Hall.

21. H. Simon, *New Science*.

22. M. S. Scott-Morton 1971. *Management decision systems*. Boston: Harvard Business School Division of Research.

23. D. Berlew and D. Hall 1966. The socialization of managers: effect of expectations on performance. *Administrative Science Quarterly*, (Sept.): 207–223. E. H. Schein 1961. Management development as a process of influence. *Industrial Management Review* 2: 59–77, and A. Edstrom and J. Galbraith 1974. The transfer of managers in multinational organizations: why? Wharton School, working paper.

24. T. Burns and G. M. Stalker 1961. *The management of innovation*. London: Tavistock.

25. J. Woodward 1965. *Industrial organization: theory and practice*. London: Oxford University Press.

26. A. Chandler 1966. *Strategy and structure*. Garden City: Anchor Books.

27. L. E. Fouraker and J. M. Stopford 1968. Organizational structure and the multinational strategy. *Administrative Science Quarterly*, (June): 47–64.

28. R. H. Hall 1962. Intraorganization structure variation. *Administrative Science Quarterly*, (December): 295–308.

29. A. Van de Ven and A. Delbecq 1974. A task contingent model of work unit structure. *Administrative Science Quarterly*, (June): 183–197.

30. F. Fiedler 1974. *A theory of leadership effectiveness*. New York: McGraw-Hill. F. Fiedler and M. Chemers 1974, *Leadership and effective management,* Glenville, Ill.: Scott Foresman.

31. P. R. Lawrence and J. W. Lorsch 1967. *Organization and environment*. Boston: Division of Research, Harvard Business School.

32. Other studies are in J. Hage and M. Aiken 1969, Routine technology, social structure and organizational goals. *Administrative Science Quarterly* 14: 336–377, and R. B. Duncan 1972, Characteristics of organizational environments and perceived environmental uncertainty. *Administrative Science Quarterly*, (Sept.): 313–327.

33. J. Lorsch and J. Morse 1974. *Organizations and their members: a contingency approach*. New York: Harper & Row.

## QUESTIONS

1. What managerial problems are created by the division of labor?

2. Is there a limit to the span of control? Is it variable? Explain.

3. What are the advantages and disadvantages of functional and product divisionalized structures, respectively?

4. How many different bases for departments can you think of? Can they be grouped into Gulick's categories?

5. How can one defend a reduction in the vertical and horizontal division of work?

6. Explain the following point of view. Each of the stages of inquiry into organizations such as classical management was not wrong but only partially correct.

7. Why does diversity and uncertainy affect the choice of organizing mode and integrating schemes?

| ORGANIZING MODES: AN INFORMATION PROCESSING MODEL | CHAPTER **3** |
| --- | --- |

The task of this chapter is to present the framework for choices of organizing modes. Recall that Chapter 1 identified organization design as a continuous choice process covering choices of strategy, organizing modes, and techniques for integrating individual and organizational interests. Chapter 2 elaborated on each area of choice showing that organizing modes consisted of a choice of structure and information and decision process. The choice of integrating scheme consisted of choices of reward system and types of individuals. The short-run goals of the organization, resulting from choices of domain and objectives, constitute the organization's conception of its task. This task is the link between choices of strategy and organization. Recent research suggests that structure, decision process, and individual personality vary systematically with the uncertainty of that task. The objective of this chapter is to explain what is meant by task uncertainty and why it is associated with variations in organizing modes. Subsequent chapters will elaborate on these alternative modes. Finally, the link between task uncertainty and reward systems will be presented in Chapter 16 with an elaboration in following chapters.

## TASK UNCERTAINTY AND ORGANIZATION DESIGN

The organization design problem is one of achieving coherence among strategy, organizing mode, and integration of individuals. This conception defines a rich choice of alternative actions to bring about a coherence but leaves one a little confused about where to start. To eliminate some of the confusion we will begin with the task and let it vary. In so doing we will be able to follow how organizing modes can be adjusted so as to maintain coherence. However, the reader should regard this as a teaching device, not as a theoretical necessity. We could equally well see how tasks and structures vary as individual personalities vary. We choose to make use of recent research and start with the task and specifically with task uncertainty. Following this beginning, one is led to ask why task uncertainty is related to variation in organizing modes.

The basic proposition is that the greater the uncertainty of the task, the greater the amount of information that has to be processed between decision makers during the execution of the task. If the task is well understood prior to its performance, much of the activity can be preplanned. If it is not understood, then during the actual task execution more knowledge is acquired which leads to changes in resource allocations, schedules, and priorities. All these changes require information processing *during* task performance. Therefore *the greater the task uncertainty, the greater the amount of information that must be processed among decision makers during task execution in order to achieve a given level of performance.* The basic effect of uncertainty is to limit the ability of the organization to preplan or to make decisions about activities in advance of their execution. Therefore, it is hypothesized that the observed variations in organizational forms are actually variations in the alternative organizing modes to (1) increase their ability to preplan, (2) increase their flexibility to adapt to their inability to preplan, or (3) decrease the level of performance required for continued viability. Which mode is chosen depends on the type of uncertainty and the relative costs of the alternative modes. The function of the information processing framework is to identify these modes and their costs. Before articulating the framework, the concepts of uncertainty and information need clarification.

## Uncertainty and Information

Uncertainty is the core concept upon which the organization design frameworks are based. This is unfortunate because there is a great deal of uncertainty about the concept of uncertainty. On a general level, everyone understands what uncertainty is. It is the inability to predict future outcomes or states of the world. But when it comes to specifically measuring uncertainty and comparing different tasks, the concept is not understood. No two research studies have defined, labeled, and measured the concept in the same way. The concept of uncertainty has been discussed under the labels of technology, complexity, uncertainty, etc.

First, it can be stated that uncertainty is not inherent in the task and therefore cannot be determined by an analysis of the task alone. *Uncertainty is the difference between the amount of information required to perform the task and the amount of information already possessed by the organization.* Thus, the amount of task uncertainty is the result of the combination of the specific task and the specific organization performing the task. In order to determine uncertainty, the required task information must be defined.

The amount of information required to perform a task is a function of the nature of the task itself and the level of performance. The aspects of the task that are of interest are those that determine the number of variables about which the organization must collect information. The first aspect is the *diversity of goals* associated with output categories such as the number of different products, different markets, different clients, different diseases treated, etc. Each goal represents a factor in the environment about which knowledge and information must be obtained and processed in decision making. What these goals are and how many are relevant for decision making is determined by the choice of domain. The second aspect is the amount of internal diversity which is determined primarily by the *division of labor.* For example, the organization that employs electronic and electro-mechanical engineering specialists must process more information than the organization that employs electrical engineering generalists. The former must balance work loads among the specialties, sequence the movement of work between them, use two salary categories, etc. Thus, the division of labor determines the number of internal factors about which information must be processed.

The other determinant of required task information is the *level of goal performance* needed to remain viable in the organization's chosen domain. The higher the level of performance, the larger the number of variables that must be considered simultaneously when allocating resources, setting priorities, or determining schedules. For example, when funds are not scarce, universities respond to requests by professors for sabbaticals and trips by considering the merits of the professor's case. When funds are tight, however, professor A's case must be considered simultaneously with the cases of professors B, C, and D. Similarly, a capital shortage may force a job shop to increase its capacity utilization from 60 to 75 percent. At a 60 percent utilization rate, there are few bottlenecks, and scheduling consists of decisions about start dates and completion dates. Follow-up effort is a simple monitoring of progress against those dates. At 75 percent, however, many bottlenecks will arise. Decision making consists of the exploration of many more alternatives such as subcontracting, overtime, split orders, alternate sequences, etc. for the purpose of working around or eliminating bottleneck operations. The higher performance level necessitates considering more alternatives, more variables, and more variables simultaneously. Information must be collected and utilized for all these variables. Thus performance levels, similar to diversity and division of labor, increase the number of variables to be considered when making decisions and the number of decisions to be made. In addition, performance levels affect the number of factors that must be considered simultaneously when making those decisions.

Task uncertainty is the difference between the required information as defined above and the amount already possessed by the organization. The amount of information possessed by an organization is largely a function of its prior experience with the service, product, type of client or customer, or the technology used in its operations. Thus, a technology may be well within the state of the art but still be new to an organization. Generalizations about new technology must be made in reference to the focal organization and its experience.

The discussion above is summarized by Fig. 3.1. If information could be measured on a scale, which it cannot be, then the amount of information possessed by the organization and the amount of information needed for task performance could be placed on the scale as shown. The difference between these amounts is the relative uncertainty that the organization faces and the amount of information that must be acquired and processed by the decision makers. Uncertainty here means simply the absence of information.

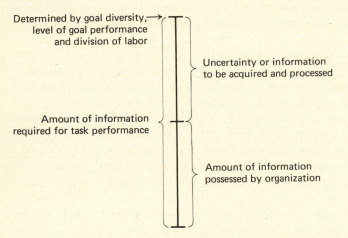

**Fig. 3.1  Determinants of information and task uncertainty.**

At the moment the information-processing load of a task and the information-processing capacity of an organization cannot be measured accurately. There exist measures for types of diversity[1] and for the division of labor[2] but no method for combining them into a measure of required information. This is due partially to the difficulty of operationalizing the measuring level of goal performance. Several researchers have developed measures of overall perceived task uncertainty.[3] Rather than measuring each of the components discussed here, they aggregate them and measure the uncertainty as perceived by the managers who must make the decisions. These researchers have been criticized by others trying to replicate their work. At the moment, the best measure is the combination of the validated task variability and task difficulty scales of Van de Ven and Lynch.[4]

These techniques do not permit the measurement of requirements and capacity so that adjustments can be made in the manner that organizations measure and match supply and demand. However, organizations can detect changes in variables affecting information. Organizations know when they adopt strategies of product or market diversification, they know when the division of labor increases, and they know when they increase performance levels by pursuing shorter schedules, tighter quality tolerances, lower costs, higher productivity, etc. Thus, when the task changes, the organization must change. The organization should be planned and designed concurrently with the strategy formulation and planned resource allocations. What the design choices are will be discussed in the remainder of the book.

In summary, the complexity of a task in terms of the amount of information to be processed in decision making is a function of the division of labor, the goal diversity, and the level of goal performance required. When the organization does not have the necessary information, it must acquire the information and make and remake decisions during the actual task execution. Task uncertainty is the relative amount of information that must be acquired. The greater the uncertainty, the greater the amount of decision making and information processing. It is hypothesized that organizations have limited capacities to process information and adopt different organizing modes to deal with task uncertainty. Therefore, variations in organizing modes are actually variations in the capacity of organizations to process information and make decisions about events which cannot be anticipated in advance. In order to see how information is related to structure, let us create a model organization and follow its development when it is faced with increasing task uncertainty.

## THE MECHANISTIC MODEL

In this section, the basic model is created and the overall structure of the framework is outlined. Subsequent chapters will expand upon the organizing modes put forth in the framework. Of necessity, the remainder of the chapter is fairly abstract. The purpose is to conceive of organizations as information-processing networks and to explain why and through what mechanisms uncertainty and information relate to structure. In order to accomplish this explanation, a basic mechanical model is created. The value of the model is not that it describes reality but that it creates a basis from which various organizing modes are followed to adapt the mechanistic structure to handle greater complexity.

In order to develop the model and the design strategies, assume we have a task which requires several thousand employees divided among many subtasks. For example, the task of designing and manufacturing an aircraft or space capsule requires a group to design the capsule, a group to design the manufacturing methods, a group to fabricate parts and components, a group to assemble the parts, and a group to test the completed unit. The creation of specialized subtasks shown in Fig. 3.2 has all the benefits that the classical theorists claimed. On the other hand, it creates new problems which are nicely illustrated by Bavelas.[5]

> When a job is made up of separate parts, and parts fit together, small errors accumulating in different parts may easily ruin the final product. Any beginner in woodworking will attest to that. He learns early, and often sadly, to study his plans and consult them frequently, to work slowly, and to check his measurements.
>
> When the interdependent parts of a job are distributed among many different persons, all of the usual problems remain and new ones appear. The new problems stem from the nature of distributed work.
>
> A single workman who finds that the interlocking faces of a joint that he is building do not quite match will decide which face to modify or will scrap them both and began again. When two men are involved, questions may arise as to which one of them will make the adjustment, and which of the two of them was in error. When work is distributed such problems are always latent in the relationship among men and functions. And the more a job is fragmented, the more numerous and the more difficult these problems may become!

This little scenario gives a good feeling for the *interdependence* that arises when work is divided. The problems are more difficult when the product is intangible such as a curriculum or a therapy policy.

In order to coordinate interdependent roles, organizations have invented mechanisms for collecting information, deciding, and disseminating information to resolve conflicts and guide interdependent actions. The collection of mechanisms used constitutes the organizing mode of the organization. A number of theorists have proposed schemes for choosing mechanisms. Child suggests that there are two strategies of control, a personal centralized one and a decentralized bureaucratic one, and that size determines which is more appropriate.[6] When organizations are small, decisions are centralized at the top and personally communicated to the implementers. Large organizations decentralize decisions but control choices through rules, procedures, and performance measurements created by specialists. Thompson proposed that there are qualitatively different types of interdependence for which a different coordination mechanism is appropriate.[7] Pooled interdependence is coordinated by rules and standards; sequential interdependence, by planning; and reciprocal interdependence, by mutual adjustment. March and Simon and more recently Hage, Aiken, and Marrett have identified programming, planning, and feedback (transmission of new information) as the basic mechanisms and one chooses the mechanisms based on routineness of task situations.[8] The less routine and more diverse the situations, the more one chooses feedback as opposed to programming and planning. In the following sections, parts of all of these schemes are used. Each of the mechanisms will be discussed by returning to a fictitious organization and using the information-processing model as the vehicle.

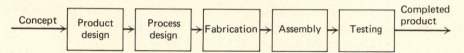

**Fig. 3.2  Horizontal work flow across a functional division of labor.**

In order to complete the task in Fig. 3.2 at a high level of performance, the activities that take place in these various groups must be coordinated. The behavior of the product design engineer must be coordinated with process design engineers, etc. While the behavior of the several thousand people must be coordinated, it is impossible for them to communicate with each other. The organization is simply too large to permit face-to-face communication to be the mechanism for coordination. The organization design problem is to create mechanisms by which an integrated pattern of behavior is obtained across all the interdependent groups. In order to see what these mechanisms are and the conditions under which they are appropriate, let us start with a very predictable task and slowly increase the degree of task uncertainty.

Thus, we have a task, like the one represented in Fig. 3.2, in which there is a high degree of division of labor, a high level of performance, and relatively large size. A good deal of information must be processed to coordinate the interdependent subtasks. Then as the degree of uncertainty increases, the amount of information processed during task execution increases. Organizations must evolve mechanisms to process the greater amount of information necessary to maintain the level of performance. Let us follow the history of a fictitious organization performing the task represented in Fig. 3.2 and observe the mechanisms that are created to deal with increasing information loads caused by increasing task uncertainty.

## Hierarchy of Authority

Every organization in every society selects some of its members to play coordinating or managerial roles and arranges these roles in a hierarchical form. The primary variable is the selection mechanism. In most of our organizations, managers are selected by the owners, legislators, or boards of trustees/directors on the basis of demonstrated performance. In the Civil Service, competitive examination is used. In still other organizations, seniority acts as the selection mechanism. In traditional societies, family connections are the bases for selection. In egalitarian cultures, workers vote for the managers. In an Israeli kibbutz or in Red China, steps are taken to prevent status differences from developing between managers and workers. Rules are that managers are elected for two or three years and cannot succeed themselves or that they spend half their time managing and half their time working. But in each case, the selection produces a representative with legitimate authority who can influence other members' behavior in resolving conflicts and coordinating interdependence. (The concepts of authority and legitimacy will be treated in depth in Chapter 16.)

Once managers are selected, they are invariably arranged in a hierarchical form as shown in Fig. 3.3. This form clearly identifies the person or group (if a committee or council is used) to whom an appeal must be made in resolving a conflict and thereby preserves legitimacy. In Fig. 3.3, a problem between assembly and fabrication is handled by Manager 2 while a problem between assembly and process design goes to the general manager. The hierarchy form is chosen because it is also an efficient information-processing mechanism.[9] If communication to coordinate interdependence takes place through direct communication channels, then

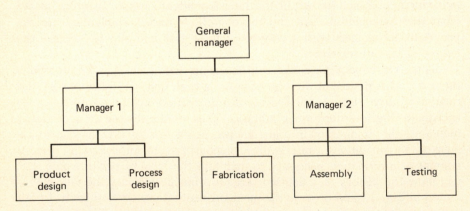

Fig. 3.3  Hierarchical organization structure.

$1/2n(n-1)$ communication channels are needed, where $n$ is the number of subunits. This number grows with the square of $n$ and gets very large even for moderate values of $n$. However, hierarchical channels reduce the number of channels that each subunit must maintain and yet ties together all interdependent units. If the structure has a uniform span of controls equal to $s$, then there are $(n-1)(s/s-1)$ communication channels. This number increases with $n$ rather than the square of $n$; a result which permits the linkage of larger numbers of subunits. Thus, hierarchies preserve legitimacy by identifying clearly who has authority over whom and by economizing on the information-processing capacity.

There is a price for the economy on information-processing capacity, however. Each channel has a limited capacity for processing information and each position can communicate directly only with those above and below. Other contacts must take place through one or more intervening nodes. An increase in task uncertainty overloads these channels and introduces delays and distortions. In order to overcome this disadvantage, organizations have invented other mechanisms which achieve coordination, preserve legitimacy, and economize on information-processing capacity.

### Rules, Programs, or Procedures

All organizations employ rules or procedures which are simply decisions made in advance of their execution. That is, to the extent that decisions are repetitive, a procedure is worked out in advance of encountering the situation. The virtue of rules is that they eliminate the need for communication between interdependent parties and between superior and subordinate. In order to make effective use of programs, the organization's employees are taught the job-related situations with which they will be faced and the behaviors appropriate to those situations. Then, as situations arise daily, the employees act out the behaviors appropriate to the situations. If everyone adopts the appropriate behavior, the resultant aggregate response is an integrated or coordinated pattern of behavior. Thereby decisions for those situations that can be anticipated in advance are decentralized to the lowest levels and the vulnerable hierarchical channels are reserved only for those decisions that cannot be anticipated in advance.

A couple of points need to be emphasized concerning the use of rules and procedures. First, the overall effect is to move repetitive decisions to lower levels of the organization. This movement to lower levels has been described as decentralization. However, it should be noted that there is little decentralization of discretion. Whether workers are guided by a superior's directive made in real-time or in advance, they are still guided by a directive from a superior. The primary effect is an information-processing one—the elimination from hierarchical channels of communications concerning routine events. Rules serve the same function as habits for individuals. They preserve the scarce information-processing, decision-making capacity for novel, consequential events.

Second, it is important to point out that rules are employed in addition to the use of the hierarchy, not instead of it. The uniform repetitive events are handled by rules while the new and unique events are treated as exceptions and referred to the hierarchical position where a shared superior exists for all affected subordinates. This combination guarantees an integrated coordinated response from the organization both for routine and nonroutine situations. While there exist trade-offs between mechanisms as we shall see, they are added to existing mechanisms to expand information-processing capacity.

The combination of rules and hierarchy, like hierarchy alone, is vulnerable to task uncertainty. As the organization's subtasks increase in uncertainty, fewer situations can be programmed in advance and more exceptions arise which must be referred upward in the hierarchy. As more exceptions are referred upward, the hierarchy will become overloaded. Serious delays will develop between the transmission of information about new situations upward and a response to that information downward. In this situation, the organization must develop new processes to supplement rules and hierarchy.

### Discretion Guided by Planning or Professionalism

As the task uncertainty increases, the volume of information from the points of action to points of decision making overload the hierarchy. In this situation, it becomes more efficient to bring the points of decision down to the points of action where the information exists. This can be accomplished by increasing the amount of discretion exercised by employees at lower levels of the organization. However, as the amount of discretion exercised at lower levels of the organization is increased, the organization faces a potential behavior control problem. That is, how can the organization be sure that the employees will consistently choose the appropriate response to the job-related situations with which they will be faced?

The increase in discretion is significant for both the choice of organizing mode which is concerned with information needed to coordinate interdependent activities and for devices to integrate individual and organizational goals. Later chapters will discuss the choice of reward systems to integrate these goals. Here we shall continue with the cognitive portion.

In order to increase the probability that employees will select the appropriate behavior, organizations make two responses to deal with the cognitive portion of the behavior control problem. The first change involves the substitution of craft or professional training of the work force for the detailed centralized programming of the work processes.[10] This is illustrated by a comparison between manufacturing industries and construction. In mass production, the work processes that are planned in advance are:

1. . . . the location at which a particular task will be done,

2. the movement of tools, materials, and people to this workplace and the most efficient arrangements of these workplace characteristics,

3. sometimes the particular movements to be performed in getting the task done,

4. the schedules and time allotments for particular operations, and

5. inspection criteria for particular operations.

In construction these characteristics of the work process are governed by the worker in accordance with the empirical lore that makes up craft principles.[11]

The shift to craft or professional workers represents a shift from control based on supervision and surveillance to control based on selection of responsible workers. Workers who have the appropriate skills and attitudes are selected.

Professionalization by itself may not be sufficient to shift decision making to lower levels of the organization. The reason is that, in the presence of interdependence, an alternative which is based on professional or craft standards may not be best for the whole organization. Thus, alternatives which are preferred from a local or departmental perspective may not be preferred from a global perspective. The product design that is technically preferred may not be preferred by the customer, may be too costly to be produced, or may require a schedule which takes too long to complete. In order to deal with this problem, organizations undertake planning processes to set goals or targets to cover the primary interdependencies.

An example of the way goals are used can be demonstrated by considering the design group responsible for an aircraft wing structure. The group's interdependence with other design groups is handled by technical specifications elaborating the points of attachment of the wing to the body, forces transmitted at these points, centers of gravity, etc. The group also has a set of targets (not to be exceeded) for weight, design man-hours to be used, and a completion date. They are given minimum stress specifications below which they cannot design. The group then designs the structures and assemblies which combine to form the wing. They need not communicate with any other design group on work-related matters if they and the interdependent groups are able to operate within the planned targets.

Thus goal setting allows coordination to be maintained between interdependent subtasks and yet allows discretion at the local subtask level. Instead of specifying specific behaviors through rules and programs, the organization undertakes processes to determine targets to be achieved and allows the employees to select behaviors appropriate to the target.

The ability of the design groups to operate within the planned targets, however, depends upon the degree of task uncertainty. If the task is one that has been performed before, the estimates of man-hours, weight, due date, etc. will probably be realized. If it is a new design involving new materials, the estimates will probably be wrong. The targets will have to be set and reset throughout the design effort.

The violation of planned targets usually requires additional decision making and hence additional information processing. The additional information processing takes place through the hierarchy in the same manner as rule exceptions were handled. Problems are handled on an exception basis. They are raised to higher levels of the hierarchy for resolution. The problem rises to the first level where a shared superior exists for all affected subunits. A decision is made and the new targets are communicated to the subunits. In this manner the behavior of the interdependent subunits remains integrated.

Thus our fictitious organization operates by delegating routine decisions guided by rules to lower levels, by delegating local discretion guided by planned targets and goals, and by the use of the hierarchy when goals are not met and rules do not apply. While organizations use all three (and others to be added shortly), some choice of mix is made by organization designers. Holding task uncertainty constant, increases in size increase the amount of programming, planning, and decentralization.[12] In addition, organizations begin to create staff or nonwork-flow specialties such as accounting and personnel who maintain the planning and programming systems. As size increases, the addition of staff specialists is an efficient design choice. Let us follow the addition of administrative services to an organization.

Our fictitious organization is assumed to be growing. At an intermediate size, each of the first-line managers spend some fraction of their time on administrative matters such as budgeting and personnel. After the organization increases in size, there exists enough work for a full-time administrative service manager. The immediate effect of the added manager is better administrative decisions by a specialized full-time manager. The secondary effect is the freeing of other managers from some administrative tasks leaving them more time for supervision. The effects are shown in Fig. 3.4.

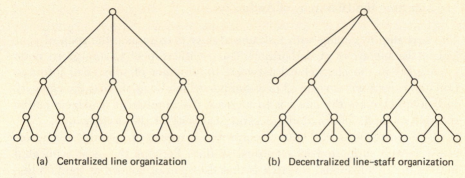

(a)  Centralized line organization        (b)  Decentralized line–staff organization

Fig. 3.4  **Effects of a staff specialist with uncertainty held constant.**

Organization A represents a line organization in which managers make all types of decisions. Organization B has added a specialist in a particular area which frees the line managers to supervise additional personnel. Thus, the same number of personnel can be managed by fewer supervisors. Organization A has ten managers while B has seven managers and a staff specialist. If the total of the three managers' salaries is greater than that of the staff specialist, this is an efficient design even if there is no difference in administrative decision quality.

This explanation is consistent with the empirical results. Increasing size is associated with increasing staff specialization, standardization, the recording of role performance, and decentralization.[13] Increases in staff specialists and the recording of role performance is associated with proportionally fewer line managers.[14] Similarly, studies on span of control show that the span increases with increasing size of organizations and with the supervision provided by others. Thus, other things being equal, increases in size permit the hiring of staff specialists and the reduction in proportion of managers thereby exploiting economies of scale of large organizations. The problem is that other things are rarely equal.

Two features change along with the changes in size which reduce the economies cited above. First, the expansion brings in new customers or clients whose needs are not exactly the same as the needs of old clients. Usually new services or products are introduced to satisfy these new consumers. Thus, diversity increases simultaneously with size. Second, the increased volume of activity permits greater specialization within the work organization itself. This increased division of labor increases interdependence. Thus, changes in size occur with changes in diversity and division of labor which increase the degree of task uncertainty. As uncertainty increases, we encounter the overloaded hierarchy.

### Adjusting the Hierarchy of Authority

The next step in coping with task uncertainty is to reduce the span of control in the hierarchy of authority.[15] Thus, with respect to any given node (manager) in the hierarchical network, the number of sources of information and exceptions is reduced to a number which he or she has the capacity to handle. Overall, the effect is to increase the number of managers or the decision-making, information-processing capacity of the organization.

The reduction of the span of control as a means of coping with uncertainty is well supported by empirical studies. Perhaps the most replicated finding in organizational research is that the span of control of the first-line manager, be it foreman, registered nurse, or finance supervisor, decreases with increases in task complexity, uncertainty, or professionalization and skill of the workers.[16] Thus, uncertainty decreases and size increases the span of control. This relationship is demonstrated by data collected by the author from United States and Canadian oil refineries. Spans of control of first-line supervisors were correlated with size (number of workers in the department) for the production, maintenance, and engineering departments. It is assumed that the engineering task is more uncertain than maintenance which in turn is more uncertain than production. The results are shown graphically in Fig. 3.5. At any given size, the span of control in engineering is less than that in the other two departments. The same phenomenon occurs as one moves up in the hierarchy. As the number of subordinates increases at a particular level, the span of control of the superior increases.

But at each higher level, the span decreases. The effect is shown for the production department in Fig. 3.6. Thus, if we assume that uncertainty increases as we move up the hierarchy, the greater the uncertainty, the smaller the span for a given number of subordinates.

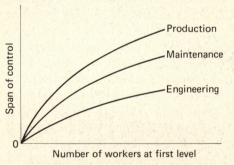

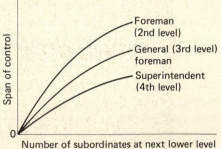

Fig. 3.5 Effects of size and uncertainty on span of control.

Fig. 3.6 Effects of size and level of uncertainty on span of control.

The decreases of the span of control, like the previous measures, has a limited usefulness. If each increase in uncertainty is matched by a decrease in span, the effect is to increase the number of people who do not do the work. The hierarchy gets taller and the amount of the managers' salaries increases. At some point it becomes more economical to adopt another mechanism or organizing mode. The organization must adopt a mode to either reduce the information necessary to coordinate its activities or increase its capacity to process more information. In the next section, these strategies are identified and integrated into the framework. Subsequent chapters explain the strategies in detail.

### Alternative Organizing Modes

The ability of an organization to successfully utilize coordination by goal setting, hierarchy, and rules depends on the combination of the frequency of exceptions and the capacity of the hierarchy to handle them. As the task uncertainty increases, the number of exceptions increases until the hierarchy is overloaded. Therefore, the organization must again take organization design action. This action constitutes the strategic choice taken by the organization. As suggested above, it can proceed in either of two general ways. First, it can act in three ways to reduce the amount of information that is processed. And second, the organization can act in two ways to increase its capacity to handle more information. The three ways for reducing the need for information and the two ways for increasing processing capacity are shown in Fig. 3.7. The effect of all these actions is to reduce the number of exceptional cases referred upward into the organization through hierarchical channels.

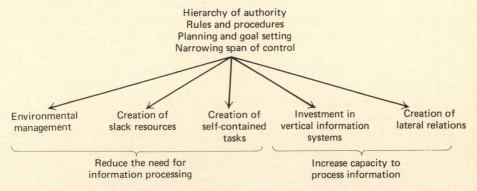

**Fig. 3.7 Organization design strategies.**

### Environmental Management

Instead of modifying its own structure and processes, the organization can attempt to modify the environment. The attempts are to reduce uncertainty about critical events. If demand is very uncertain and fluctuating demand causes problems for highly mechanized facilities requiring 24-hours utilization, the organization can buy the prior or demanding stage in the product flow. Thus, through vertical integration the organization can reduce the potentially disruptive uncertainty.

There are a number of mechanisms by which an organization can relate to its environment. First, there are a number of voluntary responses to environmental demands. These are the (1) competitive response, i.e., being efficient in order to guarantee continual access to scarce resources; (2) public relations response, i.e., influencing the environment through the mass media; and (3) voluntarism, i.e., the voluntary management in the public interest of market imperfections and externalities. If these do not reduce the uncertainty of the environment, the organization can enter various cooperative schemes such as implicit cooperation, contracting, coopting, and coalescing. Finally, if the organization cannot manage a given environment, it can search for a new one through various forms of environmental maneuvering.

This environmental maneuvering consists of adjustments to strategy. That is, the organization modifies its domain and relations with elements in its domain. All of these responses have costs for the organization. Whether it chooses one depends on the amount of uncertainty and costliness of the other four strategies.

### Creation of Slack Resources

The organization can reduce the number of exceptions that occur by simply reducing the level of performance. In the example of the wing design, the scheduled time, weight allowance, or man-hours could be increased. In each case more resources would be consumed. These additional resources are called slack resources.[17]

The slack resources are an additional cost to the organization or the customer. However, the longer the schedule time available, the lower the likelihood of a target being missed. The fewer the exceptions, the less the overload on the hierarchy. Thus the creation of slack resources, through reduced performance levels, reduces the amount of information that must be processed during task execution and prevents the overloading of the hierarchical channels. Whether the organization chooses this strategy or not depends on the relative costs of the other four strategies for handling the overload.

### Creation of Self-contained Tasks

The next method for reducing the amount of information processed is to change from the functional task design to one in which each group has all the resources it needs to perform its task; that is, change the way the task is decomposed into subtasks. For the example, self-contained units could be created around major sections of the aircraft—wing, cabin, tail, body, etc. Each group would have its own product engineers, process engineers, fabricating and assembly operations, and testing facilities. In other situations, groups can be created around product lines, geographical areas, projects, client groups, markets, etc., each of which would contain the input resources necessary for the task.

The strategy of self-containment shifts the basis of the authority structure from one based on input, resource, skill, or occupational categories to one based on output or geographical categories. The shift reduces the amount of information processing through several mechanisms—two are described here. First, it reduces the amount of output diversity faced by a single collection of resources. For example, a professional organization with multiple skill specialties providing service to three different client groups must schedule the use of these specialties across three demands for their services and determine priorities when conflicts occur. But, if the organization changed to three groups, one for each client category, each with its own full complement of specialties, the schedule conflicts across client groups disappear and there is no need to process information to determine priorities.

The second source of information reduction occurs through a reduced division of labor. The functional or source-specialized structure pools the demand for skills across all output categories. In the example above, each client generates approximately one-third of the demand for each skill. Since the division of labor is limited by the extent of the market, the division of labor must decrease as the demand decreases. In the professional organization, each client group may have generated a need for one-third of a computer programmer. The functional organization would have hired one programmer and shared the programmer across the groups. In the self-contained structure, there is insufficient demand in each group for a programmer, so the professionals must do their own programming. Specialization is reduced but there is not the problem of scheduling the programmer's time across the three possible uses for it.

Thus the first organizing modes reduce overloads on the hierarchy by reducing the number of exceptions that occur. The reduction occurs by reducing the level of performance, diversity of output, division of labor or by increasing the amount of information available to the organization prior to task execution. According to the theory put forth earlier, reducing the level of performance, etc., reduces the amount of information required to coordinate resources in creating the organization's services or products. Thereby the amount of information to be acquired and processed during task execution is reduced. The second class of modes takes the level of information as given, and creates processes and mechanisms to acquire and process information during task execution.

### Investment in Vertical Information Systems

The organization can invest in mechanisms which allow it to process information acquired during task performance without overloading the hierarchical communication channels. The investment occurs according to the following logic. After the organization has created its plan or set of targets for weight, stress, budget, and schedule, unanticipated events occur which generate exceptions requiring adjustments to the original plan. At some point when the number of exceptions becomes substantial, it is preferable to generate a new plan rather than make incremental changes with each exception. The issue is then how frequently should plans be revised—yearly, quarterly, or monthly? The greater the uncertainty, the greater the frequency of replanning. The greater the frequency of replanning, the greater the resources, such as clerks, computer time, input-output devices required to process information about relevant factors.

Providing more information more often may simply overload the decision maker. Investment may be required to increase the capacity of the decision maker by employing computers, various man-machine combinations, assistants-to, etc. The cost of this strategy is the cost of the information-processing resources.

The investment strategy is to collect information at the points of origination and direct it to the appropriate places in the hierarchy. The strategy increases the information processing at planning time while reducing the number of exceptions which have overloaded the hierarchy.

### Creation of Lateral Relations

The last mode is to selectively employ lateral decision processes which cut across lines of authority. This mode moves the level of decision making down to where the information exists rather than bringing the information up to the points of decision. It decentralizes decisions but without creating self-contained groups. Several mechanisms are employed. The number and types depend upon the level of uncertainty.

The simplest form of lateral relation is direct contact between two people who share a problem. If a problem arises in testing in Fig. 3.3, the manager of testing may contact the manager of assembly and secure the necessary change. Direct contact avoids the upward referral to another manager and removes overloads from the hierarchy.

In some cases, there is a large volume of contact between two subtasks such as process design and assembly. In these circumstances a new role, a liaison role, is created to handle the interdepartmental contacts.

As tasks of higher uncertainty are encountered, problems are detected in testing which require the joint efforts of product and process design, assembly, and testing. Rather than refer the problem upwards, managers of these areas form a task force or team to jointly resolve the issue. In this manner interdepartmental group problem solving becomes a mechanism to decentralize decisions and reduce hierarchical overloads.

As more decisions of consequence are made at lower levels of the organization through interdepartmental groups, problems of leadership arise. The response is the creation of a new role, an integrating role.[18] The function of the role is to represent the general manager in the interdepartmental decisions for a particular brand, product line, project, country, or geographical unit. These roles are called product managers in commercial firms, project managers in aerospace, and unit managers in hospitals.

After the role is created, the issue is how much and what kind of influence does the role occupant need in order to achieve integration for the project, unit, or product. Mechanisms from supporting information and budget control all the way to dual reporting relations and the matrix design are employed in various circumstances described in later chapters.

The empirical study by Van de Ven, Delbecq, and Koenig reveals a number of the characteristics of the coordination mechanisms described in this chapter.[19] They measured the extent to which departments in an organization used the various mechanisms described above—rules, planning, hierarchy, horizontal channels, unscheduled meetings, and formal scheduled meetings. The results are shown graphically in Fig. 3.8. The graph shows that the use of horizontal channels and meetings increase with increases in task uncertainty. Second, the use of rules and planning declines with increases in uncertainty. Thus, there is a trade-off between the various modes. Third, the use of the hierarchy remains constant at all levels. This channel is used to its maximum and is supplemented by other mechanisms as needed. Fourth, an organization uses all mechanisms of coordination. They are added to the organization's repertoire rather than substituted for other

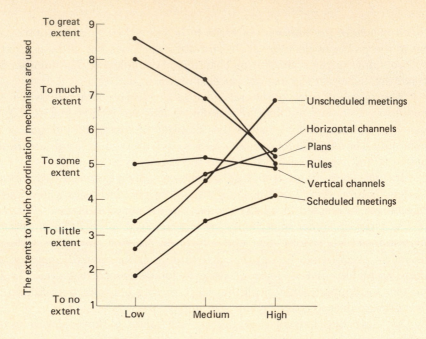

Fig. 3.8  Profile of coordination mechanisms on classified task uncertainty showing the extent to which coordination mechanisms are used.

| | Classified task uncertainty | | | | | |
|---|---|---|---|---|---|---|
| | n = 43 | | n = 125 | | n = 29 | |
| | $\overline{X}$ | $\Gamma$ | $\overline{X}$ | $\Gamma$ | $\overline{X}$ | $\Gamma$ |
| Total coordination (Grand mean) | 4.4 | 0.9 | 4.9 | 0.9 | 4.7 | 0.8 |
| A.  Impersonal coordination mode | 8.4 | 1.7 | 7.2 | 1.4 | 5.1 | 1.2 |
| 1.  Rules, policies, procedures | 8.6 | 1.5 | 7.4 | 1.8 | 5.0 | 1.8 |
| 2.  Plans, schedules, forecast | 8.0 | 2.0 | 6.9 | 1.8 | 5.2 | 1.8 |
| B.  Personal coordination mode | 4.2 | 0.9 | 5.0 | 1.1 | 5.1 | 1.2 |
| 3.  Vertical channels (hierarchical) | 5.0 | 1.2 | 5.2 | 1.6 | 4.9 | 1.5 |
| 4.  Horizontal channels | 3.4 | 1.4 | 4.7 | 1.3 | 5.3 | 1.7 |
| C.  Group coordination mode | 2.1 | 1.0 | 3.7 | 1.8 | 4.9 | 1.8 |
| 5.  Scheduled meetings | 1.8 | 0.9 | 3.4 | 1.8 | 4.1 | 1.8 |
| 6.  Unscheduled meetings | 2.6 | 1.6 | 4.5 | 2.3 | 6.7 | 2.7 |

mechanisms although some substitution takes place between using decisions made in advance (rules and plans) and decisions made on an as-needed basis (horizontal channels and meetings). Every organization maintains a repertoire as indicated by the profile, and the profile is a function of task uncertainty.[20]

In summary, lateral relations permit the moving of decisions to lower levels of the organization and yet guarantee that all information is included in the process. The cost of the strategy is greater amounts of managerial time spent in group processes and the overhead expense of liaison and integrating roles.

### Choice of Organizing Mode

Each of the five organizing modes has been briefly presented. The organization can choose to follow one or some combination of several if it chooses. It will choose that mode which has the least cost in its environmental context. However, what may be lost in all of the explanations is that the five strategies are hypothesized to be an exhaustive set of alternatives. That is, if the organization is faced with greater uncertainty due to technological change, higher performance standards, increased competition, or if it diversifies its product line to reduce environmental dependence, the amount of information processing will be increased. *The organization must adopt at least one of the five strategies when faced with greater uncertainty.* If it does not consciously choose one of the five, then slack, reduced performance standards will happen automatically. The task information requirements and the capacity of the organization to process information are always matched. If the organization does not consciously match them, reduced performance through budget overruns, schedule overruns, etc. will occur in order to bring about equality. Thus, the organization should be planned and designed simultaneously with the planning of the strategy and resource allocations. But if the strategy involves introducing new products, entering new markets, etc., then some provision for increased information must be made. Not to decide is to decide, and it is to decide upon slack resources as the strategy to remove hierarchical overload.

### SUMMARY

This chapter introduced the basic theory upon which the remainder of the book will build. Starting from the observation that uncertainty appears to make a difference in type of organization structures, it was postulated that uncertainty increased the amount of information that must be processed during task execution. Therefore, perceived variation in organization form was hypothesized to be variation in the capability of the organization to process information about events that could not be anticipated in advance.

Uncertainty was conceived as the relative difference in the amount of information required and the amount possessed by the organization. The amount required was a function of the output diversity, division of labor, and level of performance. In combination the organization's current knowledge, division of labor, diversity of output, and level of performance determine the amount of information that must be processed.

Next the basic mechanistic, bureaucratic model was introduced along with explanations of its information-processing capabilities. It was shown that hierarchical communication channels can coordinate large numbers of interdependent subtasks but have a limited capacity to remake decisions. In response, five organizing modes were articulated which either reduced the amount of information or increased the capacity of the organization to process more information. The way to decrease information was to reduce the determinants of the amount of information. Thus, reduction of performance levels, diversity, and division of labor were indicated. The modes to increase capacity were to invest in the formal, hierarchical information process and to introduce lateral decision processes. Each of these modes has its effects and costs. The subsequent chapters will discuss each mode in more detail. In addition, case studies will be presented which highlight the choice.

## NOTES

1. M. Gort 1962. *Diversification and integration in American industry.* Princeton: Princeton University Press.

2. L. Pondy 1959. Effects of size, complexity, and ownership on administrative intensity. *Administrative Science Quarterly,* (March): p. 52.

3. R. Duncan 1972. Characteristics of organizational environments and perceived environmental uncertainty, *Administrative Science Quarterly,* (September), pp. 313–327.

4. A. H. Van de Ven and A. L. Delbecq 1974. A task contingent model of work unit structure. *Administrative Science Quarterly,* (June): 183–197. B. P. Lynch 1974. An empirical assessment of Perrow's technology construct. *Administrative Science Quarterly,* (September): 338–356.

5. A. Bavelas 1960. Communication and organization. In G. P. Schultz and T. L. Whisler (eds.), *Management organization and the computer.* Chicago: Free Press, p. 319.

6. J. Child 1972. Organization structure and strategies of control. *Administrative Science Quarterly* 17: 163–177.

7. J. D. Thompson 1967. *Organizations in action.* New York: McGraw-Hill, Chapter 5.

8. J. March and H. Simon 1958. *Organizations.* New York: Wiley, pp. 158–169. J. Hage, M. Aiken, and C. B. Marrett 1971. Organization structure and communication. *American Sociological Review,* (Oct.): pp. 860–871.

9. J. Emery 1969. *Organization planning and control systems.* New York: Macmillan, pp. 5–16.

10. A. Stinchcombe 1959. Bureaucratic and craft administration of production: a comparative study. *Administrative Science Quarterly,* (September): 168–187.

11. *Ibid.,* p. 170.

12. J. Child 1973. Predicting and understanding organization structure. *Administrative Science Quarterly*, (June): pp. 168–185.

13. *Ibid.*

14. D. Pugh, D. J. Hickson, C. R. Hinings, and C. Turner 1968. Dimensions of organization structure. *Administrative Science Quarterly* 13: 65–105. P. Blau and R. A. Schoenherr 1971. *The structure of organizations*. New York: Basic Books.

15. Blau and Schoenherr. J. Udell 1967. An empirical test of hypotheses relating to span of control. *Administrative Science Quarterly*, (Dec.): 420–439.

16. J. Woodward 1965. *Industrial organization: theory and practice*. London: Oxford University Press. P. Blau, W. V. Heydebrand and R. A. Stouffer 1966. The structure of small bureaucracies. *American Sociological Review*, (April): 179–191. P. Blau 1968. The hierarchy of authority in organizations. *American Journal of Sociology*, (Jan.): 453–467. G. Bell 1967. Determinants of the span of control. *American Journal of Sociology*, (July): 100–109. M. Meyer 1968. Expertness and span of control. *American Sociological Review*, (Dec.): 947–950.

17. J. G. March and H. A. Simon 1958. *Organizations*. New York: Wiley. R. Cyert and J. G. March 1963. *A behavioral theory of the firm*. Englewood Cliffs, N.J.: Prentice-Hall.

18. P. Lawrence and J. Lorsch 1967. *Organization and environment*. Boston: Harvard Business School Division of Research, Chapter 3.

19. A. H. Van de Ven, A. L. Delbecq, and R. Koenig 1976. Determinants of coordination modes within organizations. *American Sociological Review*, (April): pp. 332–338.

20. R. Duncan 1973. Multiple decision-making structures in adapting to environmental uncertainty. *Human Relations* 26: 273–291.

## QUESTIONS

1. Why does structural form vary with task uncertainty?

2. What is the relation between uncertainty and information? Isn't uncertainty simply the absence of information?

3. How does a change in a performance level increase or decrease information processing in an organization? Give an example.

4. Are manufacturing operations always less uncertain than research tasks? Why or why not?

5. Why are hierarchies efficient information-processing instruments? Why are they inefficient information processors?

6. Some recent research findings suggest that greater use of rules, programs, and plans result in greater delegation and perceived control on the part of subordinates. How can this result be explained?

7. Why do (a) environmental management (b) slack resources, and (c) self-contained tasks reduce information processing?

8. Explain how vertical information systems and lateral relations expand information processing capacity.

<table>
<tr><td>CHANDLER'S RESTAURANT:<br>A CASE OF<br>STRATEGIC CHOICE</td><td>CHAPTER<br>4</td></tr>
</table>

This chapter presents a description of the communication and supply problems of a restaurant. The purpose is to analyze this organization as an information processing system so as to illustrate the concept of strategic choice of organizing modes introduced in the last chapter. The restaurant is large enough to have information processing problems and small enough so that we can comprehend it in its entirety. The case is a modification of an actual restaurant described by Whyte.[1] Much of the description is quoted directly but the charts and work flows have been added to facilitate the analysis to follow in the next chapter.

## ORGANIZATION AND WORK FLOW

Chandler's Restaurant is a fairly large restaurant employing 100 persons and serving medium quality food. Chandler's operates on three floors. The second and third floors are devoted to dining areas. The bottom floor is the kitchen. The pantries are on the floor of the dining room that they supply. Dishwashing is on the bottom floor. Figure 4.1 represents the work flow and information flow relevant to the supply system. The system is directly analogous to a durable good distribution system in which the kitchen represents the fabrication or job-shop stage; the pantry, the assembly operation; and the dining rooms, the distribution of the product. This supply system is coordinated through an authority structure which is diagrammed in Fig. 4.2.

There is a dining room supervisor who manages the admission, seating, serving, and customer request functions. A kitchen supervisor is in charge of the pantry, kitchen, and dish provisioning functions. And finally, the ad-

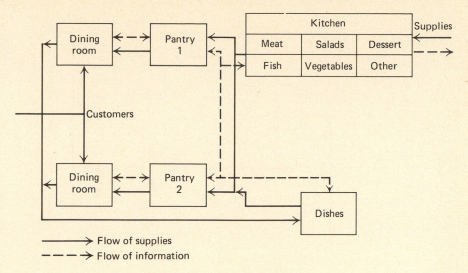

Fig. 4.1  Schematic of information and supplies flows.

ministrative function of bookkeeping, financial, and personnel activities are placed in a third group.

While reading Whyte's description, the reader should try to identify the problems of supplying food at Chandler's and to think of as many methods as possible to alleviate these problems. It should be mentioned that the description is relevant only to the supplying function. The management is also concerned with menu and recipe selection, selection of suppliers, selection and purchase of foodstuffs, supervision of preparation and quality of food, handling of food, quality complaints, advertising, etc. These are issues, but are not considered to be problematic in the described situation.

## CHANDLER'S RESTAURANT*

In discussing the kitchen as a status system, we have only incidentally taken account of the fact that the kitchen is part of a communication and supply system, which operates to get the food from the range onto the customer's table. Looking at it this way will bring to light other problems.

Where the restaurant is small and the kitchen is on the same floor as the dining room, waitresses are in direct contact with cooks. This does not eliminate friction, but at least everybody is in a position to know what

* From *Human relations in the restaurant industry,* copyright 1948 by McGraw-Hill, pp. 47–60. Reprinted by permission of the author.

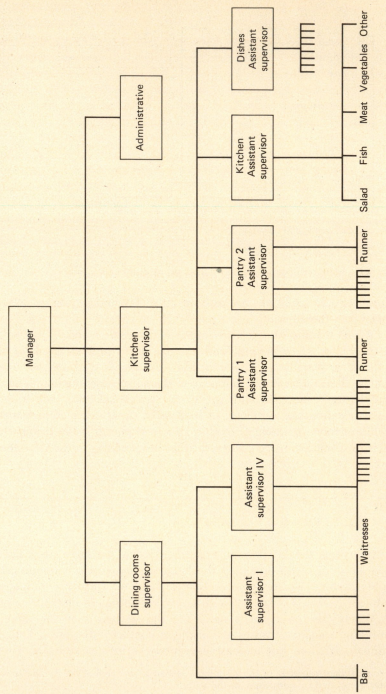

Fig. 4.2 Authority structure of Chandler's Restaurant.

everybody else is doing, and the problems of communication and coordination are relatively simple.

When the restaurant is large, there are more people whose activities must be coordinated, and when the restaurant operates on several floors, the coordination must be accomplished through people who are not generally in face-to-face contact with each other. These factors add tremendously to the difficulty of achieving smooth coordination.

The cooks feel that they work under pressure—and under a pressure whose origins they cannot see or anticipate.

As one of them said,

> It's mostly the uncertainty of the job that gets me down, I think. I
> mean, you never know how much work you're going to have to do.
> You never know in advance if you're going to have to make more. I
> think that's what a lot of 'em don't like around here. That uncertainty
> is hard on your nerves.

For a cook, the ideal situation is one in which she always has a sufficient supply of food prepared ahead so that she is never asked for something she does not have on hand. As one of them said, "You have to keep ahead or you get all excited and upset."

Life would be simpler for the cook if she were free to prepare just as much food as she wanted to, but the large and efficiently operated restaurant plans production on the basis of very careful estimates of the volume of business to be expected. Low food costs depend in part upon minimizing waste or left-over food. This means that production must be scheduled so as to run only a little ahead of customer demand. The cook therefore works within a narrow margin of error. She can't get far ahead, and that means that on extra-busy days she is certain sometimes to lose her lead or even to drop behind.

When the cook drops behind, all the pressures from customer to waitress to service pantry to runner descend upon her, for no one between her and the customer can do his job unless she produces the goods. From this point of view, timing and coordination are key problems of the organization. Proper timing and good coordination must be achieved in human relations or else efficiency is dissipated in personal frictions.

While these statements apply to every step in the process of production and service, let us look here at the first steps—the relations of cooks to kitchen runners to the service pantry.

When the restaurant operates on different floors, the relations must be carried on in part through mechanical means of communication. There are three common channels of this nature, and all have their drawbacks. Use of a public address system adds considerably to the noise of the kitchen and service pantries. The teleautograph (in which orders written on the machine on one floor are automatically recorded on the kitchen machine) is quiet but sometimes unintelligible. Orders written in a hurry and in abbreviated form are sometimes misinterpreted so that sliced ham arrives when sliced toms (tomatoes) were ordered. Besides, neither of those channels operates easily for two-way communication. It is difficult to carry on a conversation over the public address system, and, while kitchen runners can write their replies to orders on the teleautograph, this hardly makes for full and free expression. The telephone provides two-way communication, but most kitchens are so noisy that it is difficult to hear phone conversations. And then in some restaurants there is only one telephone circuit for the whole house, so that when kitchen and pantry runners are using it, no one else can put in a call.

The problems that come up with such communication systems can best be illustrated by looking at a particular restaurant, Chandler's, where teleautograph and phone were used.

A kitchen supervisor was in charge of Chandler's kitchen, and pantry supervisors were in charge of each pantry, under her general supervision. There was also an assistant supervisor working in the kitchen.

The supplying function was carried on in the kitchen by two or three runners (depending upon the employment situation) and by a runner on each of the service-pantry floors. Food was sent up by automatic elevator.

The kitchen runners were supposed to pick up their orders from storage bins, iceboxes, or direct from the cooks. When the order was in preparation, the cook or salad girl was supposed to say how long it would be before it was ready, and the runner would relay this information by teleautograph to the service pantries. When the cooking or salad making had not been begun, the runner had no authority to tell the cook to hurry the order. Before each meal, the cook was given an open order (a minimum and maximum amount) on each item by the kitchen supervisor. She worked steadily until she had produced the minimum, and, from then on, she gauged her production according to the demands that came to her from the runner. That is, if the item was going out fast, she would keep producing as fast as she could until she had produced the maximum. Beyond this point she could not go without authorization from her supervisor. Ideally, the supervisor and cook would confer before the maximum had been reached in order to see whether it was necessary to set a new figure, but this did not always happen.

While the runner could not order the cook to go beyond her maximum, his demands did directly influence her behavior up to that point. He originated action for her.

That was at the base of his troubles. Among kitchen employees, as we have seen, the cooks have the highest status. In Chandler's, runners had a low status, just above potwashers and sweepers. The jobs were filled by inexperienced employees, women or men who, if they performed well, were advanced to something of higher status. Their wages were considerably lower than the cooks', and the cooks also had a great advantage in seniority. In this particular case, the age difference was important too. The runners were a young man, a teen-aged boy, and a young girl, while the cooks were middle-aged women.

The runners would have been in a more secure position if they had been in close touch with a supervisor, but here the communication was sporadic and ineffective. The supervisor was inclined to let the runners fend for themselves.

When the runners put pressure on them, the cooks were inclined to react so as to put the runners in their place. For example, we observed incidents like this one. One runner (Ruth) asked another to get some salmon salad from the salad girl. The second runner found that the salad girl had no more on hand.

"They want me to get some more of that salmon salad," he said. "Could you make it, please?"

"Who told you that?" she asked.

"Ruth did."

"You can tell Ruth that I don't take no orders from her. I have a boss, and I don't take no orders from nobody else. You can just tell her that."

Now it may have been that the salad girl had made her maximum and could not go on without authorization from her supervisor, but the runner had no way of knowing that this was the case. He put his request to her politely, and she could have responded in kind by saying she was sorry that she could not make more without consulting the supervisor. Instead she responded aggressively, as if she felt a need to make it clear that no mere runner was going to originate action for her.

Even when they complied with the runner's requests, the cooks some-times behaved so as to make it appear as if it were really they who origi-nated the action. They always liked to make it clear that they had authority over the foods after they had been prepared, and that they could determine what should be done with them. While this was a general reaction, the salad girl was most explicit in such cases.

A runner went to look for some boiled eggs. The salad girl was not present at the moment, so he could not ask her, but after he had got the eggs from the icebox, he saw that she was back at her station. He showed her the pan of eggs, asking, "What about that?"

"I don't like that," she said belligerently. "You have no business taking them eggs out of the icebox without asking."

"Well, I'm asking you now."

"I have to know how much there is. That's why I want you to tell me. . . . Go on, you might as well take them now that you have them."

On other occasions when he asked her for salad, she would say, "Why don't you people look in the icebox once in a while?"

In such a case, whatever the runner did was wrong. The salad girl's behavior was irrational, of course, but it did serve a function for her. Behaving in this way, she was able to originate action for the runner instead of being in the inferior position of responding to his actions.

The runners also had difficulty in getting information out of the cooks. When there was a demand from the service pantries, and the food could not be sent up immediately, the runners were always supposed to give an estimate as to when they could furnish the item. This information they were expected to get from the cooks. The cooks sometimes flatly refused to give a time and were generally reluctant to make an estimate. When they did give a time, they nearly always ran considerably beyond it.

Incidentally, time seems to be used as a weapon in the restaurant. It is well known that customers feel and complain that they wait for a table or for service far longer than they actually do. Waitresses, as we observed them, estimated their waiting time on orders as much as 50 to 100 percent more than the actual time. While they were not conscious of what they were doing, they could express impatience with the service-pantry girls more eloquently by saying, "I've been waiting 20 minutes for that order," than by giving the time as 10 minutes. In the front of the house, time is used to put pressure on people. In the back of the house, the cooks try to use time to take pressure off themselves. They say that an item will be done "right away," which does not tell when it will be done but announces that they have the situation well in hand and that nobody should bother them about it. Giving a short time tends to have the same effect. It reassures the runner, who reassures the service pantries. When the time runs out, the pantry runners begin again to demand action, but it may take a few minutes before the pressure gets back to the cooks, and by that time the item may really be ready for delivery. Furthermore, the cook's refusal to give a time turns the pressure back on runners and other parts of the house—a result that she is not able to accomplish in any other way.

In the case of some of the inexperienced cooks, it may be that they simply did not know how to estimate cooking time, but that would hardly explain the persistent failure of all the cooks to cooperate with the runners in this matter.

The management was quite aware of this problem but had no real solution to offer. One of the pantry supervisors instructed a kitchen runner in this way:

"You have to give us a time on everything that is going to be delayed. That is the only way we can keep things going upstairs. On our blackboards we list all our foods and how long it will take to get them, and most of the time we have to list them 'indefinite.' That shouldn't be. We should always have a definite time, so the waitress can tell the guest how long he will have to wait for his order. We can't tell the guest we're out of a certain food item on the menu and that we don't know how long it will take to replace it. They'll ask what kind of a restaurant we're running."

The runner thought that over and then went on to question the supervisor. "But sometimes we can't get that information from the cooks. . . . They won't tell us, or maybe they don't know."

"Then you should always ask the food-production manager. She'll tell you, or she'll get the cook to tell you."

"But the cooks would think we had squealed."

"No, they wouldn't. And if they did, all right, it's the only way they'll ever learn. They've got to learn that, because we must always have a time on all delayed foods."

"Yes, surely we couldn't tell on them if they refused to give the information."

"Yes, you could. You have to. They'll have to learn it somehow."

The efficiency of this system depended upon building up a cooperative relationship between cooks and runners. For runners to try to get action by appealing to the boss to put pressure on the cooks is hardly the way to build up such a relationship. It is clear that, considering their low status in relation to the cooks, runners are not in a position to take the lead in smoothing out human-relations difficulties.

Some of the runner's problems arise out of failure to achieve efficient coordination and communication between floors. For example, on one occasion one of the upstairs floors put in a rush order for a pan of rice. With some difficulty, the kitchen runner was able to fill the order. Then, 15 minutes later, the pan came back to the kitchen again, still almost full, but apparently no more was needed for the meal. The cooks gathered around the elevator to give vent to their feelings. This proved, they said, that the rice had not been needed after all. Those people upstairs just didn't know what they were doing. After the meal was over, the kitchen runner went up to check with the pantry runner. The pantry man explained, "I ran out of creole, and there wasn't going to be any more, so I had no use for any more rice."

This was a perfectly reasonable explanation, but it did not reach the cooks. As a rule, the cooks had little idea of what was going on upstairs. Sometimes there would be an urgent call for some food item along toward the end of the meal-time, and it would be supplied only after a considerable delay. By the time it reached the service pantries, there would no longer be a demand for it, and the supply would shortly be sent back. This would always upset the cooks. They would then stand around and vow that next time they would not take it seriously when the upstairs people were clamoring for action.

"In the service pantries," one of the cooks said, "they just don't care how much they ask for. That guy, Joe [pantry runner], just hoards the stuff up there. He can't always be out of it like he claims. He just hoards it."

A kitchen runner made this comment:

> Joe will order something and right away he'll order it again. He just
> keeps calling for more. Once or twice I went upstairs, and I saw he
> had plenty of stuff up there. He just hoards it up there, and he has
> to send a lot of stuff downstairs. He wastes a lot of stuff. After I
> caught on to the way he works, I just made it a rule when he called
> for stuff and the first floor was calling for stuff at the same time, I
> divided it between them.

On the other hand, when Joe was rushed and found that he was not getting quick action on his orders, his tendency was to make his orders larger, repeat the orders before any supply had come up, and mark all his orders *rush*. When this did not bring results, he would call the kitchen on the phone. If all else failed, he would sometimes run down into the kitchen himself to see if he could snatch what he needed.

This kind of behavior built up confusion and resentment in the kitchen. When orders were repeated, the kitchen runners could not tell whether additional supply was needed or whether the pantry runners were just getting impatient. When everything was marked rush, there was no way of telling how badly anybody needed anything. But most serious of all was the reaction when the pantry runner invaded the kitchen.

One of them told us of such an incident:

> One of the cooks got mad at me the other day. I went down there to
> get this item, and boy, did she get mad at me for coming down there.
> But I got to do *something!* The waitresses and the pantry girls keep
> on yelling at me to get it for them. Well, I finally got it, or somehow
> it got sent upstairs. Boy, she was sure mad at me, though.

Apparently the cooks resented the presence of any upstairs supply man in the kitchen, but they were particularly incensed against Joe, the runner they all suspected of hoarding food.

One of them made this comment:

> That guy would try to come down in the kitchen and tell us what to do. But not me. No sir. He came down here one day and tried to tell me what to do. He said to me, "We're going to be very busy today." I just looked at him. "Yeah?" I said, "who are you? Go on upstairs. Go on. Mind your own business." Can you beat that! "We're going to be very busy today!" He never came down and told *me* anything again. "Who are you?" I asked him. That's all I had to say to him.

Here the runner's remark did not have any effect upon the work of the cook, but the implication was that he was in a superior position, and she reacted strongly against him for that reason. None of the cooks enjoy having the kitchen runners originate action for them, but, since it occurs regularly, they make some adjustment to it. They are not accustomed to any sort of relationship with the pantry runners, so when they come down to add to the pressure and confusion of the kitchen, the cooks feel free to slap them down.

It was not only the pantry runners who invaded the kitchen. The pantry supervisors spent a good deal of time and energy running up and down. When an upstairs supervisor comes after supplies, the kitchen reaction is the same as that to the pantry runners—except that the supervisor cannot be slapped down. Instead, the employees gripe to each other.

As one kitchen runner said,

> I wish she would quit that. I wonder what she thinks she's doing, running down here and picking up things we're waiting for. Now like just a minute ago, did you see that? She went off with peaches and plums, and we'd never have known about it if I hadn't seen her. Now couldn't she have just stepped over here and told us? . . . She sure gets mad a lot, doesn't she? She's always griping. I mean, she's probably a nice person, but she's hard to get along with at work—she sure is!

There were other pantry supervisors whose presence in the kitchen did not cause such a disturbance. The workers would say that so-and-so was really all right. Nevertheless, whenever a pantry supervisor dashed into the kitchen to look for supplies, it was a sign to everybody that something was wrong—that somebody was worried—and thus it added to the tension in the atmosphere and disturbed the human relations of the regular supply system—such as they were.

In this situation, the kitchen runner was the man in the middle. One of the service-pantry girls we interviewed put it this way:

> Oh, we certainly are busy up here. We don't stop even for a moment. I think this is the busiest place around here. It's bad when we can't get those foods, though. We get delayed by those supply people downstairs all the time. I could shoot those runners. We can be just as busy up here—but down there it's always slow motion. It seems like they just don't care at all. They always take all the time in the world.

On the other hand, the cooks blamed the inefficiency of the runners for many of their troubles. They felt that the runners were constantly sending up duplicate orders just through failure to consult each other on the progress of their work. Actually, according to our observation, this happened very rarely, but whenever a runner was caught in the act, this was taken as proof that duplication was common practice. The failure of the runners to coordinate their work efficiently did annoy the cooks in another way, as they were sometimes asked for the same order within a few seconds by two different runners. However, while this added to the nervous tension, it did not directly affect the flow of supplies.

Such were the problems of supply in one restaurant where we were able to give them close attention. However, as it stands, this account is likely to give a false impression. The reader may picture the restaurant as a series of armed camps, each one in constant battle with its neighbor. He may also get the impression that food reaches customers only intermittently and after long delays.

To us it seemed that the restaurant was doing a remarkable job of production and service, and yet, in view of the frictions we observed, it is only natural to ask whether it would not be possible to organize the human relations so as to make for better teamwork and greater efficiency.

According to one point of view, no basic improvement is possible because "you can't change human nature."

But is it all just personalities and personal inefficiency? What has been the situation in other restaurants of this type (operating on several floors) and in other periods of time?

Unfortunately we have no studies for other time periods, but we do have the testimony of several supervisors who have had previous experience in restaurants facing similar problems, and who have shown themselves, in the course of our study, to be shrewd observers of behavior in their own organizations. Their story is that the friction and incoordination we observed were not simply a war-time phenomenon. While increased business and inexperienced help made the problem much more acute, the friction came at the same places in the organization—between the same categories of people—that it used to. The job of the kitchen runner, apparently, has always been a "hot spot" in such an organization.

This, then, is not primarily a personality problem. It is a problem in human relations. When the organization operates so as to stimulate conflict between people holding certain positions within it, then we can expect trouble.

---

## SUMMARY

The preceding has been a quotation taken from Whyte's observations of the restaurant supply function. The student is asked to describe the underlying or basic causes of what Whyte describes as human relations problems. Whyte also asks the question as to whether there is not a better way of organizing the human relations so as to be satisfying to the participants and more efficient in terms of service to the customers and food resources that are wasted. How would you intervene in the system? Would you change the task, the structure, the information system, or the human system? Is there more than one way to solve the problem? How many different ways can you think of?

## NOTE

1. W. F. Whyte 1948. *Human relations in the restaurant industry*. New York: McGraw-Hill.

| ANALYSIS OF CHANDLER'S RESTAURANT: STRATEGIC CHOICE ILLUSTRATED | CHAPTER 5 |
| --- | --- |

In this chapter we will analyze the capability of the Chandler's organization to function as a supply system. First, the supply task is analyzed and then the coordination of the task is described. The intention of the description is to allow the identification of problems which can be treated by some type of organization design intervention. Finally, several different changes are described and evaluated in terms of the problem description.

### THE SUPPLY TASK

The supply requirements at Chandler's stem from the division of labor which has been adopted. First, the time value of the product and the geographical separation of activity areas force the creation of separate subtasks to prepare, assemble, and distribute the food. That is, the time value or perishability prevents the same work force from preparing and assembling the food prior to distribution. Thus, these activities must be performed almost simultaneously at the last minute. In addition, the economies of cost per square foot that the multistory operation offers also require that the subtasks be performed by different people in different locations. Second, the desired quality level is best achieved by further dividing the preparation function around common skills and equipment availability. This further division leads to separate groups who specialize in preparing meat, fish, salads, etc. Thus, the physical nature of the product, the desired quality level, the economics of physical location, the volume of activity, and the market availability of skills and equipment all influence Chandler's to choose the existing pattern of work division.

While the chosen division of labor satisfies economic and technological constraints, it creates problems for the coordination and integration of the subtasks for the successful completion of the whole task. That is, the output of the system is a customer order which requires some distribution activities, some assembly activities, and several of the preparation activities. Since these activities are performed by different people on different floors, the cooperative, combined efforts of several people are required for the successful completion of the order. The securing of these combined efforts is made difficult because the optimal basis of the kitchen operation is different from those of the pantries and dining rooms, there are tight time requirements, the perishability of the product makes inventory accumulation difficult, food wastage is expensive, there is a large variety of items, the items are interdependent, and there are priority questions in serving two pantries. Let us look briefly at each of these.

The problems of coordinating the work flow from the pantry to the dining room are minimized by using the customer order as the focus around which the combined efforts are concentrated. They can work toward a common, clear goal. This is not the case for many activities in the kitchen. The reason is that kitchen activities require only a little more time to prepare 20 orders than to prepare one order. Therefore, the most efficient way for the kitchen tasks to operate is to pool customer orders and prepare batches. The batches disrupt the continuity of flow around customer orders.

The conflict between operation modes is problematic only because of the severe time pressures under which the restaurant operates. These pressures arise from the unwillingness of the customer to wait very long for the preparation and delivery of the order and from the need to serve the order very quickly after its preparation. Both these factors require the smooth quick flow of orders from the kitchen to the dining room.

The conflict between operation modes of sequential activities is common in manufacturing industries and is resolved by accumulating inventories to allow each activity to operate in its most efficient manner and still meet customer delivery requirements. The restaurant must also accumulate some inventory to uncouple the kitchen and pantry operations. Like the manufacturer, the restaurant incurs substantial storage costs. Steam tables and refrigerated storage are expensive. But still there are other pressures because the items perish over short periods of time and the cost of wasted food is substantial. Indeed, the cost of wasted food is the only variable cost in the short run because the work force and physical capacity are known. Thus perishability and food cost create pressures to minimize the amount of food stored between the kitchen and the pantry and in the pantry itself.

The minimization of the inventory is made difficult because Chandler's serves a variety of menu items and must be prepared to serve all of them.

The large variety of items and the uncertainty as to which ones will be ordered complicate the decision. It is further complicated by the fact that there is interdependence among items. This interdependence is indicated by the rice-creole episode. The amount of rice ordered is not independent of the amount of creole. The orders for these items and others need to be coordinated and ordering decisions must be taken simultaneously.

The final complication for the inventory management arises because there are two pantries. The two pantries create conditions where one can be out of stock while the other has an oversupply. Rather than prepare a new batch, the stock should be transferred from one pantry to another. On other occasions, both pantries will run out of stock and present a priority problem to the shared kitchen facility. Thus, the stocks of the two pantries need to be coordinated as well.

In summary, the division of labor, the diversity of output, and the cost and delivery requirements create a highly interdependent work flow system which needs to be coordinated. Let us now examine the information and decision process which coordinates this work flow.

## CURRENT ORGANIZING MODE

The interdependent work flow is coordinated with a periodic planning decision process. Each day the kitchen supervisor forecasts the evening's activity and prepares maximum and minimum production levels for each menu item. As described in the previous chapter, the cook works up to the minimum in order to create an inventory. Further production up to the maximum depends on the observed outflow from inventory. Cooks cannot go above the maximum without the authorization of the kitchen supervisor. This control presumably is to see that reorder decisions are made from the global perspective of the kitchen supervisor.

The plan is a global comprehensive one in that it considers all the interdependent factors (menu items, pantries, and kitchen subtasks) simultaneously from the point of view of the system as a whole. The kitchen supervisor maintains a global data base so that exceptions to the maximum levels can be handled effectively. The plan is periodic in that it is prepared once at the beginning of the evening and updated only on an exception basis. There is no comprehensive replanning during an evening. The next comprehensive plan is made for the next evening.

## EVALUATION OF THE CURRENT SYSTEM

The effectiveness of the system at Chandler's, like all period planning systems, depends critically upon the ability of the organization to forecast accurately over the period of the plan and to generate meaningful targets (max. and min.). For Chandler's, this means they must forecast the total volume of activity and its distribution over a large number of items. From the case, we can conclude that quite often these forecasts are inaccurate. The described interactions between cooks and runners occur on the evenings when the volume is high and the mix forecasts are poor. What happens specifically?

On busy evenings, items begin to reach maximums and generate exceptions to be handled by the kitchen supervisor. The first few exceptions are probably handled in the prescribed manner. However, the press of normal duties, exceptions such as returned items from the dining room, menu changes, etc., very soon take up all the supervisor's available time. The upward referral process stalls. In most organizations this situation would cause delays in decisions or expansion of executive time through longer hours or time taken from planning activities. In the restaurant the time pressure forces immediate decisions. Thus, the decisions to order or not to order fall to lower levels until decisions "happen" at the waitress, runner, and cook level. The information and decision process becomes a local, real-time type. The decay in the plan caused by the demand uncertainty and the time pressure force a real-time process on the restaurant and render the global plan ineffective.

The information system at Chandler's, however, is inadequate to support an interdependent real-time system. The system becomes a series of two-way verbal links which are shown in Fig. 5.1. This system has two

Customer ⟷ Waitress ⟷ Pantry ⟷ Runner ⟷ Cook

**Fig. 5.1   Serial information flow to support the real-time decision process.**

major defects. First, it does not have the channel capacity to transmit the volume of information necessary to support decisions which must consider simultaneously all of the interdependent factors. For example, a cook may prepare an order for one pantry only to have the other pantry order the same item after the completion of the first order. Another is that a cook may refuse to prepare another batch of an item which could be used in the next night's menu because she is ignorant of that menu. Many other examples could be given but in every case a decision must be made with incomplete knowledge of relevant circumstances.

The second defect of the information system is that some of the limited channel capacity is wasted by the transmission of noise in addition to signal. Even under benign circumstances, the sequential transmission of a message between five people will result in some distortion. In this case, there is also time pressure, status differences, different perceptions of the situation, differences in goals, and differences in costs of a mistake. These factors create the overordering, overstatement of needs, misquotation of times, misperceptions of valid requests, etc., which were reported in the previous chapter. The result is that many messages are simply not believed or are regarded as noise. A pantry must order something three times before the cooks believe the pantry "really" needs the item. Reordering consumes additional capacity which could be used for sending other messages.

In summary, the uncertainty of demand for the many menu items causes the global plan to decay over the evening. Overloads on the supervision and time pressures force the decisions to be taken at the runner–cook level of the organization. In a situation of interdependence, decisions are made with local information and local goals. The result is reduced customer service and/or wasted food. Now it's quite possible that Chandler's is a profitable operation and no different from other large restaurants. But as Whyte asks, is there not a better way to organize for more effective teamwork and efficiency?

## ALTERNATIVE ORGANIZATION DESIGNS

The continuation of the chapter is evidence that it is believed that there are better ways of organizing. It is suggested that there are many ways to intervene in the organization to improve the situation. The alternatives will be presented within the organization design framework.

Before the design alternatives are described, it should be said that a simple intervention through the human system may be possible. If the removal of noise from the information system shown in Fig. 5.1 would create enough capacity to support the real-time decision process, the human system intervention may be the preferable one. Some team-building sessions, daily or weekly meetings, and job rotation may reduce goal differences, increase the awareness of the others' problems, increase trust and validity of communications so that the current technology, structure, and decision processes are more effective. However, if channel capacity is still insufficient after improving the quality of the sequential verbal system, other changes would be necessary in addition to improved interpersonal relations.

### Change the Environment

Another way of eliminating the necessity of changing the structure and processes of the restaurant is to change the sources of the problem. A substantial portion of the coordination problem stems from the time pressure and uncertainty originating in the customer. Why not try to reduce these factors to tolerable levels?

The uncertainty may be reduced in a number of ways. First, the number of menu items could be reduced. It is easier to forecast demand for five items than for 20 items. The reduction will increase forecast accuracy and thereby reduce both the number of exceptions and the number of items about which one must communicate when an exception occurs. Second, the restaurant could seek out large parties for banquets and fix the menus in advance. This strategy altogether eliminates the need to forecast. There are some restaurants which ask you to choose a menu when you make a reservation. Again uncertainty is reduced and the life of the global plan is extended through the decision period.

These strategies are not without their costs, however. Limited menus may lose customers who also want reasonable quality. The party giving the banquet will probably demand a lower price quotation. The menu selected in advance may contain requests for greater variety as the selector will want a larger voice in the menu creation. Thus, while each alternative is effective in reducing the magnitude of the problem, it may not be efficient from the overall viewpoint of the restaurant.

Similarly, the restaurant may try to provide atmosphere, entertainment, drinks, etc., to reduce the time pressure. All these strategies attempt to extend the time between when a customer enters and orders and when the order is delivered without making the time appear to be long. Like reducing uncertainty, reducing time pressure is effective in alleviating the problem (expands time available for communication, less distortion, etc.) but has its costs (less eating space, greater cost of facilities, etc.). Whether these strategies are chosen depends on their relative costs and relative effectiveness in dealing with the communication problem.

### Creation of Slack

The second class of alternatives are those which reduce the difficulty of performance levels. The obvious alternative in this case is simply to raise the maximums for the given forecast levels. The result will be more inventory, good customer service, fewer exceptions, and smoother interactions all along the work flow because the global plan can provide the basis for cooperation. The cost is, of course, more food spoilage. However, if it is recognized that menu items are not equally perishable and not equally costly, the maximums could be raised only for low cost and less perishable items. Then all communication and coordination would be concentrated upon high cost, highly perishable items. The restaurant may, however, already employ this practice.

### Increase the Degree of Self-Containment

The coordination requirements can be reduced by reducing the division of labor. Chandler's could follow the European tradition of moving some of the preparation and assembling of orders into the dining room to be performed by a waiter at the customer's table. This strategy combines the preparation, assembly, and delivery of an order into a single role. The coordination among the three subtasks is performed by a single individual. The cost of this strategy is finding people with the necessary skill and paying them the wages that the skill demands.

There is also the possibility of moving some preparation tasks into the pantry and creating self-contained units around the two pantry–dining room combinations. The cost to Chandler's will be the duplication of resources in two pantries where now these resources are shared. However, those activities for which there is sufficient volume, low skills, or low economies of scale in the equipment can be moved forward at minimal costs. Those activities requiring special skills and equipment and which cannot be purchased outside remain shared in the kitchen. This strategy reduces the division of labor which in turn reduces either the number of subactivities which must be combined to produce an order or to bring all the divided subtasks into a single unit where communication and coordination are rendered more easily. These are structural changes which facilitate real-time decision making. The decay of the global plan is assumed and the capability to respond and make decisions at the local level is enhanced by reducing some of the interdependence (shared resources) between the two local units. The autonomy of the local units permits the exercise of greater influence by first-level participants which may be preferable from a motivational standpoint.

### Investment in the Formal Information System

If Chandler's cannot change its strategy, cannot tolerate more waste, and must keep the current division of work, then it can also solve its problems by changing its information system. There are two possibilities. First, Chandler's can augment its current periodic planning system by formalization and a different decision mechanism. Second, it can increase the frequency of making global decisions and move toward a global, real-time system. Let us look in detail at each of these.

**1. Augmented periodic planning system.** The capacity of the information system could be expanded if the languages for ordering and reordering were formalized and standardized. The process could start by standardizing the menu items and assigning numbers to them. Printed forms would allow more accurate messages for ordering and provide a historical record as well. One restaurant currently employs a system of metal discs on which numbers are stamped. Different sized discs represent different sizes of reorders. These are dropped through a pipe between floors to provide an ordering system. The formalization also depersonalizes the initiation of reorder preparation.

The formalization steps permit the transmission of more information with fewer symbols. It expands the channel capacity for responding to changes in the plan. But by itself formalization may not be sufficient.

A second and complementary change would be to improve the decision mechanism which forecasts and assigns maximum and minimum levels. One could employ operations research techniques to reduce the forecasting error. A model which accounted for cyclical demand changes during the week, month, or year may improve upon the current forecast.

The new forecast could feed into an algorithm which chooses optimal amounts of inventory by trading off the cost of food spoilage and customer service. To some degree the restaurant's decision is a classical operations research problem referred to as the newsboy problem or the Christmas tree problem. Chandler's has a multistage version of that classical problem.

The effect of these changes is to create some mathematical models which reduce the forecast errors and select inventory levels which minimize the expected costs which are affected by the level of inventory. The change is to improve the initial global planning decision. Decision rules could be generated for decisions of when and how much to order during an evening as well. When combined with increased formalization of data flow, the planning models may reduce significantly the communication problems that are facing Chandler's. The global plan is more likely to be valid and the subsequent changes to it are facilitated by the formalized language and procedures. This strategy of formalization and models augments the current global periodic system for managing the interdependent work flow.

**2. Global, real-time system.** The second alternative is to regard the initial planning decision as one of many that will be made during the night and to modify the information and decision process so that subsequent reordering decisions are made using a global data base. There are many ways to implement this strategy but all of them involve making the global decisions more often, creating a decision mechanism to make them, and creating a global data base to support the decisions. One method of implementing this strategy will be described here but there are others.

One method of implementing the real-time strategy is to create a new role—a supply management role. The decision mechanism is simply the person who will act out this new role. Currently this role is partially played by the runners. The runners however perform the role by accident, not by design. They do not have the information or knowledge to make good decisions. And the rest of the organization does not regard their decisions as legitimate. The new role performer must overcome these difficulties.

The new role may be performed by someone in the existing organization. The case does not give information as to what the assistant supervisors and kitchen supervisors are doing while the runners and cooks are having their problems. But assuming it can be performed by someone in the existing organization, who should perform the role? The assistant supervisors do not appear to be the appropriate choice. The essence of the role is making trade-off decisions between food costs and customer service. The assistant supervisors in the pantries, who bear little cost if there is too much food but face frantic waitresses when there is too little, would be biased toward overproduction. The assistant supervisor in the kitchen who faces overworked cooks but never sees a waitress would be biased towards too little production. Thus, the kitchen supervisor appears to be one with the appropriate goal orientation to exhibit the needed decision-making behavior.

After the decision mechanism is designed, the design of the information flows and data base is accomplished by seeing that the role occupant participates in buying and menu preparation decisions and stays informed of developments throughout the evening. Staying informed merely means relying on verbal and visual information systems by walking around the restaurant and talking and observing the activity. The information system for supply decisions becomes the one shown in Fig. 5.2.

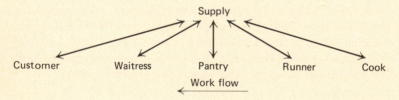

**Fig. 5.2** **Representation of global information system for supply decisions.**

The supply supervisor can reorder, observe stocks, reforecast activity, change minimums and maximums for cooks, feed information to waitresses to promise faster service for items not moving fast, shift supplies from one pantry to another, etc. In this manner adaptive decisions are made in an uncertain, interdependent situation. The new role has the time, authority, and information to perform this task.

This section has described a global, real-time information system. The global data base being necessary to manage the interdependence brought about by the division of labor, time pressure, and food cost, and the real-time decision making being necessary for the uncertainty. The information system may be regarded by some as no system at all. However, one purpose of this section was to talk about information systems independent of computers and paper-processing mechanisms. Too often discussions of information systems consider only computers. It may be that if Chandler's is large enough, a computer and closed circuit television can provide an on-line, real-time system to coordinate the work. But the supply supervisor with the appropriate behavior provides the same capacity for moderately sized restaurants.

Like the other strategies, the two strategies for changing the information systems have their costs. It costs to build and sustain formalized information flows and operations research models. The cost of the supply role depends on whether and what type of person is hired by the restaurant. A clerk could be hired to free some time so that the current kitchen supervisor performs the role. In any case more wages are paid.

### Lateral Relations

The last organizing mode is to employ lateral relations between the interdependent roles. The informal and spontaneous direct contacts are currently being used by runners, cooks, pantry workers, etc., and are insufficient. A liaison role may be employed by upgrading the status of the runners. However, a global perspective is required to coordinate the whole system. The next logical mechanism is a group formed by combining the interdependent roles. Meetings would pool all the information needed to manage the supply system. However, the time pressures operating in the restaurant make this option unfeasible. Some other form is needed.

The most feasible alternative is to create a new role, an integrating role, to perform the supply function. If some of the current supervisors have sufficient time to perform the supply function, an integrating role will work. The new position would be at a level of assistant supervisor. In several large restaurants which use an assistant supervisor of supply, the position reports to the kitchen supervisor. In this manner, the restaurant, like manufacturing organizations with difficult supply problems, creates an integrating role to coordinate interdepartmental work flows. In manufacturing, this position is referred to as the production controller or scheduler.

The new role is an integrating role since no one works for the occupant. Occupants of this role are expected to coordinate the work of people who do not work for them. They are to coordinate because the current organization cannot. They coordinate only with respect to supply problems which are the major source of interdependence.

## SUMMARY AND DISCUSSION

In this chapter Chandler's Restaurant was analyzed as a supply system. To some degree we ignored the quality of food preparation and some of the motivation issues in order to highlight the information processing aspects. The chapter illustrates the use of the organization design framework in generating alternative forms of intervention in an organization. About seven or eight alternatives were described, any one of which could be adopted by a restaurant like Chandler's. For example, the slack alternative may be adopted by a restaurant in an airport. The additional food cost could be covered by raising the price. Since customers are usually on expense accounts, the price is less important than quality and speed of service. In another environment, one of the other alternatives must be chosen.

The application of the framework to Chandler's gives us the opportunity to be clearer about the logic of the framework. The different modes of the framework are continually referred to as "alternatives." In one sense the strategies are not alternatives but in another sense they are. First, the strategies are not mutually exclusive alternatives. That is, the restaurant could choose to create a new supply role *and* use operations research techniques to forecast demand and choose inventory levels. Indeed, as long as the strategies do not work at cross-purposes, Chandler's could adopt all the suggestions described in this chapter. Thus the strategies of the framework can be combined and more than one of them chosen. However, each of the alternatives has a cost in addition to producing a desired effect. At some point the improvement of operations diminishes so that the effect produced fails to offset the cost of the change. Therefore the strategies and combinations of strategies are alternatives. The organization should choose the strategy that produces the desired effect at the least cost. Which alternative is chosen is also determined by preferences of the people in positions of influence. They may prefer the decentralization that is achieved by self-contained units. If costs are substantially different between the alternatives, the strategic choice may be determined by preferences or ideologies of the group in power.

And finally, this chapter demonstrates the richness of organization phenomena. Seven or eight viable strategies for handling uncertainty were discussed. Someone more familiar with restaurant operations could easily double that number. The richness should lead to a healthy skepticism of research studies which report simple correlations between uncertainty and decentralization or size and decentralization. In this chapter it was shown that uncertainty could lead to decentralization if self-contained groups were chosen, to centralization if either of the global information systems were chosen, or to no change if slack is employed. Thus, there is no simple relationship between uncertainty and structural attributes.

| INFORMATION REDUCTION<br>MODES: ALTERNATIVES 1 AND 2 | CHAPTER<br>**6** |
|---|---|

The organizing modes (Alternatives 1 and 2) discussed in this chapter are those that reduce the amount of information that must be processed. In terms of the information-processing theory presented in Chapter 3, the amount of information is reduced by reducing the level of goal performance, the division of labor, or the diversity of goals. Information processing is reduced by the creation of slack resources and the creation of self-contained authority structures. Let us look at the effects and costs of each of these strategies.

## ALTERNATIVE 1: CREATION OF SLACK RESOURCES

The concept of slack is one of the core concepts of Simon's cognitive limits theory of organization.[1] The concept is best illustrated by a practical example.

In the late 1950s and early 1960s a good deal of research was devoted to finding a solution to the job-shop scheduling problem.[2] This is a very complex combinatorial problem. For example, if there are five parts, each requiring work on a sequence of five different machines, then there are 25 billion possible ways to schedule the parts which need to be evaluated prior to choosing the best one. Even this extremely simple example would require computer time amounting to several centuries of 24-hour days to solve it. The research was directed therefore to operationalizing more efficient evaluation techniques such as dynamic programming, integer-linear programming, and Monte Carlo simulation.[3] However, none of these produced any practically useful results for large problems.

The research interest then shifted to the use of artificial intelligence to evaluate schedules. The original interest in artificial intelligence came from attempts to write computer programs which played chess. One approach was to have a chess expert verbalize thought process while playing a game. Then a computer program would duplicate the thought process. Since computers can manipulate symbols faster than can the human brain and have larger and more accurate memories, the computer should play better chess than the human. The problems involved in this area have proved to be quite difficult. But it was within this context that the job-shop problem was tackled. If the job-shop scheduler could verbalize the sequencing of jobs on machines, then a computer program could be written which would do it better. One researcher describes in the following way his experience at trying to discover the thought process used to solve the problem:

> To say that I did not succeed in this effort would be something of an understatement. If these trips accomplished anything, they convinced me that there was something about this problem that I did not quite understand. Since I now believe this to be an important point, I shall attempt to describe the source of my confusion.
>
> In all my plant visits, I arranged to spend most of my time with the man in the organization responsible for the detailed sequencing of production orders. This seemed sensible to me since this was the man who everyday somehow dealt with the vast complexity of the job-shop problem—this was the man who should be able to tell me what I needed to know.
>
> Upon meeting this gentleman, therefore, it was with considerable anticipation that I would say that I had come to discuss with him his very complicated job-shop scheduling problem. Without exception, he would look somewhat perplexed and ask, "What job-shop scheduling problem?"
>
> Despite my explanations . . . he never could see my definition of his problem. He showed me records which indicated in great detail that he met virtually all his promised deliveries, and he showed me other records which revealed his precise control of costs, but he never admitted any problem of scheduling.
>
> Now, as I said, my inability to elicit any recognition of a scheduling problem from people who schedule discouraged me. But I can now report that I have found the explanation.
>
> The job-shop problem is not recognized by most factory schedulers because *for them,* in most cases, no scheduling problem exists. That is, there is no scheduling problem for them because the organization which surrounds the schedulers reacts to protect them from strongly interdependent sequencing problems.[4]

Thus, the sales department knows that the scheduler cannot solve the complex scheduling problem. As a result, they quote to customers delivery times which are sufficiently long that the complex scheduling problem does not arise. The organization can remain competitive because they compete with other job shops facing identically complex scheduling problems. Their competitive market interaction determines a standard delivery time in the same way that it establishes a price. If all customers wanted shorter delivery times, the job shops could respond by hiring more workers and under-utilizing them or by working overtime to remove bottlenecks. Or they may buy more machines and incur a lower level of machine utilization. Other examples could be given but the result in each case is the same. *The organization responds by increasing the resources available rather than utilizing existing resources more efficiently.* It does this not because of poor management but because it does not have the information processing and computational capacity to deal with the coordination requirements of interdependence. Instead, it creates additional resources by reducing performance standards. These additional resources are called slack resources. The slack resource takes the form of additional time that the customer must wait, in-process inventory, underutilized man-hours and machine time, higher costs, etc.

The quotation presented above was chosen because it illustrates several features of slack resources. First, it illustrates that slack can be functional. It is usually regarded as bad and as something of which we must rid ourselves. While it does have its costs, it can be less costly than other alternatives in allowing rational action in the face of complexity. Second, the example illustrates the fact that we are seldom consciously aware of slack. It is so pervasive that most of us are not aware of it unless something happens to force us to look for it. But it can be increased or decreased just as any other policy variable. And finally, the examples illustrate how slack can reduce complexity so as to create problems that we are capable of solving. Let us look more precisely at the information-processing effects and costs.

## Information Processing Effects

Let us continue using the job shop as our example. For the job shop the combination of task uncertainty, diversity of parts, division of labor in the form of different labor skills and machines, and the interdependence between them create an information-processing problem which overwhelms the decision-making apparatus. The increased delivery time both reduces the number of factors that must be considered simultaneously when making a decision and the likelihood that another decision will be required. The longer the delivery time, the higher the probability that the organization will complete the job on time. The more jobs that are completed on time, the fewer the number of exceptional cases requiring decision making. Thus the delivery time can be increased until the number of exceptions is within the capacity of the hierarchy to handle them. When exceptions do occur, fewer factors need to be considered simultaneously. The longer delivery times permit the creation of in-process inventories between machine centers. Therefore machine breakdowns, quality rejects, or any other type of schedule disruption are not instantaneously transmitted to other departments. Over short periods of time the department is independent of other departments and can act autonomously. This means the decision makers do not have to collect information about first- and second-order effects of their decisions on the other departments. The inventory absorbs them.

Similar results can be obtained by changes to other targets. In the example of the wing design group, they too could lengthen due dates. In addition the allowable weight or man-hours consumed could be increased. Allowable stress could be decreased. In each case, the probability of an exception and the complexity to be considered when an exception occurs is thereby reduced. The reduced performance standards increase the resources consumed in the design process. The additional resources are the slack resources.

The amount of slack required depends on the degree of task uncertainty. The less the organization knows about its task, the greater the reduction in performance that is required. The performance level must be reduced until the number of exceptions is within the capacity of the organization to process them.

The use of slack may result in decentralization of decision making or in centralization depending on how management chooses to use things like slack time. Additional time can uncouple sequential operations, make the operations more autonomous, and permit the people in the operations to exercise discretion and self-control. In this manner, the autonomy structurally created can be used to permit job-design modifications to integrate individual and organizational goals. On the other hand, the slack time can be used to see that all decisions go through channels. The slack reduces the need for quick response and permits centralized decision making. Either choice may be viable.

### Costs

While a change to each target can produce the same information processing effect, they will have different costs depending on the context. Increased delivery time means the customer must wait longer. In manufacturing organizations, increased lead times generate inventories which absorb capital which could be used in other alternative investments. Increased budget has the obvious cost of more money or man-hours consumed in producing the product. Changes to weight, stress, or other design specifications reduce the worth of the item to the user. In each case there is a cost. The greater the uncertainty, the greater the cost. Whether slack is chosen as the policy with which to absorb increased uncertainty depends on the relative costs of the other three strategies.

## ALTERNATIVE 2: CREATION OF SELF-CONTAINED TASKS

The second method of reducing the amount of information was explained earlier as a shift from a functional group or input-based task design to one in which each group handled a category of output and contained all major resources needed to provide that output. For example, many business firms pursuing strategies of product diversification developed problems with their functional organizations.[5] Many found that by creating self-contained product divisions many of the overload problems disappeared. Chandler's work describes the situation at Du Pont during this period. Sears, Roebuck decided upon self-contained geographical divisions as have many state university systems such as those of California and New York. Some aerospace firms have created self-contained divisions around major projects. So regardless of the type of organization there is an output task around which self-sufficient resource groups can be created.

### Information Processing Effects

Some of the effects were described in Chapter 5. First, the output diversity faced by a single collection of resources is reduced. Reduced diversity reduced the information processing needed to schedule and reschedule the demands for shared resources. The problem was eliminated by eliminating the sharing. Second, there is usually a reduction in the division of labor and therefore fewer distinctly different resources whose work needs to be coordinated and scheduled. Both result in less information being required to coordinate work across interdependent, specialized resources and to set priorities across demands for scarce, shared resources.

A third effect is that the point of decision is moved closer to the source of information. Exceptions have to travel through fewer levels before reaching a shared superior. Decisions can be taken at lower levels while supported with only local information, the reason being that other departments are relatively less affected since few resources are shared and each task is more or less independent. The creation of self-contained groups permits local discretion based on local information only.

A variable to be considered is the degree of self-containment and thereby the degree of decentralization. First of all, no group is completely self-contained or else it would not be part of the same organization. Therefore, the variable is the degree of self-containment and consequently the degree of decentralization that is permitted. For example, if the services of 15 different specialties are required to produce an organization's product lines, then a choice must be made when product divisions are created as to which services will be contained in the divisions and which will remain centralized in the corporate office. In general the greater the diversity of the outputs and the greater the task uncertainty, the greater the self-containment. For example, if the outputs are moderately diverse and tasks moderately unpredictable, then perhaps 8 to 10 services will be allocated to the divisions. The finance, accounting, research and development, legal and industrial relations may remain functional and centralized at corporate headquarters. Under extreme diversity and uncertainty, only the financial and legal may remain in corporate headquarters. This latter type is usually labeled a "conglomerate." In order to complete the discussion of which functions remain centralized, we must examine the costs of the self-containment strategy.

## Costs and Benefits

The creation of self-contained units, like each of the four strategies, has its cost. The costs are basically those which are connected with a reduction of skill specialization. In the case of physical equipment, there is a loss of economies of scale. If a manufacturing organization is broken down into product divisions, then several smaller pieces of equipment must replace the one large piece. It is always more expensive to buy several pieces of equipment than to buy one large piece of equipment of the same total capacity.

There are also costs associated with the division of labor. In a functional engineering organization there can be two electrical engineers—one electromechanical and one electronics. If the structure is changed to two product groups, two electrical engineers are still needed but they will be required to generalize across electromechanical and electronics applications. (This assumes that more knowledge is required to generalize across disciplines than across products.) If a high level of expertise is necessary, the organization can maintain one electromechanical and one electronics engineer for each product group. But now there is duplication involved. Four engineers are required instead of two. Expertise is maintained by the use of slack resources in the form of two additional engineers. In addition, functional or skill-based structures provide career paths for people who remain in the same occupational group. They are physically located together and interact with members of their own specialty. These features disappear or are reduced in the self-contained structure.

The costs above apply differentially to the individual subtasks or functions. Some functions such as R & D, finance, and fabricating operations have economies of scale in the form of specialized manpower, borrowing leverage and risk pooling, and economies of scale in physical processing equipment. These functions tend to remain centralized and separate from the relatively self-contained groups. Thus, for a given level of diversity and uncertainty, the greater the economies of scale, the less the degree of self-containment. Serious problems develop if a function is critical to providing the output, and therefore should be a part of the self-contained group, and also possesses economies of scale, and therefore should be centralized. This case is best handled with lateral relations.

There are benefits associated with the self-contained mode in addition to·bringing information-processing needs and capacity into line. First, the mode permits greater amounts of local discretion thereby allowing the organization to design jobs in which the occupants can exercise more discretion, participate in decisions affecting their work, and influence the pace of their work. It is the type of structural adjustment which is necessary to accommodate the preferred reward system. The work of Eric Trist is most illustrative of this type of reward system and structural adjustment.[6]

The other benefit is that the organization can use tailor-made systems and procedures to adapt to the differences in products, regions, customers, clients, projects, or whatever basis constitutes the group. For example, psychiatric hospitals separate patients into those groups who can respond to treatment and those who cannot. A treatment ideology then determines the structure and processes of the former while a more predictable, custodial ideology dominates the latter. Similarly manufacturing firms place stable product lines in one product group and unstable lines in another. The first is characterized by predictability, cost consciousness, economies of scale, large batches, utilization of resources, and the elimination of disturbances. In the second group, the processes are designed to adapt and respond to disturbances. Every order is a rush order, engineering changes are continuous, and the employees rarely do the same thing twice. The separation permits a better matching of people, structure, systems, and task.

### Empirical Studies

There is some empirical evidence accumulating to support these assertions. Some of it comes from Chandler's work which was quoted in Chapter 2. Recall that he showed that those large American industrial firms that pursued a strategy of product diversification were the ones that assumed the decentralized multidivision form. Those large firms that expanded output in the same product lines retained or centralized to a greater extent their functional forms. These conclusions have been supported and expanded by Stopford[7] in a more recent study utilizing a large sample and a more quantitative analysis. The study was performed as part of the Harvard study of the multinational corporation. The sample of firms on the study were those organizations that were part of the *Fortune 500* and "that had manufacturing subsidiaries in six or more foreign countries at the end of 1963 where the parent company owned 25 percent or more of the subsidiaries."[8] When these firms are classified by the type of structure they have, it turns out that 122 have the product-divisionalized form and 17 have a functional form. So the vast majority of firms handling diverse international markets are of the divisionalized type. Table 6.1 shows a further classification of these firms by total product diversification. Diversification is measured by the percentage of total sales outside the firm's primary industry classification. For example if Procter and Gamble's primary industry is soap and 20 percent of their sales are outside that industry, they would be 20 percent diversified. The data reveal that there are no functional organizations with product diversification above 6 percent. There are some divisionalized structures below 6 percent indicating that there are other factors at work. They could also be geographic divisions rather than product divisions. However, the data support the conclusion that the functional form cannot handle the information-processing and decision-making load that is associated with area and product diversity.

Additional evidence is revealed by the sequence of reorganizations. Chandler's case studies indicate that the vast majority of American enterprise had the centralized functional form at the beginning of this century. Then as each firm pursued a strategy of product diversification, there was

Table 6.1    Structures classified by product diversification*

| Total product diversification % | Functional form | Multidivisional form |
|---|---|---|
| 0 | 12 | 19 |
| 1–6 | 5 | 14 |
| 1–17 | 0 | 17 |
| 18–45 | 0 | 37 |
| 46–71 | 0 | 35 |
| | 17 | 122 |

* From J. M. Stopford 1968, *Growth and organizational change in the multinational firm*, Boston: Harvard Business School, p. 45.

the invariable sequence of a profit decline, a reorganization to the multi-national form, and a subsequent profit improvement.

Stopford expands upon this finding by analyzing structural changes following the strategy of expansion into international markets. The initial structural response to the international expansion strategy is the establishment of the international division. Figure 6.1 depicts the multidivisional form with an international division which is responsible for foreign sales and manufacture of all products. This form economizes on a critical resource by requiring only one international general manager.

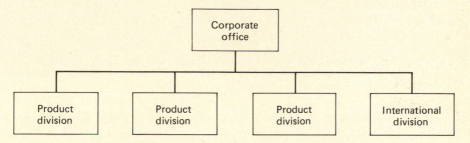

**Fig. 6.1    Product divisionalized form with international division.**

The divisional form with the international division however is a transitional form which gives way to some other multidivisional structure. The type of structure depends on the kind of international expansion strategy. The hypothesis is that as organizations expand product lines and move into international markets they evolve higher level structures by moving from functional (II) to divisional (III) to divisional with international division III(i), and finally to some other form (III other).

Table 6.2 presents the reorganization experience of the firms in the sample up to 1966. The data reveal that the direction of the changes in structure are overwhelmingly in the predicted direction. If this is true, then the question becomes, "What are the other forms and what are the strategies that lead to the abandoning of the international division?"

There are two pure forms of self-contained divisions. One is the worldwide product division form where the division is given worldwide profit responsibility for the manufacture and sale of a product line. The other is the area division. The area division has profit responsibility for the products manufactured and sold in a geographical area. In addition, there are mixed structures which may have area divisions with one or two products set up on a worldwide basis. The products are usually sufficiently different and have a large enough volume to justify independent operation.

**Table 6.2   Observed directions of structure change up to 1966***

| Sequence of change | Number of observations in predicted direction | Number of observations not in predicted direction |
|---|---|---|
| II to II(i) | 45 | 3 |
| II to III | 64 | 0 |
| II to III(i) | 17 | 1 |
| II to III other | 13 | 0 |
| II(i) to III(i) | 29 | 2 |
| II(i) to III other | 3 | 1 |
| III to III(i) | 60 | 1 |
| III to III other | 8 | 0 |
| III(i) to III other | 31 | 0 |
| | 270 | 8 |

* From J. M. Stopford 1968, *Growth and organizational change in the multinational firm,* Boston: Harvard Business School, p. 32. The symbol (i) indicates structural form plus an international division.

There are different strategies available for the firm going into international markets. One strategy involves carrying its full product line abroad. It can diversify in foreign markets as well as at home. The other strategy involves building volume in only one or two products abroad. Table 6.3 shows the relationship of foreign product diversity to types of structure. Keep in mind that diversity is foreign sales outside of the firm's primary industry.

Once again the functional form is associated with low diversity. The multidivisional form with an international division also shows that diversity cannot be contained within a single structure. The interdependence with other divisions yields a coordination problem which cannot be handled by

**Table 6.3   Structure classified by foreign product diversity***

| Foreign product diversification % | Functional form | Multidivisional forms | | | Mixed form |
|---|---|---|---|---|---|
| | | International division | Worldwide product div. | Area div. | |
| 0 | 13 | 26 | 1 | 5 | 1 |
| 1–5 | 4 | 14 | 1 | 2 | 4 |
| 6–25 | 0 | 5 | 7 | 1 | 2 |
| 26–71 | 0 | 3 | 8 | 1 | 3 |
| Total | 17 | 48 | 17 | 9 | 10 |

* From J. M. Stopford 1968, *Growth and organizational change in the multinational firm,* Boston: Harvard Business School, pp. 47 and 64.

the international division. The division is disbanded and distributed among the product divisions which now assume worldwide profit responsibility. Thus, product diversification in foreign markets is associated with the worldwide product division form.

The worldwide product division form also operates the largest R & D functions. They are also concerned with the highest levels of new technology and product innovation. The firms operate by continually introducing new products first domestically, then in foreign markets. Domestic diversification is always greater than foreign diversification. Therefore, their primary task is one of communication and technology transfer. This task is highly uncertain in addition to being diverse and requires a considerable amount of decentralization. The data indicate that this is true. The R & D is still centralized to some degree but most other functions are contained within the product divisions.

The other international strategy of introducing a few high-volume products is associated with the area division form. As foreign volume expands, the international division is disbanded and area divisions are established—one of which is the United States. Interestingly it is not absolute volume but relative volume that leads to disbanding the international division. The division disappears when its sales are equal to the largest domestic product division. It is hypothesized that the domestic product divisions form a coalition against the rapidly expanding and threatening international division. It was originally thought that area diversity would overload the decision-making apparatus. Unfortunately the only measure of area diversity was the number of countries in which manufacturing was carried out. Since marketing is the basic concern of standardized high-volume products, the results were inconclusive.

The area division structure operates with low foreign product diversity (they still have high domestic diversity) and low levels of technology. They sell in high volume a few mature, standardized products. Competition revolves around marketing considerations of price, promotion, and brand differentiation. Unlike the worldwide product divisions, the area division form has large centralized functional staffs. Since the same standardized products are sold by all divisions, centralization is economically viable. Thus, a degree of centralization occurs when the task of technology transfer is more predictable.

It seems that the two divisionalized structures are transitory forms also. Some of the area division forms are beginning to diversify in foreign markets. As they do, they run into the problems of coordinating diversity within a single structure. Similarly, product divisions expand their volume in new world markets and are faced with area diversity. The problem facing these organizations is how to deal simultaneously with product and area diversity. An initial response is the mixed structural form. However, in the long run, the way to deal simultaneously with two sources of diversity and uncertainty is to resort to other forms of influencing the decision making rather than relying on the authority structure as the prime determinant of influence. They are moving to grid or matrix structures which will be discussed in later chapters. Figure 6.2 portrays graphically the domains in which the various structures predominate. As the organizations expand volume and diversity, they pass boundaries in which they change form. In area A all organizations with low levels of diversity and relatively small foreign sales volumes are represented. Invariably these organizations have a functional or divisional structure with an international division.

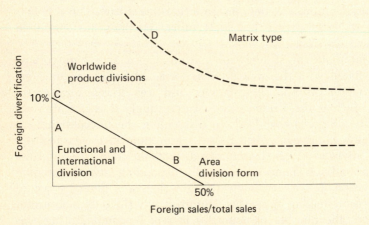

Fig. 6.2 The Stopford model of diversity, relative size, and structure. Adapted from J. M. Stopford 1968, *Growth and organizational change in the multinational firm.* Boston: Harvard Business School, p. 108.

If the organization moves into area B by expanding volume of a single product line, it adopts the area division at about the point where foreign sales are 50 percent of total sales. This structure is shown in Fig. 6.3.

If the organization begins to carry its full diversified product line abroad, it moves into area C. These organizations adopt worldwide product divisions as shown in Fig. 6.4. And finally as organizations move from B to D by diversifying or from C to D by volume expansions, pressures are created to adopt a matrix or grid type of structure.

The preceding discussion of a specific organizational problem was introduced not to present international strategy but to present specific evidence of a general phenomenon—the effect of diversity and uncertainty. The effect of diversity was to overload the decision-making apparatus at a particular level of the organization. The response was to reduce interdependence by setting up self-contained divisions. The effect of uncertainty

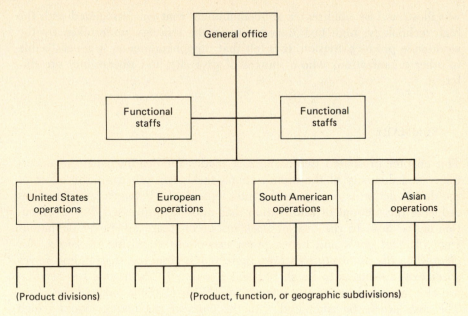

**Fig. 6.3 Multinational organization with area divisions.**

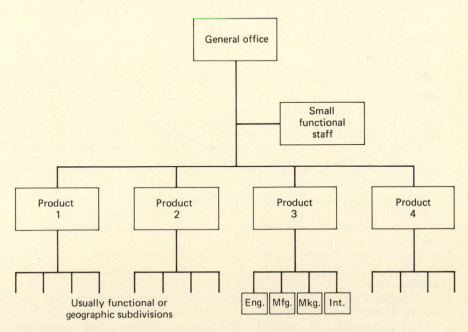

**Fig. 6.4 Multinational organization with worldwide product divisions.**

was illustrated by the greater self-containment that was associated with the high technology, high task uncertainty in the strategy undertaken by the worldwide product division. It is felt that this phenomenon is generalizable to other organizations whose sources of diversity and uncertainty are different.

## SUMMARY

This chapter presented two organizing modes for dealing with the uncertainty and diversity of the organization's tasks. In both cases the effect of the design action is to reduce the interdependence between subunits, thus reducing the amount of information that must be processed during execution of the task. In the case of *slack resources*, there are fewer deviations from planned goals and hence fewer exceptions requiring decisions. For *changes in the authority structure*, there is less resource sharing and fewer specialized resources to be shared and scheduled. The points for decision are also moved closer to the information. Each of these modes have costs. The costs are to be compared with the costs of organizing modes which increase the capacity to process information. The next several chapters will articulate the effects of such designs.

## NOTES

1. J. G. March and H. A. Simon 1958. *Organizations.* New York: Wiley. R. Cyert and J. G. March 1963. *A behavioral theory of the firm.* Englewood Cliffs, N.J.: Prentice-Hall.
2. A job shop is a manufacturing facility in which all machines performing a similar process, such as drilling, grinding, and cutting, are placed in the same department. There may be 15 to 50 such machine centers in a shop. As orders arrive they must be loaded on available machine time and also must meet customer delivery requirements. An order requires various types and amounts of machine time in various sequences. There may be 500 to 3000 orders in the shop. The magnitude of the scheduling of 3000 orders across 50 machine centers is a formidable problem.
3. J. F. Muth and G. Thompson (eds.) 1963. *Industrial scheduling.* Englewood Cliffs, N.J.: Prentice-Hall.
4. W. F. Pounds 1963. The scheduling environment, in Muth and Thompson, *op. cit.,* pp. 7 and 8.
5. A. Chandler 1962. *Strategy and structure.* Cambridge: M.I.T. Press.
6. E. L. Trist, G. W. Higgin, H. Murray, and A. B. Pollack 1963. *Organizational choice.* London: Tavistock.
7. J. M. Stopford 1968. *Growth and organizational change in the multinational firm.* Boston: Harvard Business School. Unpublished D.B.A. thesis.
8. L. E. Fouraker and J. M. Stopford 1968. Organization structure and multinational strategy, *Administrative Science Quarterly,* (June): 57.

## QUESTIONS

1. Give some examples in which organizations employ slack resources. Explain the impact on information processing.
2. Does the use of slack resources result in centralization or decentralization of decisions?
3. Is slack positive or negative in its effects?
4. Give some examples of self-contained units. Explain which resources are still shared.
5. If you were a technical specialist, would you want to work in a product or project divisionalized firm? Why or why not?
6. Take an organization and trace at least eight steps in its structural transition from a functional organization in the United States to a worldwide matrix form.

| INVESTMENT IN THE VERTICAL INFORMATION SYSTEM: ALTERNATIVE 3 | CHAPTER 7 |
| --- | --- |

This chapter presents the third organizing mode (Alternative 3) which is the investment of resources in the vertical information system. The investment takes the form of increasing the capacity of existing channels of communication, creating new channels, and introducing new decision mechanisms. These investments increase the capacity of the organization to make use of information acquired during task execution. The chapter is primarily concerned with design choices involving computers and the new information technology.

The effect of the investments is the same as the creation of slack resources and self-contained tasks—there are fewer exceptions referred upward in the hierarchy. The critical factor limiting an organization's attainment of high levels of performance in the presence of the division of labor, size, and diversity is its ability to make decisions and communicate about unique, nonroutine, consequential events which could not be foreseen. While the result is the same, the nature of the design choices and their costs are quite different. The chapter proceeds by first introducing the policy dimensions. The dimensions are combined into some prototype information systems. Some empirical evidence supporting the theory is then reviewed. And finally a brief case study is used to summarize the chapter.

## DIMENSIONS OF THE VERTICAL INFORMATION SYSTEM

Before discussing policy changes, the policy variables need to be identified. In Chapter 2, the four variables of interest were briefly introduced and some of them were discussed again at the end of Chapter 3.[1]

The variables of interest are as follows.

1. *Decision frequency* or *timing* of information flows to and from the decision mechanism.

2. *The scope of the data base* available to the decision mechanism.

3. *The degree of formalization* of the information flows to and from the decision mechanism.

4. *The capacity of the decision mechanism* to process information and select the appropriate alternative.

Let us look at each of these dimensions individually.


### Decision Frequency or Timing

The first dimension that can be changed is the length of time between decisions. Although the length of time is a continuous variable, let us dichotomize it for ease of discussion and look at the extreme types of decision frequencies. At one extreme of the dichotomy is the *periodic* information flow. For example, the job shop may schedule its operation once a month. At that time the status of orders and machines is relayed to the decision mechanism. A new schedule is created and communicated to those who must effect it. The distinctive feature is the fixed interval between successive collections of data and/or making of decisions. The other extreme is the *continuous* collection of information and the making of decisions whenever decisions need to be made.

The timing or frequency of the goal-setting process affects the number of exceptions that are referred upward in the hierarchy. Every set of goals or plan begins to decay in usefulness immediately after it is created. For example, the schedule for the job shop begins to decay as unplanned events occur such as machine breakdowns, worker absenteeism, engineering design changes, quality control rejects, and order cancellations. These events cause exceptions which are referred upward and which overload the hierarchy. When this occurs, it becomes more efficient to create a new plan than to make incremental changes to the old one. As the uncertainty of the task increases, the interval between plans decreases. The shorter the interval between plans, the fewer the number of exceptions. There are fewer exceptions because most exceptions occur late in the planning cycle when the decay has been greatest. The reduction in exceptions is gained at the cost of more processing of information at planning time. For example, reduction of the planning cycle from one month to two weeks doubles the amount of information processed at planning time. More clerks and/or computer time are required. But this option may be cheaper than using slack or creating self-contained structures.

### Scope of the Data Base

The second dimension is the scope of the data base available to the decision mechanism. The scope, like timing, is dichotomized into pure types. If the decision mechanism has access to information pertaining only to its immediate location, the data base is called *local*. On the other hand, if the decision mechanism has access to information concerning the state of affairs in all resource groups and for all output categories, the data base is *global*. The scope of the data base available to the decision mechanism affects the ability to direct activities in one part of the organization so as to be consistent with the activities taking place in other parts of the organization. The decision alternative which appears best from a local perspective may not be best from a global one. Furthermore, there is no guarantee that the summation of a series of local optima will add to a global optimum when interdependence exists. This phenomenon has been termed *suboptimization.*[2] Therefore, the greater the interdependence between subunits, the greater the need for a global data base.

Like the other attributes, the scope of the data base is increased with an increase in cost. The costs are incurred by the creation of the new information channels that are needed to bring together at one decision mechanism all the information pertaining to an interdependent set of subunits. One of the ways in which a global data base is implemented is by creating new *direct* information channels to a position in the hierarchy which has the global goal orientation required to reach high quality decisions. This kind of global system avoids the sequential processing of the hierarchical channels and reduces filtering and delays. The cost is the resources utilized to maintain another information channel.

Care should be taken to point out that taking information from its points of origin and collecting it into a global data base to be presented at a level high in the hierarchy is one method of operationalizing this dimension. Bringing information up to points of decision has as its primary virtue the avoidance of the problem of behavior control. That is, if the information is presented to the manager responsible for all the units involved, the manager will probably choose the alternative that is best for the entire unit. However, the policy dimension is to increase the scope of the data base available to the decision mechanism independent of what it is or where in the hierarchy it is located. But if global data is presented to a manager of a subunit, will that manager choose the alternative which is in the best interest of the global entity rather than the one which is best for the manager's own subunit? At this point, the organization is no longer limited by cognitive factors but by goal factors. The situation requires a global goal orientation to be brought down to lower levels. Global goal orientations can be created by using mode 2 to employ self-continued, autonomous groups at low levels of the organization. Another way is to design global incentive and reward systems. And the third method is to employ lateral relations which are discussed in the next chapter.

The reason for this apparent side discussion is that too often the expedient of avoiding the behavior control problem is chosen. The power of computers and their use in nonhierarchical, democratic organization designs is virtually unexplored. The fact remains that once computers are employed, many of the cognitive limiting factors disappear or no longer limit effectiveness. Organizations become limited by motivation, cooperation, and conflict-resolving technologies.

## Formalization

A third dimension of the information system is the degree of formality of the collection and reporting processes. The formalization of categories for collecting and reporting information creates a language with which members of the organization can communicate about events that the organization faces. The most obvious example is the accounting system which every organization has.

The primary effect of the formalized languages is to permit the transmission of information with fewer symbols thereby expanding the communication channels to carry more information.[3] The ability of an organization to coordinate diverse outputs across specialized resources depends critically upon having an efficient means to identify all the factors and record changes to them in the face of uncertainty. For this monitoring some formalization of language is necessary. Also the resources consumed in reporting information more often and through new channels is probably proportional to the number of symbols transmitted. Therefore, for a given information content, the more formal the information system, the fewer the resources consumed in transmission.

Formalization also has its costs and limitations. First, staffs are required to design and maintain these languages. Systems analysts and cost accountants are expensive personnel to maintain. A second limitation is that not all information lends itself to being formalized. To the extent that activities are ambiguous and require qualitative rather than quantitative measures, they are difficult to formalize. Formalization is therefore limited by the type of uncertainty that it can handle. Situations in which the organization is uncertain about what the variables are and how they are related do not lend themselves to formal languages. It is the other type of uncertainty when known factors may assume unknown values, that can be effectively handled by formalization. Therefore the unique, nonroutine events still require the nonformal, usually verbal, channels. Finally, when used by itself formalization is limited in its ability to reduce overloads. Providing more information does not always improve the situation without a means to process it. More information may simply overload the decision mechanism.

### Decision Mechanism

The fourth policy dimension is the capacity of the decision mechanism to process information and select an alternative. As suggested above, providing more information, more often, and more efficiently may simply overload the decision mechanism. Therefore, the capacity of the decision mechanism must be expanded with timing, scope, and formalization. This section suggests some different types of mechanisms.

Several years ago there would have been no need for a section entitled "Decision Mechanism." Managers were the decision makers. The structure of organizations was determined by the capacity of the managers to handle the decision situations with which they were faced. The only way to improve decision making was to select those managers who made better decisions than other managers. Since that time, there have been two major thrusts for improving decision making. One from the behavioral sciences has operationalized the process of group decision making. The use of a group for a decision mechanism affects not only the quality of a decision but the motivation to implement it. The next chapter will discuss the choice of group mechanisms. The second has come from the new information technology which was made possible by computers.

The use of machines to reach routine decisions is now well known.[4] The use of machines as decsion mechanisms has been credited with substantial reductions in slack in manufacturing firms. It is also known that computers have been limited in their use in less structured problems at middle and top levels of management. This recognition has led to research on man-machine decision mechanisms. The division of labor results in the worker concentrating on alternative creation and consequence evaluation while the computer performs manipulations on large volumes of quantitative data in order to compute consequences of alternatives.[5] More recently it has been recognized that in order to include all global data, both machine readable and verbal, group-machine decision mechanisms are needed. The use of visual displays in joint decision making appears to hold significant promise.[6] Figure 7.1 represents the possible decision mechanisms in increasing capacity to process information and make decisions and also in increasing cost.

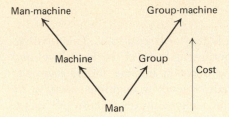

**Fig. 7.1  Decision mechanisms.**

## PROTOTYPE INFORMATION SYSTEMS

The attributes can be combined into some prototype information systems. The primary attributes will be the timing and scope which are depicted schematically in Fig. 7.2. The systems will be presented in sequence of increasing cost; a more costly system being required when faced with greater task uncertainty and task interdependence.

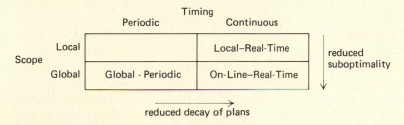

**Fig. 7.2  Typology of information systems.**

### Local–Periodic

The first logical system is the local–periodic which is not used extensively. It can be illustrated by the warehouse clerk who places orders every Friday to replenish inventory. The clerk places orders for those items whose actual stock level has fallen below a preset minimum level. The ordering is periodic and based only on local information available to the clerk. The system ignores interdependence. If a work center at the plant has a low work load, the clerk will not place an order to utilize that capacity because of the limited scope of the data available to the clerk. In addition if an unforeseen increase in demand occurs, the warehouse will stockout and not be replenished until the next Friday. So while the system is simple and inexpensive, it ignores interdependence and is not responsive to uncertain environments.

## Local–Real-time

The second type of information system is the local–real-time. This involves largely informal data collection on a continuous basis at the local level and person-dominated decision making. The decision making differs from the local–periodic in that decisions are made whenever decisions need to be made. This type is best illustrated by the sequencing decision in job shops. The decision concerns the choice of which one of a number of waiting jobs should be processed next on an available machine. The decision is made by either the foreman or a dispatcher at the moment a machine becomes available. Therefore, the decision is made in light of the most current information concerning the status of the department. This allows a last-minute matching of job, machine, and worker to permit the most efficient functioning of the department. Many of the prevailing conditions may not have been predictable in advance. The current data base allows a responsiveness to uncertain environments.

The system has the defect of a local data base. For example, the dispatcher may choose an order to load on a machine which appears best from the department's viewpoint. However, the order goes next to a machine center experiencing a machine breakdown while another order could have gone to a machine center experiencing a temporary underload. A more global data base would prevent this accentuation of load discrepancies.

The virtue of this system is that it is inexpensive to sustain. Prior to the use of computers such a system was the primary way to respond to task uncertainty. The interdependencies were handled by reducing their impact through the use of slack resources and self-contained authority structures which eliminated the need for global data.

## Global–Periodic

The third information and decision system is the global–periodic structure. This structure has also been applied to the scheduling of job shops. A typical process would begin with the collection of information concerning the status of completion of all orders in all machine centers. This information would be fed into a computer. The computer would be equipped with a simulation program or similar algorithm which would compute start dates for all jobs on all machines. The program would be written so as to meet the promised delivery dates and to keep the machine centers loaded. These new start dates would be transmitted to all foremen and would be the basis for loading machines for a period of one week. At the end of the week, the process would be repeated.

Such a system is characterized by formalized information collection and machine-aided decision making which are necessary in order to expand the capacity of the information channel and the decision mechanism to handle the larger volumes of data. This type of structure is typical of batch-processing computer systems.

Global–periodic structures vary in application in two ways—the nature of the review period and the comprehensiveness of the plan. The review period can be either fixed or variable. In the example above it was fixed and the interval was one week. While variable lengths are possible, review periods are almost always fixed with the interval length being a design variable. There are several reasons for desiring a fixed interval. First, there is a desire for predictability and regularity in the usage of batch-processing computers. Second, it allows the making of a number of decisions simultaneously which affect a number of departments. For example, the decisions are made simultaneously for production labor capacity and personnel hiring. Finally, we do not know when conditions have changed sufficiently to re-make a decision. Instead, we fix an interval whose length approximates the needs for adaptation on the average.

A plan is comprehensive to the extent that the decision process considers the bulk of the economically and physically relevant variables. The job-shop schedule is comprehensive to the extent that it considers limited machine capacities, technically feasible machine substitutes to smooth work loads, the possibility for splitting orders to bypass a bottleneck, etc. Such comprehensiveness requires formalization and computerization to handle the large volumes of data needed to support the decision. Since this is expensive, organizations vary in the comprehensiveness of their plans. Those factors not considered in the global plan are either ignored or left to be resolved at the local level.

The global–periodic structure has characteristics opposite of those of the local–real-time. By simultaneously determining schedules for all orders, full account is taken of the interdependencies between departments. In addition, the computational power of the computer is exploited. The result is a schedule which is best from the point of view of the organization rather than a schedule which is the summation of best decisions, each made from a departmental point of view. However, the schedule is subject to the decay process mentioned earlier. After it is put into effect on Monday morning, a series of machine breakdowns, quality rejects, and engineering changes may render the schedule ineffective by Wednesday. Thus, the global data base and computational power reduce suboptimal decision making but the periodicity subjects the decisions to decay.

The global–periodic structure has been used extensively in applications where uncertainty is low to moderate. The applications have exploited the power of the computer and the global data. The decay process in these applications is a minor irritant, not a major disadvantage. Most of the research and some of the speculation has been the result of observations of changes from local–real-time to global–periodic structures. Let us look at the results from the most comprehensive study available.[7]

Whisler has reported a study of 23 insurance companies. The insurance industry has made extensive use of computers for a long period of time. The applications studied were almost all concerned with batch-processing computers. The changes have been from local–real-time to global–periodic structures. The following organization changes have resulted:

1. Reduced Personnel—There is usually an impact on the *configuration* of the organization in the form of fewer clerical personnel. This is usually difficult to measure because the firms grow during implementation and also take on new activities. The best indicator is the estimated number of additional personnel that would be needed to perform current activities without computers. They are:

   | | |
   |---|---|
   | Clerical | 60% |
   | Supervisory | 9% |
   | Managerial | 2% |

   These data show both the magnitude and location of the effect. Computers have had their greatest impact at the routine, operating level of organizations.

2. Integration and consolidation of subtasks—In addition to reduced numbers of clerks, the most ubiquitous phenomenon was integration of subtasks or increasing interdependence.

   Without exception, the companies in this study reported that computer applications have consolidated or will soon consolidate decision-making areas that were previously separate. In no case has the reverse effect occurred, they say . . . computer systems reverse the effects of organizational growth and development, restoring fragmented decision systems to the state of integration that would have been logically and economically desirable had it not been for acute problems of information overload.[8]

   The ways in which this increased interdependence was coordinated varied. The organizations seem to have chosen different design strategies. Let us see the overall results before speculating.

3. Reorganization from self-contained departments into functional departments—Integrating subtasks usually was accompanied by organizational consolidation of the departments responsible for the subtasks. The use

of the computer in the decision process reduced the information overload and allowed a functional organizational structure to operate efficiently. For example, one company regrouped its two self-contained accounting departments into two functional departments as follows:[9]

| *Before computer* | *After computer* |
|---|---|
| Premium and commission (First-year policies) | Commission accounting (All policies) |
| Accounting (First-year policies) | Premium accounting (All policies) |
| Premium and commission (Renewed policies) | |
| Accounting (Renewed policies) | |

These changes permit greater specialization of skills due to a greater division of labor. The computer permits the coordination of the specialization units.

Not all the organizations changed to functional structures. Those who had the systems installed the longest and who were growing at slower rates changed to functional structures. The organizations dealing with greater uncertainty maintained self-contained structures or, as we shall see, shortly achieved global decision structures without changing the formal authority structure.

4. Centralization of decision making—Most of the organizations reported a centralization of control or that choices were made at higher levels of the organization. This is consistent with the change to a functional organization and an increase in subtask interdependence. An exception now has an impact on more departments and is more consequential. In addition, many decisions were programmed into the computer. There was greater rationalization and quantification of decisions in many organizations.

All of these findings fit together. The increase in interdependence, the increase in information processing capacity, the change to a functional organization, centralization of decisions, and quantification appear as parts of one total strategy.

5. More group decision making—Several organizations indicated that tying together subtasks need not result in consolidating under a single authority those units that perform the work. Coordination takes place by using the strategy described in the next chapter—"Group Decisions."

On the other hand, one of the greatest benefits of computer automation, in my opinion, has been the development of group decision
making as a staff function rather than hierarchical decision making
through line relationships. The unifying relationship in these varying
groups assembled for decision making usually is either a consolidated
record file (i.e., personnel and payroll functions joined procedurally
through a common master record but separate organizationally)
or a series of separate record files that are joined together procedurally
in a continuous computer operation with input and output cutting
across existing organizational lines.

The trend toward group decision making has evolved largely on a
voluntary basis, I believe. What probably began as a "getting together"
for the purpose of coordination and communication has subtly evolved
into something more like "consensus decision making." Generally,
however, the person upon whom the responsibility for a decision
would be expected to fall, from an organizational standpoint, would
be considered by the group as having actually made the final decision.
This, again, points up the increasingly complex line-and-staff relationships now involved in decision making in highly computer-oriented
organizations.[10]

These findings support the theory being developed in this book. The
use of computers in the modification of the vertical information system is
an alternative to the creation of self-contained structures in handling information overloads.

The increase in group decision making suggests that computers need
not lead to centralized, functional structures. With a sample size of 23,
Whisler had limited opportunity for multivariate analysis, but it is probable
that group decision making is an alternative to centralization as was suggested earlier. The least centralized organizations are probably those using
group decisions. All of which suggests alternative structures for exploiting
the advantages of computers and global data bases.

### On-line–Real-time

The last prototype would logically be called the global–continuous but in
the current vernacular it is known as on-line–real-time. It is characterized
by the continuous flow of formalized, global data and man-machine involvement in decision making. The best examples of such systems are airline
reservation systems and Ticketron systems for sports and theater events.
These systems allow rapid updating of a constantly changing status and
make the information available everywhere.

An example of what can be done is illustrated by the use of computers at the new Volvo factory at Kalmar.[11] There is a sequential work flow through semiautonomous groups as shown in Fig. 7.3. Interspersed are inspection groups for quality control purposes.

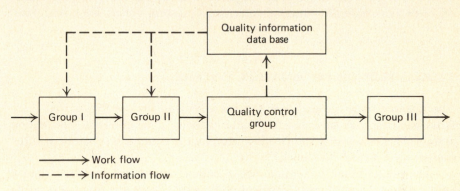

Fig. 7.3   On-line, real-time system at Volvo Kalmar plant.

Normally, the occurrence of errors of a particular type would be reported to the quality control supervisor who in turn would inform the supervisor of the responsible group. The group supervisor would relay the problem to the workers along with whatever instructions would be necessary to correct the problem. At Kalmar, the information is entered into the computer system data base and made available on the terminal of the responsible group, who in this instance is in fact responsible. It is the task of the group without supervisory intervention to remedy the problem. This approach removes the supervisors as information processors, eliminates their selective access to information and therefore reduces the power difference between supervisors and workers.

The on-line–real-time structure is perfect in theory. It permits interunit consistency of action and reduces decay of plans by responding to new situations. In addition when using remote-access computer terminals, the computational power of the computer can be brought to bear at the moment of decision and at the convenience of the manager.

On-line–real-time structures have two problems. First, the remote-access and time-shared computers are very expensive to acquire and maintain. The second is our inability to create new organization structures to utilize them. The cultural lag is very evident here. We cannot foresee the ramifications of information instantaneously available everywhere in the organization. Information is a source of power and the entire power structure is threatened. Most of our attitudes and behaviors still reflect hierarchical and sequential processing of data.

Despite these costs, there are some systems in application which approximate the prototype structure. Two job shops have implemented systems which utilize global data and provide updates every one and three days, respectively.[12] The result is a reduction of slack time. Average lead times to complete work were reduced 20–30 percent. Once again we see the trade-off of design strategies—vertical information system versus slack resources.

## EXAMPLES OF INFORMATION SYSTEMS

The research reviewed earlier in this book leads to the conclusion that there is no one best way to organize. Similarly there is no one best information system. This conclusion can be illustrated by the comparative study of three multispecialist medical clinics.[13]

The clinics allow patients to see a number of specialists rather than a single general practitioner. A typical clinic might have five to six specialists in each of ten to twelve departments. There are usually three or four laboratories and X-ray facilities. These specialized resources, both doctors and equipment, are expensive. Therefore, it is important to achieve full utilization of their time. A scheduling problem arises because patients must see a number of doctors. The specialization causes interdependence. The scheduling is problematic because there is uncertainty as to which doctors a patient should see, in which order, and for how long. In order to schedule a patient, a diagnosis is needed before he or she arrives. This is the case for returning or referred patients, but not for new ones. The problem becomes one of trying to schedule doctors to be fully utilized under considerable uncertainty.

Rockart has attempted to design a scheduling system for one clinic, based on a comparative study of several other clinics. The first clinic operates on a *local–real-time* basis. The patients arrive, are examined by a doctor, and are routed to other doctors on the basis of the examination. There is no detailed prescheduling. The diagnosis is made and the schedule determined when all the facts are in. However, the schedule is based on local information. In order to prevent schedule conflicts and underutilized doctors, this clinic uses slack time. The situation is analogous to the job shop. Instead of parts flowing through machine centers, patients flow through medical departments. The waiting lines guarantee full utilization of doctors and equipment. The cost is that the patient spends a good deal of his or her time waiting. This cost is minimized because patients travel to this clinic which is located in a rural setting. Patients arrange their affairs so as to have time available. While they are at the clinic there are few competing uses of their time and they have the expectation of a relaxing wait.

The other two clinics have a more difficult problem. They are located in large metropolitan areas. The result is that patients do not like to wait. They have alternative uses for their time. Hotel accommodations are expensive. So these clinics must find a way to keep doctors fully utilized without long delays to patients.

Any solution must accept the level of specialization as given. Since slack cannot be used, the clinics must either reduce uncertainty or devote more resources to coordination. One clinic is trying to reduce uncertainty by sending an elaborate questionnaire to new in-coming patients in order to reveal symptoms, perform a diagnosis, and schedule the appropriate doctors. Success would allow a *global–periodic* scheduling procedure. The last clinic studied by Rockart used a global–periodic structure but without reducing uncertainty. A central staff of 20 received in-coming phone calls and mail and tried to schedule the requests on global listings of doctor availability. However, the decay process was significant and doctors averaged fifteen minutes a day of idle time and patients waited thirty minutes per appointment. The decay was caused by patients failing to meet their apointments, doctors being called away, changes in doctor assignments, etc. To adapt to this situation, Rockart designed an *on-line–real-time* system to allow global data to be used in scheduling patients through multiple doctors without a significant decay process invalidating the schedule. It can now be updated rapidly and rescheduling can take place as needed. This increases costs by about $75,000 a year, but permits specialization.

This illustrates quite clearly the two points of emphasis. First, there is no one best information system. The clinics mentioned above operate identical technologies with different information systems, yet all are effective organizations. The second point is that the information system is only one of several organization design variables. In this case, the basis of departmentalization is fixed and the task uncertainty, slack, and information systems must be combined into a consistent system. The rural clinic is able to operate under high uncertainty and a simple information system by using slack time. The second clinic is attempting to reduce uncertainty to permit a global–periodic information system and thereby reduce slack time. This may be done also by operating from referrals only. The third clinic accepted the high uncertainty and is trying to reduce slack time with an on-line–real-time scheduling information system. All these combinations are internally consistent and can lead to effective operations.


## SUMMARY

This chapter discussed the use of the new information technology as an organizing mode. As with the previous modes, the effects are discussed with respect to information overloads. The controllable design attributes were identified and cast into some prototype information systems. The effects and costs were discussed. The empirical studies highlighted the alternative nature of the modes of organizing.

## NOTES

1. This framework comes from the work of D. C. Carroll 1967. On the structure of operational control systems. In J. Pierce (ed.), *Operations research and the design of management information systems.* New York: Technical Association of the Pulp and Paper Industry, pp. 391–415.
2. C. Hitch 1953. Suboptimization in operations problems. *Journal of the Operations Research Society* (May): 87–99.
3. J. G. March and H. A. Simon 1958. *Organizations.* New York: Wiley, pp. 161–166.
4. H. A. Simon 1960. *The new science of management decision.* New York: Harper & Row.
5. D. C. Carroll 1966. Man-machine cooperation on planning and control problems. *Industrial Management Review,* (Fall): 47–54.
6. M. S. Scott-Morton 1971. *Management decision systems.* Boston: Harvard Business School, Division of Research.
7. T. L. Whisler 1970. *The impact of computers on organizations.* New York: Praeger.
8. *Ibid.,* p. 60.
9. *Ibid.,* pp. 62 and 72.
10. *Ibid.,* p. 74.
11. B. Hedberg 1974. Computer systems to support industrial democracy. Paper delivered at IFIP Conference, Vienna, April. Available from International Institute of Management, Berlin.
12. E. Buffa 1968. *Production-inventory systems.* Homewood, Ill.: Richard D. Irwin, Chapter 12.
13. J. Rockart, 1967. Scheduling in multispecialist group medical practice. Unpublished Ph.D. Dissertation, Cambridge: M.I.T. Press.

## QUESTIONS

1. Give an example of each of the following information system types and suggest the costs and benefits of changing it to another type.
   a) local–periodic          b) local–real-time
   c) global–periodic        d) global–real-time
2. Give an example of a formal information system which can (a) decentralize and (b) centralize decision making.
3. What do you predict will be the structural consequences of increased computer applications?
4. Assume the creation of an inexpensive minicomputer. How could it be used to help coordination at Chandler's Restaurant?

| CREATION OF LATERAL RELATIONS: ALTERNATIVE 4 | CHAPTER 8 |
|---|---|

The final organizing mode (Alternative 4) is to employ lateral forms of communication and joint decision-making processes. That is, instead of referring a problem upward in the hierarchy, the managers solve the problem at their own level, contacting and cooperating with peers in those departments affected by the new information. In this chapter lateral forms of direct-contact liaison departments, task forces, and teams are discussed. A case study illustrating the design and use of these processes follows in Chapter 9.

## LATERAL PROCESSES

As with the other organizing modes, the purpose is to reduce the number of decisions being referred upward. As in the case of vertical information systems, the effect is to increase the capacity of the organization to process information and make decisions. Lateral relations accomplish this by increasing discretion at lower levels of the organization in contrast to some computer applications which transmit information from points of origination to a central decision point to exploit global information. Such computerized information systems are effective when the decision in question requires formalized, quantitative data. However, if the information relevant to a particular decision is qualitative, it is more effective to bring the point of decision down to the points of information origin. Lateral processes should also be contrasted with the creation of self-contained groups. This strategy also increased discretion at lower levels of the organization. Discretion was permitted at a low level because there was little sharing of resources across groups. A group did not need information about another group when solving a problem. However, if discretion is to be increased at lower levels without reducing resource sharing, lateral relations are required. They are necessary in order to acquire all the information relevant to the shared resources and the possible uses of shared resources.

Some of the forms of lateral relations make use of what is referred to as the "informal organization" or cliques.[1] These informal processes are thought to arise spontaneously and are the processes through which the organization accomplishes most of its work despite the formally designed structure. A typical point of view is, "If we had to go through channels, we would never get anything done." The point of view being taken here is that these processes are necessary but their use can be substantially improved by designing them into the formal organization. At the very least organizations can be designed so as not to prevent these processes from arising spontaneously, and reward systems can be designed to encourage such processes.[2] But a more important reason for formalization is that these processes do not always arise spontaneously from the task requirements, especially in highly differentiated organizations. When the relevant participants have different and sometimes antagonistic attitudes, come from different countries, and are separated geographically, the effective use of joint decision making requires formally designed processes.

There are several forms of lateral relations. Some are simple, obvious, and inexpensive. Others are more sophisticated and costly and also require more design attention. The forms are listed below in order of increasing cost. It is hypothesized that in order to be effective, organizations will utilize these forms in proportion to the amount of task uncertainty. Thus, as task uncertainty increases, the organization will sequentially adopt these mechanisms up through the matrix organization. The forms are also cumulative in the sense that higher forms are added to, not substituted for, lower forms. The forms, from simplest to most complex, apply the following strategies:

1. Utilize *direct contact* between managers who share a problem.

2. Establish *liaison roles* to link two departments which have substantial contact.

3. Create temporary groups called *task forces* to solve problems affecting several departments.

4. Employ groups or *teams* on a permanent basis for constantly recurring interdepartmental problems.

5. Create a new role, an *integrating role,* when leadership of lateral processes becomes a problem.

6. Shift from an integrating role to a *linking-managerial role* when faced with substantial differentiation.

7. Establish dual authority relations at critical points to create the *matrix design.*

The first four of these relations are discussed in this chapter.

### Direct Contact

The simplest and least costly form of lateral relationship is direct contact between managers jointly affected by a problem. For example, in Fig. 8.1 if department A is about to overrun its schedule on an item which goes next to department D, the manager of A, instead of referring the problem up-

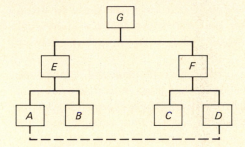

**Fig. 8.1   Hierarchy utilizing direct contact.**

ward to G for resolution, could contact D directly and they could reach a mutually agreeable joint decision. If problems can be resolved in this manner, the number of exceptions flowing upward and downward in the hierarchy is reduced. The top managers are then left free for those decisions that cannot be solved by direct contact between managers.

From an information-processing view, direct contact relieves overloads by moving decisions from high in the hierarchy to lower levels. Such contact should improve the quality of the decision making because managers A and D have more information relevant to the decision. However, A and D may reach a decision which is not in the best interest of the organization as a whole. To ensure good decisions, the organization should have a reward system which rewards cooperative behaviors,[3] should have managers who are interpersonally competent, norms which make such collaboration legitimate, and clearly visible departmental targets. If these supporting factors are not present, they should become the objectives for Organization Development (OD) activities.

There is another way to improve these informal practices. Many organizations engage in the practice of laterally transferring personnel from one department to another. This practice is usually part of the management development program. If an individual has a series of experiences in specialist departments, then he or she is prepared for a general management position. The effects of such transfers on attitudes and communication behavior have been tested.[4] The findings clearly indicate that managers having interdepartmental experience communicate laterally to a larger number of colleague managers than managers not having interdepartmental experience. Similar findings were reported for a Japanese R & D organization.[5] In the second study it was discovered that the effects of the transfer diminish with time. People transferred ten years ago behave the same way as individuals who have had no experience.

A second finding is that individuals having interdepartmental experience use more informal means to communicate when engaging in a lateral contact. They will use a telephone call, a face-to-face contact, or an informal meeting. Those not having the experience are more likely to use a memo. Therefore the transfer increases the probability that the individual will engage in a problem-solving dialogue rather than use a less effective one-way communication means.

The last finding is that managers with interdepartmental experience tend to establish reciprocal relations. That is, they receive as many contacts as they initiate. Therefore, they are less likely to be always pushing someone or always being pushed. Most satisfaction producing relationships are reciprocal.

The lateral transfer apparently improves lateral relations by reducing the impersonality of the contact. Managers with interdepartmental experience had the same attitudes as managers without the experience. They pursued parochial departmental goals to the same degree as other managers. However they were more likely to perceive the presence of conflict. This may be why they choose a more personal approach to the contact. In addition, no one likes to call a department. Everyone prefers to call a person. If one calls a department, he or she is likely to get low-level personnel and a predictable, rule-oriented response. It is difficult to ask people you do not know for favors. However, if you know Paul works in the department, he may not be able to help you but can set you up with someone who can. This is why the transfer effect decays over time. The promotion, transfer, and turnover process causes a loss of personal contacts.

Therefore, it appears that lateral transfers result in more lateral contacts and more effective contacts. In addition the organization gets something for nothing if it already uses lateral transfers. The only thing needed is to transfer between interdependent departments and to transfer often enough to offset the diminishing time effect. If transfers are not used currently, they should be evaluated against the costs of lost specialization and lost productivity due to learning time.

## Liaison Roles

When the volume of contacts between any two departments grows, it becomes economical to set up a specialized role to handle this communication. Liaison people are typical examples of specialized roles designed to facilitate communication between two interdependent departments and to bypass the long lines of communication involved in upward referral.

The best example of this role is the engineering liaison person in a manufacturing plant. The liaison is part of the engineering organization but is physically located in the plant to serve the production organization. These roles link two functional departments at low levels of the organization. This is shown in Fig. 8.2. Other examples are expediters or stock chasers in firms with fabricating and assembly operations.

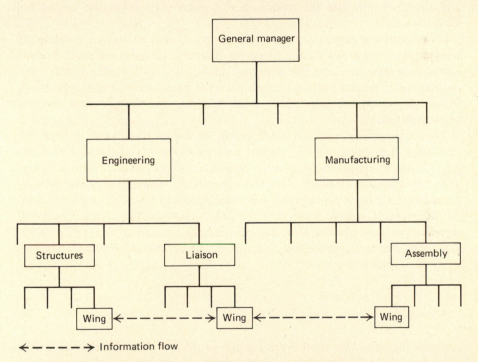

Fig. 8.2  Example of engineering liaison linking two functions.

## Task Forces

Direct contact and liaison roles, like the integration mechanisms discussed before, have a limited range of usefulness. They work when two managers or functions are involved. When problems arise involving seven or eight departments, direct contacts are not sufficient to reach a joint decision. These problems must be referred upward. For uncertain, interdependent tasks such situations arise frequently. Task forces are a form of horizontal contact which is designed to solve problems of multiple departments.

The task force is made up of representatives from each of the affected departments. Some are full-time members; others may be part-time. The task force is a temporary group. It exists only as long as the problem remains. When a solution is reached each participant returns to his or her normal tasks.

To the extent that they are successful, task forces remove problems from higher levels of the hierarchy. The decisions are made at lower levels in the organization. In order to guarantee integration, a group problem-solving approach can be taken. Each affected subunit contributes a member and therefore provides the information necessary to judge the impact on all units.

These groups may arise informally or on a formal basis. In one company when a problem arises on the assembly floor the foreman calls the process engineer, a member from the company laboratory, and quality control and purchasing if vendor parts are involved. This group works out the problem. When an acceptable solution is created, group members return to their normal duties.

On other occasions the establishment of the group is more formal. An aerospace firm holds weekly design reviews. When a significant problem arises, a group is appointed, given a deadline, a limit to their discretion, and asked to solve the problem. Quite frequently the functional hierarchies of manufacturing firms are supported by task forces to introduce new products or processes. The task force is a temporary patchwork on the functional structure used to short circuit communication lines in a time of high uncertainty. When the uncertainty decreases, the functional hierarchy resumes its guiding influence.


## Teams

As tasks become less predictable, more problems arise during the act of execution. At some point, the combined use of rules, plans, direct contact, task forces, and upward referral may no longer be adequate to the task of maintaining integration. If the delays in decisions become long, lines of communication become extended, and top managers are forced to spend more time on day-to-day operations; the next response is to use group problem solving on a more permanent basis. Teams are typically formed around frequently occurring problems. Such teams can meet daily or weekly to discuss problems affecting the group. They solve all the problems which require commitments that they are capable of making. Larger problems are referred upward.

Teams can be formed at various levels. Actually an entire hierarchy of teams could be designed. The design of team structures present the same kind of departmentalization problems that are involved in the design of the formal hierarchy of authority. They could be formed around common customers, clients, geographic regions, functions, processes, products, or projects. If the hierarchy of authority is based on common functions such as engineering, production, and marketing, the teams could be formed around products with representatives from each function. Thus the teams involve design decisions concerning the basis of the team, the composition of membership, the levels at which they are to operate, the extent of their decision, and the frequency of their meetings. The pattern of interdependence and basis for the authority structure should determine the basis and composition of membership. In addition the greater the task uncertainty, the greater the number of levels at which teams should operate, the more frequent should be their meetings and the greater should be their discretion.

An interesting example of teams can be found in an aerospace firm's manufacturing operations. The formal authority structure is based on common functions and is illustrated in Fig. 8.3. Teams were formed around the

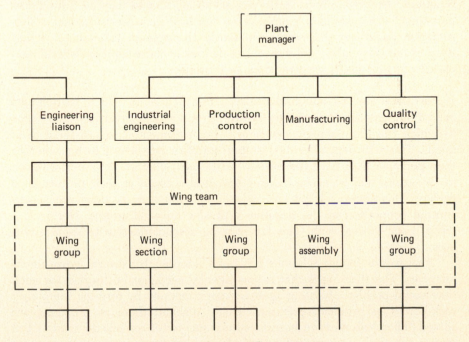

Fig. 8.3   Wing team overlaid on a functional structure.

major sections of the aircraft that were being produced. In addition, the groups were physically located around common aircraft sections. All groups working on the wing are located in the same area of the plant. Thus the physical location facilitates the lateral communication process and team structure. The design is an attempt to achieve the benefits of both a functional form and a task or project form.

## MAKING LATERAL PROCESSES EFFECTIVE

The use of group decision making in organizations is a topic that never fails to elicit strong opinions—pro and con. There are usually good reasons for these opinions. Good and bad examples of groups are readily available. However, some learning has taken place from these good and bad experiences so that something can be said about when groups are most and least effective. This section attempts to articulate which factors must be changed so that lateral relationships "fit" into the mosaic of the organization's processes rather than work at cross-purposes.

In addition there are some operational decisions which affect team effectiveness. Even if there is a supportive managerial climate, questions remain about representation. Who should participate in the team? which functions? from what level in the organization? Should they be full-time or part-time? What kinds of people make the best members? Or does representation make any difference? Obviously the opinion taken here is that these factors *do* make a difference. Let us look at those representational and climate factors which seem to make a difference.

**1. Perceived reward and importance.** The degree to which participants are willing to commit themselves to the group task depends on the degree to which the group's performance will be instrumental in satisfying their needs. This will depend on how important they perceive it to be, whether they perceive they have the needed skills, and whether their performance in the group will be evaluated or taken into account at their performance review. This feature, despite its apparent obviousness, accounts for a substantial proportion of the negative attitudes towards groups. Nor is it a trivial issue to deal with. This fact can be demonstrated with some examples.

The use of lateral relations has been adopted by several government agencies. The thinking is that a new agency need not be formed for each new social problem. Existing agencies can cooperate by forming temporary task forces as problems arise and easily disband them as problems are solved. These efforts have been less than successful for several reasons but one is the perceived reward system. In one of the participating agencies not using Civil Service, a questionnaire was used to assess which activities were perceived by the managers as most likely to lead to a promotion.[6] Out of twenty possible activities, participation in interagency projects was ranked last. Similar conditions prevail among university professors.[7] How do these conditions arise? How can they be changed so that the individuals are willing to commit themselves?

Individuals' perception of task activity is a function of the process by which assignments are made to the task force. The assignment process is the mechanism by which superiors communicate their expectations about task importance. If participation is unimportant and therefore not part of the reward system, the superior will make assignments which communicate that fact. One approach is to assign the low performers. Since the task force is thought to be a waste of time, the boss will not want to waste any resources. Therefore the assignment goes to whomever can be spared. The astute employees get this message very quickly. In addition, the practice staffs the task force with those people who are most likely to make it fail.

A second assignment approach is to take turns. Individuals are made to feel that it is their "turn in the barrel." This perception is created when subordinates object to an assignment on the basis that they are already very busy. The response of the superior is not to relieve them of previous tasks but to ask that they take on this other assignment because it is their turn. The department is expected to provide staff, and rotation is an equitable way to handle the assignment. Again the message is clear. It is also reinforced by other members of the group.

In order to change the reward system and assignment process, the attitudes of the assigning managers need to be changed. It may be pointed out to the managers that their experiences appear valid but their behavior determined the outcome they expected. Therefore, the OD effort must deal with the manager's attitudes toward group decision making. The managers must get to a point where they are willing to try to make it work. They are the ones who will assign competent participants, reward performance, relieve participants of previous assignments, and communicate importance. But these behaviors occur only if managers believe there is a reasonable chance that the task force will accomplish something. The OD educational effort must deal with the attitudes brought about by the self-fulfilling prophecy.

**2. Assignment of line managers.** At least a substantial minority of the team or task force must consist of managers who will subsequently be held responsible for the implementation of the joint decision. If all the Department of Defense task force studies were separated into those that were implemented and those that were discarded, the discarded task force studies would be characterized by exclusive participation of staff groups and outside consultants. It is not that these groups are useless but that they lack the insight of the person who has the problem and the commitment from the person who has to make it work.

The problem is not always the result of experts working in isolation. Quite often staff experts seek the help of the managers but are told they are too busy to work with the staff experts. This is partly due to the reward system effect discussed above. Work on task forces and teams is perceived to be costly and time consuming, and usually this perception is true. However, at this point lateral relations must be viewed in the perspective of being one design strategy of four possible alternatives. The theory being put forth here is that *as organizations introduce new products, new processes, or diversify product lines, the organization must incur greater costs. It has no choice. The choice relates only to the form in which the cost is incurred.* It can be incurred in the form of extended schedules (slack), reduced specialization (self-containment), more computer time and clerical effort (vertical information system), or of time and effort from line managers (lateral managers). Thus, participation on a task force or team is a cost but it is a natural consequence of the task being performed by the organization. Objections must show that alternative costs are in fact smaller.

One consequence is that the cost of lateral relations must be reflected in the budgets of the managers so that they can legitimately be expected to provide staff for task forces and teams. It will mean that they are more likely to send competent personnel rather than someone they can spare. It also communicates to the manager that the organization as a whole thinks that teams are an important part of the decision process. These changes to the budget and reward system have substantial effects on the organization norms which support decision processes.

The participation of line managers is essential if task forces or teams are to reduce information overloads. This means the group must arrive at an action decision. Therefore the manager who is responsible for performing the action must participate.

**3. Participants must have information relevant to the decision.** If an action decision is to be reached, the participants in the group must have the information relevant to the decisions with which the group is charged. This is another commonsense statement that is frequently violated. In one sense this means all the departments who are significantly affected by a decision should be there. One of the advantages of PERT networks is that they portray the activities to be performed and who is to perform them. This allows easy identification of affected units.

A more subtle aspect of this point is the choice of level of the organization from which a participant must come. The level will vary with each department depending on the pattern of interdependence and task uncertainty within each department. For example, a frequent violator of the appropriate level is the technical function of an organization. The technical representative sometimes comes from too high in the organization. Then during a problem-solving session the representative is too far removed from the technology to be able to evaluate consequences of others' suggestions or to create technical alternatives to satisfy the criteria of other departments. One response to the lack of detailed knowledge is to bring subordinates in with the manager. This has the defect of enlarging the size of the group solving the problem. In one company, such a meeting brought out 40 people. The appropriate solution is to have lower level personnel represent the department. These people are usually first- and second-level technical people. They are the ones who are in day-to-day contact with the technology.

**4. Participants must have the authority to commit their department.** If an action decision is to be reached, the participants must be able to commit the resources necessary to carry out the agreed-upon solution. A typical violator of this requirement is the production or operating department. In one company a task force was formed to help manage the introduction of a new product. After one intense, confronting meeting concerning a schedule slippage, the group decided the best response was for manufacturing to work 100 hours of overtime. The manufacturing representative then stated that he could not commit his organization for that magnitude of resource usage. When the solution was presented to his superior for consideration, it was vetoed. This had a disastrous effect on the group. It achieved effectiveness only when the superior became the representative from manufacturing.

All of the factors above are necessary if the task forces and teams are to reach effective action decisions. This does not mean that task forces are not useful for other purposes such as recommendations, fact finding, information sharing, etc. But if information overloads are to be relieved by lateral relations, the groups must arrive at and carry out decisions that would normally have been made at higher levels. This means that line managers must participate, be willing to participate, and come from that level of the organization which has both the relevant information and the authority to commit resources. The result will be a high-quality decision and the necessary commitment to implement it. If any of these factors is missing, the team will become one more case of "we tried it and it didn't work."

**5. Influence based on knowledge and information.** One of the consequences of having representatives with authority and relevant information is that the team may be composed of people from different levels of the organization. This will occur if there are differences in subtask uncertainty and interdependence. Recall that structural variations that are found between organizations also exist within organizations but between departments. Therefore the predictable, interdependent tasks of the operating department lead to the concentration of information and authority at high levels. The uncertain diverse tasks of the technical function concentrate authority and information at low levels. Therefore, the task forces should represent diagonal cuts across the organization. In order to be effective, the status differences must be dealt with so as not to constrain the problem-solving process. This requires a norm in the organization that influence is based on knowledge and information rather than a norm that influence is based on hierarchical position.

In organizations with stable and repetitive tasks and with a reasonably effective managerial selection process, there is not likely to be a conflict between hierarchical influence and knowledge-based influence. But in organizations characterized by change and high technology, a single manager cannot know enough about all decision factors. The influence structure for one decision is not the best for another decision. The best influence distribution varies with the decision in question. The organization has to have norms which support knowledge-based influence. If the organization is going to use diagonal-cut teams and does not have the supporting norms, then the Organization Development effort should be aimed at a culture change to create these norms.[8] If status barriers remain, then the groups will not be effective problem-solving, decision-making units.[9]

**6. The lateral processes must be integrated into the vertical processes.** The team-decision processes are not intended to undermine but rather to complement the normal budgeting resource allocation decisions. The lateral processes are used in addition to the vertical processes. They are not replacements. The lateral processes are necessitated by the need for more decision making at low levels. Therefore these processes need to be integrated into the normal day-to-day decision processes.

Nothing irritates managers more than to have information about their responsibilities "go around" them. For example the company represented in Fig. 8.3 had this problem. The wing team met and discovered a quality problem. The solution to the problem required some substantial schedule changes. Much of this work was performed by the production control representative. Later in the day the plant manager held his normal staff meeting. At the meeting the production control manager was asked by the plant manager how the changes were proceeding. This was the first time the production control manager had heard of the changes. The manager's reaction was to limit the discretion of the team representatives. Since a limit to the discretion of team members would limit the decision effectiveness of the teams, the change was not carried out. Instead a procedure was instituted whereby team representatives came in each morning of a meeting, checked the information relevant to their function and team, checked with their superiors if necessary, and then went to the team meeting. Following the team meeting each function holds its meeting to review team actions and unresolved problems. The unresolved problems then become part of the agenda for the plant manager's meeting in the afternoon. The result is a global information system for the plant decision process.

This is also a good example of a systemwide Organization Development effort. Working only with the production control manager would not have resulted in the final solution achieved. The integrating of team decision processes into existing decision processes requires a systemwide intervention. The lack of integration will generate several actions like the production control manager's initial solution. The result will be "We tried it and it didn't work!"

**7. Part-time, full-time composition.** When a task force is formed which will operate for a substantial period of time (more than a couple of months), there is a choice of assignment methods. A member can be totally relieved of departmental duties and assigned full time to the task force. Alternatively the member can be partially relieved and work part time for the department and part time on the task force. This is a constant decision in project-oriented organizations. Even though the organization may be functional or matrix, employees may work on several projects at a time or only one at a time. Marquis reports some data shown in Table 8.1 which bears on this question.[10]

Table 8.1

| Composition | Number of projects | Project performance* |
|---|---|---|
| All Full-time | 12 | 4.6 |
| Over 50% Full-time | 6 | 3.8 |
| Under 50% Full-time | 13 | 2.2 |
| All Part-time | 6 | 3.9 |

* The lower the rating, the better the performance.

The study concerns ratings of overall technical, cost, and schedule performance for 37 projects performed for DOD and NASA. The data suggest that a small core of full-time people and a majority of part-time participants will lead to superior performance.

The projects on which all participants are full time make use of the motivational forces which permit people to identify with a complete piece of work and with the group of people performing it. This advantage is offset by a loss of contact with people within the same department or, in this case, in the same technical specialty. There is a greater lack of contact with one's specialty if all people on the project were physically located together. Collocation frequently happens around a project. The result is that scientists are cut off from the pooled resources of their specialty departments. Since most technical information is transmitted verbally through personal interactions, these scientists are cut off from information sources which can provide problem solutions.[11]

The other extreme, all part-time, maximizes contacts with colleagues but loses the motivational and integrative advantages of identification with a project. A mixture of full time and part time will provide the best of both worlds. However, there is a substantial difference between the over 50 percent and under 50 percent full time. Although this is admittedly post hoc reasoning, it seems little is gained from a motivational and cooperative standpoint by expanding the full-time core. If we have a project employing 50 people, a full-time core of 5 to 10 seems sufficient. If expanded to 25 or 30 full-time people located together, little is gained motivationally. The larger the size of the group, the more likely are subgroups to form and the less each individual participates in overall group decisions. Thus, it seems that motivational effects may be subject to diminishing returns while information sources are cut off as each additional individual becomes full time. In addition, from an overall organizational point of view, higher proportions of part time permit greater manpower flexibility.[12] This allows the use of more specialized resources without the expense of partial utilization. This flexibility is one of the primary advantages of matrix-type organization designs.

Some qualifications are in order. The cost of being cut off from colleagues in a technical specialty is a function of how rapidly the knowledge base underlying the specialty is changing. Under this reasoning the cost of separation is small for an accountant but large for a plasma physicist. Thus full-time task force assignments may be preferable for purely administrative questions.

**8. Conflict resolution practices.**   All of the previous points dealt with factors which are contextual or antecedent to the actual group decision process. The intent was to remove as many barriers as possible which might constrain the individual from choosing behaviors that are most conducive to effective group problem solving. The reason these factors were treated at some length is that there will be conflict, sometimes considerable conflict, to be resolved when the group convenes. That is, the decision alternative which is most preferred using one department's criteria may be the least preferred using another department's criteria and vice versa. However, it is assumed that the conflict is good. It is assumed that the individuals when faced with conflict will share information about their preferences, about why they have these preferences, and then search out new alternatives which satisfy the criteria of as many departments as possible. The result will be a high-quality decision from the point of view of the overall organization.

In order for people to behave as described above, in the face of conflict, they must invest a great deal of emotional and intellectual energy. The appropriate changes suggested in the previous factor discussions all increase the probability that the individual will be willing to incur these psychological costs.

In addition to the problem-solving or confrontation mode, there are other resolution practices which can be used and are predicted to be less effective.[13] One approach is for individuals to push for acceptance of the alternative which is preferred by their department and occasionally "give in" by making incremental changes to it, i.e., a bargaining or compromise approach. It is less effective because the conflict does not trigger a search for new alternatives. In addition the likelihood of getting the department's preferred alternative accepted is increased if information is withheld rather than shared. Under this mode individuals are less likely to search for better solutions and are less likely to find them if they did search.

A bargaining approach arises when solving the problem is less important than gaining an advantage over the other persons. This occurs when there is competition among the departments from which the participants come. Then each participant represents a constituency whose rewards depend on how closely the solution resembles the departmentally preferred alternative rather than on solving the problem in the best interest of the organization. Therefore, reward systems and resource allocation practices should not stimulate competition among interdependent departments.

Another strategy is the prevention of conflict or smoothing over of differences. This sometimes results from bad experiences with the bargaining approach. It can also result from a culture where politeness is valued or from individuals who do not want to bear the emotional costs of confrontation. Therefore conflict is regarded as bad. The approach is less effective because it eliminates the search which is triggered by conflict. In addition, the conflict is still present but is driven underground and acted out in ways which may not contribute to organizational goals.

The last approach is called forcing. This results when the power of position or knowledge is used to force a preferred alternative on the rest of the group. Although forcing is not generally recommended, it can result in effective decision making. This will be true if the forced alternative is consistent with organizational goals and the act of forcing does not limit future confrontation and information sharing. Forcing will lead to ineffective decisions if it is the dominant mode. If one function or dominant department always forces, then there is no need for a group decision and information from other departments is ignored. This leads to suboptimal decisions and poor implementation because a forced solution is based on local information in the presence of interdependence.

The preferred approach to conflict resolution therefore is to use confrontation and problem solving backed up by occasional forcing when lack of agreement stymies the group.[14] Indeed, there may be occasional instances when bargaining and smoothing are necessary. Occasionally situations arise which approximate a fixed resource pool which triggers bargaining. Similar smoothing might be used to allow some to preserve their self-respect so that they can confront and problem solve in the future. But the predominant mode must be confrontation.[15]

**9. Group and interpersonal skills.** The successful use of confrontation as a conflict resolution mode requires that participants have skills to deal with the interpersonal and group decision issues which arise. It is assumed that the process will consider all facts in the situation. This includes feelings as well as so-called objective facts. The conflict resolution process causes individuals to be confronted, to place their egos on the line, to accept criticism, and to deal with role conflict due to multiple group memberships. In order to deal with these feelings, interpersonal competence is required. It must result from either selection or training. Therefore, OD activities are required to support the team decision process. Team-building activities reduce threat and create a climate in which confrontation can be accepted.

**10. Leadership.** The occasional use of force from a leadership position raises the question about who should be the leader of the team or task force. The problem-solving approach is intended to achieve a consensus which obviates the need for a powerful leader. Consensus is not unanimity but a state of affairs where the individual who disagrees with the preferred solution feels as follows:

> I understand what most of you would like to do. I personally would not do that, but I feel that you understand what my alternative would be. I have had sufficient opportunity to sway you to my point of view but clearly have not been able to do so. Therefore, I will go along with what most of you wish to do.[16]

However, this state of affairs is not always achieved. Sometimes a forced solution is required to achieve some collective action. Then from whose point of view does the decision get forced?

There are several models. One is that a decision is forced from the point of view of an obviously high-status, dominant department. This may be made up of physicians in hospitals or scientists in aerospace. The group process gives other departments their "day in court" but the burden is on them to convince the high-status department. This process can be effective if the goals of the organization are congruent with those of the high-status department. When they are not, the high-status department adjusts on the basis of information provided by other departments.

Another model occurs when the decision in question predominantly affects one department more than the others. Then the manager of that department becomes the team leader. If consensus is not reached and the leader forces, the organization is still likely to achieve a high-quality decision. The leader must be clear, however, that it is lack of consensus that causes forcing. Otherwise problem solving may be discouraged in future meetings. The leader still needs information from interdependent departments.

A variation of this model arises when the predominantly affected department varies with time. For example, in the early stages of introducing a new product, the decisions are primarily technical. A little later they have impact primarily on the production department. Finally the major decisions bear on marketing strategy. The leadership function will pass from one department manager to the next as the questions vary. At each stage, if a decision is forced, it is forced from the point of view of the predominantly affected department but after other departments have had a chance to influence the decision. There is a high probability that these decisions will be in the best interest of the organization.

These models are not sufficient as more decisions and more decisions of consequence are made and carried out at low levels in the organization.

Thus, as uncertainty increases, greater concern is taken for the quality of decisions reached through group processes. Other factors change also. There may not be an obviously dominant function. It becomes important to get marketing influence into new products at an early stage. Departments with exclusive access to information may inordinately dominate decision making. When these pressures occur in the presence of increasing differentiation between departments, a need arises for an integration function to bring a global viewpoint into the decision process. In addition someone works full time on maintaining the quality of the decisions. This is the integrator role which is one of the topics of Chapter 10.

## SUMMARY

This chapter introduced the concept of lateral relations and their design. Direct contact, liaison roles, task forces, and teams were discussed in this chapter. They were identified as mechanisms by which the organization can move decisions down into the organization towards the points of information origin. This reduced the information overload by moving decisions to lower levels freeing higher levels for consequential and long-range decisions only. In order to bring global information to bear on the decisions, the organization has to engage in joint decisions. From an information-processing point of view, this works in the sense that the overload is reduced. But it work only if people behave in a confronting, problem-solving manner.

Most of the chapter was concerned with climate, representational, and process factors which must support the joint-decision process. The joint-decision process must include line managers from the level of the organization which has both the information relevant to the decision and the authority to commit the resources to implement the decision. The processes of assigning people, rewarding performance, and budgeting resources must support the group processes. These formal organization practices "communicate" to individuals how important these groups are and influence their willingness to incur the psychological costs of confrontation. The group processes must also be integrated into the organization's decision process. Even if the climate is supportive, participants must have the skills to deal with interpersonal issues which necessarily rise. Finally the leadership should come from the department whose viewpoint is most congruent with organizational goals relevant to the decision. If this department cannot be found and decisions reached by groups are consequential, it pays to design the role of integrator to perform the leadership function.

All of these factors can facilitate the joint-decision process. The Organization Development effort of the organization must diagnose which factors need to be changed and engage in interventions to make them support the joint-decision process.

## NOTES

1. M. Dalton 1957. *Men who manage.* New York: Wiley.

2. G. F. Farris 1971. Organizing your informal organization. *Innovation,* (October).

3. A. Zander and D. Wolfe 1964. Administrative rewards and coordination among committee members. *Administrative Science Quarterly,* (June): 50–69.

4. W. M. Newport 1969. The interdepartmental transfer: an integrative strategy. Unpublished M.S. thesis. Cambridge: M.I.T. Press.

5. M. Kanno 1968. Effects on communication between labs and plants of the transfer of R & D personnel. Unpublished M.S. thesis, Cambridge: M.I.T. Press.

6. H. Weiner 1970. Role perception and organization ineffectiveness in the foreign service. Unpublished M.S. thesis. Cambridge: M.I.T. Press.

7. E. Schein 1970. The reluctant professor: implications for university management. *Sloan Management Review,* (Fall): 35–50.

8. R. Beckhard 1969. *Organization development: strategies and models.* Reading, Mass.: Addison-Wesley, Chapter 4.

9. E. M. Bridges, W. J. Doyle, and D. J. Mahan 1968. Effects of hierarchical differentiation on group productivity, efficiency, and risk taking. *Administrative Science Quarterly,* (September): 305–319.

10. D. Marquis 1969. Ways of organizing projects. *Innovation* **5**: 26–33.

11. T. J. Allen and S. Cohen 1969. Information flow in research and development laboratories. *Administrative Science Quarterly,* (March): 12–20.

12. R. A. Goodman 1968. Organization and manpower utilization in research and development. *IEEE Transactions,* (December): 198–204.

13. R. R. Blake and J. S. Mouton 1964. *The managerial grid.* Houston: Gulf Publishing.

14. P. Lawrence and J. Lorsch 1967. *Organization and environment.* Boston: Harvard Business School, pp. 73–78.

15. The management of conflict is treated in depth elsewhere. See R. Walton 1969, *Interpersonal peacemaking: confrontations and third party consultation.* Reading, Mass.: Addison-Wesley.

16. E. Schein 1956. *Process consultation: its role in organization development.* Reading, Mass.: Addison-Wesley, p. 56.

## QUESTIONS

1. How do teams and task forces increase the information-processing and decision-making capacity of an organization?

2. Explain how lateral forms of coordination decentralize decisions.

3. How would you increase the likelihood that direct contact or other informal practices would spring up around mutual problems?

4. Give examples of liaison roles. How are they different from integrating roles?

5. Discuss the suggestion that in designing teams one confronts many of the same problems encountered in designing self-contained forms.

6. Select a group in which you participated and discuss how the ten group-effectiveness points were handled.

7. Discuss other variations of handling leader roles (i.e., rotating leader function) and critique them.

| | CHAPTER |
|---|---|
| A CASE STUDY—TEAMS | **9** |

The concepts of the previous chapter can be illustrated by a case example. The chapter first presents the organization structure, technology, and current state of affairs facing a manufacturing company. Then the various organizing modes are presented as alternatives to relieve the current situation and finally the alternative that was actually chosen is discussed.


### SITUATION BEFORE THE CHANGE

The manufacturing company produces a number of different assembled mechanical devices for the aircraft industry. Many of the devices were used to actuate the flaps, ailerons, stabilizers, and other moving parts of the airframe. About 75 percent of the production went to the airframe manufacturers while the other 25 percent went to the airlines as replacement parts. The company had been working with the airframe manufacturers for many years and was quite profitable.


#### Organization

The 1100 employees were organized in a basic functional structure which is depicted in Fig. 9.1. The department of administration handled the accounting and personnel functions. The process engineering function was responsible for the development and design of manufacturing processes and tools. In addition they managed the construction, maintenance, and set-ups of all tooling. This function was very important since between 20 percent and 30 percent of the products changed each year. Each change required a retooling effort.

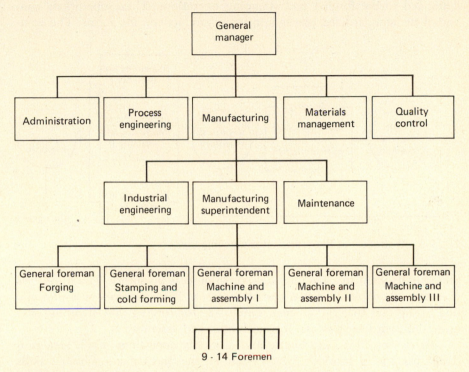

Fig. 9.1 Organization chart for the manufacturing company.

The materials management unit is responsible for the scheduling of the work flow from vendors to customers. The purchasing department, receiving, shipping, and parts control make up the remainder of the materials function. They also coordinate with the corporate marketing function. The quality control unit is responsible for inspection of material when it arrives, at intermittent points and prior to shipping. The high-quality standards of the aircraft manufacturers have made this unit an important one.

The majority of the people were in manufacturing. Each of the general foremen worked with from 9 to 14 foremen. Each foreman had an average of about 16 workers in his group. The industrial engineers were concerned with work methods, time standards for costs and schedules, and plant layout. The maintenance unit was responsible for maintaining all physical facilities other than tooling fixtures.

## Work Flow

The flow of work from vendors to customers is shown in Fig. 9.2. The flow begins with raw materials in the form of homogeneous, standard steel forms being fed to the forging and stamping operations. These operations converted the standardized pieces into more product-specific forms. The com-

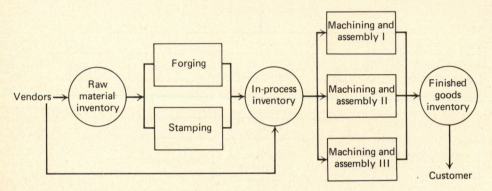

Fig. 9.2   Work flow at the manufacturing company.

pleted parts went to a holding area for in-process inventory. The in-process inventory uncoupled the two operating areas. This inventory was partially due to the fact that the efficient batch size for forging and stamping was quite different from the one for machining and assembly.

There were three machining and assembly operations. Each area produced a range of products which required the particular machining skills peculiar to the area. These were not product-specialized areas, however. No products had sufficient volume to set up a machining line for that product. Therefore the layout had some features of a job shop in that orders were sequenced through process centers, and some of the features of a flow shop in that the three areas capitalized on the regularities in sequences of processes which existed among groups of products.

Some of the high-volume items were held as finished goods inventory. Most production was to customer order, however. The inventory was also used for holding replacement parts for which quick delivery was necessary.

## Assessment of Decision Processes

In late 1969 a new general manager assumed office. In the process of learning the business, he discovered among the management a dissatisfaction with the prevailing state of affairs. On the surface there was little reason for the dissatisfaction. The profits were at planned levels. The costs were under control. The growth in volume was adequate. But with a little analysis it was discovered that managers felt that today's performance was being achieved at the expense of tomorrow's performance.

Most of the top-management group felt they were spending almost all their time on day-to-day problems. They were continually being drawn into "now" problems on the shop floor that they felt should be handled at lower levels. The longer run tooling and capital investment programs were not receiving even a fraction of the attention they required. If their programs were not handled well, the neglect would generate more "now" problems next year.

The general manager and the top-management team took the analysis of current decision processes as their first order of business. They first analyzed the environment in which they were operating. Everyone was aware of the year-to-year market changes but was surprised when the ten-year history was compiled. Although they still offered the same basic product lines, the individual variations had grown from 400 to 800. The number of parts from 5000 to 8000. The proportion of products requiring retooling had jumped from 20 percent to 30 percent. Thus there was a greater variety of products and more frequent changes to the line.

In addition there were some qualitative changes as well. The airframe manufacturers were hard pressed financially. They reduced their inventories but tried to get their vendors to hold the inventory for them or to decrease the delivery time and increase delivery reliability. The quality specifications and tolerance limits continued to get tighter. At the same time, the manufacturers and their suppliers had to acquire some expertise in working with titanium. This lighter metal was being used extensively on the larger and supersonic aircraft. As with any new technology there were many mistakes and rejected lots.

In the face of these substantial changes, the general manager was surprised that the plant was doing as well as it was. He recognized that the key to success for the plant was efficient scheduling. They had to meet airframe assembly schedules and simultaneously get full utilization out of their capital-intensive, high-skilled labor operations. One response to this state of affairs was to expand by adding multiple shifts. The machines were running 24 hours a day. In order to determine how the plant was scheduled, the general manager began an analysis of the production scheduling system in the materials management unit.

The materials management group was primarily concerned with aggregate scheduling for the entire plant. They worked from aggregated forecasts and smoothed out the fluctuations in demand to avoid layoffs and overtime. They did this by building up and depleting inventories, using subcontracting for occasional peak periods, and negotiating more favorable delivery schedules with the customer.[1] Their procedures generated a full load for each department, a smooth flow from raw materials to finished goods, and the required coordination between purchasing, production, and marketing.

The materials department did not assign specific orders to specific machines. They tried to centralize the detailed scheduling many years ago. A number of scheduling boards were mounted on the wall. The boards maintained the availability of each machine group. As orders came in, due dates were negotiated, and the order was scheduled in the time available. However, the staff assigned to maintain the boards was very quickly overloaded. In addition to the arrival of customer orders and cancellations, they had to make changes for machine breakdowns, absenteeism, quality rejects, and engineering changes. After that experience it was agreed that the materials group would see that the total available time in each shop matched the demand for that shop's services. The detailed job assignment was left to each shop. They employed a procedure referred to as "scheduling to infinite capacity."[2] The materials department assigned due dates for operations which served only as guides for production personnel. The due dates were based on historical average lead times and standard times worked out by industrial engineering. As customers requested work by a certain date, the materials function would simply subtract the average lead times from that date and generate start dates which, on the average, were necessary to complete the order on time.

The assessment of the top-management team was that this procedure worked well as long as material was available, the aggregate demand equaled the capacity available, and the shop personnel had sufficient flexibility to adapt to short-run schedule conflicts. Since material availability and short-run capacity were not problematic, the team's attention shifted to the shop floor.

The scheduling procedure mentioned above was defective in that it created schedule conflicts. In subtracting average lead times from delivery dates, the materials function did not consider the load existing on a machine. It was possible to schedule three or four jobs on the same machine at the same time. These conflicts were no problem if the production personnel had some short-run flexibility to shift manpower, to schedule overtime selectively, etc. However, analysis of the management team revealed very quickly that the foreman and general foreman did not have the flexibility required. The market changes had increased the number of machine set-ups and tooling changes. Since set-up men and tooling personnel were part of process engineering, the changes increased the dependence of manufacturing upon the service of engineering. Also the quality control unit was required to inspect the first few units produced to check the new set-ups and tooling fixtures. While the machine was idle because of the set-up and inspection, the foreman would try to get maintenance to perform machine repairs. The coordination was necessary to minimize machine idle time and still meet tight schedules. Thus, there was little flexibility and an increasing amount of interdependence.

In the day-to-day scheduling process, the foremen and general foremen were continually seeking the services of the support units. Quite often two or more demands upon the support unit could not be met simultaneously. Process engineering, quality control, and maintenance were forced into making priority decisions. If there was disagreement, the situations were referred upward to top management. These schedule-related priority issues were the ones that were burdening the top management. This is a general problem present in all organizations when operating units share service and support resources. The problem is one of determining priorities among the requests for service.

The normal way to handle the problem is with a schedule. Requests for service are matched against service resources and priorities are determined at a global level by those knowledgeable about the total situation. Short-run priorities are determined by which job was scheduled first. In the present situation, the number of factors and the rate at which they changed caused the schedule to decay and become useless. Priorities were set through personal contacts. But the head of maintenance could not make priority decisions. He knew his resource availability but not which request for service was more important. Hence, the question was escalated to higher levels where priority decisions could be made.

The case description illustrates how external changes are translated into information processing overloads. There were increases in diversity (number of product variations), uncertainty (30 percent tooling changes and titanium technology), required performance levels (tighter schedules, greater delivery reliability, and stricter tolerances), and interdependence (engineering-production-maintenance). The increased information processing and decision making overloaded the hierarchy. Therefore, some kind of organization design action is required. In the next section, the alternative actions are created and described.

## ORGANIZATION DESIGN ALTERNATIVES

In order to relieve the overload, the manufacturing firm must choose one or some combination of the four organizing modes. Each of the available strategies will be described in this section along with the predicted effects and costs.

## Slack

The first strategy that could be adopted would be to employ various forms of slack resources. Three examples will be discussed here. First, the average lead times could be extended. Instead of allowing six weeks from start to finish for an order, the lead time could be extended to eight or nine. The additional time would be effective in removing the overload. The additional time would reduce the necessity of having all support units present simultaneously on a tooling change. Production could tolerate more machine idle time and still meet delivery dates. They could schedule set-ups independent of maintenance work because two work stoppages would not be disruptive. The additional time reduces the interdependence between production and the support units.

The increased lead time has its costs, also. On the average there will be two or three weeks demand in in-process inventory tying up additional working capital. However, the real cost is asking the customer to order eight weeks prior to planned usage rather than six. The current situation in the industry is one of reducing lead time to four or five weeks rather than six. Thus, increasing lead time is very costly. If a finished goods inventory could be accumulated, then the production could be uncoupled from the customer's usage. An extended lead time and quick delivery would both be possible. However, the large variety of products and parts and frequent engineering changes make the carrying of finished goods expensive. In addition, uncertainty about customer specifications means production is undertaken only when an order is received rather than in anticipation of demand through inventory accumulation.

A second approach would be to employ additional resources in the form of machines rather than inventory. Additional machines would have the same effect as longer lead time. It would increase the amount of planned machine idle time. The greater the amount of idle time, the less the necessity to perform simultaneously all those activities which require the machine to be idle. A greater number of machines reduces the interdependence between production and support activities. However additional machinery is expensive. Current technology requires computerized and numerically controlled equipment. It is simply too expensive to leave this equipment underutilized.

A third approach is to employ more resources in the support units. The first two approaches adapted production operations for the convenience of scheduling support resources. This is letting "the tail wag the dog." With the majority of resources employed in the manufacturing unit, it makes greater economic sense to adapt the operation of the support units. One way is to employ more engineers, inspectors, and maintenance personnel.

The more resources in the support units, the fewer the priority problems. The fewer the priority problems, the less the load on the hierarchy. Dalton's analysis of production and maintenance activities reveals that production frequently supports the demands of maintenance for more personnel at budget time in order to remove possible priority problems.[3] However, skilled maintenance specialists and process engineers are also expensive. Whether additional support personnel should be employed depends on the cost of other feasible alternatives.

The costs and effects of employing slack resources should now be clear. Coordination problems arise out of the scarcity of specialized resources. The scheduling and priority problems are eliminated by eliminating the scarcity. The scarcity of specialized resources is eliminated by employing more resources or by eliminating the time pressure. The design problem is to determine which is the scarcest or bottleneck resource and what is the least costly way to increase the availability of that resource.

### Self-contained Departments

The second possible organizing mode is to create self-contained units. This strategy also reduces the interdependence between production and the support units. The design problems are to select the basis on which the autonomous departments will be created (the departmentalization problem) and the level of the organization to which they will report.

The usual alternative departmental arrangement to the functional design is the product divisional design. However, this is not the case in the present situation. Product divisions are the alternative when coordination problems are caused by new product introductions which pass through functional departments. New products contribute to the scheduling problem but are not its primary cause. Also the costs of equipping each product line with its own machinery would be prohibitive.

Instead of product divisions, the departmental arrangement should place together those roles whose interdependence is causing the priority problem. It is the process engineer, set-up man, quality control inspector, maintenance crew, and production personnel whose activities need to be coordinated in order to simultaneously meet delivery schedules, utilize capital equipment, meet aircraft quality standards, prolong the life of expensive equipment, and utilize skilled labor. If these roles are placed in the same unit, the department will contain all the resources necessary to maintain the schedules. It will be self-contained with respect to meeting due dates set by the materials department. It should be noted that the arrangement will not be self-contained with respect to personnel and industrial relations issues, new product introductions, accounting, information, aggregate scheduling, etc. These decisions will still be coordinated by higher level management.

Once the basis for grouping roles is established, there is the question of organizational level. Should each foreman have a set-up man, engineer, maintenance crew, etc.? This question is constrained by the technology of the work flow. Figure 9.2 shows that the in-process inventory creates two units which are independent of each other with respect to detailed scheduling decisions—the forging and stamping unit and the three machining and assembly units. In addition, within each unit, the work flows are parallel. Thus, there is no sequential interdependence within the two units. The work flow and inventory location create five independent units corresponding to areas assigned to general foremen. Each unit can function independently in the structure shown in Fig. 9.3.

The self-contained structure shown in Fig. 9.3 will eliminate the overloads caused by priority decisions on the use of support groups. The problem is solved by dividing up support groups and giving them to the general foreman. Each general foreman resolves the priority issues for his or her

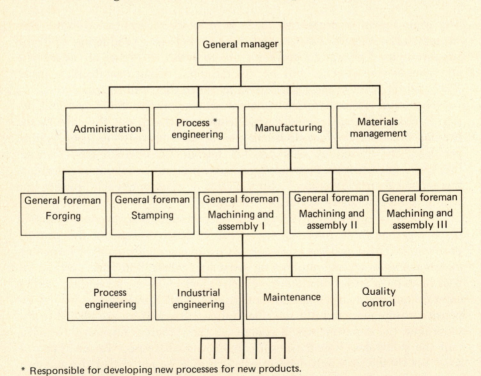

* Responsible for developing new processes for new products.

**Fig. 9.3  Self-contained structure.**

department. The assignment of jobs to machines can now be decentralized to the general foremen who also have the resource flexibility to make the short-run adjustments required by the scheduling to infinite capacity procedure.

The structure has its costs also. There are a number of cases of fractional usage of specialized resources within the self-contained units. For example, there are three specialists for handling numerically controlled machine tools. However, four of the five units make substantial use of numerically controlled equipment. The firm must either duplicate the specialized resource by hiring another specialist or reduce specialization by employing generalists who handle other equipment in addition to numerically controlled machines. The functional structure pools the fractional usages of specialized resources. But the duplication or lost benefits of specialization may be less costly than the additional slack resources required by the functional structure.

There are further costs due to lack of career paths for the personnel in the support units. The organization may have difficulty in holding competent engineers and maintenance personnel if promotions to general foreman go to production personnel. In the functional structure there are promotion possibilities within the function. One can remain an engineer and rise to manager of engineering. But the self-contained structure encourages engineers to leave or become generalists. Both options further reduce the benefits of specialization.

In summary, the strategy of creating self-contained units reduces overloads caused by priority decisions by reducing the amount of sharing of specialized resources. Sometimes reduced sharing is accompanied by a reduced number of specialized roles. The design problem is to decide upon which roles are to be combined into a self-contained unit and at what level of organization the combination will report.

### Vertical Information System

The third mode available to the organization is the employment of the new information technology in the detailed scheduling process. Unlike the two previous modes, implementing the new information technology seeks to adapt the organization's decision processes to the new task requirements. The demand characteristics, technology, lead times, and division of labor are accepted as given.

The mode requires the creation of a current, global data base and a decision mechanism capable of manipulating the data in order to reach decisions concerning the scheduling of all the resources. At the moment, resource availability information is scattered. Each unit has the information about its own resources. It is possible however to construct a computer program and file structure to record the status of all machines, maintenance crews, set-up men, engineers, and quality-control inspectors and to schedule their utilization of time.

The key to the effectiveness of this strategy is to keep the schedule current in the face of a multitude of changes. The earlier attempt at centralized scheduling was overwhelmed and attempted only to schedule machines. A real-time computer system with remote terminals in all departments can keep a current status on the availability of all resources. In addition it must record changes in customer orders, quality rejects, and engineering changes, and adapt schedules to erroneous time estimates for production jobs, set-ups, and machine repair. The maintenance of a current data base and schedule will require a great deal of computer time, input-output units, and supporting personnel. However it will remove the overload problem. While the author is aware of no operating systems for this problem, there is a comparable research project concerned with scheduling aircraft maintenance.[4]

The effects and costs of this strategy are straightforward. The priority decisions concerning the use of specialized resources is solved by bringing together in a single place, probably the materials management function, all information about resource availability and resource demands. The global information is gathered from the shop floor, maintenance crews, engineers, and inspectors via terminals scattered throughout the plant. The information is manipulated and a schedule produced by a man-machine, problem-solving combine. The result is efficient scheduling and a management structure relieved of day-to-day decisions. All this is gained by means of a substantial investment in computer hardware, peripheral equipment, programming effort, and computer time.

### Lateral Relations

The fourth organizing mode is to employ and formalize decision processes which cross lines of authority. The purpose is to move priority decisions down to lower levels of the organization. The design issues revolve around who should be represented, what should be the mechanism, and at what organization level should the mechanism operate.

The current organization uses lateral relationships of the informal type. Indeed, these personal contacts and upward referral resulting in the overload are the manifestation of the current problem. When there were fewer set-ups and tooling changes, easier schedule deadlines, and fewer products, the informal direct contacts and task forces were adequate to secure coordination. But currently these processes are not adequate. When two or three people get together, they never seem to have all the information needed to make a decision. Attempts to gather all informed parties is all but impossible. It is easier to refer the problem up to the next level. Thus, the informal, spontaneous personal contacts which worked well in the past need to be supplemented. But what form should the supplemental effort take?

The first mechanism on the list is the liaison role. Liaison personnel, particularly in process engineering, would help relieve some of the priority problems. If process engineering would formalize a linking role, that role occupant would perform engineering work and also be responsible for co-ordinating engineering and manufacturing activities. Similarly, linking roles could be formalized in the other support functions as well. These changes would aid the coordination between manufacturing and engineering and between manufacturing and maintenance, etc. However, this is not suffi-cient. The current problems do not stem from function to function links but from multifunction links. Quite often foremen, engineers, maintenance foremen, and inspectors gather together only to find they need schedule information from materials management or standard times from industrial engineering. A mechanism legitimizing multifunction problem solving is re-quired.

The next mechanism would be task forces. Each time a problem arose in manufacturing, the foreman could call together all liaison personnel concerned with his area. The response of the manufacturing manager to this problem was that the liaison personnel should be equipped with two-way radios because such problems arose daily. The manufacturing man-ager's half-humorous remark led to the proposal of daily meetings of all functional personnel concerned with the work of a manufacturing area. Thus, it was suggested that teams were the mechanisms for handling the multifunctional interdependence at low levels of the organization.

As soon as it was decided that teams were to be the mechanism, some new design questions arose. The same factors that were relevant to the de-partmentalization and level decisions for self-contained structures are rele-vant for teams. Thus, the work flow and inventory locations make the five general foremen areas the most likely basis and level of organization at which the teams should operate. Thus the team model provides the general foreman with a temporary staff rather than the permanent one provided by the self-contained model but avoids some of the costs. Once the basis and organizational level are determined the question arises as to who should go to the team meetings.

The type of functions that should provide representatives was a decision that was quickly resolved. The functions of manufacturing, quality control, process engineering, maintenance, industrial engineering, and materials management were chosen to be permanent members while accounting and industrial relations would be called on an "as-needed" basis. A design problem did arise when the selection of functional representatives was being discussed. If the teams were to arrive at decisions, the participants must have the information relevant to the decisions and the authority to commit their function to the team's choice of alternatives.

All the functions except process engineering could handle the selection very easily. Each of these functions had an authority structure like that shown for maintenance in Fig. 9.4. The organizational units in maintenance were identical to those in manufacturing. To each manufacturing area there corresponded a foreman and maintenance crew to handle most machine repair problems that could arise in that area.

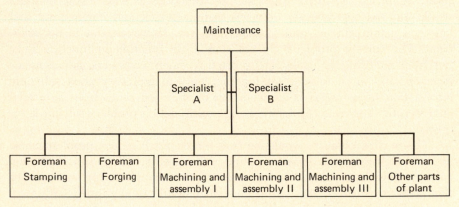

**Fig. 9.4  Functional structure which is a mirror image of manufacturing.**

Some specialist skills for which there was not enough work in the individual areas were collected into specialist pools and shared among the areas. In addition there was some maintenance work performed in areas other than manufacturing. The functions of quality control, industrial engineering, and materials management had similar "mirror image plus specialists" type of structures. The maintenance foreman and his counterpart in the other functions were the team members. They had the necessary information and authority.

The process-engineering unit had chosen to divide its work on the basis of common technical problems. A partial organization chart is shown in Fig. 9.5. This structure permits engineering to maximize the expertise that can be brought to bear on different manufacturing processes. The department was able to keep abreast of the latest technological changes and quickly convert them into the form of tooling and manufacturing processes when these changes were beneficial. This same process knowledge was necessary for the custom-design market strategy and for the introduction of new products. Each time a new customer order came in, engineering had

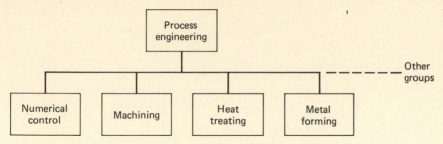

Fig. 9.5  Before organization chart for process engineering.

to create a way to produce it and still meet price constraints. When a process engineer encounters a problem, the information to solve that problem usually comes from personal experience or the experience of a colleague who had a similar problem in the past because there is no body of literature which deals with unique process problems. The specialist structure facilitated these process-design problems by placing together those people with common technical problems.

The company was quite pleased with the performance of the process engineering function. The manager of process engineering shared the perception of the top-management group on the nature of the shop floor problem but did not want a solution to that problem to be at the expense of the technical excellence of the process designs. Engineering had to maintain links with the technical community as well as manufacturing. The knowledge base underlying the work of maintenance or quality control was not changing as rapidly. Therefore, they could adapt their structures to facilitate coordination with manufacturing without much loss of excellence in their specialty. The manager of process engineering suggested appointing an engineer, with the approval of the general foreman, to each team. However, it was pointed out that if the engineer came from machining, and a problem arose concerning heat treating, the engineer would not have the technical knowledge, the information about resource availability, nor the authority to change job assignments if the problem required it. This structure satisfied the requirements for skill specialization, but not for team coordination. The "mirror-image" structure satisfied team coordination requirements, but not skill specialization.

After much deliberation, the top-management group decided upon the structure shown in Fig. 9.6. Five new roles were created for engineering managers which corresponded to the five teams. The other half of the engineering group maintained its current form and would concentrate on new processes, processes for new products, and processes for custom-designed orders. For these tasks specialization is required. All subtasks for which there was less need for specialization, such as set-up men, became

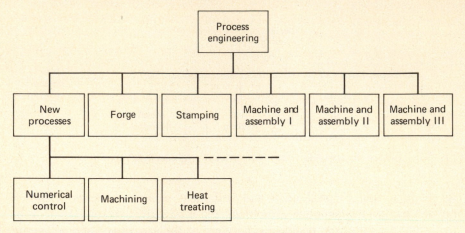

**Fig. 9.6 Differentiated structure for process engineering.**

part of the five new departments. When there was enough work for a full-time position, specialists worked for the five new managers. But it was agreed that specialists would be rotated from these units to the new process unit to minimize loss of skill specialization. Thus, by splitting engineering into two units, one support and one design, the requirements for specialization and coordination can be met simultaneously. This design was agreed upon and implemented.

The chosen design has its cost, also. There are new roles to staff in engineering and perhaps in the other functions. There are costs of disruption in engineering. The positions must be staffed, generalists must be trained, and new training needs and career patterns arise throughout the function. But it was judged that these costs and disruptions were less than those that would be required by the other design alternatives.

It should be pointed out that there are several possible designs which would accomplish the same result. Another organization may not be able to staff the five new roles in engineering immediately and may create an interim design. Still another may create two assistant engineering managers, one in charge of new designs as indicated and one in charge of support to which the five new roles would report. These alternatives reflect the fact that the organization may not have the people to staff an ideal organization. Therefore the organization must be designed around the people as well as the task requirements. It is variations such as these that generate the unique features of an organization's structure. The engineering people in the organization represent a unique set of individuals which will be reflected in a unique structure. However, the alternatives represent variations in degree rather than in kind. All of them represent some variation on the split between design and support.

Also ignored were questions of the process to be used to arrive at the structure. Given the nature of the issues, lower level engineering personnel should have been involved in order to create an acceptable solution.

In summary, teams, like the other three alternatives, will solve the problem of hierarchical overload. Decisions will be moved to the general foreman level. By creating teams with members who have the information and authority to commit resources, the general foreman will have the necessary flexibility to adapt to changing floor problems. The teams may still encounter problems they cannot solve, but these will be much fewer than before. The implementation of teams will create additional staffing costs for new roles.

## TEAMS IN OPERATION

The manufacturing firm actually implemented the team design discussed in the previous section. At the end of a year's operation, the teams had relieved the previous situation and were operating satisfactorily. Several minor changes were made to the team decision process and probably would continue to be made in the future. The critical adjustment was to make the team processes consistent with the traditional hierarchical processes and with existing personnel.

Early in the implementation some individuals were having difficulty in working first as a member of a function, then as a member of a team, and back again. When the problem was confronted it was found to originate partially within the functions. Some participants were not informed about their function's activities and could not share information they did not have. Others were unsure of the kind of commitments they could make. The problem is not one of having authority or not having authority but one of degree. The attempted solution was to initiate staff meetings within functions prior to the team meetings if this was not done already and to improve those that were held. What was needed was more information and problem sharing within functions so that team participants could be more effective across functions. Thus, by meeting within functions prior to team meetings and a reporting back after the team meeting removed the pressures for some participants.

Other individuals still disliked the team role either because they felt they were being put between two groups or they disliked generalizing and preferred quality control or engineering problems. Several individuals transferred out of the team roles. It was felt that no one should be penalized for not remaining in the linking position. Thus, through self-selection, individuals who were comfortable with linking roles found their way into the teams.

## SUMMARY

The case study which constitutes this chapter is one more illustration of the concept of strategic choice although a fifth course of action, that of modifying strategy, domain, and objectives, was not explicitly considered. The problem encountered was a general one. A primary or operating portion of an organization required the services of several specialists from the support portion in the creation of the output. Slow, cumulative change in the environment rendered the organization's previous design inadequate. The problem manifested itself in an overload on the top managers. A thorough diagnosis by the general manager defined the problem in basic enough terms to permit the creation of multiple solutions representing the variations on the four organizing modes. Thus, we have the case of a manufacturing firm in which there is no single best solution or technological imperative to follow. A rich set of choices of organizing modes exists. The richness permits an effective solution to be found which fits the ideology of management, the technology, the particular set of people involved, the structure, the culture, etc. For example, when using this case in management development programs, American and British managers prefer the solution of teams while Italians prefer the self-contained option. However, the richness of solutions does not mean that any solution will work and structure and process are therefore not significant. The current structure was not effective, for example, nor was the self-contained, product-group structure. Choice makes a difference, but a rich set of solutions exists for blending structure, task, process, environment, people, and rewards.

This case was used to illustrate both the concept of teams and strategic choice. The analysis was to give better understanding to the information-processing framework being developed here. The framework has been applied to a restaurant, to medical clinics, and to a manufacturing firm to show the generality of the framework. Further examples will be given in later chapters.

Let us now move to the problem of employing integrating roles.

## NOTES

1. For an analysis of organizational implications of smoothing problems, see J. R. Galbraith 1969, Solving production smoothing problems. *Management Science*, (August): B–665 to B–674.

2. For a more complete description, see J. C. Emery 1961, An approach to job-shop scheduling using a large scale computer. *Industrial Management Review*, (Fall): 78–96.

3. M. Dalton 1959. *Men who manage.* New York: Wiley, Chapter 3.

4. S. M. Dreyner and R. L. Van Horn 1968. Design considerations for a computer-assisted maintenance planning and control system. *Research Memorandum*, P–3765, the Rand Corporation, (February).

| LATERAL RELATIONS CONTINUED: INTEGRATING ROLES, MANAGERIAL LINKING ROLES, AND MATRIX DESIGNS | CHAPTER **10** |
|---|---|

This chapter continues the discussion of the use of lateral relations as an organizing mode. The need for something more in the way of coordinating skills to back up teams and task forces was alluded to at the end of Chapter 8. A new role, i.e., an integrating role, is introduced in this chapter with the variations in which this role appears. As the power of the role increases, the organization utilizes concurrently two bases for its departmental structure. These concurrent structures or matrix designs are then explained. Subsequent chapters discuss some evidence for these structures and analyze case examples.

### NEED FOR AN ADDITIONAL ROLE

The use of lateral relations—direct contact, liaison roles, task forces and teams—permits the organization to make more decisions and process more information without overloading hierarchical communication channels. These channels are reserved for the unique consequential problems which increase in number as uncertainty and diversity of the task increase. Further increases in task uncertainty and diversity result in greater amounts of decision making at lower levels through joint-decision processes.

The increase in the number of decisions and the number of decisions of consequence made at lower levels of the organization increases the dependence of the organization on the quality of the decisions reached through such joint processes. On the one hand, the process increases the *quality* of the decisions. If participants come from the most interdependent departments and from the appropriate level in that department, the potential quality of the decision can be increased. The process involves those individuals who are most knowledgeable about the decision in question. In addition, by involving individuals who are responsible for performing the work, the process increases the motivation to accept and *implement* the chosen alternative. But inasmuch as the participants represent a collection of people who individually have necessary but only *partial* information, a high-quality decision will result if, and only if, the partial information is shared, built upon, and used to search for and create new alternatives.

To convert a collection of individuals into a problem-solving team requires interpersonal and group skills and a climate in which group problem solving can take place. Some of the factors determining skills and climate were introduced in Chapter 8. The chapter concluded by suggesting that effective problem solving took place by confrontation backed up by forcing modes of conflict resolution. If this is true, then decision quality depends upon the power source from which a forced solution occurred. It was suggested that if a solution is forced from a power base whose goals are consistent with organization goals and in a manner which does not discourage future problem solving, this process can lead to high-quality decisions. Further, it was suggested that by selecting a leader from the appropriate places in the organization structure, the power source could be controlled and the organization designed to achieve high-quality decisions.

This chapter expands upon the power bases in the joint-decision process.[1] There is greater dependence on the quality of joint decisions due to the fact that there are more decisions and more decisions of consequence reached through joint-decision processes. At moderate levels of uncertainty a few mistakes were not critical and periodic reviews could correct some of the low-quality decisions. This is not adequate at higher levels of uncertainty and diversity. In addition to the greater number of decisions of consequence, the organization's ability to engage in problem-solving activities decreases. The reason is that the changes in task uncertainty differentially affect subtasks. Some departments experience large increases in subtask uncertainty while others experience little or none. For example, if a firm undertakes a strategy to introduce new products, the technical function experiences a greater increase in subtask uncertainty than the production or accounting function. Two new problems are generated by the increasing differences in subtask uncertainty. (1) Differences in subtask uncertainty create differences in power of participants to joint decisions. Since the organization must take some coordinated action, it requires estimates of future states of affairs from functions concerned with uncertain subtasks. Since these estimates can rarely be challenged, those functions with uncertain subtasks have greater power to influence decisions than functions performing routine predictable tasks.[2] The organization design problem is to create a set of conditions such that power differences due to selective access to information do not diminish the quality of decisions reached through lateral decisions processes. (2) Differences in subtask uncertainty create or attract people with differences in attitudes. This creates greater differentiation among the participants to joint decisions. There is some evidence to suggest that the attitudes and personalities of decision makers are related to the uncertainty of the tasks they perform.[3] Then as tasks differ in uncertainty, the attitudes of the managers differ also. Another organizational design problem is to see that these differences in attitudes, called differentiation, do not reduce the quality of solutions generated by the joint-decision process.

Thus, the organization design question becomes: What factors can the organization change so as to create a distribution of power and influence in order to arrive at high-quality joint decisions? Very briefly, the organization (1) creates a new role and (2) designs enough power and influence into it to bring about high-quality joint decisions. Before describing the role, however, the concept of differentiation needs to be explained and related to the framework being developed here.

## Differentiation

Differentiation as defined by Lawrence and Lorsch is ". . . the difference in cognitive and emotional orientation among managers in different functional departments."[4] The concept suggests the attitudes of managers become differentiated on several dimensions to the degree that the tasks they manage differ in uncertainty and time span of feedback.[5] In Chapter 9, one of the dimensions of differentiation, not necessarily related to uncertainty, goal orientation, was discussed. The fact that different departments preferred different alternatives as a solution to the same problem was the basic source of conflict to be resolved. Now as subtasks increase in uncertainty, differences on other dimensions become large enough to be a potential cause of conflict.

First, departments will vary in the formality of their structures. The highly predictable tasks in operations will lead to explicit measures of performance, well-defined procedures, narrow spans of control and well-defined areas of authority and responsibility. In contrast the technical function with its uncertain task does not have the clarity of definition of procedures, responsibilities, and performance measures. They do not because they cannot, given the nature of their task.

Secondly, individuals in these departments vary in their orientation toward time. Technologists spend hours analyzing the ambiguous problems and uncertain relationships to complete a design due in three months. They will not know if it is successful until a moon shot is completed two years from now. Contrast technologists with the operations foremen who quickly load three jobs on their machines, shift manpower assignments, ship two completed lots, and know at the end of the day how well they have performed. Each of these time perspectives is necessary for their respective tasks.

Finally each department develops a language of its own. As groups of people continuously share a common set of problems, they develop shorthand ways of referring to activities and events. Technical departments hire people who have been trained and know the language of the department's specialty. This allows people to communicate more efficiently by transmitting more information with fewer symbols. While these specialized languages increase communication efficiency within a department, they decrease efficiency between departments.

There may be other dimensions, e.g., risk-taking propensity, which may be relevant in specific situations, but these dimensions are general enough to illustrate the concept of differentiation. In addition each attribute satisfies the following conditions:

1. The relation between the dimension and task uncertainty is necessary for effective subtask performance.[6] The better the fit among the subtask, the formality of structure, and the orientation toward time and the language, the more effective is the subtask performance.

2. While differentiation is associated with effective subtask performance, it is also associated with difficulty in establishing collaboration between differentiated departments.[7] It makes it more difficult to employ lateral relations to coordinate interdependent tasks. It makes a consensus solution more difficult to obtain.

The problem facing the differentiated organization is how to obtain overall task integration among departments *without reducing the differences that lead to effective subtask performance*. The relationships between engineering and production can be made more cooperative by having engineering work on day-to-day quality problems, taking a short-run orientation and using cost rather than technical elegance as a choice criterion. While this will improve cooperation, it will not create new technology for tomorrow's products. Similarly, conflicts should not be resolved by changing goal orientations (although sometimes an operational global goal can be found) but by searching for new alternatives which satisfy differentiated subgoals of the interdependent departments. Thus, as organizations adopt strategies which result in more task uncertainty, the departments performing subtasks become more differentiated since subtasks vary in task uncertainty, language, and goals. So at the very time that the organization needs more effective interdepartmental decision making, cooperation becomes more difficult.


### Integrating Role

The response of the organization to the concern for decision quality is to create a new role in the organization structure. These roles are called integrating roles.[8] The managers who occupy these roles do not supervise any of the actual work. Instead they are to assist those who do, so that the work is coordinated in the best interest of the organization. This is the general manager's job but he or she does not have the time when the organization tasks become diverse and uncertain. The integrator becomes a little general manager with respect to the particular decision process for which he or she is responsible.

Integrating roles are a general phenomenon but the labels vary in particular situations. In manufacturing firms with significant logistics problems, the integrator is a "materials manager." If the functional departments involved in the work flow such as purchasing, manufacturing, and traffic and physical distribution each minimized its own costs, this minimization would not lead to an overall optimum for the entire logistics system. The task of the materials manager is to coordinate all the scheduling and inventory-related decisions to see that they are made in the best interests of the firm. For business firms with diverse product lines that change rapidly, the integrator is a "product manager." Product managers coordinate decisions made in each function that relate to their product or product line. In aerospace firms and government agencies the integrator is a "project or program manager." In hospitals, the "unit manager" coordinates and integrates the decisions of doctors, nurses, dieticians, and service personnel for a particular ward or building.

In each case, the task of the integrator is not to do the work but to coordinate the decision process. In each case, it is a decision which is consequential for the organization and whose decision factors are diverse and uncertain enough to overload the general manager. Rather than change the authority structure to contain the decision process, a role is created to coordinate the process across the interdependent departments. In order to coordinate a decision process the integrator needs to be able to influence the decision-making behavior of individuals who do not work for him or her. The organization design question becomes one of how much and what kind of power and authority should be designed into the integrating role.

As this role first evolves, occupants generally report to the general manager as indicated in Fig. 10.1. Integrators have no formal authority and

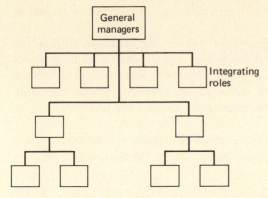

**Fig. 10.1 Integrating roles representing little general managers.**

no staff working for them. It is their function to bring the general-manager perspective to bear on joint-decision problems arising at various levels of the organization which concern their decision area. They do this by acting as leaders of task forces and teams considering joint problems, by pulling information together in one place, and providing full-time attention to problems arising due to uncertainty. However, the question is how do they exercise influence if they have no formal authority or position power?

1. The integrating role has a wide range of contacts and exposures. Its most significant contact is the general manager. The integrators, by their reporting relationship, have the ear of the most powerful individual in the organization. A mention of the fact that Paul Jones from engineering is doing a superb job on the product team can give Paul Jones, four levels down, an exposure he would not have otherwise. Similarly, integrators can influence the reward system by passing on the same information to the engineering manager. This provides an unsolicited, outside evaluation which has to be considered.

The integrator should also have wide contacts across departments. For example, Paul Jones mentions a new idea that he has but his boss is not helping him push it. The integrator however takes it to marketing and finds a sales manager who has a customer with a similar need. The result is that Paul Jones has a project of his own. The example could be multiplied many times. The point is that the integrator is at the crossroads, or should place himself or herself at the crossroads, of several information streams. What might appear as an interesting but useless fact to a marketing manager may be a valuable piece of information to the technical function. By identifying these situations and following through with them, the integrator performs useful functions for the departments. He or she becomes a useful rather than a "pushy" type and exercises influence based on access to information. Integrators make deals. They are idea brokers. The influence is in the direction of meeting both individual and organizational goals and is based on access to information.

2. The integrator equalizes power differences and increases trust in the joint-decision processes. The need for power equalization and trust arises because of the differential effect of task uncertainty. Some subtasks become more uncertain than others. The departments managing these uncertain subtasks acquire power due to the process of uncertainty absorption.

> Uncertainty absorption takes place when inferences are drawn from a body of evidence and the inferences, instead of the evidence itself, are then communicated.[10]

As subtasks increase in uncertainty, the amount of uncertainty absorbed increases because information enters organizations at specific points and recipients of communications often have neither the time nor knowledge to judge the validity of a communication. Since they rarely can check the validity of a communicated fact, the participants to a joint decision are dependent upon the uncertainty-absorbing department to draw inferences in an objective and valid manner. Thus, the greater the subtask uncertainty, the greater is the dependence upon and therefore the power of the uncertainty-absorbing department.

The quality of joint decisions is a direct function of how this power is exercised and how the dependent participants perceive the exercise of power. Since the participants cannot examine the evidence directly, their perception of the inferences rests squarely upon the confidence and trust in the uncertainty-absorbing department and their knowledge of its biases. If they perceive that the inferences are consistently drawn in a manner to benefit the department rather than the organization, they will counter this power with coalitions and the joint-decision process will degenerate into bargaining. Then the best self-interest strategies are information concealment and distortion. The search for alternatives is deprived of the information needed for high-quality decisions. Therefore, when uncertainty absorption takes place, the quality of the joint decisions is more dependent on the confidence and trust among the participants.

The necessary confidence and trust is difficult to maintain in the context of high differentiation. The production superintendent finds it difficult to have confidence in a bearded, tieless scientist who does not arrive at the office until 9:30 A.M., is five minutes late to meetings, and does not know who won Sunday's football game. However, it is possible to establish trust in this context without reducing the essential attitudinal differences by the use and proper staffing of the integrator role.

The integrating role is ideally staffed when the occupant has demonstrated competence in the areas of greatest uncertainty absorption and has an orientation towards organizational goals rather than a parochial set of goals including his or her own self-aggrandizement. Then when an inference is communicated as a fact in the presence of the integrator, there is greater confidence among the recipients in the source of the communiqué. The reason is that the mere presence of the integrator eliminates the possible distortion of inferences to the parochial interest of the uncertainty-absorbing department. For example, during a problem-solving session a manufacturing manager might suggest that if the product could be redesigned in a particular way, the manager's problems could be made easier. The engineering participant might suggest the change cannot be made because of some law of aerodynamics. The manufacturing manager may know nothing about aerodynamics and therefore has no way of validating the engineer's response. But the manufacturing manager may doubt the engineer and may believe that engineers never accept ideas that they did not create themselves. He or she may challenge the engineer. The problem for the engineers becomes one of defending themselves rather than solving the problem. If, however, an integrator is present who knows the laws of aerodynamics and who is part of the general manager's office rather than a member of engineering, the manufacturing manager is more likely to believe the engineer. The presence of an integrator eliminates the possibility of using access to knowledge and information as a power source in bargaining.[11]

The integrators equalize power and increase trust, however, only if they are *knowledgeable* in the uncertainty-absorbing areas and *unbiased* with respect to the participating departments. If they are biased, the integrators have the same trust problem as the uncertainty-absorbing department. If they are not knowledgeable, the participants will trust them but they are no more able than the participants to detect a power abuse. Thus the integrator role occupants need to be both unbiased and knowledgeable because their influence rests upon those attributes. The attributes increase the level of trust and confidence among the participants to a joint decision. This increases the likelihood of a confrontation mode of conflict resolution and therefore of high-quality decisions.

3. Integrators exercise influence by managing the joint-decision process rather than making the decision themselves. They should perform the integrative or leadership function that has been shown to be necessary in reaching high-quality joint decisions.[12] It was mentioned earlier that merely bringing people together who possess the necessary information to solve a problem does not guarantee that they will use the information. The problem-solving process needs to be managed. Some attributes of joint-decision participants may be either an asset or a liability depending on how the process is managed. For example, differences of opinion can lead to hard feelings and bargaining or to confrontation and problem solving. Whether

this latter set of attributes becomes an asset or a liability depends critically on the performance of the discussion leadership function. This requires a role that is different from the roles of the other participants to the joint decision.

> For a leader, such functions as rejecting or promoting ideas according to his personal needs are out of bounds. He must be receptive to information contributed, accept contributions without evaluating them (posting contributions on a chalkboard to keep them alive), summarize information to facilitate integration, stimulate exploratory behavior, create awareness of problems of one member by others, and detect when the group is ready to resolve differences and agree to a unified solution.[13]

The integrators' role is not to make the best decision but to see that the best decision gets made. The point is best illustrated by a quote from a product manager in a consumer products firm describing the attributes of a good product manager.

> Creativity is very important; but it's not necessary that the guy be creative himself with new and appropriate ideas. It's more important that he be able to recognize appropriate creativity in others when he sees it. He should continually be running across things others do with the reaction, "Gee, I wish I'd thought of that." The important thing is that the fact that he didn't come up with it doesn't bother him—that he is delighted to accept an idea someone else has.[14]

In order to perform this role, integrators need to be knowledgeable in the areas in question, to be capable of crossing the attitudinal barriers and see things from different points of view, and be able to speak the languages of the different specialties which are party to the decision. This multilingual ability is needed so that summaries and restatements can prevent misunderstandings. Integrators must be able to listen to a proposal in "marketing talk" and restate it in "engineering talk." Thus, the use of integrators achieves coordination without eliminating the differences—languages, attitudes, etc.—that promote good subtask performance.

Thus integrators with no formal authority do have a power base from which they can influence the decision process for which they are responsible. It is expert power based on knowledge and access to information. Integrators will be effective only if their influence facilitates the coordination of those individuals who have the formal authority and if the integrators' power is not seen as contrary to or as a replacement for the formal authority of the participants to the joint decision. This occurs when the integrators conceive of their roles as facilitating ones rather than as doing ones. Integrators are not to do the work but to see that the work that is done is performed in a manner which gives integrity to the product, program, unit, etc.

The organization controls the amount of power exercised in the integrator role by its staffing decision. Integrators have power only if they have the knowledge and behavioral skills to act as information collectors, summarizers, and group-discussion leaders. Some of the attributes required by the role occupants are obvious from the preceding discussion. Integrators must have credibility among the specialties to be integrated and especially the specialty absorbing the most uncertainty. Integrators must be unbiased, which can be controlled by the reward system for the integrators and where they report in the hierarchy as well as by the selection of the individuals. But integrators also must have personalities which permit them to use expert power to complement the power of authority. They must not assume advocacy positions and stifle problem-solving behavior. They must only summarize, suggest, and restate alternatives. The behaviors which are described as strong, quick, and decisive in line managers are dogmatic, close-minded, and bull-headed when exhibited by integrators. Thus, selection is the organization design variable.

There is some indication that individuals with high needs for affiliation measured by Thematic Apperception Tests perform better as integrators than those with low needs for affiliation.[15] While this finding makes some intuitive sense, it is also suggested that individuals with high needs for achievement do not perform well as integrators. It seems reasonable that individuals who have both a high need for achievement and a high need for affiliation might be superior integrators. Both needs could be satisfied by working through others successfully.

Another body of personality research is relevant to the selection of individuals for integrating roles.[16] The findings suggest that individuals vary in their ability to stand between two conflicting groups without being absorbed into one of them while being accepted by neither of them. Integrators must have credibility in all groups and be seen as unbiased. These are the attributes of the "marginal individual personality." Predictions from the theory show that "marginal people" are less dogmatic and more open-minded than other individuals. These theories may be useful in providing a more effective basis for selection of integrators.

An information system tracking performance with respect to agreed-upon goals and objectives can be of immeasurable value to the integrator. If top management uses the planning process to get consensus on product, project, unit, etc., goals and short-run targets, the integrator can use the gap between planned and actual to initiate activity and influence the behavior of functional people. The integrator can enter in a problem-oriented way and is less likely to be perceived as encroaching on functional territory. Instead the integrator is more likely to be perceived as a person with a problem who needs functional help.

A second method to increase the influence of the integrating role is to increase the amount of supporting formal information that is available to it. Usually the information system reports actual expenditures against functional or departmental budgets. Integrators can wield more influence if they can isolate costs and revenues attributable to their decision area, whether it be product, program, or unit. They can then identify problems and evaluate alternatives more easily. The organization must maintain a dual information reporting system by summarizing the same information system which is used to support project managers in guiding projects across functional departments.

A third method for increasing the influence of the integrating role, should more influence be necessary to perform the coordinating activities, is to use several status substitutes for position power. For example, physically locating the integrators in an appropriately sized office adjacent to the office of the general manager cues the organization as to the status and centrality of the role. It also makes them more accessible and more directly in contact with information. The role can command a sizeable salary to augment its status. Several organizations that have made extensive use of integrators have placed the role strategically in the career system. Most general managers have come from that position and/or it is placed in the "fast track" route to top positions. The implication is that while the integrators are not now the bosses, next year they may very well be. There are other ways, which vary from one organization to another, to confer status on the integrator role to increase the likelihood that the integrator can successfully influence the behavior of people who work in other departments as a substitute for using formal or position power. In summary, then, the power of the role is designed by the staffing choice, an information system, and the amount of status conferred upon it.

Thus, integrators are formal embodiments of expert power. They exercise influences based on access to knowledge and information. The role requires the individual to behave in ways which remove possible impediments to sharing information and behaving in a problem-solving fashion. Such individuals are difficult to find and training technologies are not yet developed to create them. Yet this role is becoming increasingly important in a variety of organizations.

## Managerial Linking Roles

The use of an integrating role, like the coordination mechanisms already discussed, has its limitations. These limits are the limitations of expert power. The limitations come into effect due to greater uncertainty and greater goal diversity. Both of these factors will be discussed prior to suggesting the design changes that are required.

When organizations perform highly uncertain tasks and face unique circumstances, there are never enough facts to determine solutions to decision problems. In these circumstances there is no body of knowledge or valid theory to explain the phenomena in question. Thus, there is little basis upon which one can become expert. The leverage of expert power is diminished vis-à-vis the legitimate power of hierarchical position and its complementary reward system. In order to achieve coordination across functional areas the integrating role requires another source of influence.

A second limitation arises as organizations confront phenomena in which the difficulties arise because of disagreement or uncertainty about ends or goals rather than means.[17] Admittedly, it is difficult to separate ends and means, but there are situations, particularly political situations facing government organizations, where the inability of participants to agree on a joint decision rests on questions of values rather than lack of knowledge of cause and effect. Questions about busing school children and redistribution of income are examples of the kind of situations in which expert power is less effective. It is difficult to be an expert on value questions.

Other goal differences stem from the environmental context in which an organization operates. In some government projects which cut across agencies, it becomes difficult to get joint agreement on funds reallocation from one agency to another. This is because Congress is influenced in its budgeting process by the size of last year's budget. Therefore any reduction in funds reduces the likelihood of getting more in the future. Like it or not, the agency must adapt to this fact. The integrator needs greater power to reallocate resources among agencies when new information demonstrates a need for reallocation. The accomplishment of organizational goals requires more integrator influence in decision making. The issue is how do you increase the power of the integrator role?

The approach suggested here is that the role becomes more like a normal managerial role. Influence can be increased by increasing formal position power through a number of changes which are listed below. The role is no longer an integrating role. The role occupant begins actively to enter the decision process. This role is called a managerial-linking role for lack of a better label. It is still different from the normal managerial role because the people who perform most of the work for which linking managers are responsible do not report to them. If people do not work for the linking managers, how do the linking managers exercise influence?

**1. Approval power in decision process.** The first step in increasing the formal power of linking managers is to enter them into the decision process. For example, when departmental budgets are prepared, they can be sent to the linking managers prior to being sent to the general manager. Linking managers can suggest some interdepartmental trade-offs which cannot be seen from the local perspective of each department. Subsequent changes to the budget in light of new information must get the approval of the linking managers. This increases the amount of influence that is exercised by the linking managers in the decision process in question. Most of the influence still remains in the departments, however.

**2. Earlier entrance into decision and planning process.**   Linking managers can have greater influence in the decision process by entering into it at an earlier stage. The earlier they enter into a decision process, the greater the effect they can have on the final choice.[18] If they can choose which problems to work on and generate the alternatives to solve these problems, they have greater influence on the final outcome than those who merely approve and suggest incremental changes.

The way this concept is operationalized in an organization is to begin the yearly budgeting process with the linking managers and then send these plans to the departments for approval and to check resource availability. Take for example the linking managers in the hospital: the unit managers. They would forecast activity in their area or ward for the upcoming year. Then they would prepare resource budgets to carry out the activity. They would do this with the help of the physicians, nurses, dieticians, and service people who work in their ward but do not report to them. Unit managers would send the plan to the heads of nursing, dietary, services, etc., to see if resources are available and then begin reconciliation if there are resource discrepancies. Similar processes exist for product managers who formulate product strategies and prepare product budgets.

Beginning the planning process with the linking role increases the influence that can be exercised by the role occupants by allowing them to initiate tasks more easily. This does not mean that linking managers could not initiate changes before. But it does mean it is easier to do so when the formal process begins with them. In the past, they had to go get all department heads to change. It was easy for any one of them to say no. It was the linking managers' job to justify why the change should be made. When linking managers initiate a change formally, it becomes the job of the department head to justify why the change cannot be made. Early entry in the planning, budgeting process makes change initiation a legitimate behavior of the integrator.

The effectiveness of approval authority and entering the planning process depends upon having an information system to support the decision process. Therefore these factors are not alternative ways to attribute power to the role. They are complementary and cumulative. Linking managers doing the planning also have approval power and an information system.

The extent to which the factors are used depends upon the task uncertainty and priorities among organizational goals.

**3. Budget control.**   If the linking role requires more power, it can be given control of the budget for its decision area. The dollars flow through the linking managers into the departments. In effect, the linking managers buy resources from the departments. So after preparing the plan, they receive the budgeted amount of money to gain more control over the use of resources and personnel who do not report to them.

This has taken place in aerospace industries where project managers received the contracted amount of money for their projects. They then purchased the resources, inside the organization and out, to perform the project. They could also reallocate resources during project performance. For example, if it appeared that a device could be actuated electronically, they would buy some resources of the electronics lab. If it later appeared cheaper to actuate the device hydraulically, resources would be shifted from the electronics to the hydraulics laboratory. The lab budgets would be changed accordingly. The laboratories still receive money over which they have control. This is for independent research and development work, equipment purchase, training, and other activities related to the development of the resources of the lab. Thus the labs are not entirely dependent on project work for funds.

This change gives the linking managers greater influence in the decision process. They become more active in the decision process. They become planners, decision makers, and resource allocators. However, none of the resources is their responsibility. They have only information, knowledge, approvals, and money with which to influence the activities in their area of responsibility. For many organizations, this design is sufficient to guarantee efficient resource specialization, utilization, and development and at the same time effective integration of specialized resources to maintain product or program integrity. Still others require more power in the linking role to effect program integration.

### Matrix Organization

Some organizations, or units within an organization, are faced with performing tasks which require specialized resources in an environment which requires programmatic integration. Therefore, the organization would like greater integration of specialized resources without organizing around self-contained programs, projects, products, etc. Such a move would either reduce specialization or require duplication of resources. Another alternative is to increase the power of the role that champions integration.

The integrating role acquires more power through the establishment of a dual reporting relationship. That is, at some level of the organization, linking managers become both members of the resource department and members of the product or program office. They have two bosses. An example of an aerospace matrix is shown in Fig. 10.2. It shows a project manager and, for very large projects, an assistant project manager. Reporting to the assistant or on small- and medium-sized projects to the project

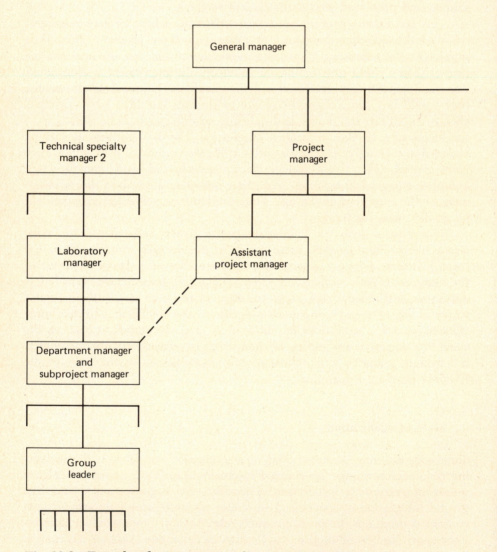

Fig. 10.2 Formal authority structure of matrix organization.

manager is the subproject manager who is also a department manager for the laboratory. All the project work in that lab is performed in the subproduct manager's department. The subproduct manager therefore plays the dual role of representing both the project and the laboratory. Above and below this manager in the structure is the normal single reporting system.

The primary design issue in the matrix is where to establish the dual reporting relation in each laboratory, department, etc. This is determined mostly by technological determinants of work divisibility. In Fig. 10.2 a departmental package is feasible. All work in that department is for that project. This does not mean that individual scientists and engineers do not work on several projects, however. If there is a fixed departmental structure and the project needs work in several departments of a lab, there are a couple of alternative designs. One is to have the department manager who is responsible for the largest proportion of laboratory work be the subproject manager. Another is to create an integrating role for the laboratory at an equivalent status to department manager. This means that the group leaders will have dual reporting relations as well. They will report to department managers and subproject managers. For small packages of work, group leaders may function as subproject managers. Thus, the size and divisibility of work determine the level at which the dual relation is established.

The simple act of drawing a line on an organization chart does not confer influence on anyone. It *does* establish some legitimacy, but integrators become more influential because the department manager is evaluated by both the project and the laboratory manager. They jointly determine the integrators' chances for promotion and their salary increases, and they also determine performance goals with the integrators. This is the mechanism by which more project influence is brought to bear at lower levels of the organization.

The effect of this change is to create a power balance between department managers and integrators, both of whom champion different sets of goals.

In aerospace, project managers encourage performance within budget, on schedule, and within contract specifications. Laboratory managers encourage full utilization of resources, long-run resource development, and highly sophisticated technical performance. For some organizations these goals are of equal importance in general, but they vary in importance in specific instances. Each circumstance, which cannot be predicted in advance, needs to be resolved on its own merits. Rather than refer each circumstance to a general manager, the matrix design institutionalizes an adversary system. The resultant goal conflict causes search behavior to discover current information and to create alternatives to resolve the conflict.

The joint decisions of the adversaries will reflect global considerations to the degree that power is distributed across the roles in proportion to the importance of the subgoals for global goals and to the degree that the role occupant employs behavior which leads to joint problem solving. The power balance is an unachievable razor's edge but needs only to be approximated. The power attributable to each role is determined by the selection of the occupant, the design of information systems to support the role, initiation and approval powers in the planning and control process, control of money to effect goals, and the establishment of formal authority relations. In the matrix, the resource manager and the program manager participate equally in these processes.

If external conditions require greater program, project, products, or unit integration, the power of the respective manager must be increased further. In some organizations this can be accomplished through symbols of office status. The project managers can be given a higher rank and salary than their peers managing the laboratories. But the final change is to begin to establish sole reporting relationships to the project manager. Thus, some of the dual reporting relations are eliminated. This is usually done for those resources where program specialization is less than skill specialization. This is where economies of scale and levels of technology are lowest. Thus, some of the administrative functions become program specialized and work for the program manager only. Further establishment of sole reporting relations move the organization towards a self-contained structure. This power continuum will be developed further in the next chapter.

### SUMMARY

This chapter has articulated a power continuum for integrating and linking roles in organizations. These roles are established to provide program integration under the conditions that the organization judges self-contained programs too costly and the program decision making overloads the general manager. Therefore, integration may be maintained through lateral relations. The amount of power needed to influence organizational behavior depends on the task uncertainty and the degree to which the organization's environmental context demands program integration. First, only expert power was used. This power was controlled by selecting individuals with relevant knowledge and having them behave so as to be at the crossroads of information flows. Next their power was strengthened by supporting the role with a formal information system and with various status symbols. Next, power was increased by entering the role in the decision process and thereby creating a managerial role. The managerial linking role entered the decision process first by approval, then by its initiation of the planning process in its area. The next step was to install the linking manager into the reward system in a formal legitimate manner. The final step was to transfer some resources to the linking manager on a full-time, sole-reporting basis. These steps are cumulative. Each is added to the previous powers. The question now becomes one of determining how far along the power continuum one should go. How do you choose? This is the topic of the next chapter.

## NOTES

1. The reader should be warned that most of the assertions are based on my informed opinion and working hypotheses. With the exception of *Organization and environment* by P. Lawrence and J. Lorsch, there is little research to draw upon.

2. M. Crozier 1964. *The bureaucratic phenomenon*. Chicago: University of Chicago Press, Chapter 6.

3. P. Lawrence and J. Lorsch 1967, *Organization and environment*. Boston: Harvard Business School, Division of Research.

4. Lawrence and Lorsch, p. 11.

5. Lawrence and Lorsch, Chapter 1.

6. Lawrence and Lorsch, Chapter 2.

7. Lawrence and Lorsch, Chapter 2.

8. Lawrence and Lorsch, Chapter 3.

9. J. G. March and H. Simon 1958. Organizations. New York: Wiley, pp. 164–166.

10. *Ibid.*, p. 165.

11. A. Pettigrew 1972. Information control as a power resource. *Sociology* 6, 2, (May): 187–204.

12. N. R. F. Maier 1967. Assets and liabilities in group problem solving: the need for an integrative function. *Psychological Review* 74, 4: 239–249.

13. *Ibid.*, p. 246.

14. J. Lorsch and P. Lawrence (eds.) 1972. *Managing group and intergroup relations* Homewood, Ill.: Richard D. Irwin, p. 272.

15. P. Lawrence and J. Lorsch 1967. New management job: the integrator. *Harvard Business Review*, (November-December): 142–151.

16. R. C. Ziller, B. J. Stark, and H. O. Pruden 1969. Marginality and integrative management positions. *Academy of Management Journal*, (December): 487–495.

17. J. D. Thompson and A. Tuden 1959. Strategies, structures, and processes of organizational decision, in James D. Thompson *et al.* (eds.), *Comparative studies in administration*. Pittsburgh: University of Pittsburgh Press, pp. 195–216.

18. J. D. Thompson and W. J. McEwen 1958. Organizational goals and environment: goal setting as an interaction process. *American Sociological Review* 23, (February): 23–31.

## QUESTIONS

1. How would you justify the need for an additional person, an integrator, who does not do any of the work?

2. What factors would you consider when selecting whether you need a strong or a weak integrator role?

3. Name as many different types of integrating roles as possible in as many different organizations as possible.

4. Compare the integrating role with the staff role discussed by classical authors.

5. How can integrators influence people who do not work for them?

6. What is the difference between an integrator role and a managerial linking role?

7. How does the change of starting planning with the integrator increase his or her influence?

8. How would you describe a pure matrix organization?

9. How would you answer objections to a pure matrix because it involves multiple bosses?

10. Using the case in Chapter 9, describe how you would design the role of subproduct managers reporting to two product managers working for the general manager.

| | CHAPTER |
|---|---|
| **AUTHORITY AND RESPONSIBILITY IN LATERAL RELATIONS** | **11** |

The use of lateral relations may solve problems of information overload but it can create others. When processes cut across lines of authority in organizations, there is always the possibility of obscuring who is responsible for what. Some discussion of authority and responsibility is in order.

## AUTHORITY AND RESPONSIBILITY AMBIGUITIES

The use of integrating roles and other lateral relations violates the unity of command principle of the classical management theorists and creates role conflict and stress for the individual. This is particularly true for the matrix design which builds in a dual reporting relation. The prediction of the management theorists was that the lack of a clear-cut, single line of authority would result in organizational ineffectiveness. Since most early knowledge about organizations came from the military operating under battle conditions, it is easy to see how one would predict that multiple authority would lead to ineffectiveness. But what about the effects of multiple authority in organizations where there is high uncertainty and unstructured situations?

There is no evidence to indicate that multiple authority and role conflict lead to ineffectiveness. This is partly due to the lack of work on the subject but the studies that are available do not support the assertion. The work of Marquis and of Goodman suggest that the response of organizations to multiply authority relations is one of ambiguous definition of who is responsible.[1] It is even suggested by some project managers that ambiguity is the best response.

One project manager observed, for example, that one of his subordinates may have most of his authority and interest in design. He will have other interests and perhaps some authority in other areas such as launch, quality control, or production. It is meaningless, he said, to try to define precisely areas of authority in order to prevent gaps or overlaps. For example, when his chief of design finds a relatively free moment and there are important problems in quality control, he is expected to help those directly responsible to solve them. This project manager further observed: "If you rigidly define authority, all you do is leave holes in the organization through which the big problems fall. However, if you go along with a 'Gaussian' distribution of authority, the overlaps insure that all problems are considered by someone."[2]

There is also considerable evidence of the existence of role conflict in professional organizations both from multiple authority relations and from conflicting influences of administrative goals and professional standards.[3] Thus, for organizations performing uncertain tasks, there is widespread existence of multiple authority relations and role conflict, and there is no evidence that ambiguity results in ineffectiveness. Some authorities even assert that ambiguity is good.

Like many other concepts for which there is no evidence and many strong, experience-based feelings, multiple authority depends on the conditions under which it is applied. If this is true, what are these conditions? The first condition is the one already mentioned—the nature of the task. In many organizational operations, time is of the essence. There is no time for exploration and negotiation. It is not advantageous to see who has the most information relevant to a decision. The important thing is to act and act fast. Under these conditions a single clear line of authority is needed. Many military, production, and operating situations fall into this category. If there is only minimal time pressure, then search processes can be undertaken to obtain relevant information. Here the issue is to see that the best decision gets made, and there is less concern for who makes it. Under these conditions, multiple authority can be effective if the conflicts are resolved in a problem-solving manner.

The second condition involves making use of the fact that individuals vary in their ability to handle role conflicts and roles vary in the amount of conflict to which they are subject. Role conflict has been shown to produce anxiety and stress in the individual with reduced satisfaction with the role.[4] Individuals vary considerably in how they cope with the conflict. The "marginal man" studies suggest some individuals perform the linking, conflict-laden roles quite well and are satisfied with them.[5] Likewise some individuals handle the dual reporting relation with minimal difficulty. Almost all of us were raised in the dual authority system of the family. So dual authority is not completely foreign. However, there are individuals for whom such a position would be unbearable. The organization needs to match linking roles with individuals who have a high tolerance for stress and ambiguity.

The third necessary condition for effective use of multiple authority is a problem-solving climate. Role conflict, like conflicts mentioned previously, can be good or bad depending on how they are resolved. The project manager quoted on page 168 can use ambiguity and multiple authority if his project team is more concerned with the problem than with the structure and who solves it. Solving the problem has to be more important than winning, controlling, or selling your solution. His words indicate that he thinks effectiveness can be improved more by emphasizing teamwork and problem solving than by role definition.

The best way to create a climate for reducing the negative aspects of role conflict is to maintain open communication for the sharing and confronting of conflicts. Walton points out:

> We increasingly understand that psychological and social energy is tied up in suppressing conflict, that conflicts not confronted may be played out in indirect and destructive ways, and that the differences that underlie interpersonal conflict often represent diversity or complementarity of significant potential value to the organization. An interpersonal or organizational system that can acknowledge and effectively confront its internal conflicts has a greater capacity to innovate and adapt.[6]

Such a system can also reduce the negative aspects of role conflict for the affected individual.

The implication of this section so far is that a manager whose departments engage in lateral relations can improve effectiveness more by creating a problem-solving climate than by clarifying role definition. In one sense this is true, but in another it is not. It is true that little can be gained by increasing role definition *as we have traditionally defined roles*. Traditionally most organizations have responded to information overloads by setting up self-contained units. This allowed them to take the competitive, free-market cultural values inside the organization. However, individual responsibility and competition were effective motivating forces only if there was little need for cooperation between roles. To the degree that interdependence could be self-contained, all the ambiguity, uncertainty, and conflict were contained within a single role. If self-containment was not feasible, individual responsibility could still be maintained but only if areas of jurisdiction could be precisely defined. This was feasible for predictable, repetitive tasks or ones for which a dominant operational goal could be found. Therefore, personnel departments undertook the preparation of elaborate job descriptions and organization charts. If there was still an overlap or gap, the issue was raised to the next level in the hierarchy where a single role could be found. All of these processes precisely defined the areas of jurisdiction but since interdependence, conflict, and ambiguity were confined to a single role, there was no concern for the *process* of resolving these issues. They were resolved by the greatest integrating mechanism—the human brain. Since some people were better than others at resolving these issues, the process was controlled by selecting those who were better. Thus, role definition and selection were the most important personnel management processes.

Today, and in the future, the picture is different for many tasks. Potential sources of conflict cannot be structured or defined away into a single role. Specialization results in interdependence between roles. High technology causes enough uncertainty that areas of jurisdiction cannot be defined ahead of time. In organizations such as the multinational organization, there is always something wrong with any structure it chooses—product, geographic, or function. All of these facts force organizations to work laterally. Since ambiguity and conflict exist between rather than within roles, more attention has to be given to the *process of resolving conflicts between roles*. Instead of removing the sources of conflict with role definition, the task of the personnel function is to help their organizations confront conflicts. This is to be done not by defining areas of jurisdiction but by role definitions concerning the *process* of decision making and conflict resolution. This is illustrated by the quote from the project manager. He says it is impossible to define roles in the sense of areas of jurisdiction but is quite definitive about the kinds of role behaviors he expects. He is not ambiguous in role definition concerning the behaviors in the decision process. Thus, there is a need for role definition but lateral relations require different role definitions from those which support individual responsibility.

The organization cannot get rid of ambiguity. It is inherent in the task. Traditionally, and in many current organizations performing predictable tasks, the ambiguity was concentrated within the role. The role occupant was faced with stresses caused by role overloads and priorities of diverse task elements. But today's tasks involving high technology and specialization still have the same priority questions but now they are between roles. Organizations have always left priority questions unresolved until the best information was available to resolve them. But now the resolution requires interpersonal rather than intrapersonal processes. Some of the emphasis on team building derives from the fact that organizations must explicitly deal with the role definition process across roles.

The technology of team building is still being developed. It is still developing a new definition of individual responsibility. The individual does not "go it alone" but neither is the individual to be lost in "group think" processes. In athletics individuals are rewarded for success in team contribution. In organizations, it is harder to assign rewards for team contribution because there is not the clear goal and outside threat to motivate teamwork.

## Responsibility Charting

A useful technique for use in team-building activities is the responsibility chart.[7] This has been used for a long time in defining jurisdictional areas. However, it is more useful in resolving ambiguities in decision processes and identifying areas where ambiguities must remain until more information is available.

The process begins by identifying the specific decisions that have to be made at a particular level of the organization. The list of decisions should not be so detailed that it overwhelms the group. These decisions should be listed to form rows as shown in Fig. 11.1. Along the top of the tableau are listed the participants to the decision processes which are listed along the side. Now it is a matter of simply matching the participants to the decision process. For this, the degree of participation can be indicated by any set of words that is meaningful for the organization. For example, one could be specifically responsible for a particular decision. Another role would not be responsible but must approve any decision made. Another role need not approve but should be consulted. Still another role need not be

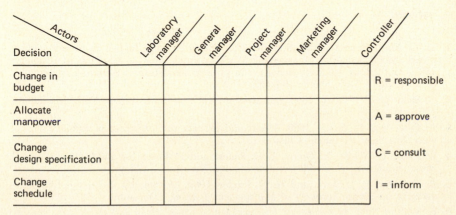

Fig. 11.1  Example of a responsibility chart.

consulted but should be informed if any change is made. These degrees of participation can be indicated by R, A, C, and I respectively.

To use the chart, the participants first identify major decision areas. Then each one fills out the form privately. The results are aggregated and presented to the group. The responses are not associated with any individual. Almost every time this is done, there will be wide variance in the responses as to who is responsible for what. This fact in itself is quite revealing. The remainder of the meeting is concerned with the gaps and overlaps. Dual responsibilities can be built in if needed. The result of the process is a completed chart that is jointly agreed upon by all participants. It is more meaningful than organization charts and job descriptions. The conflicts are confronted in the presence of all concerned and resolved to whatever extent possible. A follow-up meeting is then scheduled 3 to 6 months in the future to reconsider the decision process and to make changes to it.

The foregoing process is very useful for new teams or for introducing a change of structure. Conflicts are going to arise some time. They might as well be confronted early before a specific problem arises and before it becomes necessary to assign blame. The process eliminates role ambiguities wherever possible and pinpoints areas that must remain ambiguous. At this meeting, the group can decide upon procedures or criteria for determining which decisions will require group input and which will not.

Many consulting firms have used this approach. Some organizations have had bad experiences with it. But the problem lies with the organization climate, not with the technique. One should distinguish between improper use of the technique and flaws in the technique itself.

## NOTES

1. D. G. Marquis and D. M. Straight 1965. Organizational factors in project performance. Sloan School of Management Working Paper No. 133–65. Richard Goodman 1967. Ambiguous authority definition in project management. *Academy of Management Journal,* (December): 395–408.

2. G. Steiner and W. Ryan 1968. *Industrial project management.* New York: Macmillan, p. 32.

3. A. Filley and R. House 1969. *Managerial process and organization behavior.* Glenview, Ill.: Scott Foresman, Chapter 13.

4. R. Kahn, D. Wolfe, R. Quinn, J. D. Snoek, and R. Rosenthal 1964. *Organizational stress: studies in role conflict and ambiguity.* New York: Wiley.

5. R. C. Ziller, B. J. Stark, and H. O. Pruden 1969. Marginality and integrative management positions. *Academy of Management Journal,* (December): 487–495.

6. R. Walton 1969. *Interpersonal peacemaking: confrontations and third party consultation.* Reading, Mass.: Addison-Wesley.

7. R. Melcher 1967. Roles and relationships: clarifying the manager's job. *Personnel,* (May-June), reprinted in D. Cleland and W. King 1969. *Systems, organizations, analysis management: a book of readings.* New York: McGraw-Hill, pp. 365–371.

## QUESTIONS

1. How would you discuss the issue that authority must equal responsibility?

2. When using responsibility charting would you ever place two Rs in a row? Why? How would you justify it?

3. Can you see other uses for the techniques of responsibility charting?

4. It has been said that the result of a responsibility charting exercise is less important than the process of producing it. Explain why you agree or disagree.

# REVIEW OF MODEL AND EMPIRICAL EVIDENCE

The four organizing modes have now been presented in their entirety. This chapter reviews briefly the framework presented thus far. Then, some empirical evidence and further clarifications are discussed, particularly with reference to lateral relations. The following chapters present some case examples and discuss some operational problems with lateral relations.

## THE FRAMEWORK IN REVIEW

The theory underlying the framework was based on the premise that the observed variations in organization forms represent variations in the strategies of organizations to adapt to information-processing requirements of the task. In order to operationalize this premise, it was necessary to identify information-processing requirements, to explain how organizations process information, and to identify the organizing modes and the conditions under which the modes would be chosen.

The information-processing requirements facing an organization were primarily related to the degree of task uncertainty which was defined as the difference between the amount of information required to coordinate cooperative action and the amount of information actually possessed by the organization. The amount of information required was a function of the output diversity, the division of labor, and the level of performance. The greater each of these factors was, the greater the number of factors that must be considered simultaneously in reaching decisions. If the organization did not possess the information, then the organization must acquire it during the execution of the task. Thus, the postulate is that a critical limiting factor of organizational form is the capacity of the organization to process information and make decisions during the actual execution of the task.

To explain how information processing limited the form of the organization, the basic mechanistic, bureaucratic model was created. The model started with a large task in which the work was divided on the basis of input skill specialization. The design problem arises because the behavior that occurs in one of these subtasks cannot be judged as good or bad except as it relates to the behaviors occurring in other subtasks. The behaviors must be coordinated but the executors of the behaviors cannot communicate with all the others with whom they are interdependent. The design problem was to create mechanisms that permit coordinated action across large numbers of interdependent roles. Each of the mechanisms has, however, a range over which it is effective at handling the information requirements necessary to coordinate the interdependent roles. The mechanisms were discussed by starting with little information processing (a predictable task) and increasing the amount of information by increasing task uncertainty.

The basic bureaucratic model was one in which some behaviors were determined by rules created before their execution and communicated to role occupants; others by the discretion of the role occupant by limited goals and targets; and still others by decisions made by managers in the hierarchy after an unanticipated event occurred. The upward referral process which was needed to generate decisions as exceptional events occurred became overloaded as highly uncertain tasks generated large numbers of exceptions. The organization could then choose from among four organizing modes. Two of them reduced interdependence among the roles and reduced the need to process information while two others created mechanisms to process more information.

**Alternative 1: Creation of slack resources.** This occurred as a result of reducing the level of performance. Lower performance reduced the interdependence between roles and made it unnecessary to consider large numbers of decision factors simultaneously. Since there are many dimensions to performance, the design problem was to find the one that would reduce the overload and for which lower performance would be acceptable among the organization's clients, suppliers, owners, etc.

**Alternative 2: Creation of self-contained units.** This occurred when groups of input resources were devoted solely to one output category. By making all resource groups self-contained, there was no need to process information about resource sharing among outputs and less need to coordinate roles due to reduced division of labor. Again, interdependence was reduced making it unnecessary to consider a large number of factors simultaneously in decision making. The design choices were to select the basis of self-containment, the degree of self-containment, and the level at which the self-contained groups would report.

**Alternative 3: Investment in the vertical information system.** This occurred as a result of expanding the capacity of hierarchical channels of communication, creating new ones, and expanding the capacity of decision mechanisms. The investment occurred by employing the new information technologies and computers. The design variables were the frequency with which decisions were made, the scope of the data base available to the decision mechanism, the capacity of the decision mechanism, and the degree of formalization of language to be used in communicating about events which the organization faced.

**Alternative 4: Creation of lateral relations.** This occurred by selectively implementing communication channels across lines of authority. These channels needed to be designed because the "informal organization" did not spontaneously arise to coordinate interdependencies not encompassed by the hierarchy of authority. The lateral processes are listed below in a sequence determined by increasing ability to handle information and cost to the organization.

1. *Direct contact* between managers
2. Creation of *liaison role*
3. Creation of *task forces*
4. Use of *teams*
5. Creation of *integrating role*
6. Change to *managerial linking role*
7. Establishment of the *matrix form*

There are several design questions associated with each of these mechanisms which will not be repeated here.

It was hypothesized that as organizations take on tasks of increasing uncertainty, they must choose one or some combination of these modes in order to cope with increased information processing. If they did not consciously choose, then it is hypothesized that slack is automatically generated in order to balance the information-processing requirements of the task and the capacity of the organization to process information.

There is some evidence to support these assertions. In the remainder of this chapter some empirical studies are presented. In Chapter 13, two case studies are discussed in greater detail.

## LATERAL RELATIONS AND INFLUENCE DISTRIBUTION

The use of lateral relations which begins with direct contact and runs through the matrix design significantly alters the distribution of power in the organization's decision processes. In part, the distribution is a reflection of task uncertainty and in part a reflection of environmental influences. The effect of uncertainty is demonstrated in the findings of Lawrence and Lorsch.[1] Their findings are shown in Table 12.1. The data shown are taken

**Table 12.1 Relation between integrating effort and task uncertainty**

|  | Plastics | Food | Container |
|---|---|---|---|
| Percentage of new products in last 20 years | 35% | 15% | 0.0% |
| Integrating devices | rules | rules | rules |
|  | hierarchy | hierarchy | hierarchy |
|  | goal setting | goal setting | goal setting |
|  | direct contact | direct contact | direct contact |
|  | teams at three levels | task forces |  |
|  | integrating dept. | integrators |  |
| Percentage of integrators/managers | 22% | 17% | 0.0% |

from the most effective divisions of firms in three different industries. The industries differ in the amount of new product activity they have undertaken. It is assumed increased product activity increases the degree of task uncertainty. The comparison therefore holds effectiveness constant and high and varies the degree of task uncertainty. The extent to which lateral relations are used varies directly with the degree of task uncertainty. The container company works effectively through the hierarchy with a minimum of formal, lateral contacts. Alternatively the uncertain tasks facing the plastics firm require extensive use of lateral relations in order for them to be effective. That extensive lateral relations are more costly is reflected by the proportion of managers who perform integrating roles in integrating departments. The cost of lateral relations, more management, is quite clear.

The effect on the vertical distribution of influence is shown graphically in Fig. 12.1. The successful container firm has proportionally more influence concentrated at the top while the plastics firm has a more even distribution. The effect of task uncertainty is to overload the top levels in the plastic firm necessitating the decentralization of decisions. The combination of Table 12.1 and Fig. 12.1 indicates that the decentralization takes place through the establishment of lateral relations. It also illustrates that decentralization is not good or bad per se, but depends on the level of task uncertainty.

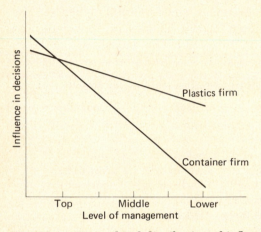

**Fig. 12.1   Hierarchical distribution of influence.**

Task uncertainty also influences the horizontal distribution of influence. Every organization requires the coordination of specialized resources. Uncertainty has the effect of making prior decisions inadequate. Decisions must then be made in light of current information. Many of these decisions require the global perspective of the general manager. However, uncertainty also has the effect of overloading the general management role. As decisions are pushed down to lower levels, the general manager controls the decision process by controlling the power bases of the participants to joint decisions. As uncertainty increases, more decisions about integrating resources around outputs are made at lower levels. Therefore, the role which champions product, unit, or program integration requires more power as uncertainty increases. The increase is obtained by the use of lateral relations and the power factors described in the previous chapter. Actually there is a continuum of relative power in the decision process which varies from a predominantly resource-based structure, like the container firm, all the way to a self-contained, program-based structure. This is shown in Fig. 12.2.

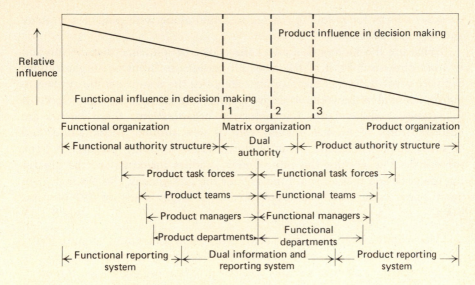

**Fig. 12.2   The range of alternatives.**

The extent to which lateral relations and the power factors are used determines where a particular organization is located along the bottom line. Figure 12.2 shows the power distribution for the product versus functional choice for a manufacturing firm. It could be project-functional or functional-geographic area as well. Starting on the far left, the decision-making influence is strictly functional. If the firm wishes to bring more product orientation into its decision process, it introduces product task forces, product teams, and then integrators (product managers). In so doing it moves along the bottom line toward the right.

In the previous chapter, the movement from a functional structure to a matrix was described. The movement could have been continued by shifting all departments to report to the original integrating position. But now the functional manager becomes the integrator who works for the goal of resource integrity across a product divisionalized structure. Similarly there can be functional teams and functional task forces. Indeed, a scenario could have been created by starting with product departments and subjecting the organization to changes in technology requiring more specialized resources.

The research on organizations has not progressed to a point at which an organization can locate where it should be on the diagram. But the research does allow us to determine the major factors to which we can add our subjective weightings. In addition, we can locate our present position and make changes in the appropriate directions as the factors change. This provides a basis for planning the organization along with plans for strategy and resource allocation.

What are the factors that affect the choice of influence distribution and in what direction? Most of the research pertains to industrial organizations but with substitutions of appropriate categories the results can be applied to noncommercial organizations as well. The first factors are the effects of uncertainty and diversity. For industrial organizations, these factors are indicated rates of market change, rate of new product introduction, and diversity of product lines. Some of the relevant research has already been presented.[2] The greater the rate of new product introduction, the greater the use of lateral relations and the greater the influence of the product manager. These same results are replicated in a larger study of 397 business firms.[3]

> Most significantly, businesses with program organizations seem to have been considerably more successful in developing and introducing new products than businesses without program organizations. For example 36.9% of the 358 businesses which had product program managers reported that more than 20% of 1967 sales were accounted for by new products, while only 19.8% of the businesses without product program managers made this claim.[4]

Similarly the diversity of product lines has the effect of overloading the decision process of functional organizations. In Chapter 4 this pressure was shown to lead to the establishment of product divisions. For small organizations or when the division itself diversifies, the same pressures exist but the costs of divisionalization are too great. Therefore, they undertake lateral relations and establish product integrators. The results were not reported quantitatively but were summarized as follows:

> There was a striking relationship between the amount of product and/or market diversity faced by a business and its use of program managers. In all industry and size classifications, the more diversified a business's products and/or markets, the more likely it was to have a program structure.[5]

Thus uncertainty and diversity create decision overloads which force the introduction of integrating roles. There is one study of hospitals which reports a higher proportion of administration staff in general hospitals than in specialized tuberculosis hospitals.[6] While there is no identification of the kinds of roles in the structure, it shows that there is a relation between the diversity of diseases and ills served and the number of managers it requires to provide the service. When combined with the Lawrence and Lorsch findings, it supports the generality of the information overload theory.

A second factor associated with the use of lateral relations and integrating roles is subtask interdependence. Using a longitudinal case study approach, Galbraith illustrates the increase in use of lateral relations after the time allowed for new product introduction was reduced.[7] The case is explained more fully in Chapter 13.

The findings from the Sloan School Project on the Management of Science and Technology help put the discussion in perspective.[8] If tight schedules, uncertainty, and diversity were the only forces operating, lateral relations would give way to self-contained program organizations. But the data from aerospace firms performing high technology projects for the government reveal that firms with technical personnel organized on a functional basis produce technically superior projects to firms organizing technical personnel on a project basis. Better technical performance is associated with resource-based organization forms. The same study also reveals that firms organizing administrative personnel on project basis and firms using PERT information systems are more likely to meet their cost and schedule targets. Therefore, in order to create high technology on tight schedules, the firm should use a matrix with technical personnel organized on a functional basis and with a project office containing administrative personnel supported by a project-related information system.

Thus, the evidence that exists supports the theory being developed here. The increases in uncertainty, diversity, and performance exert pressures to move the organization to the right in Fig. 12.2. Increases in specialization and economies of scale exert forces to move the organization to the left. Where the organization should be depends on the sum of these. When the forces are equally strong and opposing, the matrix design results.

All of these studies indicate the direction of change. They indicate use of lateral relations and integrating roles. But the data are not precise enough to specify exact power distributions. The evidence is inconclusive about power and influence of the integrating role. For example, Lawrence and Lorsch find that because all integrators have high influence, they cannot distinguish between successful and unsuccessful performance on that basis.[9] Similarly, Marquis could find no relationship between the types and amounts of influence possessed by a project manager and project performance.[10] The lack of results is partly due to the difficulty of measuring power and influence as opposed to the existence of a role and the number of people performing it.

Some anecdotal evidence is available, however, on the changes of power distributions in aerospace firms over a period of time. In addition to illustrating power shifts, the example highlights the effect of the environmental context on internal influence processes. Recall that in aerospace the tradeoffs were made among project technical performance, schedule completion, and cost. These general manager type decisions were decentralized to become joint decisions between a laboratory or functional manager championing technical performance and resource utilization and a project manager championing schedule completion and project cost.

In the late 1950s and early 1960s technical performance was the critical dimension. The environment was characterized by *Sputnik,* space race, and missile gap. It was deemed imperative by the government to produce technical accomplishments and to do it rapidly. The priorities ran technical performance first, schedule second, and cost a poor third. Data on actual performance during this time period reflect this.[11] All projects met or exceeded technical specifications while completion times were 1.5 times as great and costs exceeded targets by a factor of 3.2. In aerospace firms performing these projects, the functional managers dominated the joint decisions, but project managers were also influential due to time pressures. Since technical performance dominated, the influence distribution was approximated by the dotted line 1 in Fig. 12.2.

In the early and middle 1960s, the environment changed. This was the era dominated by McNamara. He was of the opinion that technical performance could be achieved but at less cost. The contracts changed from cost plus fixed fee to various incentive contracts and fixed price contracts. Defense department officials demanded that aerospace firms use PERT, then PERT/Cost information systems. The effect of these changes was to make the project manager more influential in the decision process. In Fig. 12.2, the influence distribution is represented by the dotted line 2.

Still another change occurred in the late 1960s. Strong pressures to reduce defense costs began operating. First there was the publicity concerning cost overruns on the giant C-5 A aircraft. Senator Proxmire began hearings on contractor efficiency practices. Finally, inflation and shifting national priorities all combined to make cost the top priority consideration as opposed to technical performance and schedule completion. In the internal workings of aerospace firms, the project managers began to dominate the joint-decision processes. The influence pattern was explicit. Project managers held vice-presidential status while laboratory and functional managers had titles of director. The influence distribution moved to dotted line 3 in Fig. 12.2.

Currently still another change is occurring. The national government is shifting spending away from aerospace projects. The effect is to reduce the size of the aerospace industry and firms in it. The firms must not only retain specialization to create the technology but must also reduce costs and size simultaneously. Thus, effective utilization of specialized resources across a number of projects has increased in importance. Firms must avoid fractional utilization of shared resources and duplication. Internally the functional managers are regaining some of their previous strengths in order to increase utilization. Reduced size influences the importance of the utilization of resources and its champion, the resource manager.

This brief account of the aerospace industry demonstrates how environmental influences affect internal decision processes. Normally general managers would watch these trends and alter their decision-making behavior accordingly. But when decisions are decentralized, the general managers must change internal power bases in addition to their decision behavior. It becomes the task of general managers to see that internal influence distributions determining joint decision outcomes reflect the external realities that the organization faces. This requires that they take an open-system view of the organization.

A similar sequence of events has taken place in hospitals over a longer period of time.[12] Decision making in hospitals revolves around the triumvirate of trustees, doctors, and administrators. Originally hospitals for the most part served those members of the community who could not afford treatment in their homes. Therefore, the hospital depended on the trustees to donate and secure donations from the community to finance its operations. The technological advances contained in sophisticated equipment for treatment and diagnosis shifted the power to the medical staff because they were the only ones trained to understand the resources used by the hospital. Also more patients were treated in hospitals than in their homes. The hospitals became financially dependent upon the physicians for referrals. Trustees were still influential because financing was required for the acquisition of the sophisticated equipment. Recently there has been a shift in power escalating the influence of the administrative staff. The increases in specialization and demands for complete utilization of facilities makes the administrator and unit manager more active in the coordination of activities. There is also an increase in external interdependence. The hospital needs to coordinate its activities with other health agencies in the community. It is the administrative staff that have the external contacts which enable them to influence external affairs to aid internal problems in the hospital. It is important for organizations to adapt to these realities. Those hospitals and aerospace firms which adapted first were the most successful. Those institutions which cannot achieve the internal power shifts are those which are most likely to fail.

Thus, as patterns of interdependence, task uncertainty, diversity, and external conditions change, the organization must change its structure for decision making in order to remain effective. The types and directions of changes have been described in this section.

It should be mentioned that this analysis assumes that organizations must adapt to their environments. In some cases, they must. However, there are other occasions in which organizations can change the environment rather than adapt to it. This possibility is discussed in Chapters 14 and 15.

## NOTES

1. P. Lawrence and J. Lorsch 1967. *Organization and environment*. Boston: Harvard Business School, Chapter 6.

2. Lawrence and Lorsch, *Ibid*. T. Burns and G. M. Stalker 1958. *Management and innovation*. London: Tavistock.

3. E. R. Corey and S. H. Star 1970. *Organization strategy: a marketing approach*. Boston: Division of Research, Harvard Business School, Chapter 6.

4. *Ibid.*, p. 54.

5. *Ibid.*, p. 52.

6. T. Anderson and S. Warkov 1961. Organizational size and functional complexity: a study of administration in hospitals. *American Sociological Review*, (February): 23–28.

7. J. Galbraith 1970. Environmental and technological determinants of organization design. In J. Lorsch and P. Lawrence (eds.), *Studies in organization design*. Homewood, Ill.: Richard D. Irwin.

8. D. G. Marquis 1969. Ways of organizing projects. *Innovation* **5**: 26–33.

9. Lawrence and Lorsch, p. 62.

10. D. G. Marquis and D. M. Straight 1965. Organizational factors in project performance. Sloan School of Management Working Paper No. 133–65, M.I.T., (August).

11. M. Peck and F. Sherer 1962. *The weapons acquisition process*. Boston: Division of Research, Harvard Business School.

12. C. Perrow 1961. The analysis of goals in complex organizations. *American Sociological Review* 26: 854–866. C. Perrow 1965. Hospitals: technology, structure and goals. In J. G. March, *Handbook of organizations*. Chicago: Rand-McNally, Chapter 22.

## QUESTIONS

1. Are the alternative organizing modes genuine alternatives or can they be combined in a design? Explain.

2. If an organization changes its strategy and thereby increases task uncertainty, it must increase its capacity to process information or decrease the need to process information. If it does not choose one of the alternative organizing modes, slack will automatically be added. Explain or refute the preceding statement.

3. Explain the view that coordination mechanisms are added to the mechanisms already in use and are not substitutes for them.

4. How would you go about choosing which mechanisms to add?

5. Under what conditions would you expect to find the matrix form operating successfully?

6. Explain how changes in an organization's environment affect its power and influence distribution. Is the change automatic?

| | CHAPTER |
|---|---|
| CASE STUDIES | **13** |

The entire framework and some supporting evidence have now been presented. Some examples have been given throughout to illustrate specific points. In this chapter, two case studies will be presented. They are intended to highlight the trade-offs articulated in the theory and also to demonstrate practical usefulness.

## RESPONSE TO A MARKET CHANGE

The history of the Commercial Airplane Division of the Boeing Company can be used as a case to illustrate the design choices that have been derived in the theory.[1] The Commercial Airplane Division is responsible for the generation, design, and production of aircraft for the world's airlines. The organization is shown in Fig. 13.1. It reflects the product divisionalized structure with functional integrating departments. After experiencing substantial growth and introducing new models in the early 1960s, the Commercial Airplane Division reorganized to the divisionalized form. This illustrates the effect of diversity and size on the organization. However, since all product branches were concentrated in the Seattle area and most labor markets were tight, the functional integrating departments were influential in manpower allocation. Our interest however concentrates on the product branch organization which designs and produces a single type of aircraft.

### Coordination in a Product Branch

A typical product branch organization is shown in Fig. 13.2. The branch employed about 10,000 people and produced about ten aircraft a month.

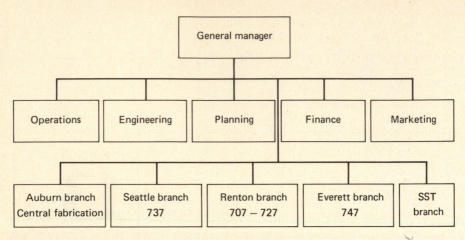

**Fig. 13.1   Commercial airplane division organization chart.**

Each aircraft required about 14 months to two years for completion. The branch engaged in the sequential process of design of product, design of the process, acquisition and fabrication of parts, assembly of parts, and finally testing and delivery. Invariably the branches chose the functional form illustrated in Fig. 13.2.

The functional form placed the design of the aircraft in a unit under a single authority structure. This was done because the design process involves uncertain and reciprocally interdependent activities of the highest priority. The design must meet the specifications guaranteed to the airlines

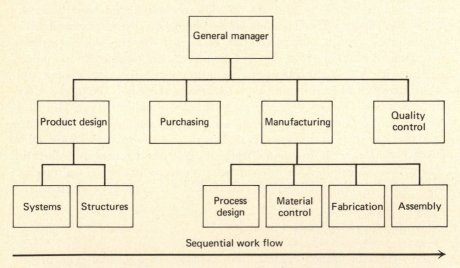

**Fig. 13.2   Functional organization of product branch before the change.**

and meet the safety requirements of the government or there will be no sales. Thus, the activities which were most difficult to coordinate were also the most consequential. The product design unit was structured to coordinate the design activities most effectively. Similarly purchasing and manufacturing were functional to exploit common vendor groupings and economies of scale in equipment and tooling, respectively.

The effect of the functional organization was to create for the branch manager the problem of coordinating the sequential work flow between the functions. The mechanism for coordination is a schedule which provides targets for each function to guide its completion of the work. The schedule must allow each function enough time to do its work and still complete the work in the time desired by the customer. The task of scheduling is a problem of considerable magnitude both within and among the interdependent functions. Let us analyze how this scheduling function was performed in a branch.

**1. Functional integrating departments.** The two primary functions, product design and manufacturing, each had its own integrating department which was responsible for scheduling between the departments within the functions. The cost and schedules group within product design collected detailed information for the decisions concerning technical performance, cost, and schedule completion. The scheduling function in manufacturing scheduled the flow of some 100,000 parts into final assembly. Those were the locations of information concerning schedules and status of operations. Therefore, a good deal of the scheduling was decentralized within the two primary functions.

The functional scheduling departments handled the sequential interdependence within the functions but left the problem of coordinating sequential interdependence between functions. The manner in which this coordination was carried out varied with the type of decision. There was one mechanism for establishing the original schedule for each airplane and others for handling deviations from it.

**2. Branch integrating department.** There was an overall schedule established for each aircraft upon its order. This schedule was determined by a team formed by representatives from product design, manufacturing, purchasing, division marketing, and a customer representative. An integrator, called a program manager, served as chairman of this team in order to achieve a schedule that was in the best interest of the branch. He was the representative of the branch general manager. Negotiations began by having (1) manufacturing's scheduling department work backward from the date desired by the customer and (2) product design's cost and schedules group work forward from the present. The problem was to achieve a set of milestones that everyone could live with. These milestones then guided the subsequent scheduling within the functions.

The program manager's integrating department was responsible for getting the schedule established and for monitoring schedule progress but only in an aggregate way. It provided information for the general manager's review of major milestones rather than detailed information to guide the scheduling effort.

This method of coordination worked very well as long as every department met its due date or milestone. It is only when due dates are missed and missed in substantial numbers that additional coordination effort is needed. There are two possible types of schedule disruption which require additional resources—predictable and unpredictable causes. Different mechanisms are used in each case.

**3. Change board.** The predictable disruptions result from the constant flow of design changes from product design engineers. The design changes are caused by attempts to update technology, by rejects from quality control, by liaison engineers, and by customer requests. Since design changes are originated in the product design step, the change can have effects on all subsequent functional activity. The additional coordination effort took the form of a team called a change board. Each function and sales have a permanent representative on the board. It was chaired and run by the representative from product design. The board met daily to discuss schedule and budget changes. The changes were then communicated to the affected groups and the functional scheduling departments. All of these integrating positions are indicated in Fig. 13.3.

**4. Slack resources.** The unpredictable schedule disruptions usually arise due to uncertainties inherent in the task of designing and manufacturing airplanes. The uncertainty varies between functions. The design groups have the greatest uncertainty. The uncertainty varies with the maturity of the project and the state of the art of the design. Thus, the introduction of new models introduces the greatest uncertainty. What makes the problem difficult is that the schedule disruptions are most likely to occur in the design functions which are at the start of the sequential work flow. Therefore, they can potentially disrupt all subsequent activity.

During the mature stages of a program these disruptions can be handled by scheduling—rescheduling decisions with the functions, by direct contact between affected managers by informal task force activity, and with the schedule slack that has been built into the schedule. However, when a new model was introduced, the increase in uncertainty overloaded the decision process. The response was to absorb the uncertainty with slack and perform the scheduling less effectively. This was because the uncertainty was temporary and the primary problem was in achieving an effective high-

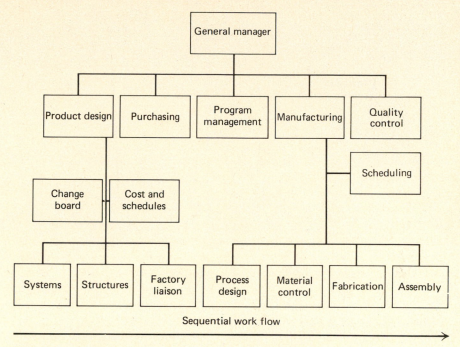

**Fig. 13.3   Typical product branch before the change.**

quality design. The effect of uncertainty on the organization is depicted graphically in Fig. 13.4. It shows the stockout history of the Commercial Airplane Division. A stockout occurs if a part or assembly is not available in the assembly at its scheduled time. Periods of high stockout activity coincide perfectly with the introduction of new models. These peak periods were tolerated as transients. Indeed, in periods of stability, the system functioned well. It was cheaper to absorb uncertainty with slack than to apply more coordination effort.

In summary, the branches operated a functional organization in order to coordinate the primary subtask of designing the aircraft. This created a problem of sequential interdependence between functions. A schedule was the plan by which the sequential activities were coordinated. The schedule was established by a functional team chaired by the program manager, an integrating role. The schedule was subsequently elaborated, implemented and controlled through integrating departments within the functions. Another team, the change board, coordinated many of the subsequent design changes. This was another interfunctional team but it was chaired by product design. Finally there was slack used to reduce the magnitude of the task particularly at times of new model introduction. Thus, the scheduling was decentralized and controlled within the two principal functions.

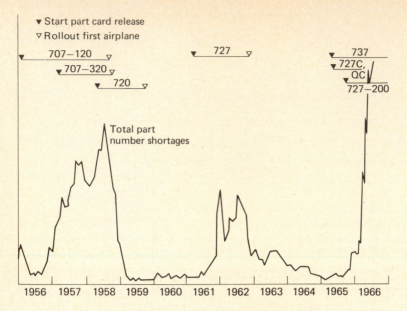

Fig. 13.4   Stockout history of commercial airplane division.

## Environmental Change

In the years from 1963 to 1966 some significant environmental changes took place. First there was an enormous increase in the demand for commercial jet aircraft. This required a rapid buildup of men, material, and facilities. Previous buildups at Boeing had been financed by the government either by progress payments prior to actual delivery of the aircraft or by using government equipment and facilities. Prior to the 747, airlines did not make progress payments. Therefore the buildup had to be internally financed. The shift from government to commercial markets combined with rapid growth made cost and financial factors higher in priority.

The other major change occurred in the market. Prior to the middle sixties, the problem to be solved in order to sell aircraft was to demonstrate the profitability of jet over propeller-driven aircraft on commercial routes. The problem was to create a market. In this environment, the cost of time and delay is small relative to a mistake in design or construction. Thus, prior to making commitments to the airlines on the 707, Boeing built, flew, and tested a prototype. The success of the 707 brought imitation from Douglas in the DC–8 and Convair in the 880. These models were directly competitive for the same airline routes. The same market problem prevailed in introducing the 727. Boeing had to demonstrate the profitability of jets on medium-range routes. However, this time they did not build a prototype. Instead, they undertook four years of wind-tunnel testing and product development to perfect the three aft-mounted engine design. The 727 was also successful but this time Douglas did not imitate. They introduced the DC–9 for short-range routes.

After 1964 the problem facing Boeing was not to establish a market but to meet the opportunities remaining as quickly as possible. They introduced the short-range 737, new versions of the 727, the giant 747, and the SST. But each of these received competitive time pressure from the DC–9, an elongated DC–9, an elongated DC–8, the DC–10, Lockheed's L1011, a possible commercial derivative of Lockheed's C–5A, and the British-French Concorde. Now a delay of a few months would result in canceled orders and fewer sales. The cost of using slack time to uncouple sequentially interdependent subtasks was prohibitive. Thus, Boeing operated under compressed schedules. The product development effort which preceded the final design effort was reduced from four years on the 727 to four months on the 747. This left considerable uncertainty to be resolved by the branches in the design stage while at the same time compressed schedules gave them less time in which to do it.

As the theory would predict, information overloads occurred. The amount of stockout activity shown in Fig. 13.4 during 1966–67 was higher than at any time in the past. During this same period, stockouts slowed production and caused a financial crisis at the Douglas Company. These facts caused the Boeing management to search for alternative solutions to what is the organization design problem.

### Choice of Organizing Mode

The increased task uncertainty (caused by less prior product development work) and interdependence (caused by compressed schedules) increased the amount of information that had to be processed during the actual design and manufacture. Therefore, according to the theory, branches had to undertake some organization design action. This is illustrated by the increase in stockouts when no action was initially taken. Therefore the policy to do nothing is tantamount to a decision to use slack. Not to decide is to decide on slack. But as stockouts increased and Douglas developed similar problems, Boeing searched for alternatives.

The theory developed here identifies four alternatives. The first, slack resources, cannot be used. Indeed, slack must be reduced. Alternatively the information processing between decision makers could be reduced by creating self-contained units within the branch. These units should be formed around the major units which come together to form the aircraft such as wing, cab, tail, and body. This alternative was not chosen for two reasons. First, the critical problem is one of product design. The design process has the greatest uncertainty, greatest amount of interdependence, and greatest consequence for overall performance of the aircraft. Splitting up the inter-dependent units would jeopardize the technical integration. There is some factual basis for this. A study by engineering showed that when the design work was subcontracted and performed at a remote site, that work was more likely to overrun its cost and schedules. Figure 13.5 shows the graph they developed. It shows that the greater the percentage of contracted design work, the greater the cost overrun of the original target. Thus, for the consequential design work, it is more effective to collocate designers and maintain them in a single structure.

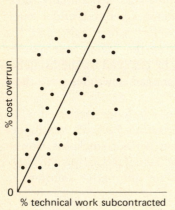

Fig. 13.5    Cost overrun history in relation to the amount of design subcontracted.

There is also the possibility of placing the design work in one unit and placing the remaining sequential interdependence in self-contained units. This would place the scheduling through manufacturing and testing in autonomous units. Such an organization is represented in Fig. 13.6. It is predicted that this change would have been effective in reducing stockouts and providing the decentralized, quick response necessitated by compressed schedules. This design alternative was not chosen, however. It was not chosen because the problem it solved was too transient and temporary to merit a change in overall structure. Figure 13.4 shows that problem exists only in the initial stages of a program. In mature stages, the functional organization and previous coordination devices will be appropriate. There-fore, other design alternatives had to be sought. These alternatives had to increase the capacity of the organization to process the information which temporarily overloads the branch. The responses varied with the program.

**1. Task forces.**    The primary response of the branches introducing the 737 and various 727 derivatives was to introduce task forces to provide the interfunctional coordination. Since the structure could not be changed as indicated in Fig. 13.6, task forces were formed around the major sections. These groups worked the sequential interdependence between functions.

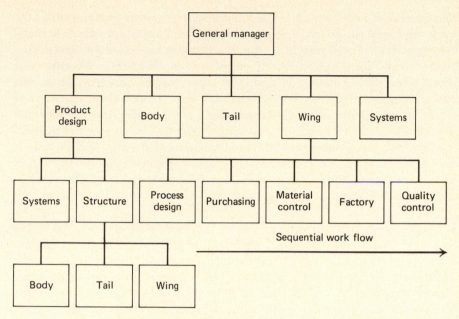

**Fig. 13.6   Product branch with sequentially interdependent clusters.**

The task forces were able to collect information on an informal basis by walking through the plant and telephoning managers. This interfunctional information gave them the basis for setting priorities. This interfunctional information was not available anywhere else. The information collected and displayed by the program manager was interfunctional, but was neither detailed enough nor current enough to provide for the setting of priorities as problems arose. Since the groups within the task forces were responsible for relatively independent tasks, they were able to collect this information and respond to problems as they arose. Also by spending a good deal of time in the plant, they were able to work with people who were most knowledgeable about the problem.

All personnel assigned to the task forces worked full time until the first six to ten aircraft were completed. They were then assigned elsewhere. The task forces were temporary patchwork on the functional structure which was vulnerable to sequential interdependence.

The task forces represented a temporary structure change which modified the authority relationship during periods of high uncertainty. During the period of new design introduction, the task force set priorities on what to do next. Since they had information which cut across functions and were not identified with any single function, the task force members were in a better position to determine priorities than were the functional managers.

The functional managers still made decisions relating to who would do the work and how to do it. During periods of task certainty, the functional managers did not need priorities other than "follow the schedule!" but during a new model introduction, the assumptions on which the schedule was based often proved wrong as problems arose. As the problems arose, the information collecting activities of the task force placed them in the position to set new priorities. As the task became more predictable, the schedule became a more reliable priority device and the task force was not needed.

The task force represents additional coordination effort and cost. It is used in addition to, not instead of, the normal means of coordination. It is necessary to replace the slack time that has been removed from the schedule with additional means of coordination.

**2. Liaison.** Another vulnerable spot in the functional organization is between the product and process design groups. It is here that the uncertainties are highest and there is reciprocal and sequential interdependence. The additional coordination was performed by a liaison group of process designers who were physically stationed in the product design area. Their first responsibility was to work with the product designer and suggest design alternatives which allow less costly manufacturing processes. Due to the environmental changes, the interdependence between these groups requires communication and interaction to achieve the necessary coordination. This is due to several factors. First, the interdependence was not completely worked out in product development. Second, the amount of communication exceeded the capacity of direct managerial contact. The increased volume of activity brought in new engineers who were not familiar with past practices. These combined to create a need for liaison engineers.

The liaison group also aided in the coordination of sequential interdependence. If the product designers were late in completing a design, this delayed the start of the process design activity. In order to put a part back on schedule, the process design group would have to resort to overtime. However, the liaison group took advantage of the fact that a part design did not have to be 100 percent complete before the process design could begin. The tool design could be started if rough dimensions and material were known. Thus, the liaison engineers kept the process designers supplied with work by bringing them partially completed parts designs. In this way the design efforts were run in parallel rather than in series with the liaison as the communication link.

Thus, the liaison group facilitated mutual adjustment and allowed the removal of slack time from the schedule without causing disruptions. The liaison group also represented an increase in coordination costs since it was used in addition to, not instead of, the schedule and direct managerial contact. However, once the design of the new aircraft was complete, the

liaison men resumed normal duties as process designers or liaison personnel elsewhere. The activity was needed only in periods of high uncertainty.
On some programs this was not a new approach, on others it was. However,
on all programs more liaison engineers and higher quality engineers were
assigned than in the past.

Thus, the reduction in slack resources was countered by allocating more
resources, liaison and task force, to coordination through local relations.
These resources were placed at critical spots in the sequential flow being
coordinated by a functional organization. The lateral relations allowed a
temporary decentralization of influence. The organization was still a functionally dominant one with an integrating role between functions.

### The 747 Program

The introduction of the 747 represented one of the largest private under-
takings ever attempted. The magnitude of the coordination task rendered
the previous mechanisms insufficient. The program still used rules, hierarchy, goal setting and planning, and direct contact. They made extensive
use of liaison, task forces, and teams. The departments working on the same
section of the aircraft were physically located together. This enhanced the
probability that direct contact and informal task forces and teams would
develop spontaneously. But more attention needed to be given to the costs
incurred and to schedule completion. The means by which this was accomplished was an organization change and a lateral shift in influence, all
of which increased the influence of the integrator—the program management office. The modified organization is shown in Fig. 13.7.

**1. Structure change.** The change in structure had two effects. The first
involved the creation of an operations manager. The structure represented
a more inclusive first-order grouping of the sequentially interdependent
functions which take place after product design. The grouping consisted
of a unit for the reciprocally interdependent product design units and a unit
for the sequentially interdependent operations functions. The change created two units within which were contained the major coordination problems. However, it still left the problem of coupling design and operations.
To accomplish this, the influence of the program office was increased.

The influence was increased by the structure change of shifting the
change board activity to the program office and enlarging the number of
boards operating. The effect of the change was to change the goal orientation of the board chairman to one which was responsive to cost and schedules as well as technical considerations.

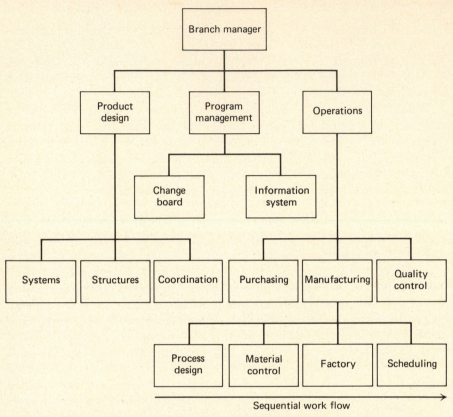

Fig. 13.7 Product branch organization responsible for 747.

**2. Information system.** The other major change was in the vertical information system. The result was an increase in the detail of global information and an increase in the currency of information utilized in the program office. Previously the information in the program office was used more for *ex post* evaluation rather than *ex ante* decision making. Detailed real-time, interfunctional information for decision making had to be acquired informally by the task forces. The change created a more formalized information system to provide this data. The formalization was accomplished by utilizing a PERT-like network diagram for planning and control purposes. The cost of the change was a large increase in clerical personnel to process the information.

Thus, the increase in task uncertainty and tighter coupling of functions was countered with more information and an increased decision-making capability. It was easy to change from this design to one required for stable operations. Under the present system as the uncertainty is decreased, the amount of information is decreased. The frequency of reporting can be reduced from daily to weekly, weekly to every other week. The PERT system will not be needed. The number of information processing people can be decreased to a normal level as the task certainty increases. Although the form of coordination is different, its intensity still varies directly with the uncertainty of the task.

The case study described here has been intended to illustrate the framework developed in the book and to highlight the trade-off between slack, authority structure, vertical information systems, and lateral relations. The example first described the mechanisms the organization used to come to terms with its environment. Then as the environment changed, the organization had to adjust its mechanisms of coordination. Whether these changes were effective is clearly a matter of conjecture. However, one possible explanation is that these changes were effective. Boeing, at the time of this writing, is the only commercial airframe manufacturer which has not failed financially. Douglas failed financially and sold out to the McDonnell Company. Lockheed failed and had to secure a government loan. If Boeing fails at some time in the future, then it can be argued that it held out longer

The Boeing case illustrates coordination problems in a functional design Let us look at some problems arising in a project-based design.

## ORGANIZATION OF A DATA-PROCESSING SYSTEM

A design change made in the computer operation of a large company illustrates a change toward a matrix form from a project-based design. The original organization is shown in Fig. 13.8. The organization consisted of about 600 people. About 400 of those were in the data-processing center which performed the computation and minor programming for the rest of

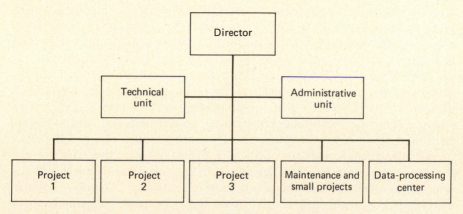

Fig. 13.8    Original organization of data-processing department.

the organization. Reporting to the director was a technical unit and an administrative unit. The technical unit consisted of computer scientists who evaluated new equipment and new languages, consulted internally on difficult programming and problems, and aided in the long-range planning for the department. The administrative unit kept the budgets, costs, and personnel information for the department. The remainder of the organization consisted of about 150 programmers and systems analysts working on three large projects and in a unit devoted to small projects and maintenance of ongoing systems.

In late 1969, the data-processing department began to be concerned about the technical quality of performance. The projects were delivered on time, but the work was not done well. In addition there were morale and turnover problems among the programmers. After investigating, a task force identified several problems.

There were several problems which were designated as phase-out problems. Every project, whether it lasts three months or three years, must come to an end. This ending or phaseout causes feelings of anxiety on the part of the project members. They are concerned whether they will have a job at the end of the project or whether their next job will be as interesting, challenging, and responsible as their present one. Therefore, many programmers spend a good deal of time looking for their next job. The result is decreased productivity and lower performance on final tasks such as documentation.

A second problem aggravated by the phaseout was turnover. An analysis of exit interviews showed that turnover was greatest near the end of a project and occurred because certain individuals were concerned about their next assignment. Besides incurring the usual turnover costs, the department was concerned because those who left were those who were competent enough to get another job.

The phaseout also caused some skill degradation. Sometimes new project jobs were not immediately available. The programmers were given what they perceive to be "staff work" or make-work assignments below their skill level until they could move on to their next project. Worse yet was the tendency for project managers to hold on to skilled personnel. As the manpower requirements declined at the end of the project, the project managers were forced to give up programmers. When they did, project managers gave up those programmers they could spare and held on to the good ones. They did this because the accounting system charged the same for all programmers and if a problem was encountered, they couldn't get the good programmers back. The work at the end of the project did not require as much skill as the work in the beginning. Therefore, people worked below their skill levels. Also, they became concerned about the next job. Since they were the last to leave a project, all the better assignments might be gone when they were ready. This fact caused some turnover as well.

The other problem was caused by the insufficient attention paid to maintaining the skill inventory. The project managers were concerned with their project only, and rightly so. No one was concerned with fitness to perform projects in the future. Project managers were not concerned with the personal development of the people that worked for them for a short time. This lack of concern contributed to the anxiety of many programmers. It was not that project managers did not care about people but rather that they were primarily concerned with short-run results. This short-run orientation also caused some skill decline. It would pay the project manager to use programmers on tasks for which they already had well-developed skills. A programmer would get to be known for being good at a specific task. Every time that task arose he would be asked to do it. While this is good for short-run productivity, it causes skill decay in the unused areas. A technical change could also eliminate the task and make the programmer obsolete.

Most of these problems could be handled by the department director. However, multiple projects, many programmers, and changing technology require decisions which overload the manager when they are added to his other duties. In order to handle these decisions to maintain skilled resources, the director introduced two resource integrators as shown in Fig. 13.9. The

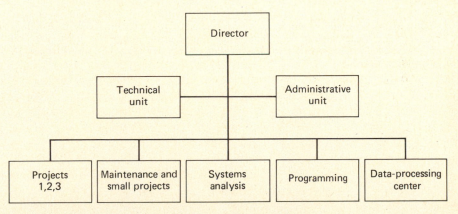

**Fig. 13.9  Data-processing department after change.**

integrating departments became a home base for systems analysts and programmers, respectively. The integrators became primarily concerned with skill mix, maintaining skill levels, and allocation across projects. The allocations were joint decisions between the integrators and project managers. The integrators were selected to be competent in their respective areas. Therefore, they were respected in the allocation process and in the work evaluation process.

There was also a change in the charge for programmers. Three skill categories were established and charges to projects were to reflect the skill level. Therefore the project managers had to make skill-cost, trade-off decisions. This also reduced potential conflict between project managers and integrators. There were still conflicts to be resolved. The project managers had to argue for the priority of the project and need for a skill. The integrators defended the skill level of the individual. Also the integrators tried to eliminate the fear that if a project released a programmer, they could not get him back. Today, this system is not entirely debugged but has satisfied its creators.

## SUMMARY

This chapter presented two examples to help illustrate the theory. One example involved a change from a functional to a more program-oriented organization. The other was a shift from a project to a more functionally oriented design.

## NOTE

1. For a more complete description and analysis, see J. R. Galbraith 1970. Environmental and technological determinants of organization design. In J. Lorsch and P. Lawrence (eds.), *Studies in organization design.* Homewood, Ill.: Richard D. Irwin, pp. 113–139.

<table>
<tr><td rowspan="2">THE ORGANIZATION AND<br>ITS ENVIRONMENT</td><td>CHAPTER</td></tr>
<tr><td>**14**</td></tr>
</table>

In this chapter we return to the concept of strategic choice and consider the option of changing strategy rather than or in addition to changing the organizing mode. The focus here will be on changing the organization's domain and relations with other organizations in the domain thereby changing objectives and goals. Thus, the chapter focuses on the environment of an organization and how the organization manages that environment.

Previous chapters implicitly dealt with the environment through the concept of uncertainty. Our treatments of uncertainty assumed that the organization did not control all the determinants of outcomes which it tried to achieve. Those determinants were controlled by others. However, we implicitly assumed that the relevant other was nature. Then, since the organization could not control, understand, or predict the effects of nature on outcomes that were desired, it had to adapt in order to achieve those desired outcomes. The previous chapters described various ways in which the organization can design its structure, information system, and reward system to adapt to the task uncertainty and diversity with which it must live. This chapter, on the other hand, describes ways the organization can change the environment, reduce uncertainty, and manage its dependence on others so that its present structure and processes are adequate. This management of environmental dependence begins with a recognition of the fact that the "other," which controls some of the determinants of outcomes thought to be desirable, is other organizations or well defined groups, not solely nature. These other organizations are themselves dependent on their environment. Out of this mutual dependence or interdependence comes the basis for cooperation and management of environmental forces.

The chapter begins by introducing some terminology with which we can talk about the environment. Then the different strategies for environmental management are discussed along with their affects, costs, and benefits, some examples and relevant evidence, if any. Chapter 15 takes a particular kind of problem of environmental dependence and traces the organizational strategies which different firms have adopted to deal with this problem.

## THE ORGANIZATION'S ENVIRONMENT

In analyzing the environment, the first task is in developing a language and set of concepts in order to talk about the environment. The task is not an easy one, because "the environment" tends to be a catchall phrase. Anything that is not part of the organization is part of the environment. But the boundaries of many organizations are rather amorphous. Most of us have little trouble deciding on the boundaries of a 100-person enterprise which is owned by the president. The customers, creditors, and suppliers are outside and the 100 employees are inside. But as ownership and management become separate, are the stockholders part of the organization or part of the environment? The customers were thought to be outside but the customers of educational institutions, students, may be considered inside. And are physicians suppliers of services to hospitals or members of the organization? The boundaries get still more confused in voluntary organizations.

The problem is, in part, generated by the insistence upon making inside-outside choices. In fact, there is continuous variation in the *degree of inclusion* in the decision-making processes of the organization. Indeed, there may be an inner circle of ten who are more included in these processes than are the other 90 within our fictitious organization.[1] Thus, our interest will be in the degree of inclusion of various groups in the goal-setting, strategy-making, and resource-allocation decisions of an organization and not in making clear distinctions of boundaries. Thus, we will try to explain why the local banker, an outsider, may be more influential in the decision processes of our fictitious firm than any of the 99 employees, all insiders.

The next step in the analysis, given that the interest is in the degree of inclusion in the decision process, is to identify *who should be included* (from the point of view of the focal organization). In order to do this we will borrow from the work of Thompson.[2] His analysis begins by noting that no organization is self-sufficient. Each organization reaches points at which it depends on others to provide inputs, absorb outputs, grant concessions, provide support, etc. which are needed to achieve outcomes desired by the people doing the work. The points of interest are then *points of dependence*. These points of dependence are determined by three choices which determine the domain of the organization.

The first and key choice which determines points of dependence is the choice of strategy.[3] For business firms the choice is one of product/market distinctive competence. Which products and services are to be offered? Which class or classes of customers/clients are to be served in which geographical areas? With the appropriate substitution of students and patients for customers, and courses and diseases for products, the concept is easily extended to universities and hospitals and then to other types of organizations. This choice establishes various dependencies. For example, a business school which chooses to become a management school by offering courses and degrees in health care administration suddenly becomes dependent upon health care institutions, to mention only one point of dependence, to send students and/or to hire graduates of the program. Traditional business schools pursuing different course/student strategies do not have those dependencies.

The second choice influencing the points of dependency is the choice of technology. Organizations choosing capital as opposed to labor-intensive technologies become more dependent upon banks and suppliers of capital funds. Labor-intensive technologies requiring professional talent become dependent on professional schools for their required inputs.

Finally, the choice of physical location completes the list of the three strategic choices.

While individual organizations vary in their freedom to make these choices, collectively these choices determine (1) who are the *consumers and users* of the organization's services, (2) who are the *suppliers* of the organization's inputs (3) who are its *competitors* for these users and resources, and (4) who are the concerned *regulatory groups* such as governments, unions, trade associations, etc.[4] These groups are the relevant others whose support is needed by the focal organization. Collectively they constitute the organization's *task environment* or what Evan calls the organization's set.[5] The expectations, attitudes, goals, preferences, and opinions of these groups must be taken into account and included in the decision-making processes of the focal organization when it sets goals and allocates resources. This "taking into account" of the task environment introduces environmental control over the focal organization and prevents unilateral choice of goals, strategy, and resource allocations.

The necessary inclusion of relevant others in the decision process raises the notion of interaction between the focal organization and the relevant others. It is this interaction process over time which determines the *organization's goals.*[6] The people controlling the organization may have their own motives of seeking profits, prestige, votes, etc., but these outcomes can be attained only if the organization provides something to those on whom the organization is dependent. The goals of an organization, the operational goals that guide its decision making, result from this interaction process and reflect what the relevant others want done as well as what they can be persuaded to accept. The question then becomes one of *how to include relevant others* in the decision process without giving up too much freedom to act. What are the mechanisms by which an organization can interact with the relevant others? Let us turn our attention to that design choice.

## ENVIRONMENTAL MANAGEMENT

In this section various strategies are discussed by which organizations interact with their environments. The preceding paragraphs argued that choices of strategy, technology, and location determined the organization's task environment. The task environment then became the set of groups which must be included in the decision-making process. In choosing mechanisms by which elements of the task environment can be included, the organization balances its needs for autonomy and flexibility against the exchange of commitments to reduce uncertainty and get cooperation and coordination. There is a need for balance. If the task environment has too much influence, the organization becomes subservient. On the other hand, not enough influence may lead to instability, unpredictability, and lack of support which may catch the organization unprepared and/or unable to react and adapt. From the point of view of society, insufficient environmental influence leads to monopolies and other concentrations of power to unilaterally allocate society's resources. Let us look at the various strategies for interacting with and managing a *given* task environment. That is, let us assume that the organization has chosen its strategy, technology, and location which determine that task environment.

The strategies can be separated, first, into two general categories—independent and cooperative. The independent strategies are means by which the organization can reduce the uncertainty and/or dependence which may threaten its existence by drawing on its own resources and ingenuity. This strategy allows some environmental influence on its decisions but environmental elements are only minimally and indirectly included. The organization retains its autonomy while being responsive. Alternatively cooperative strategies are ways that the organization implicitly or explicitly cooperates with other elements in its environment. These forms are hypothesized to be more costly in terms of autonomy reduction but are to be more necessary when uncertainty and dependency are high. Each of the categories will be described along with the subcategories before giving a more detailed comparison of the two approaches.

## Independent Strategies

There are three different independent strategies which will be described. Each one is an attempt to maintain self-control in a situation of interdependence. Each is appropriate for particular circumstances. In general the strategies are appropriate (from the point of view of the focal organization) in the presence of low to moderate levels of uncertainty and low to moderate amounts of dependency on specific outside elements.

**1. Competitive response.** The first response to uncertainty concerning environmental support is to compete with others for that support.[7] The focal organization exploits its distinctive competence, builds better mousetraps, improves internal efficiency in the use of resources, etc. It is this strategy that provides one of the justifications for a market system. The organizations while pursuing their idiosyncratic goals of profit, growth, and survival must provide something useful to consumers. Those who do not are eliminated and denied support. The environment exercises indirect control over individual firms through the process of natural selection of those who are most fit, i.e., efficient.

The competitive response appears to be appropriate when the support capacity of the environment is dispersed. The situation of many small sellers and many small buyers which economists refer to as perfect competition is an example. The actions of a single buyer or seller have little impact on the others. The organizations are dependent only on the market, and the only way they can influence it is through better offerings and internal efficiency.

The selecting-out of firms during periods of scarcity, however, creates uncertainty for them. In addition, most markets have imperfections where the organization finds that its actions can have an effect. Under such conditions one would expect the organization to attempt to manage its environment.

**2. Public relations response.** Organizations attempt to establish and maintain favorable images in the minds of those making up the task environment.[8] They foster a favorable image through the mass media and skillful use of publicity. In some cases the prestige is merited due to effective offerings or efficient utilization of resources; however, the organization does not leave its reputation to chance or "word of mouth" processes. It attempts to get the word around, the right word, faster and more completely. The strategy is implemented by employing specialists who link the organization with media and represent an expenditure of resources on the part of the organization. The use of the mass media implies that this response is appropriate when environmental support is dispersed.

Successful public relations result in better chances to attract personnel, capital, customers, donors, students, volunteers, etc. During times of shortage and scarcity the prestigious organization may still attract support while less prestigious ones cannot. Organizations such as universities and hospitals in nonmarket situations find this strategy essential in competing for donations, students, and patients. Thompson suggests that the acquisition of prestige reduces dependence without giving up anything in return other than the effort expenditure.[9]

**3. Voluntary response.**  A third response is the voluntary management of and commitments to various interest groups, causes, and social problems. These commitments may be the voluntary control of pollution, hiring of disadvantaged groups, contributions to causes, etc. Most of these activities travel under the label of social responsibility and are usually, but need not be, attributed to business organizations. There has always been a great deal of controversy about these activities. Political economists and business policy professors are chief among those who ask questions as to what firms actually do in this area, why they do it, and what they should do.

The issue arises legitimately because there are market imperfections called externalities which render the competitive response inadequate.[10] That is, the firm, in pursuing its own objectives in the most efficient manner, does not satisfy or, indeed, may dissatisfy members of the task environment. One way it may do this is by polluting water through its production methods. A firm has no economic incentive to clean wastes put into a river. The downstream people pay the price. If the dumping firm invests in cleaning equipment, it receives no economic benefit on its investment. Thus, there is an imperfection in the market. There are a number of remedies put forth to bring about congruence between the interests of the firm and the interests of environment.

Some suggest government intervention through taxes on the pollution or through standards backed up by fines for deviance. These mechanisms either convert the situation back to a competitive response through a pseudo-price or render deviance illegal and provide for direct regulation of behavior. Others cite the *noblesse oblige* of management. It is suggested that managements do and should act voluntarily for the good of society. Government intervention would be redundant. The problem would be best handled by selecting socially responsible managers. Another view admits to the voluntary response by managements but imputes a self-interest motive. This view says that management invests in cleaning equipment in order to avoid government intervention. Whether voluntarism results from social responsibility values or from the avoidance of anticipated outside interference, organizations do voluntarily make compensations for market imperfections.

The line of reasoning being developed in this chapter suggests that, independent of the motives, it is in the organization's best interest, and in society's interest too, that the organization act voluntarily on certain environmental issues and over certain ranges of dependence and uncertainty. First and most obvious, the organization may avoid the stricter, more rigid standards set by outsiders. But the other and perhaps more significant reason is that outside intervention may reduce the organization's ability to act in the future. With technical changes and the passage of time, standards may become obsolete and detrimental. In order to change them, the organization must enter the political arena. If the response was voluntary, the resulting autonomy would permit the organization to adapt its technology to the new unforeseen circumstances and still maintain acceptable standards. It is this autonomy and ability to act that organizations try to preserve while being responsive to elements of the task environment. Thus, it is predicted that on market imperfections and social issues where interest groups are strong, organizations will act voluntarily either to avoid subsequent legislation and preserve autonomy, generate arguments for public relations, or simply to be socially responsible. In any case, the power of the outside interest group will help explain which of an infinite number of worthwhile causes is voluntarily supported.

The discussion so far has centered on voluntarism as applied to outside interest groups, the community and, finally, to the various regulatory and governmental units. However, the same approach applies to other parts of the task environment where the organization, for whatever reason, does more for an element of the task environment than is expected, than is required legally, or than is commonly practical. The result, whether from the pursuit of high ideals or to "get a leg up on the other guy," is that the focal organization can call on those favored elements of the task environment when scrambling for resources and support during a time of scarcity. Organizations often leave larger than necessary cash balances with banks in order to be able to get funds during tight money periods. Special treatment of customers, donors, investors, employees, etc., all create a certain amount of goodwill on which the firm may capitalize whether the accumulation of goodwill was or was not the intention behind the treatment. The instrumental value is usually recognized, however, and some firms go so far as to place a monetary value on goodwill, capitalize it, and place it on their balance sheet as an asset.

The use of voluntarism and, indeed, the use of all response is limited. The argument can be demonstrated for voluntarism more clearly due to some empirical work by Bowman.[11] He examined pollution control expenditures by pulp and paper manufacturers and related them to the firm's profitability. However the relation was not linear. If the firms were placed in groups of high, intermediate, and low expenditures, the intermediate group turns out to be the most profitable. He suggests that one interpretation is that firms must strike a balance and that deviation in either direction reduces profitability. A second study produced the same result. Bowman assumed that the annual reports of food industry firms would give some "straight talk" about social responsibility; that is, they understood that over-inflated boasts about social responsiveness would buy very little with stockholders interested in profits, growth, and dividends. He and Haire then scored the reports as a projective test on social responsibility. Again high- and low-ranking firms were less profitable than intermediate firms.

These studies suggest that if firms need support from the task environment, too little voluntarism generates too little support. On the other hand, there may be diminishing returns to the extent that too much voluntarism generates too little in return unless the act itself carries its own reward. For example, there is only so much support from bankers that can be guaranteed with cash balances. Additional cash, which the organization may not have, may not guarantee as much support as would the act of putting the banker on the board, an approach discussed in the next section. While the point is made for business firms using a profit goal, it seems likely that each response has limitations on the amount of environmental support it will generate and sustain per unit of cost expenditure of the response. Figure 14.1 shows the

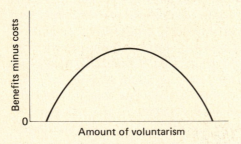

Fig. 14.1   Relation between amount of response and the returns from it.

suggested relation between voluntarism and returns to the organization. The relation suggests that there is a limited range of dependence for which voluntarism is appropriate. If dependence is too great, the organization must shift to another strategy of environmental management. The dependence may increase in any of the sectors of task environments largely due to market imperfections caused by concentrations of support in the hands of one or a few organizations. As task environment support becomes concentrated, organizations engage in strategic maneuvering and/or cooperative strategies.

In summary, three strategies for managing the environment have been suggested. They have in common the attribute that they permit responsiveness to environmental control but the control is through self-control. Responses other than the competitive one are initiated as markets become imperfect due to externalities and the concentration of support in the hands of a few. As that happens, the behavior of one buyer or seller has an influence on everyone else. The hypothesis is that organizations do not leave the consequences of that behavior to chance but engage in environmental management.

If the independent strategies do not guarantee support, or attain support at too high a cost, and the organization cannot change or judges it too costly to change task environments, it may select the alternative to engage in one of the cooperative strategies.

### Cooperative Strategies

The cooperative strategies, as their name implies, concern the coordinated actions of two or more organizations to resolve joint problems. These forms can involve competitors acting together, buyer and seller, union and employer, etc. As with the independent strategies, there are several alternatives which are appropriate under various conditions. In each case, however, the focal organization must yield some autonomy when making commitments and coordinating its actions.

In employing cooperative strategies, the focal organization recognizes that those elements of the task environment on whom it is dependent also have dependence problems of their own. Just as there are times when bank loans are scarce, there are times when loanable funds are plentiful and the banker becomes dependent on borrowers. Thus, it is interdependence that is the basis for cooperation between elements of the task environment and the focal organization. While the discussion that follows centers on the focal organization, keep in mind the fact that the elements of the environment on whom the organization is dependent are also, to varying degrees, dependent on the focal organization. The amount of dependence varies directly with the strength of the need for the support that an element can give and inversely with the abundance of elements that can give it. The amount of autonomy that the focal organization is willing to give up varies directly with amount of dependence.

**1. Implicit cooperation.** Organizations engage in forms of implicit cooperation when their behaviors become patterned, predictable, and coordinated with the behaviors of others, but when there is neither communication nor explicit attempts to coordinate those behaviors. There is no explicit communication quite often because it is illegal but also because it is redundant. These patterns of cooperation arise for a number of reasons and are sustained because they work; i.e., they reduce uncertainty in the competitive struggle for scarce resources. Quite often they arise when the independent responses by organizations become patterned. In working out their own problems, firms collectively and coincidentally arrive at a patterned response.

One of the reasons that these implicit forms arise is that managers share a common set of values and norms. There is quite often a norm of what constitutes good business practice. Indeed, Pfeffer explicitly draws the analogy between the developmental process of interfirm combines and small groups.[12] Experiments in social psychology suggest that individual behaviors become predictable to others and a pattern evolves without explicit communication. This result is pronounced when individuals are interdependent with respect to rewards.[13] Similar processes develop between firms who have interdependent reward systems or payoff functions. When there are a few other firms in the market, the focal organization can, over time, predict some of their responses. Then the other firms come to know that the focal firms knows. There is some "jockeying for position" before a stable pattern emerges where all firms know where they compete and where they cooperate. Given sufficient stability in the market, this group is just as organized as an explicitly designed group.[14] This type of implicit organization arises if there are a few firms. As the number increases, the task of predicting others' actions and implicit patterning becomes difficult.

Another model is the price leadership phenomenon. This model arises when there is a dominant firm in the industry and that firm sets the price which all others follow. The pattern is sustained by the belief that firms are better off acting together than competing separately and that deviance may be punished.

Thus, when there is a small number of firms or when power is concentrated in the hands of one or a few firms in an industry, the daily interactions in markets create enough information and communication to permit cooperation between firms. The assumption is that firms desire to use this information to reduce uncertainty which may arise from competition on sensitive or potentially disruptive issues while competing on the less essential ones. For example, large oil companies may compete for a corner gas station site but not on price increases resulting from higher crude charges from the Arabs. The ability to communicate through market interactions declines as the number of relevant firms increases and as changes affect the market. In these cases other mechanisms are needed to sustain cooperation. Pfeffer and Leblebici suggest that executive movement between firms in the same industry is such a mechanism for moderate concentrations of influence.[15] That is, if market interactions and press releases carry too little information, the hiring of executives from competing firms can bring in more. This practice is most effective for industries with modern sales concentrations. An industry where most sales are concentrated in the hands of one or two firms can achieve stability by relying on good business practice, information from market interactions, price leadership, etc. There is no need for outside recruiting. On the other hand, the industries where sales are dispersed among many firms, even intraindustry recruitment will not generate sufficient information to organize so as to reduce uncertainty. Pfeffer and Leblebici's results are consistent with this interpretation. As industries deviate from the average amount of concentration, there are proportionally fewer executives promoted from within, more from outside but from the same industry. The same phenomenon occurs for industries with high-growth rates and technological change. Both factors increase the need for information to maintain implicit cooperation. Over a range of variation in these phenomena and for moderate concentrations, executive recruitment can supply this information.

There is no assumption here that executive recruitment is a purposely planned mechanism. The recruiters are not necessarily aware of implicit organizations and probably hire the best person for the job. However in the industries above the best person for the job is an outsider from the same industry. The reason is that the outsider reduces uncertainty once he or she joins the firm. Over time, recruiters in moderately concentrated industries find that this recruiting pattern "works" while in other industries outsiders perform less well. They perform less well because they cannot reduce uncertainty any more than insiders can and have none of the insiders' local information. The assumption again is that practices that "work" for organizations are those that eliminate potentially disruptive uncertainties connected with the competitive scramble for scarce resources. Implicit cooperation also implies a loss of autonomy for the focal organization as it conforms to the accepted pattern.

This form of environmental management appears to be limited to managing relations between competitors, small numbers of competitors, and in situations of low to moderate technical change and growth. Organizations with large dependencies on other elements in the environment must seek other mechanisms. In the presence of rapid growth and technical change the information from market interactions and intraindustry executive recruitment is insufficient to agree on coordinated actions. Other more explicit cooperative forms involving more active relations between the interdependent organizations are required.

**2. Contracting.** One mechanism with a higher information capacity is contracting which is merely the negotiation of an agreement between the organization and another group to exchange goods, services, information, patents, commitments, etc., over some time period. Negotiation implies direct contact between the parties with the result being an explicit form of cooperation. Negotiation also implies a dialogue, an information exchange, and bargaining to reach the agreement on coordinated action. The agreement may be legally binding but may be based on reputation and trust as well.

Contracting between competitors in the United States is usually illegal. In Europe it is restricted but in other areas may be commonplace. Certainly contracting is a common form of interaction between buyers and sellers, unions and management, and regulator and regulated. It arises in situations "... when support is concentrated *and balanced against concentrated demand....*"[16] When support is concentrated, the support-seeking organization has fewer alternative sources and becomes more dependent on those who can provide it. When the effect is mutual, both parties can gain by an explicit agreement of exchange. For example, coal companies and electric utilities enter into long-term, 20-year contracts to reduce uncertainty for both and to permit costly, capital-intensive technological changes. Occasionally the parties cooperate by building a railroad line between the mine and the utility with specifically designed railroad cars for handling the coal in the specific situation. The 20-year commitment is necessary to reduce the potentially threatening uncertainty of the buyer–seller relationship. The geographical concentration of coal companies and utilities and power balance makes contracting the appropriate form of uncertainty reduction.

It takes greater dependence to create the motivation for contracting because contracting allows greater influence on the part of the environmental element than any of the previously discussed mechanisms. For example, the major airlines have greater influence on the design of aircraft produced by airframe manufacturers than automobile buyers have on the design of new models produced by automobile manufacturers. Pan Am directly entered the design process for the 707 and 747. Its representatives negotiated design criteria and helped create alternatives throughout the design process. On the other hand, auto companies certainly try to anticipate consumer preferences but the buyers' influence is simply one of accepting or rejecting an already designed model. There is no direct intervention in the design creation process. Indeed, some would say that the consumer has little influence and that auto companies through PR and advertising convince him or her to accept what the auto companies have created.[17] In either case, contracting gives the environmental element more influence in the decision process of the focal organization. The example shows that the airlines' demand power is concentrated in a few large carriers and their manufacturing power is concentrated in a few large companies. On the other hand, power is concentrated in the hands of a few auto companies but purchasing power dispersed in the hands of millions of drivers. The concentration of demand forces contracting rather than the implicit co-operation-competitive response as in the auto industry.

The fact that contracting is more inclusive and is seen as more costly by the focal organization can be illustrated again by the auto industry design process. The issue is safety standards. The airframe manufacturers and the FAA have for years negotiated safety standards for new designs. The negotiations were particularly intense on issues of number and location of engines on 727s, DC–9s, and 737s. However, the airframe manufacturers' engineers have always negotiated designs with NASA, the Department of Defense, Pan Am, TWA, as well as the FAA whose representatives are physically located on the manufacturers' premises. This type of negotiation, however, is seen as government intervention by auto company engineers. From the popular press, one gets the idea that it is the outside intervention rather than the safety standards themselves that is being resisted. There is good reason for resistance. While auto company engineers always negotiated with auto company marketing, it is quite another thing to negotiate with government standards people. The government people have different goals, terminology, and points of view and have not been socialized into the auto industry ideology, all of which makes conflict more likely. In addition, conflict resolution is more difficult because there is neither an operational higher level goal (profit) nor a hierarchy of authority to which to appeal. The situation calls for skills which are new to the design team.

In summary, contracting is an explicit form of cooperation involving negotiation and two-way communication between the interdependent parties. The parties negotiate only those issues that are important to the task environment and which cannot be managed through independent actions or implicit cooperation. The issues are generally around uncertainty of future actions where the signaling and cueing of implicit cooperation do not provide enough information for coordination. On the issues involved, the power is usually concentrated in the hands of a few but balanced against concentrated power. Contracting is a more inclusive form than any of the previously mentioned forms. As a result, from the point of view of the focal organization, it is a more costly form. It results in a loss of autonomy, (the organization generally gives up more), and involves a greater amount of management time and energy. Thus, contracting is used when the dependence and uncertainty are so great that independent and implicit cooperation cannot manage them or are too costly to manage them. However, contracting itself is limited. What happens when environmental support is concentrated but not balanced? The contracts can be too one-sided for the focal organization. It can still try to reduce dependence through strategic maneuvering but if it must live with dependence, it must seek another form of environmental management.

## Coopting

The next cooperative strategy of environmental management is cooptation. "Cooptation" has been defined as the process of absorbing new elements into the leadership or policymaking structure of an organization as a means of averting threats to its stability or existence."[18] For example, firms needing capital resources often have bankers on their boards of directors when these boards are used for policymaking. Thus, to the degree that boards of directors, boards of trustees, advisory boards or advisory councils perform policymaking functions, one would predict that cooptation would consist of placing representatives from the task environment on those bodies in exchange for support from the represented elements.

Cooptation, like contracting, has its cost for the focal organization. The reason is that the coopted element is in a position to exercise more influence than in any of the previous forms. By sitting on a board responsible for leadership and policy, outsiders can influence a *greater range* of issues than they can in contracting. Contracting may involve environmental control only for long-term sale agreements, for example, but may exclude the buyer's direct influence over capital structure, employee relations, who is to be the next president, where the new plant is to be located, etc., all of which are fair game for the board member. Greater influence also results from the higher level of the organization at which the contact takes place. Contracting may involve negotiations between purchasing and sales departments of the respective firms where cooptation involves top-management contact. This is not always the case, however. One would presume that contact occurred between the presidents of Boeing and Pan Am during the creation of the 747. But the majority of contact takes place between the engineers. Therefore, high-level contact on a broad range of issues gives the outsider the potential for more influence than do the previously mentioned forms if the board is used for policymaking. In return, the organization doing the coopting gets support from the coopted element. Thus, "... the strategy of cooptation involves exchanging some degree of control and privacy of information for some commitment of continued support from the external organization."[19]

The focal organization would choose to use cooptation only when other forms are inadequate. Thompson predicts that cooptation occurs "... when support capacity is concentrated *but demand dispersed* (italics supplied)."[20] Again, the best example is the banker placed on a firm's board of directors. Usually there are a few large banks in any region and a potentially large number of borrowers. The firm which depends on external funds finds it necessary to include the banker in policymaking in order to have access to funds during a scarcity. Thus it requires dependence on an external group, uncertainty concerning continuous availability of the group's support, and the inability or illegality of other mechanisms.

There is some support for portions of the argument put forth above, thanks primarily to the work of Pfeffer.[21] First, boards can be used for several functions—administration, environmental linkage, ceremony, minimal legal compliance, etc. Pfeffer's study of hospitals shows that those which are more dependent on the local community for resources are more likely to use their boards for linkage in attaining these resources. Hospitals funded by the federal government were less dependent, had smaller boards, and used them to aid in administering the hospital. In the study of business firms, he finds a greater number of directors and a greater proportion of outside directors for organizations with high debt-to-equity ratios (greater dependence on outside borrowing and funds) and for companies in regulated industries. While regulated companies cannot put regulators on the board, they can appoint socially and politically prominent people to create a favorable climate or impression. Thus, variations in dependency are associated with the use of boards as cooptive mechanisms. Second, when boards are used for linking purposes, their composition can be explained by dependency needs of the organization and the makeup of the task environment. Hospitals with needs for outside funding use people financial institutions while hospitals funded by national foundations and religious orders seek subgroup representation regardless of the economic or political clout of that subgroup. Urban hospitals have more representation from manufacturing organizations while rural hospitals appoint people from agricultural organizations. Boards of firms in regulated industries have greater proportions of lawyers. Since these organizations are dependent on the environment, variations in dependency and environmental context are associated with variations in composition of director makeup. Similarly, the size of boards varies with the number of functions it must perform, the number of links needed to provide resources, the amount of dependence on outside funding and the amount of government regulation. In short, dependence and task environment context can predict the function of, the composition of, and size of boards of directors for hospitals and corporations.

The most significant finding of the studies, however, is the relation between size and composition of boards and organizational performance. It is a contingent one. That is, given the organization's external dependence and the context of the task environment, one can predict the board size and composition of the average organization in that position by statistical means, (e.g., regression analysis). As hospitals and firms deviate from that average, their performance declines. This finding is critical to the position taken in this chapter. The organization can have too many outsiders, (i.e., it gives up too much control for the support received), or too few, (i.e., it does not get the support on which it is dependent or it can have the wrong elements represented). The important thing is to achieve a fit between the organization's dependency and the function, size, and composition of its board.

The one aspect of the argument not tested is the assertion that contracting is more costly than implicit cooperation and independent strategies while cooptation is more costly than contracting. One might accept this based on some anecdotal evidence. Most organizations appear to resist collective bargaining when they have an option to do so preferring to keep autonomous their responses to employee needs. It is only when grape picker boycotts force them to recognize organized labor groups that firms do so. One would predict IBM would prefer not to have a union and bargain collectively with it. The argument is not a clean one because one may be able to find companies that voluntarily choose to have a union. However, their behavior may be motivated by a desire to choose the union, by a recognition of the inevitable, or by a recognition that contracting is appropriate given their power/dependence position.

The argument can be bolstered by the behavior of some northern European countries. In an effort to increase the power of labor for ideological reasons or to counter the power of multinationals, Holland, Sweden, and West Germany have enacted legislation to put workers in varying percentages on boards of directors. In other words, to increase the amount of influence of workers on decisions, the governments are trying to shift from a contracting, collective-bargaining relation between labor and management to a forced form of cooptation.

In response, one can find management opposition. It is particularly obvious in, but not confined to, Britain where the legislation is now being drafted and debated following the election of the labor majority in the fall of 1974. Also in West Germany there are attempts to strengthen the legislation because organizations can successfully subvert the attempt by changing the functions of the board (much the way decision making shifts when students and nontenured faculty become members of policy committees in universities) to more ceremonial activities while the real power shifts to the executive committee or to the more amorphous inner circles. To indicate that cooptation also implies support from the coopted group, one can cite the opposition from socialist and communist unions in Latin European countries. Codetermination within the capitalist system is not what they want. Thus, some governments apparently think that representation on boards of directors gives the represented more influence in decision making than collective bargaining does. These efforts are resisted in most countries by the companies who presumably see the change as reducing their autonomy and ability to profitably allocate resources. The interpretation above of anecdotal evidence is consistent with Thompson's argument that cooptation is more costly to the focal organization than are the previously mentioned forms. More will be said about this in the summary.

## Coalition

The last form of interorganizational cooperation is for two or more groups to coalesce and act jointly with respect to some set of issues for some period of time. Each unit keeps its own identity while acting jointly. Examples are price-fixing cartels and multinational joint ventures. This form of explicit cooperation is presumed to be the most limiting on individual action. For the time period of the agreement, the organization can act jointly only on the issues at stake. Thompson suggests that the agreement is not one of exchange only but is also a commitment to joint decision making. One will not act without consulting the other partners. Therefore, it has the greatest amount of inclusion of environmental elements.

While the cartel is not explicit in the United States, the joint venture among various groups is quite common. Even the big oil companies coalesce when looking for oil in the North Sea or Alaska. Other research activities having payoffs for a group, requiring large amounts of resources, and having high risk usually result in joint ventures.

The conditions for coalescing are stated to exist "...when support capacity is concentrated and balanced against concentrated demands, but the power achieved through contracting is inadequate...."[22] The best examples of this phenomenon are the international combines or ventures that are beginning to arise.[23] Examples are the agreement for engine development work between Renault, Volvo, and Peugeot; agreement between the French aircraft firm SNECMA and General Electric to make low-pollution jet engines; and the financial combine of Italian Banco de Roma, the French Crédit Lyonnais, and West German Commerzbank.[24] A better example is the unidata combination of Siemans (West German), Phillips (Dutch), and CII (French) in order to compete with IBM in the world computer market. Contracting may have been used before to share patents and new ideas in order to reduce uncertainty in that area. Or it may have been used to divide the market so as to concentrate on IBM and not on each other. However, the choice is to jointly develop new products. The joint venture involves sharing funding for research, joint decisions on where research is to be performed, by whom, from where is the scientific talent to come, etc. If production is also joint, a whole new set of decisions arise. Where will what portions be produced? How will capital spending on new equipment be shared? What are the tax problems? How will profits/losses be shared? How will prices in different markets be set? How will export sales be shared? Who will be project manager? Thus, a joint technical-production venture requires considerable joint decision making in a large number of areas. As one moves from sharing patents, licenses, and technical ideas (contracting) to sharing technical development to sharing production, the members reduce duplication, gain economies of scale, and eliminate competition between themselves at a cost of a loss in autonomy and sovereignty. One moves to an almost total commitment to joint decision making which may be the only feasible way to compete with IBM, Honeywell-Bull, etc. Perlmutter predicts this type of interorganizational cooperation is an alternative to multinational giantism and allows the maintenance of the individual unit identities. He suggests that in the future the computer combine would eventually join with a Japanese firm and a Czechoslovakian firm to achieve a true global combine.[25]

One can find some theorists who, like Perlmutter, predict an increasing amount of organizational interdependence and environmental change.[26] As each focal organization tries to chart an adaptive course, it merely adds to the turbulence. Some form of macroorganization is necessary if societies are to be masters of their own destinies when faced with turbulent environments. There is a good deal of effort going into the search for these organization forms.[27]

If one continues with the degree of coalescing, there comes a point where the parties have lost their individual identities. This point suggests that there is a final step in the process of managing task environments, that step is to change the task environment itself. Rather than continue to coopt, contract, etc., it may be easier to merge with or absorb other elements, when that alternative is legal, or engage in other forms of strategic maneuvering. This maneuvering attempts to eliminate dependence, not manage it.

### Strategic Maneuvering

The mechanisms discussed so far attempted to manage environmental dependence for a *given* task environment. However, if the organization is not able to generate sufficient support in that task environment or can do so only at substantial costs, it can try to change or alter task environments. The obvious alteration is to carry coalescing one step further into a merger. The joint decision making can now take place under a hierarchy of authority to speed decision making if nothing else.

Once again this form of activity has been examined empirically by Pfeffer.[28] And once again his findings support Thompson's arguments that resource interdependencies between organizations can explain a good deal of merger activity and that these mergers take place to reduce uncertainty connected with competing for these resources rather than purely economic opportunistic reasons.

It is apparent after fifty years of research that if mergers are made
to increase profitability or to share prices, they are not particularly
successful in doing so. . . . It is hypothesized here . . . that mergers are
an attempt on the part of organizations to reduce uncertainty and
manage their environments.[29]

In addition to explaining large amounts of merger activity on the basis
of resource exchanges between the merged units, Perlmutter also shows
that merger activity is contingent on industry concentration and the relation
is the same U-shaped curve. That is, in highly concentrated industries, there
is little merger activity because it is either unnecessary or illegal. It can be
unnecessary because implicit cooperation and price leadership may be sufficient to generate stability. In highly competitive industries with many firms,
there is also little merger activity. This time there is none because it is
useless. The merger of several small firms still leaves a small firm among
many others with no reduction in uncertainty. It is only in the intermediate
range that large numbers of mergers take place. The contingent relation is
also consistent with the prior studies and arguments.

Merger is not the only form of strategic maneuvering. As a matter of
fact, there are an infinite number of forms which depend only on the ingenuity of the maneuvering organization. While not all organizations have
such freedom, most organizations can make and remake decisions about
their strategy, their technology, and their physical location with some degree of latitude. Organizations can try to acquire power through growth or
to reduce dependence by diversifying through new products or new markets. They can change technology to reduce dependence on a single source
of energy. And some can move to more receptive physical locations. In each
case, the organization changes the elements of the task environment presumably in a direction of less dependence, greater autonomy, or less cost
for the focal organization.

## SUMMARY

The chapter has discussed various ways in which the organization can act
on and manage its environment. These interactions with other groups in
the environment took place around points of dependency where the focal
organization required support from those groups. The uncertainty concerning continued support was reduced by including these others in the goal-
setting and resource-allocation processes of the organization. The choice
for the organization is one of getting the support it needs without giving
up too much of its autonomy to act in the future. How much autonomy it
would give up depends on the degree of dependency on the support, the

uncertainty of support, and the availability of other task environments. The choice of mechanism of interaction determines the degree to which the outside group is included in the organization's decision process, the degree to which they can influence it, and the amount of information they have about the focal organization. Thus, the mechanism determines how much control is given up to get the support on which the organization is dependent. It is this contingent relation that appears critical and untested. The arguments of Thompson and empirical works of Bowman and Pfeffer are consistent with the contingency relation. Presumably the mechanisms can be ordered as in Fig. 14.2.

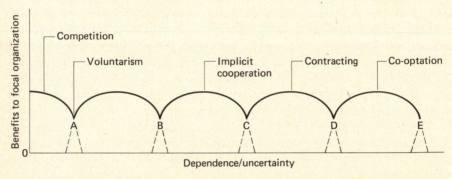

**Fig. 14.2   Graph of mechanism contingency on external dependence/uncertainty.**

Figure 14.2 suggests that for small amounts of market imperfections and externalities, voluntarism is appropriate (from the point of view of the focal organization) for obtaining support without giving up too much autonomy. The relation is consistent with Bowman's findings. The curve from points A to B signifies the range of dependence appropriate for a voluntary response. Greater dependency requires a shift to forms of cooperation represented by the curve from B to E. Subsections of the curve such as from C to D indicate where contracting secures the needed support without giving up too much. Other parts of the contracting curve are less effective at managing the dependence indicated. Either implicit forms or cooptation would be preferable.

In specific situations, the curves probably are not so clearly distinguished. Often some alternatives are not available, are illegal, or are just undesirable. The shapes of the curves and whether the peaks are on the same level (as shown), increase, decrease or increase then decrease, etc. is not known. The diagram does indicate the kinds of assertions one can draw from Thompson's theory and which cannot be rejected.

Finally, it is difficult to be normative in this chapter. The point of view of the focal organization was adopted in order to be consistent with the rest of the book, but it is not always true that what is "best for General Motors is best for the country too." More specific contexts are needed. For example, price-fixing coalitions are illegal, but a coalition between federal, local, and private organizations to create jobs and training programs for the handicapped is desirable. The movement of executives between firms in the same industry is not illegal but may be controversial. An exchange between a regulatory agency and regulated firm is illegal. The characteristics of the specific situation must be evaluated as well as the specific organization's interest.

Chapter 15 faces some of these same issues but adopts the perspective of analyzing a specific problem—the production-smoothing problem. Let us analyze the attempts of organizations to manage their external relations around the exigencies of this problem.

## NOTES

1. See E. H. Schein 1971. The individual, the organization, and the career: a conceptual scheme. *Journal of Applied Behavioral Science* 7: 401–426.

2. J. D. Thompson 1967. *Organizations in action*. New York: McGraw-Hill, Chapter 3.

3. Thompson uses the concept of domain here. However, I think strategy is usually employed for the choice of products and markets to serve. I. Ansoff 1965. *Corporate strategy*. New York: McGraw-Hill.

4. This four-way classification is what Dill and Thompson have called the *task environment*. W. R. Dill 1958. Environment as an influence on autonomy. *Administrative Science Quarterly*.

5. W. Evan 1966. The organization set: toward a theory of interorganizational relations. In J. D. Thompson (ed.), *Approaches to organizational design*. Pittsburgh: University of Pittsburgh Press.

6. J. D. Thompson and W. J. McEwen 1958. Organizational goals and environment: goal-setting as an interaction process. *American Sociological Review*, (February): 23–31.

7. Thompson, *Organizations*.

8. C. Perrow 1961. "Organizational prestige: some functions and dysfunctions. *American Journal of Sociology*, (January): 335–341.

9. Thompson, *Organizations*, pp. 23–31.

10. For example, see J. Buchanan and W. C. Stubblebine 1962. Externality. *Economica*, (November): 371–384.

11. E. H. Bowman and M. Haire 1975. A strategic posture with respect to corporate social responsibility. *California Management Review*, (Winter): 49–58.

12. J. Pfeffer and H. Leblebici 1973. Executive recruitment and the development of interfirm organizations. *Administrative Science Quarterly*, (December): 449–450.

13. H. J. Leavitt 1962. Unhuman organizations. *Harvard Business Review*, (July-August): 90–98.

14. A. Phillips 1960. A theory of interfirm organization. *Quarterly Journal of Economics* 74: 602–613. O. Williamson 1965. A dynamic theory of interfirm behavior. *Quarterly Journal of Economics* 79: 579–607.

15. Pfeffer and Leblebici.

16. Thompson, *Organizations*, p. 79.

17. J. K. Galbraith 1958. *The affluent society*. Boston: Houghton Mifflin.

18. Thompson and McEwen, p. 27. The quote follows from P. Selznick's original work 1949. *TVA and the grass roots*. University of California Press.

19. J. Pfeffer 1972. Size and composition of corporate boards of directors: the organization and its environment. *Administrative Science Quarterly*, (June): 222.

20. Thompson, *Organizations*, Chapter 3.

21. Pfeffer, pp. 218–228. J. Pfeffer 1973. Size, composition, and function of hospital boards of directors: a study of organizational environmental linkage. *Administrative Science Quarterly*, (September): 349–364.

22. Thompson, *Organizations*, p. 81.

23. See the work of H. Perlmutter, especially The multinational firm and the future, 1972. *Annals of the American Academy of Political and Social Science*, (September: 139–152.

24. *Ibid.*, pp. 142–3.

25. *Ibid.*, pp. 142–3.

26. F. Emery and E. L. Trist 1965. The causal texture of organizational environments. *Human Relations* 18: 21–32.

27. F. Emery and E. L. Trist 1973. *Toward a social ecology*. London: Tavistock. D. F. Berry, L. Metcalfe, and W. McQuillan 1974. Neddy: an organizational metamorphosis. *Journal of Management Studies*, (February): 1–20. L. Metcalfe 1976. Systems models, economic models, and the causal texture of organizational environments: an approach to macroorganization theory. *Human Relations* Vol. 27, No. 3 201–238.

28. J. Pfeffer 1972. Merger as a response to organizational interdependence. *Administrative Science Quarterly*, (September): 382–394.

29. *Ibid.*, p. 385.

## QUESTIONS

1. Select an organization with which you are familiar and identify the relevant insiders and outsiders. Illustrate how they impact decision processes.

2. Describe how a change in strategy of the organization discussed in question 1 will change the points of dependence on the environment and generate a new set of relevant outsiders.

3. Why are cooperative strategies more costly than independent ones?

4. Choose a particular form of voluntarism and discuss the pursuit of that form by referring to Fig. 14.1.

5. What is the difference between implicit and explicit forms of cooperation among organizations?

6. Explain the relationship between the number of firms in an industry and the effectiveness of implicit cooperation as an environmental management technique.

7. Explain why contracting, coopting, and coalescing represent increasing amounts of control over the focal organization by the relevant environmental parties.

8. From your experience, knowledge, or recent readings of *Business Week, Fortune, Forbes,* etc. give an example of environmental manuevering.

9. Choose an industry with significant environmental management problems and describe the environmental management techniques it uses. Discuss them in terms of Fig. 14.2.

<table>
<tr><td>ORGANIZATION AND ENVIRONMENT:<br>AN EXAMPLE OF PRODUCTION<br>SMOOTHING[1]</td><td>CHAPTER<br>**15**</td></tr>
</table>

Chapter 14 discussed the strategies by which an organization could manage its environment. This chapter illustrates that framework by analyzing a specific problem, the production-smoothing problem, and by using the concepts of that framework.

The chapter first describes the nature of the problem and how the organization becomes dependent on the user and then others in the task environment. Then the independent and cooperative strategies will be described by which some organizations manage this dependence. Finally the strategic maneuvering of organizations with critical problems will be discussed.

## THE SMOOTHING PROBLEM

The smoothing problem begins with the fact that all organizations have fixed resources—hospital rooms, classrooms, airplanes, computers, machine shops, etc. These resources produce goods and services for which there is a demand from the organization's customers or clients. The smoothing problem arises because the times and quantities of service which make up the users' desired consumption pattern seldom coincide with times and quantities which make for efficient utilization of the resource. The demands for service may vary both randomly or systematically on a daily, weekly, yearly, or cyclic basis. The resource itself is usually available continuously and at a constant rate of service. The relationship between a pattern of demand and a level of resource capacity is illustrated in Fig. 15.1.

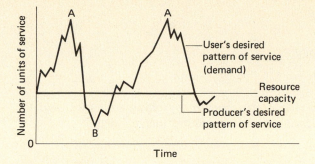

Fig. 15.1 Contrast between user's and producer's ideal patterns of resource use and availability.

If the supplying organization must provide instantaneous service, it must purchase enough fixed resource capacity to meet a peak demand (point A in Fig. 15.1). Then during a slack period (point B in Fig. 15.1) the resource is utilized at only 1/10 its potential capacity. If the organization could smooth the demand pattern to fit the resource availability, it could purchase fewer resources (enough to meet only the average demand) and use them continuously. The greater the cost of the fixed resource, the greater the need for a smooth demand pattern. However, the users may not want to alter their consuming behavior. Therein lies the smoothing problem for our focal organization. How does it smooth demand without giving too much in return? The lengths to which an organization will go depends on the nature of the output, the divisibility of the resource, the amount of resources invested in the fixed resources, and the power of the user of the resource.

The strategies for solving the problem fall into the categories already discussed.

*Independent Strategies*

1. Slack
2. Slack substitutes
3. Demand influence

*Cooperative Strategies*

1. Implicit cooperation
2. Contracting
3. Coalition

*Strategic Maneuvering*

1. Change in strategy
2. Change in technology
3. Change in location

Let us proceed by considering each response, by citing examples, and by interpreting the result in terms of environmental management.

## INDEPENDENT STRATEGIES

Most organizations are able to reach an accommodation with users of their services and with other elements in their task environment by employing the independent strategies. These strategies manipulate variables that the organization controls and permit self-control despite environmental inter-dependence.

### Slack

The first independent strategy is to employ slack to uncouple the use of the resource from the consumption of its services. The uncoupling involves the accumulation of finished product in the form of an inventory for goods-producing organizations and an accumulation of an order backlog for service providers and manufacturers with products which are difficult to store. Any discrepancy between supply and demand is absorbed by the slack resource or buffer which in this case is the inventory or backlog. This function of the inventory is shown in Fig. 15.2.

The use of inventory allows both user and consumer to behave in their desired ways but creates costs for the accumulating organization. These

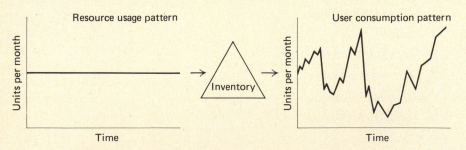

**Fig. 15.2  Illustration of uncoupling of production and consumption.**

costs must be balanced against the savings in resource utilization. There are a number of mathematical means for analyzing these trade-offs.[1] However, if the swings in demand become large, the amount of inventory necessary for uncoupling becomes quite large and expensive. Also, order backlogs require the users to wait. They may go to a competitor instead. These organizations must balance customer service against resource utilization.

In general, the organization must arrive at an acceptable state of affairs, i.e., one that the task environment and the focal organization are willing to live with, by balancing the inventory holding costs, the costs of user delay, and the costs of underutilization of fixed resources.

The balancing of the costs and benefits of buffers is the production-smoothing problem. Many organizations are able to achieve smooth operations by using buffer inventories and order backlogs. However, other organizations that face fluctuating demands for quick service while producing nonstorable or perishable outputs must find other ways to solve the smoothing problem or find ways to get rid of it. It is from these organizations that we can learn most about solutions to smoothing problems.

### Slack Substitutes

The next independent strategy is the use of slack substitutes. That is, organizations reduce inventory investment by varying factors which will trade off with inventories. For organizations with labor-intensive operations this means varying the work force or utilization of the work force. These strategies attempt to give the smoothing problem to another element of the task environment. The commonality of all the techniques in this section is that they take the demand pattern as given and adjust capacity to meet it.

**1. Work force utilization.** The first buffer substitute is work force utilization. That is, by varying the amount of overtime and undertime or the length of the workweek, organizations can reduce the amount of inventory or size of backlog to meet a given demand pattern.[2] Overtime is probably the most flexible buffer substitute in that it can be used for all types of demand fluctuations—daily, weekly, or seasonal. The best example of a user of work force utilization as a smoothing strategy is the auto industry. The high unit cost and diversity of the items make inventory accumulation costly. In addition the UAW union, through supplemental unemployment benefits, has made layoffs expensive. In order to meet seasonal and other demand fluctuations, the producers vary the length of the workweek from 32 to 50 hours.[3]

**2. Work force size.**   A second strategy is to vary the size of the work force instead of the utilization of a given size work force. As demand increases and decreases, the size of the work force is increased and decreased in synchronization by hiring and layoff. This strategy is used usually for the seasonal and business cycle fluctuations. Indeed, the classic version of the production-smoothing problem is the trade-off between inventory, overtime, and work force size in the context of a seasonal sales pattern.[4] Implicitly assumed is a work force that is willing to accept this hiring and layoff.

**3. Product mix.**   Another variable sometimes controllable by the organization is the product mix. This strategy operates by varying the labor intensity of the output in synchronization with the demand fluctuation.[5] That is, the organization produces items with high-labor content in slow periods and items with low-labor content in peak periods. In this manner, the production rate is varied while holding the work force constant. The strategy assumes that inventory is also used for smoothing.

**4. Subcontracting.**   A well-known smoothing technique in job shops is subcontracting. The amount of subcontracting is varied in synchronization with the demand fluctuations. During slow periods all work is produced internally, while in peak periods bottleneck operations are eliminated by using outside production. This strategy is usually combined with overtime in eliminating bottlenecks in job shops. Overtime is used in the short run and subcontracting for the long run. To be a viable strategy, there must be capacity available on the market at the desired times.

One of the points brought out by an examination of the smoothing problem is the process by which a problem in one sector of the task environment affects or is passed on to other elements. That is, a problem in smoothing demand, a producer-buyer relation, is shifted to the employees by varying the size of work force. If the employees have power and the customers have power, the organization can shift the problem either to suppliers through subcontracting or to stockholders by underutilizing capital resources. Thus, the smoothing problem, often analyzed as an economic problem, is also a political problem and the least powerful element in the environment usually absorbs the ups and downs.

We are now in a position to state that if the demands for organizational service vary, then one or some combination of the following factors *mus* also vary:

1. Utilization of work force
   a) overtime—undertime
   b) workweek

2. Level of work force

3. Product mix

4. Subcontracting

5. Utilization of fixed facilities

6. Inventory

7. Customer service (back orders)

For the majority of organizations, some combination of these factors can be combined into a strategy which is acceptable to the parties most affected. However, for many organizations, the variables above cannot be combined to satisfy customers, clients, labor unions, controllers, sales managers, and production managers simultaneously. It is to the strategies for solving these more difficult problems that we now turn.

### Influencing Demand

The first sections presented discussions of ways in which the supply and demand could be uncoupled and in which the capacity could be adapted to a given demand pattern. In this section we are interested in organizations that have been able to reduce smoothing costs by influencing the quantities and the timing of demand to conform to a pattern which is more consistent with the resource availability pattern. For most organizations the controllable variables which influence demand are promotion and price. The objective is to shift demand from sales peaks into the sales valleys by contracyclical pricing and promotion. Some attempts have been made to model the problem.[6]

**1. Promotion.** The first method of influencing demand is to advertise so as to increase awareness or promise better service in periods of low activity. An example of such a promotion is the NIMS (Nationwide Improved Mail Service) program of the post office. Part of this program is to persuade users to submit mail at various times during the day. Currently most mail is deposited at five o'clock, causing a surge in work load and delivery delays. The post office offers better service for complying customers. The primary objective is to level the incoming work load.

Another example is the flower grower.[7] Most flowers are purchased for special days. These days occur mostly during one half of the year (Christmas, Valentine's Day, Easter, Memorial Day, Mother's Day, June weddings). From June to Christmas there is only the normal funeral business.

Since the growers have substantial fixed costs in the form of land and greenhouses, they would like continuous use of these fixed resources. However, the inability to carry inventory means they must have capacity to meet spring peaks and remain somewhat idle the remainder of the year. Their response has been an attempt to create new demand in the form of impulse buying during summer and fall months. In this case, the organizations are not trying to shift demand from peaks to valleys but create new demand to fill the valleys.

**2. Price.** The second method of influencing the timing of demand is to offer lower prices in slow periods than in peak periods to encourage a shifting of demand from peak to slack times. The organizations with the most extensive experience with this strategy are the commercial airlines, electric utilities, and the telephone company, all organizations which must give quick service and have nonstorable output. Not all of their attempts have been successful.

The smoothing problem facing the airlines for example is quite difficult. The demand peaks on a daily, weekly, and seasonal cycle. The combination of expensive equipment and an inability to use slack make these fluctuations problematic. Thus, the airlines have attempted to influence the demand pattern by offering reduced fares at slack times. Some shifting of demand has occurred on the weekly peaks but not on the daily and seasonal. That is, the 25 percent reduction for excursion fares can persuade the traveler to start the trip on a Tuesday rather than on a Monday and to return on a Thursday or Saturday rather than on a Friday. The fare reductions do not encourage the travelers to fly at night or to fly to Europe in the winter and Puerto Rico in the summer. The airlines have evolved other techniques for these fluctuations.

**3. Rationing.** The last method of smoothing demand is to resort to rationing. This involves refusing orders from nonregular customers or granting a percentage of demand to all customers. While not a happy alternative, it does perform the function of smoothing the fillable demands to be compatible with resource availability. The so-called brownouts by electric utilities are an example.

### Summary

This section has described the independent strategies for dealing with production-smoothing problems. First, organizations simply deal with the trade-offs between the costs of customer delay (backlogs), inventory accumulation, and resource capacity utilization. If a satisfactory state of affairs cannot be achieved, organizations then attempt to vary capacity in order to meet the demand pattern. This strategy often involves giving the problem to someone else such as the work force, while reducing inventories or customer delays. If unions object to work force variation or the nature of the product prohibits accumulation of inventory, the organization tries to influence demand so as to conform to capacity availability. In each case, the organization attempts to come to terms with its task environment but does so by manipulating policies that it controls such as product mix, price, promotion, etc. Thus, responsiveness through independent action is the essence of these strategies.

For the vast majority of organizations, these techniques would achieve a very acceptable state of affairs. But if we analyze the techniques used by some firms which have particularly troublesome smoothing problems, more can be learned about ways organizations interact with their environments. Let us turn to the cooperative strategies.

## COOPERATIVE STRATEGIES

The cooperative strategies arise when a pair or a group of organizations act in a coordinated fashion in order to obtain solutions to joint problems. The strategies usually involve a synchronization of the operations of a number of organizations. These strategies are difficult to utilize since the synchronization of activities takes place in the absence of an authority relationship. This is their primary distinction from the smoothing techniques mentioned in the first section.

Three cooperative strategies are identified—implicit cooperation, contracting, and coalition. These three differ primarily on the strength of commitment between the cooperators. The coalition requires the strongest commitment in place of the authority relation.

The strategies of implicit cooperation and coalition formation usually involve cooperation between organizations in the same industry. Contracting is a strategy which involves cooperation between supplier and user.

### Implicit Cooperation

The strategy of implicit cooperation occurs when the smoothing problem affects the structure of the industry. The situation seems to evolve when the independent responses of a number of firms become patterned in order to make effective use of a smoothing technique. In the cases to be described, technological change and mechanization caused firms to adapt. The subset of original firms which remained after the adaptation survived because they fit into the patterned response. There is no evidence that there was overt collusion. The patterned response and resulting solution to the smoothing problem was obtained through the workings of the market.

**1. The coal industry.** The coal industry has always faced a seasonal pattern of demand, the amplitude of which has been reduced recently by the loss of the home-heating market.[8] The smoothing problem arises because it is difficult to hold an inventory in storage. The commodity is bulky and is subject to spontaneous combustion. Work force variation is costly, due to the unions, and of limited usefulness, due to the highly mechanized technology of coal mining. Nor is variation in capacity utilization an attractive substitute. The mechanized capacity is usually specific to a particular mine and therefore quite expensive. The alternative of acquiring capacity to meet a peak demand is to be avoided. The solution to the problem can be seen by viewing the organizational design of the vertically integrated firms.

The vertically integrated firms in the coal industry were usually steel companies that had acquired mines in order to guarantee a continuous source of high-quality coking coals. They designed the capacity of their mines, however, to produce only the minimum amount of coal as determined by the seasonal and business cycle fluctuations. In Fig. 15.3 the sales pattern shows a seasonal variation.

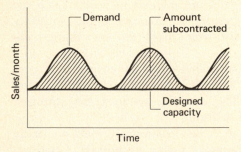

**Fig. 15.3 Productive capacity designed to meet minimum sales requirements.**

The firm faced with this pattern would design its capacity as shown and purchase from others an amount indicated by the shaded portion. The result is that the integrated firm can acquire equipment specific to rates of output and guarantee continuous utilization of capacity. The large nonvertically integrated firms have made similar adjustments to their capacities. As a substitute for vertical integration, these firms have 20-year requirements contracts with large electric utilities to provide the stable demand.

The problem which may arise when using subcontracting or outside purchases to meet peak demands was mentioned earlier in the chapter. It requires that there exist organizations that are willing to accept the fluctuations on a regular basis so that the integrated firm can depend upon them to meet its peak. It is this point that suggests the cooperativeness of the solution. In the coal industry there are many small firms which could not mechanize their facilities due to the large capital requirements. Instead they have remained very flexible. They generally are not unionized, have favorable locations which permit them to compete, or have owners willing to accept low rates of return. Their flexibility and the design of the integrated firms have allowed them to exist. Collectively this structure of large, integrated firms and small, independent firms represents an implicitly cooperative solution to the smoothing problem.

**2. The oil industry.** Technological change has brought about a similar reaction in the oil industry.[9]

The refineries of most of the integrated companies are designed to provide a large fraction of the firm's marketing requirements. The remainder is purchased from the small refineries. Further, the small refinery is designed to be flexible so that it can quickly adjust product mixes and rates of output. The flexibility of the small refinery allows the large refinery to be designed for specific rates of output and guarantees continuous use. The large refineries have cost curves such as those shown in Fig. 15.4. These are

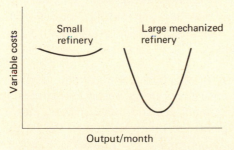

**Fig. 15.4   Variable costs reflecting flexibility.**

contrasted with those of the flexible plant. The rising variable costs make through-put maintenance a primary objective of the smoothing program, and are another reason for buffering. Again, there is a cooperative solution to what is a critical production-smoothing problem. It is also probable that the total industry cost for meeting demand is less than it would be if all plants were designed to be flexible.

The picture which emerges from these examples is that technological change can lead to expensive plants and/or rising variable costs. The result is that continuous operation at specific rates is the desired mode of operation without overcapacity. Thus, the mechanized firms become more dependent on demand and require some form of environmental management. For some industries what has evolved is an implicitly cooperative strategy of integrated mechanized units designed to provide a fraction of the next stage's needs at the peak and smaller units willing to take what is left.

### Contracting

A contracting strategy evolves as a solution to the smoothing problem when two organizations, a customer and a supplier, attempt to coordinate more closely their respective operations. The strategy differs from implicit cooperation in that the cooperators are usually not in the same industry and the cooperation is overtly sought rather than implicit. The strategy can be used to meet all the types of demand fluctuations. The strategy also needs to be distinguished from the independent strategy of demand influence.

Like the independent strategy, contracting attempts to influence demand. But the difference is that in a bargaining strategy the customer is in a position to suggest alternatives. When using price and promotion, the organization creates the alternatives and the customer accepts or rejects but does not create an alternative. The power to influence a decision is much greater when alternatives can be created as opposed to choosing among given alternatives. Thus, the organization is giving up some power to gain cooperation from a customer. This then is more costly than price and promotion but may be more effective.

**1. Box manufacturing.** An example of this strategy occurs in the production of corrugated boxes. The manufacturer operates a highly mechanized, expensive setup of equipment. The customers demand quick service. However, box sizes and printing are sufficiently unpredictable that the items are produced to order. Therefore there is no inventory nor backlog to buffer the production facility. Dutton describes such a case in which a bargaining relationship was established between the producer and major customers so that a stable work load was continuously negotiated.[10]

The smooth load was attained by a negotiation process between the producer and the customer. The producer would seek agreement from the customer to increase lots, split lots, delay delivery, or speed up delivery so that the producer could smooth the work load. In return the customer gets preferential treatment in times of shortage, quick response in emergencies, and perhaps a break in price. The objective of the negotiating is to smooth out the demand pattern. The bargaining is continual and requires an organization designed to handle the communication between schedulers, sales people, and customers.

**2. The post office.** The post office is another organization that utilizes the contracting strategy. It does so in order to smooth the weekly and monthly fluctuations in work load.

The post office has a customer relations department which negotiates the timing of billing and advertising mailings of all major users. The objective is to smooth the demands for service made by users requiring large amounts of service. The bargaining is to work out the timing to the satisfaction of the user and the post office's operations.

The post office will also bargain concerning the amount of work performed by the user and the department. The users can reduce their postal rate by doing a large portion of the sorting and packing. This process varies the department's work load by a mechanism similar to subcontracting except the work is performed by either the user or the producer.

**3. The meat packing industry.** In the meat packing industry, management and union in some firms have agreed upon a contract which eliminates temporary wage variations.[11] With most workers having fixed financial obligations, the variation in the workweek resulted in variation in take-home pay. The workers found this variation to be objectionable. The solution is the guaranteed annual wage. With considerable variation on the input side, the packing industry varied the length of the workweek to absorb the fluctuations. Since consumption did not follow the input pattern, the firms did a lot of canning during peak periods to build up a finished-goods inventory. The carrying of an inventory on the input side is costly enough to force workweek variation as the alternative to absorb the variation. By adopting a guaranteed annual wage, the firm can vary the workweek in a pattern consistent with input availability, build up finished-goods inventory, and yet eliminate wage variation for the work force. What happens is that the firm has to make a longer commitment for labor-cost control. The problem becomes one of forecasting yearly requirements.

**4. Subcontracting.** Quite often firms cannot find subcontracts to absorb their fluctuations. To solve this problem it has been suggested that cooperative arrangements be continuously maintained so that shops can help each other.[12] This type of contracting involves competitors in a legal combination that reduces uncertainty of availability of capacity for both.

Both of these last two examples show solutions to smoothing problems involving elements of task environment other than the user or supplier who is the cause of the variation. The producing organization found the variation objectionable and tried to pass it on, in these cases, to workers and competitors. They, too, found the variation objectionable. They had enough power, while also being dependent on the focal organization, to force a cooperative solution in which the parties, acting together, could eliminate many of the features that each found objectionable.

**5. The coal industry.** As previously mentioned, the integrated coal companies designed the output capacities of their mines to meet the minimum or trough demand which they themselves often controlled. The nonintegrated mines increased mechanization in a similar manner but reduced demand uncertainty by drawing up 20-year requirements contracts with major users such as electric utilities. The utilities in return got a guaranteed supply and a favorable price.

In summary, in each of the cases above a contract was arranged with a customer, a competitor, or a union to arrive at a satisfactory solution to the smoothing problem. In return the other party got privileged access to capacity, reduced uncertainty about availability, and/or a favorable price.

### Coalition

A coalition is formed when a group of organizations acts as a single unit to solve a common problem. Although the antitrust laws severely limit the forms of coalitions, some examples have evolved. Coalitions are more overt in their operations than implicit cooperation.

**1. Electric utilities.** The first example of a coalition designed to solve a smoothing problem is the electric power networks consisting of many independent electric utilities. Normally the utilities are forced to vary capacity utilization to meet fluctuations in demand. However, if every firm had to provide capacity to meet rare occurrences of peak demand, the investment would be substantial. By coalescing, the utilities are able to pool resources and jointly meet rare peak occurrences. The total investment of all firms is thus reduced.

**2. The coal industry.** The second example of coalition action is the coal industry. Earlier it was discussed as an example of implicit cooperation and contracting. Recall that large and integrated firms had designed their organizations to meet estimated minimum requirements in order to guarantee continuous operation. In 1954, 1958, and again in 1961, recessions depressed the level of demand below the level for which the integrated mines were designed. Rather than reduce output, the large coal companies coalesced along with the mine workers union to try to enforce minimum wage laws to apply to the nonunion firms. This was followed by attempts to close marketing channels which the small producers needed to transport their output. Both attempts went under labels compatible with the enforcement of wage legislation (the Walsh-Healy Act and the National Bituminous Coal Wage Agreement of 1950). However, the real purpose was to reduce the output of the nonintegrated mines.[13] The coalition behavior was necessary to achieve continuous operation. With the return of economic prosperity, the collective action declined.

**3. Commercial airlines.** More recently a coalition was announced between TWA and Eastern Airlines in order to share the costly jumbo jet and SSTs.[14] The cost of the equipment is significantly greater than the cost of the 707s. This change has made underutilization of capacity a very costly smoothing solution. Even though the airlines have tried a number of independent strategies, they can still save by sharing equipment. TWA and Eastern have route structures with contracyclical demand patterns. TWA gets summer traffic to Europe while Eastern gets winter traffic to Florida. The coalition involves TWA using the aircraft in summer with Eastern using them in winter.

### Summary

This last section has described cooperative solutions to production-smoothing problems. The examples have emphasized the fact that the mechanized technologies create conditions conducive to cooperative solutions. The higher level of mechanization and capital intensity make complete and continuous utilization imperative. If, at the same time, the organization cannot use inventories and must provide immediate service like the airlines, the organization becomes very dependent on elements in its task environment. Cooperative solutions discussed in this section were ways that such organizations have found in order to remain viable. In addition many of them have found other solutions through environmental maneuvering.

### STRATEGIC MANEUVERING

The last strategy to be discussed is strategic maneuvering by which organizations alter their task environments rather than adapt to a given one. Many of the solutions are quite creative. Let us discuss them under the three ways to change task environments—strategy, technology, and location.

## Strategy

Changes in strategy that are significant here are changes to product lines, and vertical integration. These two are illustrative of the many possibilities.

**1. Product line.** Modifications of the product line have been a fairly well-known method of eliminating the variation in the demand pattern. The usual approach is to add to the product line a product which has a contra-cyclical demand pattern and utilizes the same technology as the existing product line. Thus, manufacturers of air conditioners have introduced room humidifiers into their product lines, outboard motor firms produce snowmobiles, etc.

This has been a method used by the commercial airlines to handle their seasonal fluctuations. Unable to influence demand by pricing, they try to acquire routes having contracyclical demand patterns. This permits them to shift aircraft across routes and keep them fully loaded.

**2. Vertical integration.** As mentioned in connection with coal and oil firms, vertically integrated companies mechanize their operations and design the capacities of the sequential stages so as to permit continuous production at the mechanized stage. When paper companies mechanized, they ran their plants seven days a week, 24 hours a day. When demand fluctuations came, prices and profits fell.[15] Some of the firms worked their way out by buying the next stage in the paper-processing chain where they could control the demand on the sensitive mechanized mill. They also bought more demand than was needed to operate their mill continuously and purchased the difference in mill product on the outside market. Any fluctuation in demand is met by fluctuating the amount of outside purchase. They have moved to exactly the same solution that the integrated oil and coal companies have adopted—vertical integration with balanced stage capacities to protect the sensitive mechanized stage.

## Technology

There have been several technological changes which are very interesting. All are motivated by the need to solve the smoothing problem. It is the airlines and electric utilities that are under sufficient pressure to innovate along these lines. Both have expensive equipment, cannot store their service, and must provide quick service.

**1. Utilities.** The electric utilities have always had to meet the maximum demand that exists on any day. If their generators produced more energy than required, it was wasted. One response was to pool demands in power networks which was discussed earlier. A new response, now under construction in several locations, is to use the excess energy to pump water uphill. Then, in periods of peak demands, the utility can supplement generator production by running the water downhill and reconverting the energy to electricity. For some utilities this involves creating a lake on a hilltop. The water at a high level serves as an energy inventory. The utilities, by modifying their conversion process, are able to use a buffer to uncouple production and consumption.

**2. Airlines.** The commercial airlines have modified their production equipment to deal with their daily fluctuation. The airlines have introduced "Quick Change" 727s. These aircraft fly passengers during the day and, after a quick change, fly freight at night. The new aircraft required considerable redesign of the 727 to permit this adaptation. Thus, the airlines have found a way to keep the new expensive equipment fully utilized.

**3. The telephone company.** Some organizations have designed their jobs and technologies so as to be able to employ a work force that is not the major source of family income. Vergin describes a firm that used work force variation as a smoothing strategy.[16] However, it removed many of the objections by hiring and laying off women who were not the sole support of their families. They did not object to being laid off and rehired as they wanted part-time work only. There are many firms that provide nonstorable services that design jobs which require little training and make use of part-time help consisting of students and women. The telephone company is an example of a company that varies its work force utilization to meet daily fluctuations. However, no particular problem arises since the work force consists of young women who welcome the opportunity to shop, sunbathe, etc. All these organizations have production processes which can be staffed by individuals who do not object to a layoff and who can work on a part-time basis.

**4. Oil and chemical companies.** Other organizations that mechanize plants and operate multiplant production processes also design a plant to solve their smoothing problem. Quite often the integrated, mechanized firm cannot find small flexible plants to which they can pass the demand fluctuations. When this happens, they design one of their own plants to be flexible and concentrate all the ups and downs on that plant, while the other mechanized ones engage in continuous operation.

## Physical Location

The last choice that organizations can make is to change their physical locations. With a new location comes a new and hopefully more receptive task environment.

**1. A chocolate factory.** Some organizations have located in particular areas so as to facilitate the use of a specific smoothing strategy. An example occurred in one of the early applications of the linear decision rules.[17] The study was made in a chocolate factory that had a pronounced seasonal variation with little summer demand following the Easter peak. The firm had arrived at a strategy for smoothing which relied upon work force variation but at the same time found a way to remove the objections to hiring and layoff. The factory had changed its location to a rural area and its operative work force consisted of the area farmers. The farmers worked in the factory in the winter and on their farms in the summer. Thus, they had no objection to being laid off after the Easter peak and being rehired prior to the Christmas buildup. Since the same work force was rehired, there was no training cost. Thus a change of location, from an urban to a rural setting, made work force variation a viable smoothing strategy.

**2. Two plants.** Another example is related by Vergin.[18] An organization operated two production plants and was faced with a seasonal sales pattern. The smoothed strategy was to concentrate the swings in demand on one of the plants which was located in a rural area. This plant employed farm workers whose other occupation was seasonal but opposite to the seasonal variation at the plant. In a manner similar to that used by the chocolate factory, this organization was able to reduce the costs of and objections to smoothing by reducing the cost of variation in work force size.

### SUMMARY

In this chapter the problem of production smoothing was analyzed by focusing particularly on organizations that have the problem in its extreme form. Also the infinite variety of responses to this problem can be clarified and understood by the framework of the previous chapter. The varying severity of the problem causes all the types of environmental management to be illustrated.

In addition, the focus on a specific problem allowed us to see how firms acquire dependence. The best example was the extensive mechanization of production. Mechanization, which makes continuous through-put imperative, creates dependence on the task environment. It was shown that the organization becomes dependent on a number of elements in the task environment through its ability to pass on the problem. The problem is either absorbed by the weakest element or leads to a cooperative solution. This maneuvering shows the political as well as the economic nature of a problem that has been extensively studied and modeled by operations researchers.

## NOTES

1. This chapter is a revision of the author's earlier paper, Solving production smoothing problems. *Management Science,* (August), 1969: 665–674.

2. F. Hanssman 1962. *Operations research in production and inventory control.* New York: Wiley.

3. The trade-off between overtime and inventory has been formulated as a transportation problem. E. H. Bowman 1956. Production scheduling by the transportation method of linear programming. *Operations Research* 4, 1. It has been examined by servomechanism theory. J. F. Magee 1958. *Production planning and inventory control.* New York: McGraw-Hill, Chapter 8.

4. *Business Week,* March 2, 1963: 43–44.

5. This version of the problem has been formulated (1) as a linear programming problem by F. Hanssman and S. W. Hess 1960. A linear programming approach to production and employment scheduling. *Management Technology* 1, (January); (2) as a dynamic programming problem by K. J. Arrow, S. Karlin, and H. Scarf 1958. *Studies in the mathematical theory of inventory and production.* Stanford, California: Stanford University Press; (3) as a linear decision rule by C. C. Holt, F. Modigliani, and H. A. Simon 1955. A linear decision rule for production and employment scheduling. *Management Science* 1, 1, (October), and (4) as a computer simulation by R. C. Vergin, 1966. *Production scheduling under seasonal demand. Journal of Industrial Engineering* (May): 260–266.

6. H. B. Wolfe 1961. Seasonal production planning. *APICS Quarterly Bulletin* 11, 1, (January): 12–18.

7. R. M. Whitin 1955. Inventory control and price theory. *Management Science* 11, 1, (October): 61–68.

8. *Business Week,* April 1, 1967.

9. C. L. Christenson 1962. *Economic redevelopment in bituminous coal.* Cambridge: Harvard University Press.

10. J. B. McClean and R. M. Haigh 1954. *The growth of integrated oil companies.* Boston: Division of Research, Harvard Graduate School of Business.

11. J. M. Dutton. Simulation of an actual production scheduling and work flow control system. *International Journal of Production Research* 1, 4, (December): 21–41.

12. R. S. Eckley 1966. Company action to stabilize employment. *Harvard Business Review,* (July-August): 51–61.

13. L. M. Lawry 1967. Two-way contracting. *Harvard Business Review,* (May-June): 131–137.

14. Christenson, Chapter 7.

15. *Time,* December 8, 1967, p. 95.

16. *Forbes,* December 1, 1963, p. 27 and May 1, 1964, p. 38.

17. Vergin, pp. 260–266.

18. W. Crowston 1958. An empirical study of actual and optimum decision rules for production and employment scheduling. M.I.T. Master's Thesis.

19. Vergin, pp. 260–266.

| INTEGRATING INDIVIDUALS AND ORGANIZATIONS: REWARD SYSTEMS | CHAPTER **16** |
|---|---|

In this last part of the book, we shift our analysis to the third component of the strategic choice model: integrating individuals into organizations. The selection of individuals and change of reward systems can be considered as alternatives to changing organizing modes or strategy in order to change behavior and performance. But more important is the notion of coherence between the three concepts. As in the discussion of the other two concepts, uncertainty of the task and interdependence between roles will be our primary point of departure.

## REWARD SYSTEMS

The discussion in this book so far has conceived of the organization as something different from the individuals who perform the work. This abstraction is useful when relating design choices concerning departmentalization and configuration of the role structure to task attributes of diversity and uncertainty. However, we must now confront the issue that people must be attracted to these roles and execute the behaviors that have been assumed. To take a large number of people with diverse goals, habits, and skills and evoke an integrated pattern of behavior from them is a problem of considerable magnitude. In order to deal with this problem, organizations have evolved devices such as compensation systems, selection strategies, and job designs. Like the choices among structure attributes, there is no one best reward system. Similarly not all individual reward systems are equally effective. It depends upon the fit among the task, the structure, the information system, the people, and the reward-system policies. In the next seven chapters, the bases for choosing reward-system policies so as to maintain a fit will be articulated. The first task is to present a framework which will link the attributes of the task (uncertainty–diversity) to the choice of reward-system policies. Second, the effect of reward-system policies upon the choice of alternative role behaviors needs to be predicted. The path–goal motivation model will be employed for this purpose. Finally, some case studies will be explored to see how the design choices have actually been made.

Every organization is dependent upon its members to choose to perform those behaviors which will produce the desired effects on the environment. By definition, the more consistently individuals choose the appropriate behaviors for the role-related situations with which they are faced, the more effective is their performance. The function of the organization design is to remove as many factors as possible which would limit individuals in making these choices. So far we have dealt with two of the three limiting factors which have been articulated by Simon.

> On one side, the individual is limited by those skills, habits, and reflexes which are no longer in the realm of the conscious. His performance, for example, may be limited by his manual dexterity or his reaction time or his strength. His decision-making processes may be limited by the speed of his mental processes, his skill in elementary arithmetic and so forth. . . .
>
> On a second side, the individual is limited by his values and those conceptions of purpose which influence him in making his decisions. If his loyalty to the organization is high, his decisions may evidence sincere acceptance of the objectives set for the organization; if that loyalty is lacking, personal motives may interfere with his administrative efficiency. If his loyalties are attached to the bureau by which he is employed, he may sometimes make decisions that are inimical to the to the larger unit of which the bureau is a part. . . .
>
> On a third side, the individual is limited by the extent of his knowledge of things relevant to his job. This applies both to the basic knowledge required in decision-making—a bridge designer must know the fundamentals of mechanics—and to the information that is required to make his decisions appropriate to the given situation. . . .[1]

Earlier chapters dealt with the cognitive limits on decision behavior—factors one and three. Man–machine and group-decision mechanisms augmented the limited computational and information storage capacities of the human brain. Information systems and lateral relations brought global data to bear on interdependent decision problems or self-contained units were set up to make local data sufficient. All these policies were changes or adaptations to cognitive limits. This leaves the goals limit or what McGregor termed the integration problem;[2] that is, the problem of creating a situation in which members of the organization perceive that they can achieve their own goals best by directing their efforts toward the goals of the organization. Elsewhere, variations of this problem have been called the establishment of a psychological contract,[3] striking an inducements–contributions balance,[4] designing an organizational control structure,[5] or creating an organizational climate.[6] In this book it is the problem of integrating organizational and individual interests by designing a reward system and selecting and training people.

Organizations must design reward systems to remove the goal limitations to performance because they cannot rely upon the voluntary and spontaneous selection of the behavior which will produce the most effective task performance. This premise is not based on an assumption that people are lazy or recalcitrant. It simply means that organizations cannot rely upon a perfect matching of personality and role requirements without devoting additional administrative effort. We also do not assume that organizations cannot rely on voluntary cooperation. The key phrase in the sentence above is "without devoting additional administrative effort." For example, the Forest Service relies a great deal on voluntary compliance with its policies, but it does so by expending a large effort on recruitment and selection of individuals who have acquired conservationist values. In this way the Forest Service utilizes socialization processes in the society to reduce the conflict between individual and organizational goals. Similarly, through selection and self-selection processes, the model airplane builder arrives in the design group of an aerospace firm, the hot-rodder on the General Motors test track, and the athlete in the office of athletic director. But even in these cases, there is still an incomplete matching of individual personality and organizational roles. There is less matching for roles which require behaviors such as operating a keypunch, conducting an audit, taking an inventory, or making a five-year forecast. For these and many other roles, individuals are faced with a choice among alternative physically possible behaviors for which their previous extraorganizational experiences have not provided them with the values to choose spontaneously the organizationally preferred act. And for some behaviors, such as removing a person from his or her job, most people would prefer not to choose the organizationally preferred alternative. Therefore, selection and self-selection are not sufficient to remove goal limitations, although individual and role matching can reduce significantly the amount of effort devoted to other devices.

One of the other devices used by organizations is the authority relationship. This removes the goal limitations by removing the choice from the role. All individuals give up some of their autonomy when they join an organization and accept an authority relationship. Then as individuals face job-related situations, they merely act out that behavior that they have been instructed or directed to perform.

Although the use of authority implies the loss of individual control and autonomy in job situations, it is not alienating. It is not alienating because the socialization processes in the larger society instill in the individual a respect for and an obedience to persons in positions of authority. This means that most societies provide their members with a generalized acceptance of all relevant directives, (i.e., those directives emanating from a role upon which authority has been bestowed), while not necessarily providing for the internalization of any specific directive into the individuals' own value systems. The result of the internalized acceptance is that directives from authoritative roles are perceived to be legitimate. Persons occupying these roles have the right to issue directives and expect obedience. In this way organizations are bestowed with a capability to elicit goal-relevant behaviors without relying upon previous socialization processes to make the specific behaviors gratifying.

Authority, as described above, appears to be an all-powerful influence device. In one sense, it is. Acceptance of authority is the generalized acceptance of directives independent of the specific behavior which is required. This gives the organization greater flexibility in adapting to new task and environmental situations. However, the use of authority is not without its limits. One set of limits is cognitive. This is because the information-processing devices needed to implement a reward system based solely on authority are rules and upward referral. Just as information overload caused the use of integration mechanisms in addition to rules and upward referral, it also necessitates the use of other devices in addition to authority. Another limit arises because the acceptance of authority is not completely generalizable to all behaviors. Most individuals have zones of acceptance within which they will allow their behaviors to be determined by directives from an authoritative role.[8] If a directive requires a behavior which lies outside the zone, the organization must offer other incentives or expect disobedience. The size and makeup of the zone are both culturally and individually determined. For example, most people in our culture perceive as legitimate a directive concerning time of arrival at the work place. However, most people would not consider legitimate a directive to change the location of one's home without the reality or anticipation of a salary increase and/or promotion. There would be considerable individual variation in response to a directive specifying clothing to be worn at the work place. Thus, both information overload and the zone of acceptance place limitations on the use of authority. The result is that even the combined use of selection and authority is insufficient to remove most of the goal limitations.

The organization still faces situations in which goal accomplishment requires behaviors which lie outside the zone of acceptance and for which the individual has not been socialized. Since goal accomplishment is dependent upon the behavior choices of organization members, the organization must allocate additional administrative effort toward removing goal limits. Organizations vary both in the magnitude and direction in which this additional effort is channeled. The problem of determining the types and amounts of effort is the problem of designing the organization's reward system. Its function is to increase the probability that the members of the organization will choose those behaviors which lead simultaneously to the accomplishment of the organizations' goals and the satisfaction of the individual. The reward system which will best serve these ends depends on the nature of the task to be performed and the type of individual who performs them.

## A CONTINGENCY THEORY OF REWARD SYSTEMS

The contingency theory states that there is no one best way but that any way is not equally effective under all conditions. It depends on the situation. This book specifies under what conditions what type of organization is preferred. In this section this concept is expanded to reward system.

In Fig. 16.1 the steps in the analysis of reward system design are por-

**Fig. 16.1   Steps in reward-system analysis.**

trayed schematically. The basic assumption underlying the schematic is that reward systems are differentially effective in eliciting various types of behaviors. Therefore, as tasks vary in uncertainty and interdependence, the behaviors necessary for effective performance also vary. Since behaviors vary, the type of reward system also varies with the task. The manner of proceeding in the analysis will be first to identify the kinds of behaviors necessary for goal accomplishment and then to relate them to the organization's task. Next, different reward systems need to be identified along with the components of which they are composed. Finally, the link between the reward system and the behaviors needs to be established.

It should be pointed out that the analysis can run in either direction as is indicated by the arrows in Fig. 16.1. Critics of modern organizations and technology assert that all too often the analysis runs from left to right, that humans are considered mere appendages to the technology and are assumed to adapt their behaviors to the technological requirements. Alternatively, it is suggested that reward systems vary in the degree to which they lead to psychological growth and health. Therefore, organizations should design or redesign jobs to require behaviors that lead to this growth.[9] The point is that there must be a fit among the task, the behaviors, and the reward system if there is to be high productivity and high individual satisfaction.[10] This is independent of the direction of the analysis. It may proceed in either direction as long as the analysis terminates in the equilibrium fit between individual and task.

| Behavior<br>Reward system | Join and remain | Dependable role behavior | Effort above minimum | Spontaneous behavior | Cooperative behavior |
|---|---|---|---|---|---|
| Rule compliance | | | | | |
| System rewards | | | | | |
| Group (wage) rewards | | | | | |
| Individual rewards | | | | | |
| Task involvement | | | | | |
| Goal identification | | | | | |

Fig. 16.2   Matrix of rewards and behaviors.

The remainder of the chapter is devoted to identifying the task behaviors, describing different reward systems, and creating a scheme for analyzing how reward systems and behaviors are interrelated. Figure 16.2 is a matrix of the categories that will be used. The next sections will explain the behaviors which constitute the columns and the reward systems which are the rows. Subsequent chapters will then be devoted to filling in the boxes.

## ORGANIZATIONAL BEHAVIORS

This section identifies the role behaviors which are necessary to achieve the goals of the organization. Different organizations and, indeed, different roles in the same organization require different behaviors. This obvious statement has significance only if the motivational bases of the behaviors are different. This is our working hypothesis.

The literature on empirical studies of job and role description is not very helpful for our purposes.[11] Most of the studies are observations of actual behavior which are analyzed for developing job descriptions. The goal here is to identify behaviors which can be generalized across roles and organizations and for which the motivational bases are different. March and Simon distinguish between the motivational bases of decisions to join or leave an organization and decisions as to whether to produce at a high or low level.[12] This scheme has been extended by Katz.[13]

> Three basic types of behavior are essential for a functioning organization: (1) People must be induced to enter and remain within the system. (2) They must carry out their role assignments in a dependable fashion. (3) There must be innovative and spontaneous behaviors in achieving organizational objectives which go beyond the role specifications.[14]

Thus does Katz distinguish between routine and nonroutine behaviors. The remainder of this section draws heavily on Katz's framework and extends it where necessary. Let us look now at the set of behaviors. They are not necessarily a mutually exclusive and exhaustive set of categories. For any specific application, they will need to be expanded. But for our general purpose, they are satisfactory.

### Join and Remain

Every organization must attract people to perform the roles in its structure. In addition, the role occupants must derive sufficient satisfaction so that they do not leave for another organization. Such voluntary turnover costs the organization in terms of recruitment, selection, training, lost productivity, and administrative effort. The long-run costs of turnover depend on who is leaving, however. The organization is also dependent upon the members to attend regularly. Absenteeism is another significant cost for the organization. Thus, the measures of join-and-remain behaviors are rates of turnover and absenteeism.

### Dependable Role Performance

Simply showing up on a regular basis is not enough. Members must also adopt reliably and consistently the same behaviors that others expect of them. Out of the range of physically possible behaviors, individuals must perform only a few predictable ones to coordinate their activities with those of others. Members must perform these behaviors so as to achieve minimal levels of quality and quantity of performance. The role of secretary, for example, usually involves behaviors such as arriving at a specified time, opening and distributing mail, answering telephones, typing correspondence, and filing paperwork. The organization is dependent upon the role occupant to perform these behaviors consistently and at reasonable standards of quality. Other role occupants assume the secretary will perform them and base their actions on that assumption.

### Effort above Minimum Levels

The dependable role behaviors have a certain discretion about them. The secretary either opens the mail properly, improperly, or not at all. It is hard to excel in the opening of mail. Some roles require no more than join-and-remain and dependable role behaviors. The auto assembly line requires individuals to arrive and stop at the same time and to perform the same act 45 times an hour—no more, no less.

In contrast to these machine-paced, highly programmed roles, others are man-paced and allow some discretion as to what that pace is going to be. Consider the role of machinists in a job shop. The machinists work within a well-described role. However they have a choice of levels of job related effort. There is some minimal level of effort below which they cannot produce. The minimal level may be hard to determine precisely but there is a level below which the union will not defend them. They will either lose their jobs or, more likely, be assigned one requiring less skill. Let us say this minimum is 150 units per day. At the other extreme is some maximum amount above which machinists cannot produce. This maximum is determined either by the technology of the operation or by the physical skills and abilities of the operators themselves. Suppose the maximum is 300 units per day. Therefore a range of physically possible behaviors exists within which the operators can choose to perform and still keep their jobs. The organization is dependent upon them to choose to perform at a level above minimally acceptable levels. To the extent that workers choose to perform above minimal levels, the organization more effectively accomplishes its goals. Thus behaviors classified as "effort above minimal levels" refer to effort within the prescribed role when the role occupants have some discretion over what that level of effort will be. These behaviors are measured by units of output, output per unit of time, and other efficiency measures.

## Spontanous and Innovative Behaviors

For some roles in an organization, the behaviors necessary for effective performance cannot be anticipated in advance. Therefore, the organization cannot make them part of the job description except in a vague manner. In these situations the accomplishment of organizational goals requires behaviors that go beyond role requirements. The organization is dependent on its members to recognize that something needs to be done and to see that it is done even though they are not necessarily expected to do it or held accountable for it. The organization is also dependent on its members to offer creative suggestions for the improvement of operations. These suggestions can often permit the accomplishment of organization goals more effectively and efficiently. Again, these behaviors are not necessarily expected of individuals and nothing will happen to them if they don't offer suggestions. All of these situations have in common the fact that an unanticipated event has occurred and some action is required from a role occupant who is not necessarily held accountable for the action. In addition, the appropriate actions may not be obvious and require search behavior, information collection, etc. And usually if the role occupant does nothing, the situation will either not be discovered or will be noticed at a later date with the consequence that the organization accomplished its goals less effectively.

## Cooperative Behaviors

It seems redundant to speak of cooperative behavior in a book on organizations. Indeed, the term organization implies a cooperative, collective effort. However, much of the administrative activity is undertaken so as to obviate the need for cooperation. The use of rules, programs, and goals that make up job descriptions, upward referral, and self-contained authority structures are all attempts to create roles for which the individual alone is responsible for the outcomes. But there are task situations in which the organization is dependent on its members to recognize a need for action that was not anticipated and the situations affect more than just one role or department. Thus, there are situations where the spontaneous behaviors are joint-decision behaviors. Successful goal accomplishment requires behaviors which are both beyond role requirements and involve other units.

## TASKS AND REQUIRED BEHAVIORS

Five different types of behavior have now been identified. They are

1. Join and remain,
2. Dependable role performance,
3. Effort above minimum levels,
4. Spontaneous and innovative, and
5. Cooperative.

An important feature of these behaviors is that they are cumulative. If a role is designed to require cooperative behavior, then it also requires joining and remaining, spontaneous and innovative behavior, effort above the minimum levels, and dependable role behavior. If a role is designed to require effort above the minimum levels, then it also requires dependable role behavior and that people join and remain. It does not necessarily require spontaneous or cooperative behaviors. The auto assembly line has roles designed for people to join and remain and to perform dependably. It does not require and, indeed, considers it detrimental to have a higher rate of production. It requires role occupants to produce at the same rate, not at their highest rates. Due to rigid formats and predictable inputs, most computer centers do not want innovative keypunch operators. Therefore, the list of behaviors constitutes a cumulative scale.

A second feature is that the cumulative scale can be related to the task attributes of uncertainty and interdependence. As one moves along the scale of behaviors from number 1 to numbers 4 and 5, there is a steady increase in the discretion exercised by the role occupant. Similarly, the greater the uncertainty of the task, the greater the discretion of the task performer. Thus, the greater the uncertainty of the task, the higher on the scale are the required behaviors. Highly uncertain tasks require spontaneous behaviors on the part of the task performer while predictable situations require dependable, known behaviors only. Similarly the greater the interdependence, the greater the need for cooperative behaviors. However, the need exists only if there is high uncertainty since the programming of roles can reduce the need for cooperative behavior. Thus, the greater the uncertainty and interdependence, the higher on the scale are the required behaviors.

Finally, it is hypothesized that the scale represents increasing costs to the organization. As one moves from number 1 to numbers 4 and 5, there is a greater need for discretion and responsibility. The greater the discretion, the greater the need for skills, competence, and training. The greater the discretion and responsibility of task, the higher the salary for the task performer. Thus, the economics of the situation may create pressures to eliminate discretion from some jobs.

In summary, different types of task behavior have been identified. These behaviors represent a cumulative scale. They represent an increasing amount of discretion for the individual and an increasing amount of administrative and salary costs for the organization. Finally, the scale was related to the contingent variables of uncertainty and interdependence which distinguish between alternative structures and alternative information systems. It now needs to be shown how these behaviors relate to alternative reward systems.

## TYPES OF REWARD SYSTEMS

The ways of talking about reward systems have progressed in much the same way as the classification of types of behavior. Rewards or satisfactions were first classified as being extrinsic or intrinsic. Extrinsic rewards were outcomes which were added to the behavior being executed so as to influence the individual to choose it. The satisfactions gained were not a natural result of executing the behavior. They were artificially added. In contrast, intrinsic rewards were satisfactions which followed as a natural consequence of performing the behavior. These categories correspond roughly to Herzberg's empirical work which sorts rewards into hygiene factors (extrinsic), such as pay, supervision, and working conditions; and motivators (intrinsic), such as achievement, responsibility, and advancement.[15]

Etzioni, a sociologist, has presented a three-factor classification.[16] He suggests that organizations can rely neither on voluntary adoption of goal-related behaviors nor on willing compliance with directives. They must apply other means to motivate the goal-related behaviors. The first means are through the administration of punishment. In this way, the organization applies coercive power to the individual members. Alternatively organizations can grant material rewards on the basis of performance. This is the extrinsic-reward category. And finally they can offer symbolic rewards. This is a little broader concept than intrinsic rewards but not substantially different from it. While organizations usually offer mixtures of these reward–punishments, Etzioni suggests that organizations can be classified on the basis of the motivational pattern on the lower-level participants. Prisons and custodial institutions use coercive means, business firms use material rewards, and universities and religious organizations use symbols.

The importance of Etzioni's work is not that he added another category but that organizations vary in their use of rewards and can be classified on the basis of the predominant category. He did not, unfortunately, relate these to the kinds of behaviors or tasks required. The earlier theorists seem to suggest that the only way to successfully motivate behavior is to use intrinsic job satisfactions. Etzioni provides some differentiation but is descriptive, rather than prescriptive.

The work of Katz shows how different motivational patterns relate to different behaviors.[17] He does this by identifying five basic patterns. In the subsequent sections, his framework is followed and expanded to six.

### Rule Compliance

The use of rule compliance to gain acceptance of organizationally preferred alternative behaviors is an extension of the previous concept of authority. Recall that individuals were the focus of the analysis. They were faced with physically possible alternative behaviors for which their life experiences have not necessarily provided them with a value system which would make the organizationally preferred alternative satisfying. In order to increase the probability that the required acts are performed, the oganization eliminates the choice made by the individual and substitutes an authority relationship to provide the preferred alternative. When individuals join organizations they expect to have their behavior, within some bounds, determined by others in authority. In order to assess this method of influence in terms of the kinds of behaviors it can motivate, the concept of authority needs more definition.

Authority is a relation between two roles—one superior and one subordinate. This relation exists whenever four conditions exist. First, there must be an imperative statement from the organization concerning the choice of a particular behavior in a specific situation and the expectation on the part of the superior that the particular behavior will be adopted by the subordinate. The imperative statement may be a verbal command from the superior, the anticipation of a verbal command in a repeat situation, a written instruction, a point in the union contract, a rule voted on by the workers' council, or an instruction learned in a training course. This is a necessary condition but the crux of the relation lies in the subordinate's behavior, not the superior's.

The second condition for an authority relation to exist is actual compliance with the directive or imperative statement. If there is no compliance, there can be no authority relation. The organization can issue statements and draw lines on a chart indicating reporting relations, but if there is no compliance, there is not an authority relation in the specific situation.

There are other occasions where there is compliance with a directive and yet no authority relation is present. Superiors may rely on their expert power by using their knowledge and information to change the subordinate's perception of cause-effect linkages in the choice situation. Or superiors may rely upon their reward power by subtly reminding the subordinate that they control salary increases, chances for promotion, and pleasant job assignments. In either case, superiors persuade their subordinates thereby influencing them to choose the behavior indicated in the directive.

In the third condition for an authority relation, however, subordinates suspend their judgment which eliminates the need for persuasion. Thus, an authority relation exists when the subordinate ". . . holds in abeyance his own critical faculties for choosing between alternatives and uses the formal criterion of the receipt of a command or signal as his basis for choice."[18] Implied in the above is also an element of voluntary compliance or a willingness to obey.

Authority exists only when there is voluntary compliance with directives and suspension of judgment as to the goodness of the directive in the specific situation. More clarity is still required, however. Most of us can conceive of situations in which there is willing compliance and suspension of judgment, but in which it would be difficult to call the relation one of authority. This is partly due to the fact that there are a number of motives which can explain any observed behavior. Also, in any power situation, the lesser role is influenced as much by the anticipated use of power as it is by the actual use of the power. The power of the presidential veto, for example, is brought to bear as much by its threat as by its actual use. One would need to know what the behavior would be without the presence of the other power source. Would there be willing compliance on the chain gang without the guard's gun? Most of us would agree that there would not be— hence no authority. However, this differs only in a matter of degree from the case of the organization that maintains economic and career dominance over its employees. Yet many would call this an authority relation.

It takes a fourth distinguishing factor to differentiate authority from the coercive examples given above. Blau and Scott have suggested that a major reason for the borderline cases as to whether or not an authority relation exists is that many other power relations develop into authority.[19]

In order to be an authority relation, the exercise of power or social control must acquire another, or fourth, condition.

> This condition is that a value orientation must arise that defines the exercise of social control as legitimate, and this orientation can arise only in a group context. A single individual forced to comply with the commands of another may seek to adapt to this situation by rationalizing that he really wants to be guided by the other's directives. That this attitude is a mere rationalization would be indicated by the fact that once the coercive power was withdrawn he would not continue to comply. If, however, an entire group finds itself in the same situation, and if its members share the beliefs that it is good and right

and, indeed, in their best interest to obey, the rationalizations of individuals become transformed into a common value orientation. For group agreement and approval of what is right constitute a social value that validates the beliefs of individuals and thereby makes them "really" right. Given the development of social norms that certain orders of superiors ought to be obeyed, the members of the group will enforce compliance with these orders as part of their enforcement of conformity to group norms. The group's demand that orders of the superior be obeyed makes such obedience partly independent of his coercive power or persuasive influence over individual subordinates and thus transforms these other kinds of social control into authority.[20]

This fourth condition is one of legitimacy. It means that the subordinate willingly complies and suspends judgment because of internalized social constraints exerted by the social unit, not primarily because of influences the superior can bring to bear. Authority results from the consent of the governed. Thus, authority can exist only in social units and when the units' norms require compliance with directives of the superior.

In conclusion, an authority relation exists between two roles when (1) there is an imperative statement to guide the choice of behavior alternatives of the subordinate and an expectation by the superior that the imperative will be adopted by the subordinate, (2) there is willing compliance with the imperative statement, (3) there is a suspension of the subordinate's own judgment concerning the merits of the imperative and (4) there is a collective whose norms require such a compliance. An example would be the professor–student relation in a situation in which the professor assigns a chapter to be read by the class in preparation for a discussion in a particular session. First, there is an imperative statement that the student choose the behavior "read the chapter," and there is an expectation by the professor that it will be read. Second, there is, by and large, willing compliance. This is not to say that some students do not read it or read it for other motives. In those cases, either no authority exists or other power bases are brought to bear. Third, there is almost always a suspension of judgment by the student. He or she does not seek other opinions to see if there are chapters in other books which may be preferable to the one assigned. Finally, the class regards the assigning of reading material a legitimate behavior on the part of the professor who is usually asked for readings if he or she fails to assign some. Or another indication is that we are embarrassed when asked a question and we are not prepared. True, this is partly due to being "found out" by an authority figure, but it is also due to the fact that most students believe that they should read assignments. This norm would be stronger in a Ph.D. seminar than in an undergraduate class. While assigning readings is regarded as legitimate, the holding of a special session on Saturday night would not be regarded as legitimate and would be accompanied by noncompliance or compliance at the cost of alienation. Authority as defined here is not alienating and it is not alienating because it is accepted as legitimate. But where do the common value orientations come from which establishes the legitimacy?

Sociologists have been concerned with the basis on which legitimacy is established. The basis for most modern organizations is the rational–legal form that was articulated by Max Weber.[21] Legitimacy derives from a need for order of some kind. Everyone benefits from having some "rules of the game" articulated. To achieve a collective purpose, it is important that everyone adopt the same premises for the behavior choices they make. In the rational–legal form, the individual is obedient to a body of laws or rules which is designed to organize conduct for the accomplishment of specified goals. Obedience is not owed to a person but to the body of rules which pertain to everyone. Directives that are perceived to lie outside the need for order or to be for the selfish interest of the superior are not legitimate. These are held to be not for the "good of the order," but rather for the good of an individual.

In our culture we are socialized into a general acceptance of conforming to the rules of the game. We accepted directives from our fathers not only because they were stronger, more persuasive, or would exchange favors for obedience but also because of the culturally defined role expectations that we should obey. This was enforced and reinforced by teachers, ministers, relatives, and other relevant roles. All of this prepared us for assuming roles in the organizations we choose to join.

This discussion has been undertaken to introduce the concept of rule compliance. Rule compliance is broader than authority. This is because authority, as we have defined it, is an analytical abstraction. Authority in any real situation is accompanied by other influence forms. However, the use of these other forms will be alienating while authority will not be. Thus, rule compliance motivates the adoption of organizationally required acts through the internalized acceptance of legitimate authority or the generalized acceptance of the rules of the game and by the sanctions available to positions of authority. These sanctions include rewards such as promotions, salary increases, and job assignments—and punishments such as suspensions and dismissal. As mentioned before, it is difficult to know whether a behavior is adopted because it is legitimate or because it is a means to a reward or to avoid a penalty. One can only conclude that sanctions are necessary to enforce and bring about legitimacy.

The sanctions are also needed to enforce the appellate use of authority. The lines on the organization chart do serve the purpose of delineating "lines of authority" for the purpose of terminating debate in joint decisions. This allows a solution to be forced when consensus is not achieved. Thus, it is a conflict-resolution device.

Rule compliance is limited, however. It was previously mentioned that authority is limited to an area of acceptance. Forced compliance by the use of sanctions is alienating. For these reasons, organizations have employed other motivational bases to generate goal-related behaviors.

### System Rewards

System rewards are extrinsic rewards which are given to members of the organization based on their membership in the system. They are distributed usually on the basis of seniority in the system and maintenance of membership in good standing. They accrue to all members. Examples of these rewards are vacations, retirement benefits, sick leaves, cost-of-living raises, access to recreation facilities, working conditions, and other fringe benefits. The distinguishing feature is that these rewards are available to all members and if they are differentially distributed, it is usually on the basis of seniority.

### Group Rewards

A second type of extrinsic reward is one which is given to all members of a group or unit in an organization. This differs from the system rewards in the manner in which the reward is distributed, the nature of the unit receiving it, and the type of reward that is given. First, the reward is given to all members of a unit, but it is based on some measure of the unit's performance. Thus, it serves to influence unit members to choose behaviors leading to high unit performance. Second, the term group or unit reward raises the question of what is a group. Depending on the pattern of interdependence inherent in the technology, a group can vary from several individuals to the entire organization. If it is a large organization in a profit-sharing plan, there will be virtually no difference between the group and system rewards. But the motivational effects will be different when the unit is a division, department, or immediate work group. In one sense, this reward fills in the middle ground between system and individual rewards. Third, these rewards differ in that they are usually monetary. They take the form of group incentives that determine the individual's wages or a year-end bonus.

### Individual Rewards

The last type of extrinsic rewards is that based on differential individual performance. These rewards are supplied by those people who are affected by the individual's choice of behavior. That is, the performance level chosen by an individual will affect the satisfactions of others and these others will influence the individual to choose the level he or she desires. First, there is the organization. It provides in addition to fringe benefits and working conditions, monetary compensation. The most obvious example is a wage incentive or piece-rate incentive which determines an individual's pay in proportion to the amount of production that is turned out. There are also merit salary increases, bonuses, and commissions of as many varieties as there are organizations.

A second person affected by the individual's choice is the supervisor of the work group. The supervisor can give interesting assignments, provide help, offer support, etc. These considerations can be rewarding and can be distributed in order to influence the individual's choice of performance levels. As such, they are extrinsic rewards.

Finally, the individual's choice is influenced by the peer group. The group can offer approval, acceptance, and support to its members and, in situations of interdependence, may give these rewards based on the individual's performance. Thus the organization, the supervisor, and the work group are all possible sources of extrinsic rewards which can be distributed in order to influence the individual's choice of job behaviors.

### Task Involvement

The second type of satisfaction that one derives from performing role activities is intrinsic to the task. That is, the reward is a natural consequence of the behavior and is independent of any externally mediated rewards. In these cases high performance carries its own reward. Two types of intrinsic satisfactions are described here.

The first intrinsic source of job satisfaction derives from the task itself. Individuals conceive of themselves as having certain skills. Their self-esteem is at stake in the performance of the task. These individuals do not identify with the task but with the group of people who perform that task. The skilled craftsman, the scientist, and the professional are typical examples of jobs that rely on this source of motivation. To make use of this source of motivation, organizations select individuals with the appropriate self-concept, and design roles with the opportunities for the expression of the skills and abilities that these individuals believe they have.

## Goal Identification

The second type of intrinsic reward is goal identification. In this case the individual has internalized the goals of the organization and voluntarily chooses goal-related behaviors in the job situation. The individual does not necessarily derive satisfaction from opportunities to use specific skills. By contrast to the professional, or task-involved individual, the goal-identified individual will choose behaviors independent of the type of skill they require so long as they are perceived to lead to the goals which he or she values. These goals may have been acquired in the process of growing up or acquired in the socialization processes operating in the organization.

There is some variation in the nature of the goals in the identification process. Sometimes it is the goals of the entire organization such as the Peace Corps. In other instances, one may identify with the division, agency, or department in which he or she works. If this motive pattern is used, one of the design questions must be, "With what set of goals is the individual to identify?"

These six reward patterns make a reasonably complete set of motivational bases of organizational behavior. They are listed as follows in the order in which they were introduced:

1. Rule compliance      4. Individual rewards
2. System rewards      5. Task involvement
3. Group rewards      6. Goal identification

In some cases these rewards are alternative ways of motivating the same behavior. Task involvement may be substituted for a wage incentive to motivate effort above minimum levels. In other cases they must be used in combination. System rewards may be used for join-and-remain behaviors and task involvement for effort above minimum levels. The choice will vary with the type of role and level of organization. Many patterns will be found in all organizations.

## SUMMARY

This chapter introduced the problem of motivating organizational behavior. The role occupant was portrayed as being faced with alternative physically possible behaviors. It was asserted that individuals usually will not voluntarily choose the organizationally preferred alternative. This was due to the artificial nature of the formal organization. In order to increase the probability that the individual will select the organizationally preferred alternative, the organization must allocate resources and administrative effort to this problem. This is the problem of designing the reward system.

The type of reward system adopted was hypothesized to depend on the nature of the task. As the task varied, the behaviors necessary for effectiveness varied. This has significance only if the motivational bases of these behaviors are differentially effective. This was the premise of the chapter. Five different behaviors and six motivational patterns were presented. As seen in Fig. 16.2, this creates a 30-cell matrix. Our task is to fill in those cells. But first we need some way of assessing the effects of such things as wages on individual motivation. The model of motivation to be used is introduced in the next chapter. Then we proceed to match rewards and behaviors.

## NOTES

1. H. A. Simon 1957. *Administrative behavior,* (Rev. ed.) New York: Macmillan, p. 40.

2. D. McGregor 1960. *The human side of enterprise.* New York: McGraw-Hill.

3. E. Schein 1971. *Organizational psychology,* (Rev. ed.) Englewood Cliffs, N.J.: Prentice-Hall, Chapter 4.

4. J. G. March and H. A. Simon 1958. *Organizations.* New York: Wiley, Chapter 4.

5. A. Etzioni 1961. *A comparative analysis of complex organizations.* New York: The Free Press, Chapters 6 and 7. A. S. Tannenbaum 1968. *Control in organizations.* New York: McGraw-Hill.

6. G. H. Litwin and R. A. Stringer, Jr. 1968. *Motivation and organization climate.* Boston: Division of Research, Harvard Business School.

7. A. Etzioni 1963. *Modern organizations.* Englewood Cliffs, N.J.: Prentice-Hall, p. 59.

8. H. A. Simon, p. 12.

9. C. Argyris 1964. *Integrating the individual and the organization.* New York: Wiley.

10. J. J. Morse 1970. Organizational characteristics and individual motivation. In J. Lorsch and P. Lawrence (eds.), *Studies in organization design.* Homewood, Ill.: Richard D. Irwin, pp. 84–100.

11. J. P. Campbell, M. D. Dunette, E. Lawler, and K. Weick 1970. *Managerial behavior, performance, and effectiveness.* New York: McGraw-Hill, Chapter 4.

12. March and Simon, Chapters 3 and 4.

13. The scheme first appeared in D. Katz 1964, The motivational basis of organizational behavior, *Behavioral Science* 9: 131–146, and was expanded in D. Katz and R. Kahn 1966, *The social psychology of organizations.* New York: Wiley, Chapter 12.

14. Katz, pp. 131–132.

15. F. Herzberg, B. Mausner, and B. Snyderman 1959. *The motivation to work.* New York: Wiley.

16. A. Etzioni 1961. *A comparative analysis of complex organizations.* New York: The Free Press, Chapter 3.

17. Katz and Kahn, Chapter 12.

18. H. A. Simon, p. 126.

19. P. M. Blau and W. R. Scott 1962. *Formal organizations*. San Francisco: Chandler, pp. 27–30.
20. *Ibid.*, pp. 28–29.
21. M. Weber 1947. *The theory of social and economic organization*, T. Parsons and A. M. Henderson (trans.). London: The Free Press, Collier-Macmillan, Ltd., pp. 324–341.

## QUESTIONS

1. Why do organizations need reward systems?

2. Explain what is meant by the zone of acceptance.

3. Compare and contrast the behaviors listed across the top of Fig. 16.2.

4. Choose several jobs in an organization and specify the different types of behaviors needed for task performance.

5. Explain why and how the behaviors form a cumulative scale.

6. Distinguish between rule compliance and authority.

7. What are the differences and similarities between task involvement and goal identification?

8. It has been suggested that the six reward systems listed in Fig. 16.2 represent increasingly expensive systems for the organization to employ. Do you agree or disagree?

| | CHAPTER |
|---|---|
| AN INFLUENCE MODEL | **17** |

Chapter 16 introduced the general problem of attracting people to perform organizational roles and ensuring that they select behaviors that will produce the desired effects on the environment. It was asserted that organizations cannot rely upon their members to consistently and voluntarily choose the goal-related behaviors from among those which are physically possible. Organizations therefore must design reward systems to influence the individual's choice of job-related behaviors. The design process was begun by identifying the different types of behavior required by different tasks. This had significance because the motivational bases of these behaviors also varied. This chapter introduces an influence model which will allow us to predict the effect of reward policies on the probability that role occupants will select the goal-related behaviors. Some of the evidence for this model is reviewed before filling in the squares of the behavior-motivation matrix.

## MOTIVATION-INFLUENCE MODEL

The organization's reward system results from choices of various policy dimensions under the organization's control. The organization can choose various compensation plans, promotion systems, leadership styles, selection strategies, training programs, and job designs. However, the effect of these policies is not a simple, direct stimulus-response. The same policy can generate different behaviors with different people in different contexts. What is needed is a model which will allow us to predict how a policy will affect different individuals' attitudes and, in turn, how these attitudes will combine to produce different job-related behaviors in different situations. This is portrayed in Fig. 17.1. Chapter 16 categorized groups of policy variables into different motivational bases and also categorized the different job behaviors.

There are many models that can be placed in the box in Fig. 17.1. These models cannot be evaluated as being good or bad in the abstract. They must be evaluated relative to the questions they are to answer. If a manager is

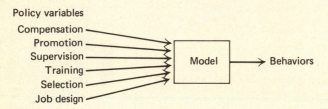

**Fig. 17.1    Relation between policy variables and job behaviors.**

planning how to conduct a performance appraisal, he or she needs a complex model of a specific individual. This model would not be appropriate for other decisions. If a plant manager is choosing between an individual incentive plan, a group-incentive, or a plantwide profit-sharing plan, he or she needs a model which will generalize across all individuals in the work force. It is the latter kind of decision that is of interest in this book. To deal with these questions, a general influence model is introduced first. This will allow the identification of different influence processes. Then a motivational model will be introduced to allow the prediction of specific behaviors.

### Influence Model

An individual's behavior in an organization has been portrayed as resulting from a choice among alternative physically possible behaviors. The task now is to explain why an individual chooses one and rejects others that are physically possible. Since there is no reason to believe that behavior in organizations is governed by processes different than those governing behavior outside of organizations, the basic theories of psychology are a relevant starting point.

It is best to begin with a base for which there is substantial agreement. Most behavioral scientists would agree that a person's behavior at any time is a function of the *interaction* between person and environment. Neither individual attributes nor stimuli in the situation can alone explain behavior. March and Simon have been most explicit about this interaction and about how influence processes operate in the interaction.[1]

They conceive of the behavior of individuals during any particular time period to be a function of their internal states and the state of their surroundings at the beginning of the time interval. In order to predict behavior the internal state and the state of the surroundings need to be more specifically defined. First, the internal state of the individual is contained in the memory. This is the summation of all past experiences. These experiences are recorded in memory in the form of different elements. The types of elements are:

1. Various physically possible behavior *alternatives* or *actions* which could be acted out by the individual.

2. Possible future states of the world or *outcomes* which could result from various actions. Associated with these outcomes are *preferences* that the individual has learned; that is, likes and dislikes concerning these states of affairs.

3. Various *connections* between actions and outcomes and between outcomes and outcomes. That is, a salesperson may believe that a particular proposal (action) will result in a sale (outcome) to a customer. Also the person believes that the sale (outcome) will lead to a bonus (outcome) and maybe a promotion (outcome). Associated with these beliefs or connections are *probabilities*. The salesperson is not certain that the proposal will result in a sale (probability $= 0.5$), but is certain that, if the sale is made, the reward will be a bonus (probability $= 1.0$). But the individual is not sure about receiving a promotion if the sale is completed (probability $= 0.3$). From a knowledge of what these elements are and from a theory which states how they are combined, one can predict which alternative the individual will choose. Subsequently the motivational model will provide this information. However, a knowledge of these elements is not enough. The definition of the internal state of the individual requires the introduction of another concept. This results from a further division of memory.

March and Simon hypothesize that the memory can be divided in another way.[2]

More specifically, the human memory content can usually be viewed as divided into two parts at any given time: a part that exerts a significant influence on the behavior at that time; and a part much larger than the first that exerts little or no influence on the behavior at that time. We will call the part of the memory that is influencing behavior at a particular time the *evoked set,* and any process that causes some memory content to be transferred from the second (unevoked) category to the first a process for *evoking* that content.

Thus, it is only a small portion of memory, the evoked set, that determines current behavior. It is the elements of the evoked set and evoking processes that are of interest here.

There is a similar dichotomy applicable to the environment. There is a small portion of the environment that affects current behavior and a portion which does not. The portions that are relevant for current behavior are called cues or stimuli. There is a strong interaction between the stimulus elements of the environment and the elements of the evoked set. Like the chicken and the egg, what is in the evoked set affects what we see in the environment and what we see in the environment affects what is in the evoked set. For example, the same individual may face the same job situation at two different times. In one case the supervisor is present while in the second the supervisor is not. In the second case the evoked set is more likely to contain extraorganizational behavior alternatives such as playing a practical joke on a fellow worker. Thus, the stimulus situation can affect what is evoked in the individual. Alternatively, the supervisor is more likely to see a mistake or an act of misconduct by the low-producing, low-trusted worker than by the trusted, high producer. Thus, the same behavior by different individuals will have different probabilities of being perceived, only because of differences in the evoked set at the moment the behavior is exhibited. Thus, the interaction between the individual and the environment is determined by the associations the individual has made between evoked set and stimuli.

The functioning of the model can be summarized here by arbitrarily starting with the environment. For each task-related situation there is a set of stimulus elements which evoke a set of elements in the individual. At least one of these elements is a behavior alternative. Others are outcomes and preferences which are believed to result from the various action alternatives. These elements of the evoked set are the determinants of current behavior.

As the task environment changes, the elements of the evoked set cause the individual to perceive a new set of stimulus elements. Associated with these new stimuli is a new evoked set with behavior alternatives, beliefs, outcomes, and preferences which will lead to new behavior and a new task environment. It is the task of the administrative process to see that the organizationally preferred behavior alternative is both contained in the evoked set and is chosen from among the other alternatives that are evoked along with it. This suggests at least two different ways of influencing behavior.

The definition of influence being used here is March's. Influence is defined as "that which induces behavior on the part of the individual at time $t_1$ different from that which might be predicted on the basis of a knowledge of the individual organism at time $t_0$."[3] The first way behavior can be influenced is by changing the contents of the evoked set. These are evoking- or attention-directing processes.[4] One type attempts to increase the probability that the organizationally preferred alternative is in the evoked set for a given stimulus situation. Training programs and on-the-job instruction are examples. Another is use of authority with willing compliance and suspension of judgment. Suspension of judgment implies that the directive is the only action alternative in the evoked set. Stimulus-response conditioning is another way of reducing the evoked set for any situation. Such habit-creating and habit-breaking processes are examples of ways to contract or expand the evoked set so as to increase the probability that the appropriate behavior is acted out for each task situation. Another mechanism is to change the stimuli. This also alters the evoked set. The presentation of new cues and information, and suggesting previously unconsidered behaviors are examples. These are primarily attention-directing phenomena. They have received very little empirical attention relative to other influence mechanisms such as wages.

The evoking processes are to be contrasted with mechanisms for changing elements already contained in the evoked set. Simon refers to these as persuasion.[5] One way is to change the values associated with perceived states of affairs or outcomes. Socialization processes in society whereby individual gain values are the best examples of this phenomenon. The values of participants are controlled partly by the selection of individuals who have been socialized to accept certain values. But there are adult socialization processes operating in organizations such as the expectations encountered on the first job experience[6] and some management development programs.[7] The other type of influence takes place by changing the probability connections between actions and outcomes and between outcomes and outcomes. The tying of wages to performance or offering promotions based on performance rather than seniority are persuasive devices of this type.

The influence model of March and Simon is a general model. It relates the person to the environment, accounts for shifts of elements into and out of the evoked set, and identifies the main elements in the evoked set. However, it does not specify the way these elements interact and does not specify a way of predicting which behavior alternative in the evoked set is actually chosen and acted out. Another model is needed for specific predictions.

## THE MOTIVATION MODEL

The influence model just presented is useful for identifying influence processes with a minimum number of assumptions. It does not, however, provide a prediction of which specific behavior will be selected by the individual. For this another model is needed. With greater specificity comes a larger number of assumptions, greater disagreement, and a greater number of models from which to choose. There are a number of versions of expectancy theory, Adam's equity theory, and two-factor theory to name just a few.[8] In this book we will adopt the path–goal version of expectancy theory. It permits the analysis of all types of extrinsic and intrinsic rewards and has received the best empirical support.

Expectancy theory is based upon a definition of motivation as being a process governing choices among forms of voluntary activity. This focus upon choice makes the theory more compatible with the point of view developed in this book. The focus in the chapters on reward systems has been the individual role occupant faced with alternative physically possible behaviors in the evoked set. As shown in Fig. 17.2, there is a set of outcomes

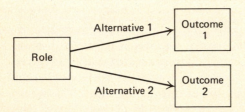

**Fig. 17.2   Role occupant with choice of voluntary behaviors.**

believed to result from these behaviors. The problem to which motivation theory addresses itself is to explain why the role occupant will choose one of the alternatives and reject the other. Approaches to the explanation of this choice process have reflected the influence of the principle of hedonism. The hedonistic doctrine is based upon the assumption that behavior is directed toward pleasure and away from pain. The history of inquiry into this problem has been one of trying to put empirical content into the hedonistic calculus. One of the primary impediments has been the difficulty of determining *a priori* which outcomes are pleasurable and which are painful. Any behavior could be explained, after the fact, by noting the probable sources of pleasure and pain. One of the primary contributions of path–goal models is that it allows the prediction of which outcomes are pleasurable and which are painful and links the concepts with empirically observable events.

The particular version of the path–goal model used here is the one articulated by Vroom.[9] His version attempts to predict which outcomes are pleasurable or painful by introducing the notion of second-level outcomes. This is shown schematically in Fig. 17.3.

The second-level outcomes are viewed as events or states of affairs to which the first-level outcomes are expected to lead. In other words, the first-

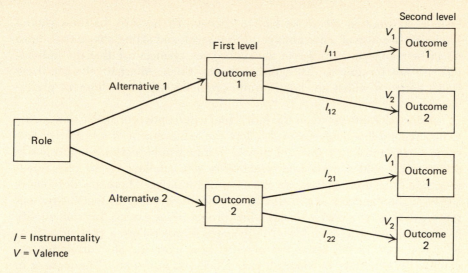

**Fig. 17.3  Choice among alternative behaviors leading to first- and second-level outcomes.**

level outcomes are viewed as means to the second-level outcomes. As in the previous example of the salesperson, Alternative 1 may be making a sales proposal. First-level Outcome 1 is achieving a sale which is expected to lead to a bonus (second-level Outcome 1), and a promotion (second-level Outcome 2). Alternative 2 may be another proposal or a proposal to a different customer.

In order to predict which behavior the role occupant will select, one needs to know which first-level outcome is preferred. In the Vroom model, preferences for first-level outcomes are determined by their expected relationship to second-level outcomes. The precise method for determining preferences for first-level outcomes makes use of two concepts—*valence* and *instrumentality.*

The concept of valence assumes that people have preferences for various states of affairs. Valence then refers to the strength of the person's desire for an outcome or state of affairs. In economics or statistical decision theory, this concept is called utility and the individual is assumed to have an ability to assign various utility values to various states of affairs. All that is assumed here is that the individual can at least assign +, 0, and − values to states of affairs or perhaps the individual possesses a five-valued function ++, +, 0, −, and −−. Human beings are assumed to have limited discriminatory abilities and may not be able to discriminate at all between preferences for states of affairs for which life has not presented them a choice in a specific stimulus situation. A man may be fond of skiing and fond of steak but may be unable to tell us which he prefers more. The reason is that he has never been in a situation where he had to choose. To be sure, he does choose implicitly because of a fixed budget. But if steak and skiing alternatives have never been objects of choice in the evoked set, chances are that the individual will not be able to distinguish between them. Alternatively, for those states between which he chooses quite often, he will have different preferences.

Instrumentality refers to the individual's perception or belief that a particular second-level outcome will follow the achievement of a first-level outcome. For example, a salesman believed that he would receive a bonus, probability $= 1.0$, and a promotion, probability $= 0.3$, following the completion of a sale. The probabilities are the instrumentalities. There are differences between the concepts of probability and instrumentality in that instrumentality can take on negative values while probabilities cannot. Instrumentality is negative when a second-level outcome will *not* follow a particular first-level outcome. In this sense, instrumentality is more like the correlation coefficient and can take on values between one and minus one. The manner in which a first-level outcome acquires valence is stated by Vroom.

> The valence of an outcome is a monotonically increasing function of the algebraic sum of the products of the valences of all other outcomes and his concepts of its instrumentality for the attainment of those other outcomes.[10]

This is formalized in Eq. 17.1.

$$V_j = F_j \left( \sum_{k=1}^{n} V_k \cdot I_{jk} \right), \qquad j = 1, 2, \ldots n, \tag{17.1}$$

where $V_j =$ Valence of first-level outcome $j$, $V_k =$ Valence of second-level outcome $k$, and $I_{jk} =$ perceived instrumentality of outcome $j$ for the attainment of outcome $k$, $-1 \le I_{jk} \le 1$.

The model can be applied to the outcomes in Fig. 17.3. The valence of first-level outcome 1 is

$$V_1 = \left( \sum_{k=1}^{2} V_k \cdot I_{jk} \right) = (V_1 I_{11} + V_2 I_{12}).$$

Similarly, the valence of first-level outcome 2 is

$$V_2 = \left( \sum_{k=1}^{2} V_k \cdot I_{jk} \right) = (V_1 I_{21} + V_2 I_{22}).$$

The second-level outcomes 1 and 2 may or may not be of the same nature for each first-level outcome. The numbering system for the summation is relative to the first-level outcome. The multiplicative relationship between instrumentality and valence and the fact that instrumentality varies between −1 and +1 allows the inclusion of both rewards and penalties. Therefore, outcomes that lead to rewards (+V and +I) and avoid penalties (−V and −I) have a positive valence and outcomes which avoid rewards (+V and −I) and lead to penalties (−V and +I) have a negative valence.

The use of Eq. 17.1 for explaining choices among alternative behaviors requires an addition to the model. The reason is that not all of the variance in the valence of an outcome can be explained by viewing the outcome as a means to other ends. Some outcomes are sought as ends in themselves. This may be the case with job-performance outcomes. Some people will seek to do well even when no externally mediated rewards are forthcoming. This phenomenon is a type of internalized motivation called ego-involvement.

> Motivation is defined as internalized to the extent that it is independent of externally mediated sanctions and is hypothesized to occur to the extent that role performance is relevant to the maintenance of an individual's self-identity.[11]

If one can determine the extent to which an individual is ego-involved with respect to a particular dimension of role performance, it can be predicted *a priori* which outcomes have greater positive valence. The modified equation becomes:

$$V_j = V_0 + \sum_{k=1}^{n} V_k I_{jk}, \qquad j = 1, 2, \ldots n, \tag{17.2}$$

where $V_0 =$ valence acquired through internalized motivation.

Other terms are as defined in Eq. 17.1. This formulation merely assumes an instrumentality of 1.0 for intrinsic rewards.

The independence and additivity of intrinsic and extrinsic rewards have been assumed. But when specifically tested, the resulting evidence suggests that they are not additive.[12] Further, the evidence suggests that one is motivated either by extrinsic or intrinsic rewards but not by both. If more evidence accumulates, the theory could be modified as shown in Eq. 17.3.

$$V_j = AV_0 + (1-A) \sum_{k=1}^{n} V_k I_{jk}, \qquad j = 1, 2, \ldots n,$$

where

$$\tag{17.3}$$

$$A = \begin{cases} 0 \text{ if } I_{jk} \neq 0 \\ 1 \text{ if } I_{jk} = 0. \end{cases}$$

That is, if the instrumentalities for extrinsic rewards are greater than or less than zero, A takes on a value of zero eliminating any intrinsic valence. When the instrumentalities for extrinsic rewards are zero, then $A$ takes on a value of 1.0 and the valence is determined by intrinsic sources. Many other forms of equations are possible and there is no evidence of the existence of a zero–one $A$ factor. In addition, there is some evidence that shows that another extrinsic reward, positive verbal reinforcement, led to increased intrinsic motivation. Therefore, we will continue with Eq. 17.2 until there is further evidence.

There are some additional connections between elements in the evoked set. These derive from the fact that the outcomes which result from actions of an individual may be affected by factors beyond the control of the individual. This introduces some additional uncertainty into the choice situation. Therefore, a person's choice among alternatives depends not only upon preferences but also upon beliefs about cause and effect. A belief concerning the likelihood that a particular act will be followed by a particular outcome is called *expectancy*. The choice situation is shown in Fig. 17.4.

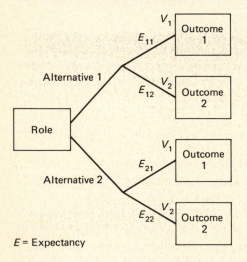

**Fig. 17.4  Choice situation with factors beyond the control of the role occupant.**

Role occupants perceive a particular behavior as leading to a particular outcome depending both on their choices and on factors beyond their control. The salesman choosing between alternative sales proposals may believe that Alternative one will result in a sale with probability equal to 0.5 (Outcome 1) and will not result in a sale with probability equal to 0.5 (Outcome 2). The reason he is not certain is that other factors such as economic conditions and proposals by other salespersons will jointly determine the outcome.

It is necessary to distinguish between instrumentality and expectancy. Expectancy is a belief about the likelihood of a behavior resulting in a par-

ticular first-level outcome. Instrumentality is a belief concerning the likelihood of a first-level outcome resulting in a particular second-level outcome.
It is important to distinguish between them since they are qualitatively different, can change independently of one another, and can be influenced by
different administrative processes.

It is the combination of first-level outcomes and expectancies which lead
to behavior choices. The directional concept of the Vroom model is the
Lewinian concept of force. The force results from a combination of valence
and expectancy. A person's behavior results from a field of forces acting
upon him or her, each force having a direction and magnitude. People
choose from among alternative acts the one corresponding to the strongest
positive or least negative force. In the Vroom model, force is defined as
follows:

> The force on a person to perform an act is a monotonically increasing
> function of the algebraic sum of the products of the valences of all out-
> comes and the strength of his expectancies that the act will be followed
> by the attainment of these outcomes.[13]

Formally, it can be written:

$$F_i = F_i \left( \sum_{j=1}^{n} E_{ij}V_j \right), \tag{17.4}$$

where

$F_i$ = force to perform act $i$;

$E_{ij}$ = the strength of the expectancy that act $i$ will be followed by outcome $j$, $0 \leq E_{ij} \leq 1$; and

$V_j$ = valence of outcome $j$ as determined by Eq. 17.2.

In Fig. 17.4, the force to perform act one can be expressed as

$F_1 = (E_{11}V_1 + E_{12}V_2)$,

and for act two

$F_2 = (E_{21}V_1 + E_{22}V_2)$.

Again, Outcomes 1 and 2 need not be the same for each act but have
the same index since numbering is relative to the particular alternative. The
role occupant depicted in Fig. 17.4 would then choose act one or two depending on which had the larger force. Therefore, force becomes the psychological concept that is linked to observable behaviors.

At this point we have identified the elements in the evoked set and how they combine to determine the choice of behavior. The task remaining is to combine the influence and motivation models in a more dynamic, realistic context. Thus far we have been assuming that behavior results from a choice from among alternative physically possible behaviors. Now introspection alone would suggest that human beings do not continuously perform instrumentality-valence-expectancy calculations in order to choose the behavior associated with the largest force. However, the notion that behavior results from choice does not necessarily imply any conscious or deliberate weighing of alternatives. It simply means that if individuals follow one course of action, there are others that they forgo. At any time there are a multitude of physically possible behaviors. Then by some process these are narrowed down to the one that is actually acted out. It is this process that needs to be described. For this purpose the path–goal model needs to include evoking phenomena. This is achieved by looking at the decision process over time.

## DYNAMIC PATH–GOAL MODEL

In this section the models are combined into one. The general dynamic models of March and Simon are combined with the specific but static Vroom model. The expanded model also draws heavily on the work of Porter and Lawler.[14] The model is shown schematically in Fig. 17.5. Each box and feedback relation will be explained individually. Then a new employee will be taken through some job history to illustrate the dynamic characteristics. The starting place for the model is the evoked set that is associated with the work place, stimulus situation.

### Elements of the Model

**1. Expectancies.** In the evoked set are alternatives of action each of which has expectancies associated with it. Expectancies are the first part (Box 1) of the sequential perception concerning the probability that effort will lead to performance and whether performance will lead to rewards. Expectancies are the effort–performance beliefs. These perceptions are partly a function of the performance measure and partly a function of the process of administering the work situation. For example, business firms have searched for years for performance measures which reflect only those factors which managers control and therefore for which they can be held accountable. But profit measures and return on investment measures, among other defects, can be influenced by general economic conditions as well as by a division's

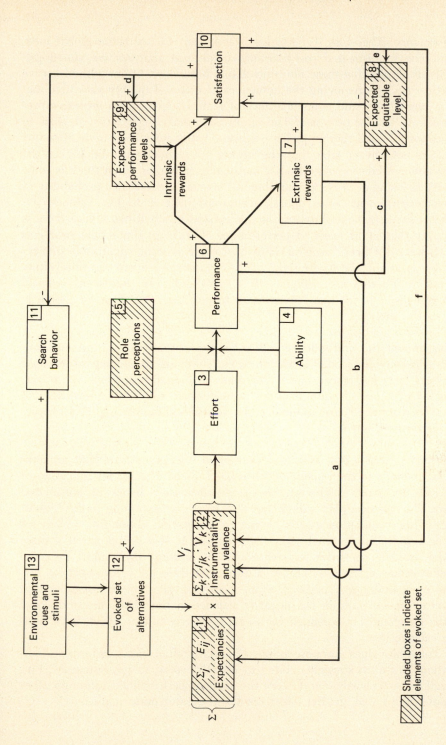

**Fig. 17.5  Dynamic path–goal model of job behavior.**

performance. Therefore, expectancy is less than 1.0 for these global measures. The sophisticated cost-accounting variance analyses are aimed primarily at eliminating these noncontrollable influences. Other administrative practices such as removing the influences of material quality variation, machine breakdown, and nonavailability of material from wage incentive programs have similar purposes. The intent is to make expectancy as close to 1.0 as possible and thereby make wage and profit incentives more effective.

It is not always true that the higher the expectancy, the higher the motivation. Atkinson suggests that motivation is higher when there is some chance of losing or of not performing.[15] This may mean that a probability of nonaccomplishment gives actual accomplishment a higher valence. Or perhaps the achievement motive is not evoked in situations where there is certainty that effort leads to performance. These are theoretical problems which have not been resolved. However, there is some qualitative distinction between uncertainty caused by defects in keeping score and uncertainty caused by inherent task difficulty. It seems the former should be removed and will result in increased motivation to perform. That is not necessarily true of the latter.

**2. Instrumentality and valence.** Box 2 is the combination of instrumentality and valence for second level outcomes. These are the perceived relations between first- and second-level outcomes and preferences for these outcomes. In the job situation it is the perception as to whether rewards will follow performance. Equation 17.2 characterizes this and Eq. 17.4 characterizes Boxes 1 and 2.

**3. Effort.** Effort (Box 3) is the amount of energy or time that an individual expends in the pursuit of job-related goals. The model conceives of the role occupant as choosing between alternative levels of job-related effort. The role occupant will choose that level corresponding to the highest force. This formulation avoids having to be specific about the evoked set for each individual in each stimulus situation. It also brings about a theoretical problem. In order to have a choice situation, there must be some conflict between the alternatives. Either something of value must be forgone or something of negative value acquired. It must be assumed that either effort expenditure has negative valence or time and energy devoted to the job could be expended for social or family affairs which have positive valence.[16]

Thus the values and perceptions of an individual which determine "motivation" are most strongly related to effort devoted to job outcomes. But, as will be seen shortly, effort is not the same as performance, although other things being equal, greater effort results in greater performance.

**4. Ability.**  One of the reasons that effort may not correlate perfectly with performance is that ability (Box 4) is an intervening variable. Individuals may be highly motivated and put forth high levels of effort but not perform well because they have neither the skills nor abilities to perform the task. It has been hypothesized that there is a multiplicative relationship between motivation and ability and there is some evidence that it exists.[17] However, these studies are all field studies and lack the experimental control for the determination of functional forms. But the studies do report the existence of a relationship rather than the lack of one.

**5. Role perceptions.**  Individuals' role perceptions (Box 5) refer to the way they define their job. This variable mediates the relation between effort and performance and accounts for differences between them. Individuals can devote considerable effort to their job but not perform well. They may allocate that effort in the wrong direction. Wrong is defined with respect to organizationally preferred directions. These perceptions arise when there are multiple goals such as costs, quality, and schedule. For example the foreman may work hard on improving quality but cost may be the biggest problem facing the organization. Thus, the role perceptions are part of the evoked set and serve to guide the direction of effort.

**6. Performance.**  Job performance (Box 6) is the end result or outcome of the application of effort. It is that portion of the individual's behavior that is relevant to the organization. It usually has several dimensions such as quantity, quality, and timeliness. For some roles, it can be measured as productivity (output/unit time), but for most managerial roles it is rated subjectively.

**7. Extrinsic rewards.**  An individual's performance can result in the actual achievement of extrinsic rewards (Box 7). This variable refers to the actual receipt of outcomes in the work situation that are mediated by others. Therefore they are extrinsic to the task. They are artificially added to influence the individual's choice of levels of effort. Wages, promotions, supervisory approval, and group acceptance are all examples of extrinsic outcomes that can have value for the individual.

**8. Expected equitable level.**  All individuals have expectations (Box 8) about how much they should receive in any exchange situation. On the job, they have these same normative orientations about what they receive in the way of organizational rewards. They have a perception of what their performance is, their education, experience, seniority, status, and other factors that they think are relevant to the job situation. The normative orientation derives from comparisons with others. Individuals have perceptions which may or may not be accurate about what others receive and how they perform. These individuals then make some judgment about what is a "fair day's pay," for example.

This variable is a perception of what they should receive. This amount may be less than what they want. They may want more money but, given their current status and performance, they may feel that they should not receive the larger amount. This expectation is an element of the evoked set in the job situation.

**9. Expected performance level.** Box 9 is another element of the evoked set which is present in the job situation. All individuals have some level of performance at which they expect to perform in a particular activity. This level, often called the aspiration level, is largely a function of individuals' history of past performances in the stimulus situation, or of the expectations of others when individuals have no personal history on which to rely. The relevant others in the job situation are primarily the supervisor and peers.[18] As individuals acquire some experience in the job situation, they compare their performance with these expectations. If they meet or exceed these levels, they begin to incorporate the role behaviors into their self-concept. They begin to conceive of themselves as persons having the skills and abilities necessary for role performance. The role performance becomes a source of self-esteem. Performance becomes a source of intrinsic satisfaction and acquires a valence. When expectations are not met or are not communicated to them, individuals fail to develop this source of self-esteem and primarily respond to extrinsic rewards.[19]

**10. Satisfaction.** Satisfaction (Box 10) is another variable that is perfectly understood in general but hard to define in particular. There is a good deal of debate over how to measure this quantity. In this book, satisfaction will simply mean the positive or negative feelings or positive or negative affects experienced from job behaviors and rewards.[20] These feelings can result from both intrinsic and extrinsic sources. Satisfaction from extrinsic rewards results from a comparison of actual reward with the expected equitable level. It is not the absolute amount that leads to satisfaction. Two individuals each could receive a $100 raise. The one who expected a $200 raise would be dissatisfied. The one who expected $75 would be satisfied and pleased with the raise.

There is some evidence that if rewards are much larger than expected, an embarrassment of riches could result.[21] This could also cause dissatisfaction on the part of the individual. Thus, the rewards must be at or near the expected equitable level in order to provide satisfaction. Dissatisfaction can result from too much or too little by comparison.

The individual can also be satisfied yet want more of a particular reward. Satisfaction results from a comparison between what is expected and what is received. What is expected can be different from what is ultimately wanted. The other source of satisfaction is the receipt of intrinsic rewards. As with extrinsic rewards, satisfaction does not result from the absolute level of performance but from a comparison of performance with aspiration level. Meeting or exceeding the aspiration level generates satisfaction. If performance is less than the expected level, dissatisfaction results. The amount of satisfaction or dissatisfaction is also a function of the degree to which the individual's self-esteem is at stake in the stimulus situation.

**11. Search behavior.** Search behavior (Box 11) is a cognitive process by which the individual changes the elements of the evoked set. This behavior is undertaken to the degree that individuals are dissatisfied with current outcomes or anticipate being dissatisfied. Dissatisfaction is not a stable conditions. Individuals will do something to remove it. They may search for new alternatives of behavior in order to improve their performance. They may collect information in order to change their role perceptions. Alternatively, they may seek out other nonperformance behaviors with which to obtain satisfaction. This may involve leaving the organization, filing a grievance, or playing politics.

On the other hand, satisfaction leads to less search behavior. Satisfied individuals will not seek out new alternatives of behavior in those areas where current outcomes meet expectations. Thus, the model predicts that changes to the evoked set and therefore changes in behavior occur when there is a dissatisfaction with the current state of affairs or anticipated dissatisfaction. The implications will be clearer when the dynamics have been described.

**12. Evoked set of alternatives.** With the evoked set (Box 12) we have come full cycle. This is the set of alternative behaviors with which we began the description. The evoked set in any situation is a function of individuals' previous history in similar situations. If dissatisfaction results, individuals search their memories and/or collect external information to create new behavior alternatives in order to remove the dissatisfaction. Similarly, if satisfaction results from current behavior, each is eliminated and the evoked set shrinks to the single alternative which has led to satisfaction. Individuals will persist in that behavior until dissatisfaction results. The dissatisfaction can result from a new role perceptions, new performance expectations, rising aspiration levels, or externally generated behavior alternatives.

**13. Environmental cues and stimuli.** In addition to internally generated search behavior, the evoked set can be altered by cues (Box 13) in the job environment. Box 13 summarizes all those effects that are not explicitly considered in the model. Others such as the presentation of new information are not explicitly shown. The effect of information is then summarized by the box.

The diagram also illustrates the interaction effect. When individuals are satisfied, they see a different set of cues than they do when they are dissatisfied. Individuals are more likely to perceive a new alternative and are more receptive to cues when they are dissatisfied. This completes the definition of the factors in the model. Let us turn now to the various feedback relations that are depicted in the diagram.

### Feedback Relations

A number of feedback relations have been added to the model in order to indicate the hypothesized cause and effect relations and in order for it to account for behavior over time. One of the relations was described above. The process of dissatisfaction leading to the search for alternative behaviors, and satisfaction leading to reduced search accounts for the expansion and contraction of the evoked set over time. The process accounts for habit-breaking and habit-establishing phenomena relevant to job behaviors. There are five other relations, each represented by a letter in the diagram.

**Performance–expectancy.** As a result of the level of effort, ability, and role perceptions, the employee achieves a level of performance over some time period. The model hypothesizes that a number of things result from this outcome. The achieved level of performance provides information on the relative ease with which the individual can translate effort into performance. Therefore, the performance level will provide some information which will permit the revision of the expectancies ($E_{ij}$). The Line **a** indicates this effect. If individuals are provided with performance information, their perceived expectancies should approach reality over a period of time.

**Performance–reward–instrumentality.** The second set of cues given individuals will come from the organization and the individuals' peers. The cues are rewards or punishments the individuals receive from others who are affected by their choice of behaviors. These extrinsic factors are wages and promotions given by the organization, approval and consideration given by the immediate supervisor, and acceptance or nonacceptance by the peer group. Then when individuals achieve a performance level, they receive a reward and perceive what others receive for their performance. This information then confirms or modifies the existing beliefs about performance–reward connections.[22] If pay increases are given to everyone after 30 days and job assignments are made on the basis of seniority, then individuals will revise their instrumentalities toward zero; that is, they believe high performance is not rewarded. On the other hand, if rewards are differentially distributed on the basis of performance, the instrumentalities will be revised upward toward 1.0. Individuals will establish beliefs on this evidence rather than on the basis of an organization's professed intentions.

Thus, Line **b** represents the effect of actual receipts of rewards on perceived instrumentalities ($I_{jk}$).

**Performance–expected equitable level.** A third effect of performance level is that it increases the expected level of reward. The higher individuals perform, the higher the reward they feel they should receive. The organization may reward for performance ($I_{jk} = 1.0$) but give rewards that are small relative to expectations. The result will be low satisfaction, low value attributed to the reward ($V_k$), and finally, lower effort and performance. Of course individuals' expected equitable levels are also functions of performance and rewards of others. The model shows only the effect of the individuals' own performances on the expected equitable levels as indicated by Line **c**.

**Satisfaction–aspiration level.** This link completes the performance–satisfaction–aspiration level loop. We need to specify how the aspiration level changes over time. Recall that the objective level of performance does not lead to feelings of success or failure. Rather, the intrinsic satisfactions result from the difference between actual and expected performance. One's feeling of success or failure depends upon whether performance is above or below this level of aspiration. Now one might be led to predict that if individuals maximize their satisfaction, they would keep their level of aspiration as low as possible. This turns out not to be the case.[23] If a task is regarded to be so easy that achievement can be taken for granted, no feelings of success are aroused. Similarly, if a task is too difficult, no feelings of failure will arise. What this means is that a feeling of failure will occur only if there is a chance for success. Likewise a feeling of success will be experienced only when there is a chance for failure. Thus, when the task permits, individuals will adjust their level of aspiration so as to create a situation where both success and failure are possible.

It is important to repeat the distinction made earlier between the probability of failure that is inherent in the relationship between the task, the aspiration level, and the ability of the task performer, and the probability of failure due to outside noncontrollable factors. A machine breakdown, poor workmanship on prior operations, or nonavailability of material may prevent machinists from reaching their level of aspiration for production quantity. However, they will have no feelings of personal failure. They may be dissatisfied but not with themselves. In order to experience success or failure feelings, individuals must be able to attribute the outcome of an action to themselves in a specific way. Increasing expectancy will increase motivation as long as it is associated with removing obstacles to translating effort into performance which are not inherent in the task itself.

The dynamics of the aspiration level were alluded to previously when it was mentioned that aspiration levels change in situations where they are permitted to change. This is indicated in Fig. 17.5 by Line **d** connecting satisfaction to the expected level. The relation is predicted to be a positive one. That is, if performance exceeds the expected level, success feelings or satisfaction results. The success leads to an upward revision of the aspiration level. If subsequent performance results in continued success, the aspiration level will continually rise. Similarly, if initial performance was less than expected, failure and dissatisfaction would be felt. This would lead to a decline in the level of aspiration. Both of these processes would stabilize when a failure in the former case and a success in the latter case was finally experienced. Individuals will vary as to whether the stable success–failure probability is 50–50, 60–40, or 70–30, but in any case an equilibrium would be reached. Thus the aspiration level, if the job design permits, will stabilize such that one's expectations of future performance are close to reality. In this case, performance is limited only by one's physical and cognitive abilities.

**Satisfaction–expected equitable level.** Extrinsic rewards produce satisfaction when rewards meet the expected equitable level. It is hypothesized that the expected level rises as a function of satisfaction as illustrated by Line **e.** Greater satisfaction results in higher expectations. Lower satisfaction results in lower expectations but expectations probably decrease more slowly than they increase. The expected equitable level is also a function of what "relevant others" are perceived as doing and what they are perceived as receiving.[24]

**Satisfaction–valence.** What happens to the valence or importance of outcomes as satisfaction varies? This relation is represented by Line **f.** Is the relation one where a little satisfaction merely whets the appetite for more, thereby increasing valence with increases in satisfaction? Or is the relationship one of satiation? That is, the more of something that one has or the more satisfied one is with a particular outcome, the less important is more of that outcome. In this case, increased satisfaction leads to decreased importance and valence of the outcome. Another question also arises. Is there any difference or relationship between satisfactions arising from intrinsic and from extrinsic rewards?

The explanation of these questions depends upon the theory of a hierarchy of needs.[25] The theory suggests that people have a number of different needs. The number and type of needs varies depending on whose list is being used. A list of five is shown here:

1. Self-actualization needs
2. Self-esteem needs
3. Social needs

4. Security needs
5. Physiological needs

The key hypothesis in the theory is that the needs form a hierarchy in the sense that higher order needs (self-actualization and self-esteem) cannot motivate behavior until lower level needs are reasonably well satisfied. And alternatively, only when lower level needs are satisfied can people be motivated by higher level needs. Thus, the greater the satisfaction of lower level needs, the less their importance and the less the valences of outcomes leading to lower level needs but the greater the importance and valences of outcomes leading to higher level needs. The available evidence supports this theory. There are still unresolved questions of how many levels and what kind of needs are involved. Alderfer suggests a three-level hierarchy.[26]

The satisfaction of lower level needs leads to reduced importance and valence, but what happens when there is a satisfaction of higher level needs? The evidence suggests that satisfaction of higher level needs, particularly self-actualization, leads to increased importance. Porter reports that satisfaction of all needs except self-actualization leads to decreased importance.[27] Satisfaction of self-actualization needs leads to increased importance. Similarly, Alderfer suggests that satisfaction of higher order needs leads to their increased importance.[28] Thus, whether satisfaction leads to increased valence of an outcome depends on the type and level of needs that the outcome satisfies.

The question that is suggested by the line of reasoning above is how are outcomes and needs related. One hypothesis, suggested by McGregor, was that extrinsic outcomes such as money and fringe benefits could satisfy lower level needs only, while intrinsic rewards satisfied higher level needs. Lawler's research suggests that this hypothesis is not entirely correct.[29] Lawler reports that the amount of pay is associated with the satisfaction of self-esteem needs which are higher level needs. But he finds no relation between the amount of pay and self-actualization. Lawler suggests that there is a difference between money, and money received as a result of job performance. It is the latter which can satisfy self-esteem needs.

The Lawler results cause one to recall the Deci experiments which suggest that one cannot be both intrinsically and extrinsically motivated by an act at one and the same time. Are these discrepant findings? They need not to be if extrinsic and intrinsic motivation are phenomena different from high- and low-level need satisfaction. There is some evidence for this assertion.[30] Thus it appears that one can be extrinsically motivated but yet can satisfy higher order needs. Lawler's findings suggest that if money is given on the basis of performance, it can satisfy higher level needs whereas if it is given independent of performance, it can satisfy only lower level needs. Deci's work suggests that if money is given on the basis of performance, performance cannot be intrinsically motivating. But his work says nothing of the level of needs satisfaction that results. Therefore, the findings of Lawler and Deci are not discrepant results.

In summary, it appears that the satisfaction of all needs except self-actualization leads to decreased importance of those needs and decreased valence of outcomes associated with those needs. Satisfaction of self-actualization needs leads to increased importance of those needs and increased valence of outcomes associated with them. Depending on how they are administered, extrinsic outcomes can lead to satisfaction of both high- and low-level needs, except self-actualization. Intrinsic outcomes are associated with the satisfaction of all higher order needs. Thus, the relation indicated by Line **f** is not a direct positive or negative relationship. The satisfaction provided by outcomes instrumental to needs other than self-actualization (or whatever the highest level of needs is) leads to reduced valence for that outcome. At the same time, increased satisfaction provided by outcomes which are instrumental to the satisfaction of self-actualization needs results in increased valence of those outcomes.

## Model Dynamics

The variables and relationships between variables (hypothesized cause and effect relations which are shown in Fig. 17.5) have been described. What remains is to explain the dynamics of the model. The dynamics are best illustrated by following new employees through the model and seeing how the model will explain the employees' behavior under various conditions.

As new employees face the job situation for the first time, a set of elements is evoked. These elements are a function of the past job experiences and expectations created upon entering the present organization. In the set is one or more action alternatives with which are associated some perceptions of the ease of translating effort into performance ($E_{ij}$) and whether performance will lead to rewards ($I_{jk}$). The rewards are believed to lead to satisfactions ($V_k$). Based on Eqs. 17.2 and 17.4, the elements are combined and the individuals choose the act which has the greatest positive or least negative force.

It is also quite possible that the evoked set for some people will be nearly empty. The new employees may not have well-formed preferences for outcomes nor clear expectations of cause and effect, yet they must choose an act to perform. Some individuals, recognizing that the current choice is the first of a series of choices, may simply choose a convenient act so as to collect information on which to base the subsequent choices. Others may abdicate choice by following the leader's advice or by imitating the immediate co-worker. In any case, a choice of level of effort is made. For these individuals, choice precedes the establishment of perceptions and preferences rather than being determined by them for the time period in question.

The choice of effort (Box 3), role perceptions (Box 5), and the individual's ability (Box 4) combine to determine a level of performance (Box 6). The achievement of a level of performance yields the first information about the ease of translating effort into performance (Line **a**). This information either confirms, modifies, or establishes the original perceived expectancy. The $E_{ij}$ will guide subsequent choices.

A second result of achieving a performance level is the receipt or non-receipt of extrinsic rewards (Box 7). This outcome provides information as to whether rewards are given on the basis of performance or are independent of performance (Line **b**). The information confirms, modifies, or establishes the first perceived instrumentality ($I_{jk}$) of performance outcomes for the receipt of reward outcomes. The instrumentalities become a part of memory which will determine future choices.

The remainder of the explanation depends on which of a number of possibilities occurs in the situations. A few possibilities will be followed here. First, assume our employees receive extrinsic rewards at the expected level and are satisfied with the outcomes. One result is that the expected equitable level rises (Line **e**). In addition, satisfaction may reduce the importance of needs served by extrinsic rewards and the valence of extrinsic outcomes will decline. In order to maintain the same level of motivation (valence in this case), the organization must pay $150 instead of $100. The upward change in the expected level and downward change in valence illustrate why some people claim that extrinsic results cannot be a sustaining source of motivation. However, the magnitudes and speeds of these changes are not known accurately. Herzberg suggests that extrinsic rewards produce momentary satisfaction but lead to higher expectations and demands for more.[31] Ultimately, extrinsic rewards can lead only to dissatisfaction in societies where people's physical well-being and security are reasonably well provided. Whether the hypothesis is true or not is an empirical question. However, it fits within the logic of the model. Over time the dissatisfaction could lead to search behavior such as looking for another job, or taking part in union activity to increase wages and fringe benefits. Or individuals could simply reduce their efforts and performance and thereby reduce the equitable level (Line c). Reduced effort will not achieve satisfaction but may reduce dissatisfaction.

Lawler suggests another possibility.[32] The individuals may receive extrinsic rewards, be satisfied, increase the expected equitable level, but may increase the valence of extrinsic outcomes. If the rewards such as money are given on the basis of performance, individuals may discover that extrinsic rewards are instrumental to the satisfaction of self-esteem needs in addition to security needs. The result would be an increase in importance and valence of those contingent outcomes. Since self-esteem needs are less likely to be satisfied, contingent extrinsic rewards provide a richer yet declining source of motivation. The decline would be slow since it is difficult to completely satisfy a higher order need. Individuals would achieve an equilibrium of high motivation, high performance, high rewards, and high satisfaction if the decline in valence was compensated by larger raises.

Highly motivated individuals would not undertake much search behavior. Indeed, satisfaction would lead to a reduction in search and a reduction in the evoked set until there was only one action alternative evoked in the work situation. The choices of level of effort would be habitual and would not involve any conscious deliberation and weighing of alternatives. Similarly, individuals in the first case who reduced effort to achieve equilibrium finally reduce the evoked set to a single alternative in which they persist until something happens to cause dissatisfaction. Before explaining dissatisfaction, let us continue to follow the employees through the diagram and consider the possibility of intrinsic rewards.

The first possibility is that performance meets or exceeds the expected level. The result is satisfaction, an increased expected level, and perhaps a perception that performance is instrumental to the satisfaction of self-esteem needs. If the job permits the upward adjustment of the aspiration level and the individuals can attribute the performance outcome to their own efforts, job performance may become a source of self-esteem and become intrinsically motivating. The expected level will rise with the increasing ability of the individuals in the task situation. Satisfaction of self-esteem needs or possibly self-actualization leads to a sustaining source of motivation and an equilibrium situation. The evoked set decreases around the single action alternative which leads to satisfaction.[33]

However our new employees may be in a situation where the aspiration level cannot change and therefore cannot stabilize so as to create intrinsic satisfaction or success feelings. For example, many jobs at lower levels of the organization have been designed so as to eliminate any possibility of failure and therefore any possibility of success feelings or intrinsic satisfaction. If the new employees' jobs were on an assembly line they probably achieved maximum performance within a few days. After that, they performed the same task 45 times an hour experiencing neither failure nor success. Or the employees could work for a supervisor who makes all decisions and wants subordinates to execute his or her choices. The boss is the only one who can make a mistake and therefore the only one who can experience success. In both situations, the tasks are the limiting factors and are too easy to arouse success feelings and intrinsic satisfaction. The individuals never develop any self-esteem from task performance and respond primarily to extrinsic rewards.

Situations may also arise which prevent the aspiration level from falling. This occurs because the performance happens in a group context. The aspiration level of individuals is not only a function of their own performance but is also a function of the expectations of others. These other expectations may be formed on the basis of the level of achievement prevailing in the individuals' reference group or may be communicated to them by people in positions of authority in the organization. In this case, individuals continually experience failure and dissatisfaction. Dissatisfaction leads to search behavior and an expansion of the evoked set. There are a large number of possibilities. Individuals may leave the organization or request another job. Both changes create a new reference group in which they may achieve self-esteem. Individuals may redefine the reference groups without moving to another job by identifying a group which supports lower expected levels. These changes allow self-esteem to be achieved.

Another possibility is that the individuals' performance is less than expected but is limited by role perceptions. In this case, dissatisfaction may trigger search behavior. The search can lead to new information and a new evoked set. Subsequently these individuals follow the same path through the model as would those who experience initial success and whose aspiration level rises and stabilizes. In this case the aspiration level rises to meet the achievement level prevailing in the organization. Success leads to satisfaction and to job performance being a source of self-esteem. The individuals incorporate role performance into their self-concept, and performance acquires a valence independent of externally mediated rewards. Again an equilibrium is attained.

Finally, individuals may remain but fail to establish job performance as a source of self-esteem. They may consider the task too difficult to arouse feelings of failure. Under these conditions, the individuals simply do not conceive of themselves as machinists or computer programmers. This alternative follows the line from satisfaction to Box 2. This implies that dissatisfaction eliminates the valence of intrinsic satisfaction in Eq. 17.2. In this case, the individuals' performance may be limited by their motivation or job-related effort. Another possibility would be that their performance would be limited by their ability but their effort was motivated primarily by extrinsic rewards. An equilibrium would be obtained through the previous reasoning for extrinsic rewards.

All of the scenarios above discuss hypothetical examples of job behavior over time. The model predicts that an equilibrium is attained through the equilibrating mechanisms of the expected level, expected equitable level, and search behavior. Equilibrium has been described as the removal of dissatisfaction and the collapse of the evoked set around a single action alternative. It is hypothesized that individuals will persist in that equilibrium behavior without the conscious weighing of alternatives and calculation of valences and expectations. The path–goal model is not a good description of the choice process at this point. However, the model is a good predictor if something happens to cause dissatisfaction or anticipated dissatisfaction, or puts employees into new job situations.

For example, employees who are motivated by extrinsic rewards may receive a cue indicating that further improvement will cause them to exceed the group's maximum of 120 percent of standard. This cue causes a choice to be made. Individuals may choose to perform above 120 percent with a chance of promotion and more money or stay at 120 percent with guaranteed group acceptance, lower probability of promotion, and current wages. Individuals may search for other alternatives such as being transferred. However, a choice must be made and the model becomes a predictor of that choice. After the choice is made and perhaps remade, the situation may again settle down to an equilibrium.

## SUMMARY

In this chapter a model was presented which describes and explains the process by which individuals choose from among voluntary alternative behaviors. This model will guide the subsequent discussion of design choices among types of reward systems. The chapter was not intended to be a complete presentation of motivation theory. Instead it presented one reasonably complete and valid model which could guide design decisions. The dynamic model will permit the integration of a number of minitheories (Maslow's needs hierarchy, path–goal, aspiration levels, etc.) and represent something more than a mélange.

Throughout the chapter the author tried to follow a precarious path between a healthy skepticism and enough confidence to base design choices on the model. The skepticism is necessary because there are unresolved issues and inconclusive evidence concerning most of the hypothesized relations. However, designers cannot wait 20 years for the research evidence to clear up these issues. Therefore, the model represents the best available basis for current design choices even though it may be modified or even overturned by future research.

## NOTES

1. J. G. March and H. A. Simon 1958. *Organizations*. New York: Wiley, especially pp. 9–11. J. G. March 1955. An introduction to the theory and measurement of influence. *American Political Science Review*, (June): 431–451. Simon 1957. *Models of man*. New York: Wiley, Chapters 14 and 15.

2. March and Simon, p. 10.

3. March, p. 438.

4. H. A. Simon 1965. Administrative decision making. *Public Administration Review* 25: 31–37.

5. *Ibid.*, p. 35.

6. D. Berlew and D. Hall 1966. The socialization of managers: effects of expectations on performance. *Administrative Science Quarterly*, (September): 207–223.

7. E. Schein 1961. Management development as a process of influence. *Industrial Management Review*, (May): 55–97.

8. For a review and discussion see E. Lawler III 1971. *Pay and organizational effectiveness: a psychological view*. New York: McGraw-Hill.

9. V. H. Vroom 1964. *Work and motivation*. New York: Wiley, Chapter 2.

10. *Ibid.*, p. 17.

11. V. H. Vroom 1962. Ego involvement, job satisfaction, and job performance. *Personnel Psychology* 15: 161.

12. E. L. Deci 1972. The effects of contingent and noncontingent rewards and controls on intrinsic motivation. *Organizational behavior and human performance* 8: 217–229.

13. V. H. Vroom, *Work and motivation*, p. 18.

14. L. Porter and E. Lawler III 1968. *Managerial attitudes and performance*. Homewood, Ill.: Richard D. Irwin, Chapter 2. E. Lawler III, Chapters 6 and 15.

15. J. W. Atkinson 1964. *An introduction to motivation*. Princeton: Van Nostrand.

16. The failure to identify the costs of job-related effort and the failure to measure individual variation in these costs accounts partially for the low correlations of some motivation studies. For job choice applications where an exhaustive set of alternatives is identified, and therefore values forgone are identified, the model accounts for a larger proportion of the variance. See V. Vroom 1966. Organizational choice: a study of pre-and post-decision processes. *Organizational Behavior and Human Performance* 1: 212–225.

17. V. Vroom, *Work and motivation*, pp. 196–204. V. Vroom 1960. *Some personality determinants of the effects of participations*. Englewood Cliffs, N.J.: Prentice-Hall. E. Lawler III 1966. Ability as a moderator of the relationship between job attitudes and job performance. *Personnel Psychology* 50: 273–279. J. R. Galbraith and L. L. Cummings 1967. An empirical investigation of the motivational determinants of task performance. *Organizational Behavior and Human Performance*, (August): 237–257.

18. A. K. Korman 1971. Expectancies as determinants of performance. *Journal of Applied Psychology* 55, (3): 218–222.

19. Berlew and Hall, p. 222.

20. For an extensive treatment see E. Lawler III, *Pay and organizational effectiveness,* Chapter 12.

21. J. S. Adams 1963. Toward an understanding of inequity. *Journal of Abnormal and Social Psychology* **67**: 422–436.

22. G. Graen 1969. Instrumentality theory of work motivation: some experimental results and suggested modifications. *Journal of Applied Psychology Monograph* **53**: 1–25.

23. K. Lewin 1936. The psychology of success and failure. *Occupation* **14**: 926–930.

24. J. S. Adams 1965. Injustice in social exchange. In G. Berkowitz (ed.), *Advances in experimental social psychology* **2**. New York: Academic Press, pp. 267–299.

25. A. H. Maslow 1943. A theory of human motivation. *Psychological Review* **50**: 370–396.

26. C. P. Alderfer 1964. An empirical test of a new theory of human needs. *Organizational Behavior and Human Performance* **4**: 142–175.

27. L. Porter 1964. *Organizational patterns of managerial job attitudes.* New York: American Foundation for Management Research.

28. Alderfer, pp. 142–175.

29. E. Lawler III, *Pay and organizational effectiveness,* Chap. 2.

30. E. Lawler III, *Ibid.*

31. F. Herzberg 1966. *Work and the nature of man.* Cleveland: World.

32. Herzberg.

33. A. C. Stedry and E. Kay 1966. The effects of goal difficulty on performance: a field experiment. *Behavioral Science* (November): 459–470.

## QUESTIONS

1. Give examples of the four methods of influencing behavior that are suggested by the March and Simon model described on pages 266–267.

2. Take a work situation and a person and identify all the factors illustrated in Fig. 17.4. Explain the choice he or she will make.

3. What organizational factors will influence expectancies?

4. If you were a manager, how many different ways could you change the instrumentalities and valences of your subordinates?

5. Using Fig. 17.5, explain the establishment and breaking of a habitual behavior.

6. Trace through the work history of a new employee using Fig. 17.5 to explain his or her behavior.

7. Use Fig. 17.5 to explain the alienated worker and the "workaholic."

# TASK BEHAVIOR
# AND MOTIVATIONAL BASES

This chapter returns to our primary concern—a contingency theory of task behavior. Chapters 16 and 17 establish that (1) different tasks require different types of behavior for effective performance, (2) organizations, due to their artificial nature, cannot rely on employees' voluntary adoption of goal-related behaviors, (3) organizations must undertake the design and administration of a reward system, and (4) the most effective reward system depends on the behaviors required by the task. This chapter relies on the motivational model discussed in Chapter 17 to help assess how the various motivational bases will affect the various task behaviors. For each motivational basis, the process by which it is implemented is discussed, the impact on the types of behaviors is predicted, and evidence in support of the prediction will be cited when it is available.

The focus of analysis is still the individual employee. The individual is portrayed as a role occupant who is faced with physically possible alternative behaviors for which life experiences have not necessarily provided the values and beliefs which would make the acts required by the organization satisfying. In order to increase the probability that individuals will choose the organizationally required alternative, organizations implement reward systems through the administrative process. Let us look at these reward systems and their motivational bases.

## RULE COMPLIANCE

Rule compliance attempts to increase the probability that the required act is performed by eliminating the choice facing individuals. The choice is eliminated by the issuance of an imperative statement indicating the preferred alternative with the expectation that it will be accepted by individuals as a determinant of their behavior. The imperative statement is communicated through a directive from the supervisor, publication of rules and procedures, or through a training course. The expectation of compliance is communicated through surveillance activities such as direct supervision accompanied with the application of rewards for compliance, and penalties for noncompliance. Thus, rule compliance consists of the issuance of an imperative statement to eliminate the choice of the individual and the expectation of compliance. It is to shrink the evoked set of the individual so that the alternative preferred by the organization is the only element evoked in the job situation.

Rule compliance can be different from the use of legitimate authority. Rule compliance is the attempt to use authority from the point of view of the organization. Authority, as defined in this book, can be legitimate only from the point of view of the individual and the group. It is like the consent of the governed. An organization cannot give supervisors authority. It can give them power. But authority can exist only when the required behaviors lie within the area of acceptance of most of the employees. Thus, if the behaviors required by the organization and specified in the imperative statements lie within the area of acceptance, rule compliance and legitimate authority are identical. The organization is successful in securing the behaviors it needs, the influence is regarded as legitimate, and the employees are satisfied.

It is also possible that the organization can issue imperatives for behaviors which lie outside the zone of acceptance. In this case the organization is implementing rule compliance which is a broader concept. The behaviors may be executed but they will be based on attaining rewards or avoiding penalties rather than based on legitimacy. Thus, rule compliance is based on two influence processes:

1. Legitimate authority in which the imperative statement is the only behavior alternative in the evoked set. Employees suspend their choice and accept the organizational imperative as a determinant of their behavior.
2. Extrinsic rewards and penalties which are attached to the adoption or nonadoption of prescribed behaviors. The compliance depends on the employees perceiving the behavior as being instrumental to these rewards and penalties.

Recall that it is extremely difficult to identify the separate effects of (1) and (2) because they always occur together. However, it is sometimes possible to identify occasions on which imperatives request behaviors outside the zone of acceptance. These imperatives result in dissatisfaction and possibly in alienation.

In order to be effective in the sense of increasing the probability that the required behaviors are performed, the implementation of rule compliance must meet several conditions. These conditions are largely necessary to maintain legitimacy. First, the rules must be seen as necessary for the good of the order. Individuals are willing to give up some of their autonomy if everyone benefits from following the rules. But if directives are seen to be for individual advantage, they will not be regarded as legitimate. Compliance must be expected to result in outcomes for the good of the order.

There must also be a good deal of clarity about the source and content of an imperative. If rule compliance is the predominant motivational basis, then there must be no conflict between imperatives. This usually results in the identification of one source as dominant if a conflict should arise. This is the concept of unity of command that was advocated by the classical management writers. There is no problem in the matrix organization because it is not based upon rule compliance.

The content of any imperative statement must also be clear as to what is the expected behavior and the conditions under which it is appropriate.

> If there is doubt about what the imperative is, or if there are many varying interpretations, then the law is not seen as having a character of its own but as a means for obtaining individual advantage. To this extent, the legitimate basis of compliance is undermined.[1]

The possibility of using ambiguity of imperatives for individual advantage reduces the legitimacy of the directives.

Finally, compliance must be enforced with rewards and penalties to reduce deviance. These could be forms of social disapproval as well as loss of pay, suspensions, etc. The breaking of rules leads slowly to total disregard for them. Imagine what would happen if parking violations were ignored. In the abstract, most people think the good of the order is promoted by restricting parking behavior. But there is always the exception when you are in a hurry. Again, if individual advantage is obtained through selective enforcement, this leads to a decline of legitimacy.

The question now becomes one of analyzing the task behaviors to see if legitimacy or compliance can be maintained under each of them.

**1. Join and remain.** There is probably a small negative relation between the use of rule compliance and turnover. This is due to the fact that individuals will probably not be attracted to roles that are constrained by rules. In addition they can be dissatisfied by being required to perform behaviors lying outside the area of acceptance. There is a good deal of evidence that dissatisfaction is associated with turnover.[2] But on the whole, there should be no strong relation between compliance and joining behaviors. If an organization had a problem of turnover, it would not employ rule compliance to reduce it.

The use of rule compliance, on the other hand, can reduce the amount of absenteeism. Most organizations have rules which define a legitimate absence. Enforcement of these rules can reduce the likelihood of one choosing to be absent. Excessive absences are usually penalized by loss of pay, suspension, and termination of employment. However, on some occasions, absenteeism can result from dissatisfaction with some aspect of the job situation. Enforcement of the rules will reduce absenteeism but not the dissatisfaction. The dissatisfaction may merely manifest itself in new forms such as grievances or strikes. Some care should be taken to diagnose the cause of excessive absences before acting through rule compliance.

**2. Dependable role behaviors.** The use of rule compliance can significantly increase the probability that individuals will choose to perform dependable role behaviors. These are repetitive, easily identifiable, and expected behaviors. It is easy to maintain legitimacy with this type of role behavior. On the auto assembly line, rule compliance is the predominant mode of influence. Employees are expected to show up at appointed times and perform their tasks reliably and consistently. Compliance is implemented through direct supervision and inspection procedures. In this way, minimal levels of quantity and quality of performance are maintained.

**3. Effort above minimum levels.** The use of rule compliance does not increase the probability that individuals will choose to perform above minimal levels. Implementation of rule compliance is probably the process of establishing the minimum level. But it also establishes a maximum.

> Emphasis on the legalities of organizational control tends in practice
> to mean that the minimal acceptable standard for quantity and quality
> of performance becomes the maximal standard. If it is legitimate
> and proper according to company and union standards to turn out
> 40 pieces on a machine, then there is no point in exceeding this stan-
> dard. One cannot be more legal or proper than the norm, though
> there are degrees of nonconformity in failing to meet it. Of course,
> individuals may be motivated to exceed the norm for various rewards
> but not for the satisfaction of properly meeting the rules.[3]

Despite the fact that rule compliance cannot motivate behaviors above minimal levels, it has often attempted to do so. Gouldner has related some of the consequences of the use of rules and their enforcement to motivate behaviors other than reliable role behaviors.[4] March and Simon have outlined the results schematically and their model is shown in Fig. 18.1.[5] The model begins in Box 1 with the demand for control. The need for control derives from the fact that organizations are artificial social forms and cannot rely on voluntary adoption of task behaviors. To fulfill this need, general and impersonal rules are articulated. The rules are the imperative statements mentioned previously. The effect of the rules and an expectation of

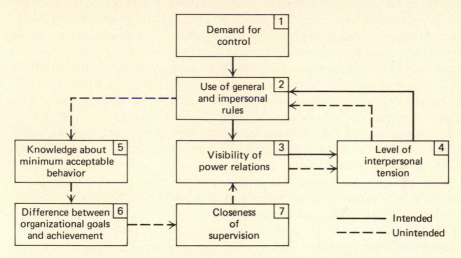

**Fig. 18.1   The simplified Gouldner model.**

their acceptance can be two-fold. First, there is the intended effect when the task is predictable. This means that behaviors can be clearly spelled out, learned, and performed. As long as the behaviors are within the zone of acceptance, they will be legitimate. Since the rules are general and impersonal, they do not lead to the individual advantage of the supervisor. The visibility of potentially alienating power differences is reduced. In cultures with egalitarian norms, it is suggested that decreased power visibility increases legitimacy of the supervisory role. The shared beliefs leading to legitimacy reduce interpersonal tensions in the group. The success in the use of rules thus reinforces their use. This process is illustrated by the solid lines from Boxes 2, 3, 4 and back to 2. This path is the intended effect and will occur when the task requires dependable predictable behaviors and these behaviors are within the zone of acceptance.

A second effect of the use of rules is an unintended one. The clarity of rules needed for legitimacy results in clarity about expected levels of performance. The hypothesis is that the clarity leads to a communication of minimal expected levels. But why is it not a high standard rather than a low one? Cannot high output be legislated? The answer is no. A standard set at a level that is the average will result in 50 percent of the work force being below standard. Deviation of this magnitude will result in a breakdown of the rule and a loss of legitimacy. Thus, the standard must be set at a level that most people are willing and able to meet if the rule is to be legitimate and enforceable. If a supervisor applies differential standards, the rules become discriminatory and lose their legitimacy. Thus, rule compliance can produce minimal levels of performance only.

If the task requires effort above minimal levels, rule compliance leads to a discrepancy between results and goals (Box 6). In some organizations, ineffective performance triggers closer supervision. Supervisors are required to exercise more control, more surveillance, more inspection, and more firmness in dealing with deviance. The result is an accentuation of the visibility of power relations. The exercise of organizational power produces employee dissatisfaction and alienation. The model predicts a reduction of legitimacy and an increase in interpersonal tensions. These changes are accompanied by increased use of rule compliance to stabilize the situation. More rules lead to a greater amount of programmed roles which eliminates the need for effort above the minimum.

In summary, rule compliance cannot motivate effort above the minimum levels. If organizations attempt to do so, they will bring about a decline in performance. So if the organization has tasks that require effort above minimum levels that cannot be designed away through the introduction of rules, it must use other rewards.

**4 and 5. Cooperative and spontaneous behaviors.** As might be expected, the use of rule compliance is not effective in motivating cooperative or spontaneous behaviors. First, it is quite difficult to create rules with the required clarity for uncertain tasks. And secondly, it is difficult to legislate creativity. Blau and Scott make this point very clearly.

> The legal authority of management to assign tasks to employees is rarely questioned—there is willing compliance—but this legal authority does not and cannot command the employee's willingness to devote his ingenuity and energy to performing his tasks to the best of his ability. Important as formal authority is for meeting the minimum requirements of operations in a complex organization, it is not sufficient for attaining efficiency. It promotes compliance with directives and discipline, but does not encourage employees to exert effort, to accept responsibilities, or to exercise initiative.[6]

Like the use of rules for effort above the minimum, rule compliance bears no necessary relationship to spontaneous behaviors. However, if it is implemented in situations requiring spontaneous behaviors, decreased performance is likely to result. The process is described by Merton.[7] A diagram of the process showing both intended and unintended effects is shown in

Fig. 18.2.[8] Again, the process begins with a demand for control by the organization. The demand for control is implemented by rule compliance or what is called emphasis on reliability. Imperatives and standard operating procedures are communicated and people are held accountable for their implementation. The intended effects do happen. That is, behavior becomes reliable and defensible, and coordination for routine activities is secured. The success reinforces the use of rules. The process is indicated by the loop from Boxes 1, 2, and 3.

There are unintended effects which can result when rule compliance is applied in dynamic situations requiring spontaneous behaviors. The emphasis upon reliability produces a rigidity of behavior. Employees fail to develop programs of action which are tailored to the unique features of each situation. (Merton uses servicing clients as the task.) In repetitive situations this process causes no problems. In uncertain situations the application of simple categories to differentiated phenomena results in reduced performance. Also, what is not covered by rules is by definition not the responsibility of the employee. Rules define what is not expected as well as what is expected. In situations where management responds to reduced performance by greater emphasis on control and accountability, there is an increased need for defensible individual action. Thus, there follows greater emphasis on reliable behavior. Both effective and ineffective performance can promote the use of rule compliance.

In both of the process models, rule compliance resulted in ineffective performance. In both cases poor performance resulted because there was compliance with directives. Management was successful in creating a situation where employees choose to perform the behavior specified by the

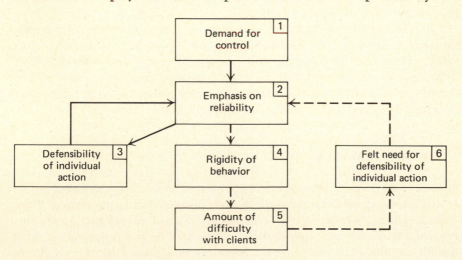

Fig. 18.2   The simplified Merton model.

imperative. Thus, rule compliance can be an effective basis of motivation. The point is that it does not result in effective performance for tasks requiring high effort and cooperative, spontaneous behaviors. The appropriate reward system depends on the nature of the task.

Another point that is suggested by the models is the paradox of control —the more management attempts to control the situation, the less control it has. The lack of control or ineffectiveness of the influence attempt comes from applying direct supervision, inspection, and accountability to tasks for which it is impossible to legislate and enforce high-effort levels. This response to low performance is partially based on the leader's assumptions about human nature. If it is thought that people need to be told what to do and checked on to see if they do it, the models of the sociologists are fairly good predictors. Other leaders with other models of human nature would respond with other motivational bases.

In summary, rule compliance is the use of legitimate authority and/or extrinsic rewards and penalties to influence individuals to choose an organizationally created directive as a determinant of their behavior. The success of this basis of influence depends on the directive to lie within the area of acceptance, to be clear and unambiguous, to be for the good of the order, and to be used for tasks requiring dependable role behaviors. In the abstract, it cannot be said that rule compliance is or is not an effective motivational basis of work behavior. It was argued that rule compliance was unrelated to some behaviors (join and remain), increased the probability of execution of other behaviors (dependable role behaviors), and could possibly be dysfunctional for others (effort above the minimum levels and spontaneous behaviors). Whether rule compliance should be chosen depends on the type of behavior required by the task.

If rule compliance is chosen as a basis of motivation, how is it implemented? In the majority of cases, compliance is obtained by direct supervision of the work by someone in a position of power and authority. This individual needs to be able to observe deviations from rules and initiate the reward and penalty system. Sometimes direct observation is augmented by inspections and audits by specialized personnel.

## SYSTEM REWARDS

System rewards are a form of extrinsic rewards, generally material rewards, which accrue to individuals based on their membership in the system. They include fringe benefits, good working conditions, cost-of-living pay increases, etc. If they are differentially distributed in the organization, it is usually on the basis of seniority. How do these rewards affect job behaviors?

**1. Join and remain.** System rewards have their largest effect on encouraging people to join and remain in the organization. They are usually designed to reward membership and longevity in the organization. System rewards are effective in attracting and holding people to the extent that the rewards compare favorably with those offered by other organizations. The path–goal model is useful in analyzing the choice of organization under these conditions. To the extent that the organization offers outcomes of positive valence and the individual perceives the taking of the role as instrumental to the attainment of these outcomes, the individual is motivated to take the role. But only if the force of the role has greater positive valence than other roles is the individual motivated to join the organization.

The model is also relevant for analyzing decisions to leave or remain. The model in the last chapter would suggest that this choice situation is not evoked until individuals are either presented another opportunity or become dissatisfied with their present jobs. Individuals may be satisfied with their present jobs but be presented with a new offer in which rewards have greater positive valence than those in the present jobs. Therefore, they change jobs. Alternatively, individuals may become dissatisfied with the present level of system rewards. The model predicts that individuals will search for new alternatives. Depending on economic conditions the employees' skills and visibility, individuals' search behaviors may or may not be productive. If they find some new alternatives, the path–goal model predicts they will select the one with the largest force. If they do not find an alternative, they may adjust their expectations downward and reduce dissatisfaction. Alternatively, they may remain dissatisfied and file a grievance to register their dissatisfaction.

Thus, turnover is the result of two factors—the dissatisfaction or satisfaction with current rewards and perceived ease of movement to another job.[9] The two factors account for the fact that some satisfied individuals leave the organization as well as the larger number of dissatisfied employees. Since search can be ineffective, some dissatisfied individuals remain along with the satisfied ones. The model can explain these phenomena with both evoking cues and search initiated by dissatisfaction. Thus, system rewards are effective at encouraging people to join and remain in an organization to the extent that they are perceived favorably when compared with rewards offered by other organizations.

**2. Dependable role behaviors.** The use of system rewards may have some effect on increasing the probability that people will adopt the dependable prescribed role behaviors. To the extent that the system rewards increase the attractiveness of the job, people will prefer not to lose an attractive position. If failure to adopt prescribed behaviors can lead to dismissal, system rewards can increase the probability of adopting dependable role behaviors. However, rule compliance is the primary motivator. System rewards have a secondary effect only. Organizations would not use system rewards to solve problems of unreliable role performance. They would use rule compliance or goal identification which will be discussed later.

**3. Effort above minimum levels.** When predicting the effects of offering or changing the amount of a system reward, one gets involved in a current debate over which theory to use. The path–goal model from expectancy theory would lead to the prediction of no direct effect on the choice of behaviors above minimum levels. The forces of the alternatives of producing above or at the minimum level are identical. Individuals receive the same reward whether they produce above or at the minimum level. Vacations, hourly wages, insurance, etc., are given independent of the individual's level of performance as long as performance is above the minimum threshold. Therefore, system rewards should have no direct effect on behavior above the minimum level. This line of reasoning, however, assumes that individuals perceive the instrumental relationship as it has been described. The assumption seems reasonable in the case of system rewards.

Alternatively, equity theory may lead to the prediction that system rewards should have an effect on behaviors above the minimum levels.[10] An oversimplified explanation is that employees have a conception of a fair day's work for a fair day's pay. If the pay (reward) is increased or decreased from that standard, individuals are motivated to increase or decrease their efforts in order to maintain the equity between effort and reward. This theory is supported by some experimental evidence.[11] However, when the theory is tested over time, either the theory's predictions appear not to hold or the expected equitable level changes quickly.[12] In either case, increasing system rewards does not serve as a sustaining motivating force for behaviors above minimum levels of effort. On the other hand, rewards below equitable levels can lead to dissatisfaction and possible reductions of effort if search behavior does not discover another means to reduce dissatisfaction. Thus, with respect to choices of behaviors above minimum levels, one would predict that system rewards cannot increase, but can decrease, the probability that individuals will choose the required behaviors. System rewards may have an indirect effect by maintaining membership in the organization. Longevity may lead to identification with the organization and identification can lead to effort above minimum levels. However, if organizations need effort above minimum levels, they should employ bases of motivation other than system rewards.

**4 and 5. Cooperative and spontaneous behaviors.** The same situation prevails for cooperative and spontaneous behaviors. Individuals receive the same system rewards whether they perform these behaviors or not. Therefore, the force acting on individuals to perform these behaviors is identical to the force acting on them not to perform the behaviors. Therefore, system rewards should have no direct effect on spontaneous and cooperative behaviors. Again, equity theory may lead to the prediction that there will be an effect if individuals remove inequity by effort allocation toward the job. There may also be an indirect effect due to identification.

In summary, system rewards are extrinsic rewards which reward membership in an organization. As such, they primarily influence the choice of individuals to join and remain in an organization to the extent that the rewards compare favorably with the rewards of other organizations. System rewards can have some other indirect or unintended effects, the most serious of which would be inequity or dissatisfaction caused by distribution on bases other than seniority. System rewards are implemented primarily through the provision of fringe benefits, working conditions, job guarantees, etc.

## INDIVIDUAL AND GROUP REWARDS

In this section both individual and group rewards are discussed together. Usually they differ only on the basis for their distribution. In addition, their juxtaposition permits us to highlight various properties of wage and salary plans. The subject matter is best divided by type of extrinsic reward. Therefore monetary incentives will be examined first, then supervisory practices.

### Monetary Incentives

The topic of monetary incentives and motivation never fails to elicit strong opinions both pro and con. These opinions result from experiences in which various incentives have been failures and experiences in which they have been successful. The goal in this section is to explain and predict when and why monetary incentives may or may not be successful in increasing the probability that employees will select the appropriate behaviors for the job situations. It is hoped that greater accuracy can be achieved by analyzing the different categories of behavior and employing the motivational model of Chapter 17.

**1. Join and remain.** Wages and salaries have the same effect upon join-and-remain behaviors as fringe benefits do. To the degree that the money package compares favorably with those offered by other organizations, monetary incentives reduce the likelihood that the individual will leave the organization and increase the likelihood that he or she will join. The likelihood of leaving or joining is primarily dependent on the amount of the reward rather than on the basis on which it is given. Therefore, there should be little difference between individual rewards, group rewards, and system rewards. Indeed, if money is not distributed on the basis of performance, it is a system reward.

In another sense, individual rewards can be tailored more to individual needs than can group or system rewards. The probability of leaving is a function of the individuals' dissatisfaction with the current state of affairs and the ease with which they can obtain other jobs. So as individuals vary in levels of satisfaction and in ease of movement, the amount of money necessary to keep them in the organization also varies. This fact leads some organizations to differentially compensate people. It raises some equity problems which are usually handled by policies of pay secrecy. But otherwise individual rewards are identical in their effect on joining and leaving decisions.

There is some evidence that bonus plans based on attendance can motivate better attendance.[13] However, the costs of administering such plans need to be weighed against the costs of absenteeism. There is also some debate as to whether hourly pay is better than salaries in motivating attendance. There is little evidence to support either opposing view. Attendance is probably best motivated by totally satisfactory rewards and intrinsic motivation.[14] Thus, it is predicted that there is little difference between system, group, and individual rewards in influencing join-and-remain behavior. It is the amount of reward rather than the basis of distribution that determines the choice of behavior.

**2. Dependable role behaviors.**   Monetary rewards can increase the probability that dependable role behaviors will be performed. If role occupants are faced with a choice of adopting a dependable behavior versus not adopting it, the probability is higher that they will adopt the behavior if adoption leads to the receipt of more money and if occupants value money. This follows directly from the model. While wages and salaries can be used in this manner, they generally are not. First, dependable behaviors are expected from everyone. Raises are not given for performing dependably because such behavior is expected. However, raises are denied for not performing dependably. In this way the administration of pay can increase the power of supervisors and increase their ability to use rule compliance.

The denial of a raise can be viewed as a penalty. Therefore the model would predict that denying a raise increases the probability of the performance of dependable role behaviors. The force has positive valence because performance avoids a penalty. However, it may also have the effect of alienating the subordinate.

The second reason pay is not used to ensure dependable behaviors is that an individual merit system is expensive relative to rule compliance for increasing the probability that dependable behaviors will be performed. It takes a great deal of management time to administer an individualized reward system. Thus, the reward policies differ in their motivational bases, their ability to motivate particular behaviors and their costs to administer. The effort involved in administering a group or individual pay system is not likely to increase the probability of adoption of dependable role behaviors by a sufficient amount to justify the expense.

**3. Effort above minimum levels.** One of the primary purposes for compensating employees on an individual or group basis rather than a system basis is to motivate individuals to contribute effort above minimally acceptable levels. Monetary incentives, merit raises, bonuses, etc. are employed because rule compliance and system rewards do not effectively influence choices of alternative levels of effort. In addition, these rewards share with the employees the profit of the organization. Let us examine the evidence to see if these assertions are supported.

The model would predict that the probability that the individual would select behaviors leading to effort above minimum levels would increase to the extent that the effort was believed to lead to performance ($E_{ij} > 0$), performance was believed to lead to increased pay ($I_{jk} > 0$), and to the degree that more pay was important ($V_k > 0$). The evidence has been reviewed by Vroom,[15] and more recently by Lawler.[16] The data strongly support the proposition with respect to instrumentality $I_{jk}$.

> When all the evidence already discussed is considered, it is obvious that there is a tremendous amount of empirical support for the proposition that productivity can be increased by making pay dependent upon performance. Admittedly, much of the evidence is from studies that have methodological problems, but some of the evidence reviewed in the discussion of individual plans is quite good. One fact stands out: Regardless of the methodology and the kind of plan considered, when individual pay is clearly dependent upon individual performance, job performance is higher than when pay and performance are not related.[17]

A good example of this evidence is the field experiment by Wyatt.[18] Starting with a work group on a fixed weekly wage, he introduced a competitive bonus system and then a piece-rate plan into the group. The assumption is that under the fixed weekly wage the instrumentality of performance for money was close to zero. Individuals received the same wage independent of their performance. Under the competitive bonus system perceived instrumentality should have increased because the receipt of wages depended on the individual's level of production. However, the receipt of wages depends on the performance of others as well. Since the outcome was not completely controlled by the individual, the assumption was that instrumentality was greater than zero but less than one. Finally under a piece-rate system, individuals are paid in proportion to their own production. The direct relation between output and wages should make instrumentality equal to one. The results showed an increase of 46 percent when the competitive bonus system was introduced and an increase of 30 percent more 15 weeks later when the piece rate was installed. The increase remained during the 12 weeks of the study. If instrumentality changed as assumed following the changes in the payment systems, output varied directly with instrumentality.

There is little evidence relevant to the expectancy hypothesis.[19] Either the studies have confounded instrumentality and expectancy or have measured only instrumentality. Thus, there is neither supportive nor contradictory evidence.

The results for valence are mixed. There is some correlation evidence showing that those people who consider money more important perform at higher levels than those who consider money less important when instrumentality is greater than zero.[20] However, in laboratory experiments under conditions where the receipt of money was contingent on performance, an increase in the amount of money sometimes increased performance and sometimes produced no changes.[21] Presumably, the greater the amount of money, the greater the valence of the outcome. But there may be intervening factors which reduce the presumed direct relation. Individuals have different preferences for money which could account for some differences. Indeed, one experiment revealed that intrinsically motivated people did not increase output when contingent monetary rewards were offered but non-intrinsically motivated people did increase their output.[22] In addition, the previously described relation between increased satisfaction and decreased importance of an outcome suggests that money outcomes need to be increased to maintain the same valence. A final interpretation might be that the relation between motivation and performance is nonlinear. An increase in money may increase valence but yield very little increase in output. In summary, there are alternative explanations within the logic of the model but the evidence is inconclusive.

Some organizations, for reasons to be discussed later, tie the pay of individuals to their group's output rather than to their own. What are the motivational effects of this pay system? The model would suggest that average individuals' productivity would decrease. The reason is that the effort of individuals is less directly related to the receipt of wages. Instrumentality should decline. Indeed, the larger the group the less directly is one's performance related to one's wages and the lower the instrumentality. An alternative explanation might be that motivation would increase. The reasoning would be as follows. The group incentive would make performance instrumental to the attainment of more wages albeit less instrumental than an individual plan, and also instrumental to the attainment of acceptance and approval from other group members. The assumption is that since everyone in the group benefits from higher production, the group would adopt and enforce norms to support higher output. Performance would become instrumental to two extrinsic rewards.

The evidence supports the first hypothesis.[23] Individuals on incentives have higher productivity than the average of individuals working in groups. Also the larger the group, the lower the average. The second hypothesis depends on the group norms. Apparently the incentive alone does not create supportive group norms. Indeed, in the Hawthorne studies, individuals were on a group incentive but still developed norms to restrict rather than increase output.[24] Thus the motivation to exert effort above minimum levels is less for group incentives than for individual incentives. But on the whole, tying pay to performance increases the probability that individuals will perform above minimally acceptable levels.

**4. Spontaneous and cooperative behaviors.** It is one thing for employees to exert effort above minimum levels within their defined roles and another to devote that effort to activities above and beyond assigned tasks. Can money motivate individuals to perform spontaneous and cooperative behaviors? From a motivational point of view, a spontaneous behavior or a cooperative behavior should be no different from any other behavior. If that behavior is believed to be instrumental to the attainment of valued outcomes, the individual will choose to perform that behavior. On the other hand, it can be argued that a pay plan to reward spontaneous behavior is difficult to operationalize. The reason is that the individual must have clear perceptions of instrumentalities and expectancies. But when the organization defines which outcomes will be rewarded, it also defines the ones which will not be rewarded. For uncertain tasks it is difficult to make this distinction between performance outcomes.

There is no evidence from research undertaken specifically to test spontaneous behavior motivation. However, there is some indirect evidence pertaining to problems of operationalizing performance measures.[25] All the cases summarized indicate that when outcomes are measured and rewarded, those outcomes occur with a high probability but they occur at the expense of unmeasured outcomes. These studies appear to be testimonials to both the strength of extrinsic rewards, (that is, they do increase the probability that people will adopt behaviors leading to measured and rewarded outcomes) and the weakness of extrinsic rewards, (they reduce the probability that unmeasured outcomes will occur). Thus, all of those necessary activities which are difficult to observe or measure and which may lead to payoffs some time in the future are unlikely to occur under monetary incentive systems. However, it should be remembered that it is the implementation rather than an erroneous motivation theory that causes the dysfunctions. As one might expect, organizations have devised strategies to overcome these problems.

The first approach is to create performance measures which are more comprehensive in terms of the number and types of outcomes. Sirota describes a case involving blue-collar workers.[26] He starts by analyzing the assumptions underlying the typical wage incentive which is based on actual output relative to some engineering standard output. That is, the greater the amount by which actual output exceeds standard output, the greater the amount of money the individual receives. However, Sirota states that:

> . . . by and large, only one determinant of worker productivity—*physcial effort*—is considered. Under this system, the major way a trained and experienced worker can increase his output, and hence his earnings, is by applying greater physical effort on his job.[27]

In repetitive, stable tasks, and with workers who choose not to be involved in their work, this may not be a bad assumption. However, in dynamic situations with changing products and processes, the worker can increase output by discovering a new method of production. The organization Sirota describes used an historical total output standard which was independent of method, and rewarded new methods, suggestions, and increases in output for the individual and anyone else who increased output as a result of adopting the new method. This plan rewards any legitimate increase in output independent of the method by which output was increased. It thereby expands the types of behaviors to include some innovative and spontaneous behaviors.

In terms of the model that has been developed, the individual has a choice of reporting or not reporting a newly discovered method. This is clearly a spontaneous behavior as we have defined it. The individual will choose to report the idea if it is believed that rewards will result. Sirota describes an organization which attempts to make spontaneous behaviors instrumental to the receipt of more wages. Company suggestion plans are examples of this phenomenon. However, their existence does not guarantee that perceived instrumentality ($I_{jk}$) will be close to 1.0. If a suggestion is rejected and a rumor starts that management keeps the ideas and tries them in other plants, the system will fail to establish instrumentalities. Whether instrumentalities are established or not depends on the administration of the program. The choice of these administrative practices can be analyzed in the context of the path–goal model.

A number of other examples could be given but all have the attribute of expanding the number of outcomes which are considered and rewarded. The result is that the measures are more subjective and ambiguous. While the measures increase instrumentality for some spontaneous behaviors, they decrease instrumentality for other repetitive behaviors. The new measures reduce the formula-like relation between effort and reward. Expectancies and some other instrumentalities decrease. To some degree that is a trade-off which cannot be avoided. One cannot define a clear, unambiguous reward system for an uncertain, ambiguous task. When such a reward system is defined, dysfunctional behaviors result. For predictable tasks, the spontaneous behaviors which are unexecuted have a minimal effect. For uncertain tasks, the spontaneous behaviors are critical. Therefore, one chooses a subjective reward in the latter case. The "best" reward system depends on the nature of the task. Extrinsic rewards must also be compared with intrinsic rewards with respect to increasing the probability of adopting spontaneous behaviors.

An alternative to using subjective rewards to motivate spontaneous and cooperative behaviors is to use more global but objective measures of performance. That is, it may be difficult to find individual criteria to reward spontaneous and cooperative behaviors but easy to find measures which reflect spontaneous and cooperative behaviors exhibited by a group. Such a reward system makes the spontaneous and cooperative behaviors instrumental to the attainment of more money. There is some evidence for this assertion.[28] Another study reports a case in which a sales group operating under individual incentives created their own group incentive to see that the spontaneous and cooperative activities were performed.[29]

There are also some costs associated with this approach. While it increases cooperation within the group to which the performance measure applies, it decreases cooperation between groups. Intergroup coordination may be a trivial problem if the groups are relatively autonomous, but if they share a common stockroom, laboratory, or maintenance function, competition may be created. Similarly if engineering introduces a new product which temporarily reduces productivity, new problems arise. If the organization is dependent on cooperation between groups it must either abandon extrinsic rewards which create competition, use subjective criteria, or expand the size of the group until a relatively autonomous grouping is attained. In the next chapter, alternative rewards will be discussed. It has already been predicted that subjectivity decreases expectancies and instrumentalities. Expanding the size of the group has two opposite effects. First, it eliminates dysfunctional behaviors caused by interunit competition. Second, the larger the unit, the less likely the individual is to see how his or her behavior relates to company profit or whatever criterion determines the individual's reward. Thus the instrumentalities drop to zero. The group incentive for large units becomes a system reward and fails to motivate job behavior. This analysis suggests that the selection of reward system and design of structure (e.g., autonomous groups) are interdependent decisions.

Another approach has been to continue to use subjective measures of performance such as supervisor ratings but to collect more information to attempt to reduce some of the subjectivity. There are a few private experiments with peer rating systems to measure cooperative behavior but no public research findings. Another organization pools ratings from supervisors, co-workers, people from other departments, customers, etc. Some of the sources are specified by the individuals themselves. The subjectivity of the rating may be reduced but there are questions of weights to ratings and the overall expense of the process.

In summary, the assertion is that in the abstract there is no reason why spontaneous or cooperative behaviors cannot be made instrumental to the attainment of money. When this is attempted in fact, the problems usually result from the implementation of the concept rather than from the concept itself. Attempts to eliminate dysfunctional side effects of these systems have involved group incentives and subjective criteria. In both cases there are reduced side effects but also reduced motivation due to lower expectancies and instrumentalities. In reality, lower expectancies and instrumentalities reflect the uncertainty inherent in the tasks.

Summarizing for all behaviors, it has been suggested that individual monetary rewards when made contingent upon the execution of particular behaviors increase the probability that those behaviors will be chosen by role occupants. Specifically, when the amounts of the reward compare favorably with those of other organizations, money influences people to join and remain in that organization. Financial outcomes are used to motivate dependable behaviors largely by being withheld when individuals behave unreliably. A good deal of evidence supported the assertion that people exert effort above minimum levels when that effort leads to performance and performance leads to monetary rewards. There was some evidence that spontaneous and cooperative behaviors could result from financial incentives but required administrative procedures specifically designed for those behaviors. There was also some evidence to suggest that those procedures are difficult to design and implement. When they are competitive, financial reward systems can reduce the probability that cooperative behaviors will be chosen. Thus, the efficacy of financial rewards for spontaneous and cooperative behaviors are dependent upon the method of implementation.

## Implementation of Pay Systems

Given the role of implementation in pay-system effectiveness a few remarks are in order. Since a scholarly work already exists, the intention is not to be exhaustive but simply to complete the analysis.[30] The reason is that there is more to a pay policy than claiming that pay should be tied to performance. Indeed, even in the place where one would expect the best implementation —the American Corporation—the research suggests that the relation between pay and performance is less than the professed intention.[31] Let us examine some of the reasons for this.

**1. Conflicting uses of pay.** Pay can be used to reward performance and it can be used to hold people in the organization. As people vary in their external visibility, the salaries reflect visibility as well as performance. The dual purpose can obscure the relation between performance and pay and reduce instrumentalities.

**2. Subjectivity of performance measures.** Another factor that obscures the relation between pay and performance is the inability to measure performance on uncertain tasks. As a consequence, individuals are uncertain as to what constitutes good performance (their perceived expectancies decline) and are uncertain as to whether rewards will follow certain performance outcomes (their perceived instrumentalities decline). In addition, subjectivity is a contributing factor to some of the following problems as well.

**3. Insufficient variance in individual rewards.** If individual performance varies, individual rewards should vary also. However, with subjective measures of performance, supervisors are reluctant to give highly variable rewards. The consequence of this practice is that the individual recognizes that pay is not directly tied to performance. Attempts to force distributions on uncertain tasks can lead to serious morale problems, however.[32]

**4. Pay secrecy policies.** One way to use pay for dual purposes and to live with subjective criteria is to employ salary secrecy policies. Perhaps it is possible to maintain instrumentalities at high levels with this policy. However, this does not appear to be the case.[33] Secrecy is associated with reduced instrumentalities and overestimation of the raises and salaries of others. Secrecy may also destroy the trust that is essential to overcome the subjectivity of the performance criteria.

**5. Infrequent distribution of rewards.** The typical pay system is one in which the pay increase is awarded once a year, divided by twelve, and distributed in the monthly check. In this manner the reward system is based on accounting convenience rather than motivational consequences. The real strength of wage incentives and sales commissions is the immediate association of the reward with the behavior. The individuals may not receive the money immediately but they know they will receive it. While the immediate association of rewards is not possible for uncertain tasks, a more frequent distribution of rewards would increase instrumentalities and perhaps promote learning.

The five categories above also identify design variables in the pay system. It can be hypothesized that the pay system will be more effective in terms of higher instrumentalities to the extent that pay is tied to performance rather than external visibility, that objectivity can be increased (perhaps through some form of management by objectives, a more sophisticated accounting system, etc.), that secrecy can be reduced, that variance in pay increases can match variance in performance, and that rewards can be distributed frequently. Supportive data exist for some of these statements, but all of the statements should be regarded as hypotheses the validity of which rests on being logically consistent with the motivation model.

A few words of caution are necessary. One of the reasons implementation of a pay system is so difficult is that changes, with good intentions, lead to side effects. One must examine the entire pay package and how this package is perceived by its recipients. For example, Thompson and Dalton describe a situation where a company was dissatisfied with the fact that there was no variance in the performance ratings and therefore little variance in raises.[34] Nearly everyone was rated as average, good, or excellent and mostly the latter two. A change was introduced to create more variance by forcing all managers to rate their subordinates and rank them in a normal distribution. The result was that some individuals increased their absolute performance but, since it was not as great as the increase achieved by others, reduced their rated performance. For them, increases in effort and performance result in lower rewards and dissatisfaction. This is not what management intended although the highly rated individuals may have increased their instrumentalities. The problem was the relative ranking system. It increased the variance in rewards but decreased the connection between performance and pay relative to an absolute performance rating.

Another example is the type of change which lets people "know where they stand" by increasing reward variance or eliminating pay secrecy. On one side, the change may increase the perceived instrumentality of performance for pay as intended. But for those people who discover they have received the lowest raises and are rated as low performers, the information provided by the change can be an ego-deflating experience. For example, in a GE study, the average self-rating placed the individual in the 77th percentile and only two out of 92 ranked themselves below average.[35] If these figures are representative, then a large number of people will find the increased information and openness a deflating and possibly a demotivating experience. Their motivation will decrease, in spite of increased instrumentality, because of a decrease in valence of pay and performance outcomes. The decrease can result from a decreased instrumentality of pay and performance outcomes for the satisfaction of self-esteem needs. After the change these outcomes may satisfy only lower order needs.[36] The effect would be to lower the importance and the valence of these outcomes. Again, an attempt to increase motivation instead creates lower motivation and satisfaction.

The point of this discussion has been to illustrate that the hypotheses stated above about secrecy, variance, etc. need qualification. Each statement should be qualified by an introduction of "other things being equal, greater secrecy promotes greater instrumentality, etc." The examples illustrate that other things are not always equal. Thus, the reward system, in this case a pay system, must not only be consistent with the required task behaviors but must also itself be internally consistent. This internal consistency must be examined from the point of view of the reward recipient. The path–goal model is one means of conducting this examination.

Before finishing the discussion of pay systems, it should be pointed out that there are alternative explanations for the phenomena above. The alternatives, however, do not detract from the basic point. It is possible to interpret the described effects of secrecy in a favorable manner. One could say that the increased openness decreased satisfaction and motivation. But the decrease would be among the low performers. There may be an increase among the high performers. In the long run, the organization creates a highly motivating, satisfying situation. The dissatisfied personnel will leave the organization, change their behavior, etc. This change concentrates the motivational leverage on the high performer.

It is quite possible that some organizations would actually prefer this system. They could argue that the previous system merely maintained the self-images of the mediocre at the expense of the high performer. The change to a high-variance, open-pay system would create a climate which rewards excellence rather than mediocrity. Indeed, the work of Roberts shows that it is very difficult to motivate innovative, risk-taking behaviors in large organizations.[37] He suggests that policies to maintain job descriptions and salary structures merely create a reward system for the mediocre but not for the excellent. Thus, many organizations create so-called venture management teams outside of the organizational context in the hopes of creating a climate to reward performance. A high-variance, open reporting system may be an alternative which rewards innovative behaviors within the organization.

The reasoning above is based partially on an assumption that performance can be objectively measured and the low rewards actually go to the low performers. In some organizations, the task is sufficiently uncertain and the goals sufficiently ambiguous that only parts of the total task can be measured. In these organizations, other forms of reward are employed rather than risk the dysfunctional aspects of pay systems.

## PROMOTION

An alternative to tying pay directly to performance is to promote individuals to higher paying jobs on the basis of performance. In this case all of the prior discussion of the instrumentality of performance to pay applies to the instrumentality of promotion. The strength and weakness of promotions is that they are given less frequently. Lower frequency of promotions permits a more time-consuming, subjective, and comprehensive review of the individuals' work. Thus promotions can minimize side effects. However, subjectivity and low frequency can blur the instrumental relation. One can usually construct a number of theories as to why a particular individual was promoted. But promotions may represent a more easily administered system of reward and may tap higher order needs than pay systems.

## SUMMARY

This chapter has been devoted to a discussion of extrinsic rewards exclusive of leadership behavior and group acceptance. The types of reward systems classed as rule compliance, system rewards, group rewards, and individual rewards were discussed. For each, the effect on the types of behaviors was discussed. Either available evidence or an implication of the model was presented to substantiate the assertions. The design variables such as pay, direct supervision, etc., were discussed as means by which the systems could be implemented.

In the next chapters, leadership and the intrinsic rewards are discussed, an example system is analyzed and, finally, a case described in which a reward system is designed.

## NOTES

1. D. Katz and R. Kahn 1966. *The social psychology of organizations.* New York: Wiley, p. 350.
2. V. H. Vroom 1964. *Work and motivation.* New York: Wiley, pp. 175–178.
3. Katz and Kahn, p. 347.

4. A. W. Gouldner 1953. *Patterns of industrial bureaucracy*. Glencoe, Ill.: Free Press.

5. J. G. March and H. A. Simon 1958. *Organizations*. New York: Wiley, pp. 44–46.

6. P. Blau and W. R. Scott 1962. *Formal organizations*. San Francisco: Chandler, 140.

7. R. K. Merton 1940. Bureaucratic structure and personality. *Social Forces* **18**: 560–568.

8. March and Simon, pp. 37–40.

9. *Ibid.*, p. 93.

10. J. S. Adams 1965. Injustice in social exchange. In Berkowitz (ed.), *Advances in experimental social psychology*. (Vol. 2). New York: Academic Press, pp. 267–299.

11. *Ibid.*

12. E. Lawler III, C. A. Koplin, T. F. Young, and J. A. Fadem 1967. Inequity reduction over time in an induced overpayment situation. *Organization Behavior and Human Performance* **2**: 122–142.

13. E. Lawler III 1971. *Pay and organizational effectiveness: a psychological view*. New York: McGraw-Hill, Chapter 11.

14. Lawler, *ibid.*, p. 195.

15. Vroom, pp. 252–260.

16. Lawler, Chapter 7.

17. *Ibid.*, p. 132.

18. S. Wyatt 1934. *Incentives in repetitive work: a practical experiment in a factory*. (Industrial Health Research Board Report No. 69.) London: Her Majesty's Stationery Office.

19. H. G. Heneman III and O. P. Schwab 1972. Evaluation of research on expectancy theory predictions of employee performance. *Psychological Bulletin* **78**: 1–9.

20. L. W. Porter and E. Lawler III, *Managerial attitudes and performance*. Homewood, Ill.: Richard D. Irwin.

21. Lawler, *Pay*, p. 134.

22. J. W. Atkinson and W. R. Reitman 1956. Performance as a function of motive strength and expectancy of goal attainment. *Journal of Abnormal and Social Psychology* **53**: 361–366.

23. R. Marriott 1949. Size of working group and output. *Occupational Psychology* **23**: 47–57.

24. F. J. Roethlisberger and W. S. Dickson 1939. *Management and the worker*. Cambridge: Harvard University Press.

25. V. F. Ridgeway 1956. "Dysfunctional consequences of performance measurements. *Administrative Science Quarterly*, (September): 143–155.

26. D. Sirota 1966. Productivity management. *Harvard Business Review*, (Sept.-Oct.): 111–116.

27. D. Sirota, p. 112.

28. A. Zander and D. Wolfe 1964. Administrative rewards and coordination among committee members. *Administrative Science Quarterly*, (June): 50–69.

29. N. Babchuk and W. J. Goode, Work incentives in a self-determined group. *American Sociological Review* **16**: 679–687.

30. Lawler, *Pay*, Chapter 9.

31. *Ibid.*, p. 158.

32. P. Thompson and G. Dalton 1970. Performance appraisal: managers beware. *Harvard Business Review*, (Jan.-Feb.): 75–84.

33. Lawler, *Pay*, pp. 174–5.

34. Thompson and Dalton.

35. H. Meyer, E. Kay, and J. R. P. French 1965. Split roles in performance appraisal. *Harvard Business Review* (Jan.-Feb.): 123.

36. Lawler, *Pay,* Chapter 3.

37. Most of the work of E. Roberts is not published but exists in working paper form from the Sloan School of Management, M.I.T., Cambridge, Mass.

## QUESTIONS

1. When is rule compliance different from legitimate authority?

2. What are the strengths and limitations of rule compliance?

3. What will be the effect on dependable role behavior of an increase in cost of living allowances?

4. If group rewards decrease instrumentality, why would you use one?

5. What would be the result of compensating faculty members based on student ratings? on number of students attracted to the course?

6. Do you think pay secrecy is a good administrative practice? Why or why not?

7. Select a job in an organization and design two different extrinsic reward systems for it. Indicate under what conditions both might be effective.

8. How many different ways can you list which will use extrinsic rewards to encourage cooperative behaviors?

<table>
<tr><td></td><td rowspan="2" style="text-align:right">CHAPTER<br>**19**</td></tr>
<tr><td>**LEADERSHIP AND GROUPS**</td></tr>
</table>

In this chapter the effects of the behaviors of others in the individual's work place are analyzed. These relevant others who can affect the choices of the individual are the peers in the work group and the formal leader of the group. The purpose of the analysis, as before, is to identify the design variables and indicate how these variables affect the choice of the different task behaviors.

The discussion of leadership and groups will complete the analysis of extrinsic rewards. Recall that the analysis is based on the premise that the individual's choice of behavior will be influenced by those who will be affected by that choice. These are the organization as a whole, the leader of the group, the other individuals making up the work group, and the individual himself or herself. The first three are considered to be extrinsic rewards and the latter an intrinsic reward. Chapter 18 developed the organization's rewards, primarily in the form of monetary compensation. Chapter 20 will discuss the types of intrinsic rewards. The discussion in the present chapter provides a transition from extrinsic to intrinsic rewards. The reason is that, in addition to affecting extrinsic rewards, some supervisory behaviors affect the degree to which motivation can be made intrinsic. Let us first examine the leadership behaviors and then the group behaviors.

### LEADERSHIP BEHAVIORS

Leadership is a subject for which there is a great deal of folklore, theoretical speculation, and even empirical evidence. But in spite of this attention, there is no single, valid theory of leadership. One can find classic works in organization theory which consider leadership to be the critical factor around which the organization should be designed.[1] In another, the word leadership is not even mentioned.[2] Among those theorists who consider leadership important, one can find several different paradigms.[3] Research within a single paradigm often shows inconsistent results and rarely if ever is more than 25 percent of the variance of a behavior or attitude explained. Thus, leadership is regarded by some as one of the most important but least understood factors in organizations.

The problem of selecting a leadership paradigm is the same as selecting a theory of motivation. The inquiry into a confused and ambiguous subject is best conducted through parallel experiments. But since the intention here is not to provide an exhaustive review of leadership, a choice must be made. In addition, those who must design organizations, unless they choose to disregard leadership, must choose one of the approaches on which to base their choices. In the following sections, the Ohio State Leadership paradigm will be followed.

### Consideration and Initiating Structure

The study of leadership has evolved from the search for traits of leaders to the search for behaviors exhibited by leaders. Specifically, the interest is in those behaviors which are likely to influence the subordinate's choice of task-related behaviors. While there are many types of leader behavior that can be exhibited, two general classes have been discovered which can explain the majority of the likely ones.[4] One set describes instrumental behaviors which create structure in a situation. The dimension includes behaviors such as assigning tasks, specifying procedures to be followed, scheduling work, etc. This dimension is termed *initiating structure* and measures the degree to which a supervisor engages in these behaviors. The second set of behaviors are those which provide socioemotional support for the dependent individual. These behaviors are ones which express warmth, support, and genuine concern for the needs of the subordinate. This dimension is called *consideration* and measures the degree to which the leader expresses genuine concern for the needs of those people who are dependent on him or her. These two dimensions have been used in numerous studies, have been found in the literature for a number of years, and are similar to dimensions used in other approaches to the study of leadership.[5]

There is another variable that has been hypothesized to moderate the relation between the behavior of a leader and the behaviors and attitudes of subordinates. This attribute is the amount of influence that the leader has outside of the immediate work group.[6] The addition of *outside influence* recognizes that the behaviors of interest take place in an organizational context. Therefore, the effectiveness of structuring and considerate behaviors may depend on the ability of the leader to affect behavior in other departments and at higher levels of the organization. Thus, the influence of a supervisor on the subordinate's behavior is a function of the degree of initiating structure and consideration shown in the leader's behavior and a function of the amount of influence the supervisor has outside of the immediate work group. Since the research has not specifically tested the effects of leadership on dependable, cooperative, or spontaneous types of behavior, let us review the research quickly and then generalize to the framework that has been developed in previous chapters.[7]

### Consideration

The studies of consideration consistently report a positive relation between subordinate satisfaction and the degree of leader consideration. This apparently strong relation needs to be qualified, however. Most of the correlations are usually low. And it is not clear whether satisfaction is related to the perception of the leader's behavior or the actual behavior. Satisfied individuals may perceive leaders to be considerate whether they are or not. While these theoretical problems remain, there seems to be a well-established relation between consideration and subordinate satisfaction.

The relationship is not quite so strong with respect to performance. Vroom summarized eleven studies in which eight revealed a positive relation; two, a negative relation; and one, no relation.[8] In addition to the mixed results, the correlations are again quite low. There is also a problem of causation. The leader of a high-producing group may be able to be considerate while the leader of a low-performing group cannot afford that luxury. Indeed, there is one experimental study which reports that changes in group output produced changes in the degree of considerate and initiating behavior of the leaders.[9] As in the case of satisfaction, there are theoretical problems but also the suggestion of a relation between consideration and performance.

One reason why a relation will consistently arise but be quite weak is that there are conditioning factors which moderate the relationship. Vroom suggests that the basis on which consideration is shown could be a moderating factor. In terms of the path–goal model, one could suggest that consideration is a rewarding outcome which carries a valence. If this reward is given independent of the level of performance, then one would predict that the subordinate would be satisfied but that performance would not be influenced. Therefore, we would not expect a relation between consideration and performance. If, however, consideration is given on the basis of performance, performance becomes instrumental to the attainment of considerate leader behaviors. One empirical study supports this contention.[10] Subordinate performance varied with the extent that subordinates desired considerate leader behavior and perceived performance as instrumental to the attainment of consideration. In addition the model explained 50 percent of the variance in subordinate physical output. Thus, individuals vary in the degree to which consideration is perceived to be rewarding, and leaders vary in the degree to which performance is instrumental to the receipt of supervisory rewards. Both factors must be positive if consideration and performance are to be related.

A second factor which is hypothesized to moderate the relationships involving consideration is the degree to which the task is intrinsically rewarding.[11] The importance and valence of consideration is less if the task is itself satisfying. Consideration is more important for dull routine tasks which provide no satisfactions in themselves. This hypothesis and the Deci results suggest that individuals cannot be motivated by two things at the same time. Authority, money, promotions, consideration, and the task itself can motivate behavior but cannot simultaneously motivate the same behavior.[12] Thus, the nature of the task can moderate consideration and satisfaction.

In summary, consideration can be satisfying and rewarding and therefore positively valent. When this reward is contingent on performance, supervisors can increase the probability that individuals will choose high-performance behaviors. The reward power is greater for unsatisfying tasks than for intrinsically motivating tasks.

### Initiating Structure

The results for initiating structure reveal the same small correlations as consideration but the results are mixed for satisfaction. The original hypothesis was that a high degree of initiating structure would be irritating and dissatisfying to the subordinate. The assumption was that no one likes to be closely supervised. Some results confirmed this initial hypothesis.[13] The greater the degree of initiating structure, the greater the number of grievances and amount of turnover. However, subsequent studies have not replicated these results and indeed have reported a positive relation between initiating structure and subordinate satisfaction.[14] On the other hand, leaders high on initiating structure are consistently rated higher by their superiors, have higher producing groups, and higher performing employees. Some of this effect, however, has little to do with subordinate motivation.

These findings have been reconciled by House as was suggested earlier by March and Simon.[15] If one controls for the type of task, one finds that initiating structure is negatively correlated with satisfaction for simple, repetitive tasks but positively correlated for ambiguous, uncertain tasks. That is, for repetitive, predictable tasks initiating structure behaviors are irritating and redundant. The supervisor instructs and directs the subordinate to do that which the subordinate would have done voluntarily. Therefore, the greater the initiating structure, the greater the dissatisfaction for repetitive, predictable tasks. On the other hand, for uncertain tasks initiating structure behaviors are helpful to the subordinate when trying to understand the job situation and to develop responses appropriate to that situation. The supervisor is not checking on the subordinate in this case but is working with him or her to solve a problem. Thus, the greater the degree of initiating structure, the greater the satisfaction and the less the role ambiguity for the subordinate performing an uncertain task.

In terms of the influence model developed in previous chapters, the initiating structure behaviors have two effects. First, the supervisor can clarify the situation for the subordinate in terms of expectancy and instrumentality. By assisting the subordinate in task definition, the supervisor also defines what is good performance, removes obstacles to the attainment of that performance, and defines performance-rewards relations. Thus, the greater the degree of initiating structure, the greater the perceived expectancies and instrumentalities of the subordinate. In this sense, initiating structure can increase subordinate motivation.

The second and possibly greater effect of initiating structure behaviors is to suggest new alternative behaviors. The supervisor expands the evoked set of alternatives by suggesting previously unconsidered behaviors. In addition to clarifying cause and effect relations between alternatives and outcomes, the supervisor should be able to expand the set of alternatives. This evoking function has received very little theoretical attention and increases in importance with increases in task uncertainty. As individuals face uncertain and diverse task situations, they must possess an equally diverse set of behaviors to act out. The supervisor can influence the behavior of subordinates to the greatest extent by suggesting or helping create these behavior alternatives. Thus, the greater the initiating structure, the greater the set of evoked alternatives.

In summary, initiating structure is not good or bad per se but depends on the uncertainty and ambiguity of the task relative to the individual performing it. That is, for predictable, repetitive tasks and/or experienced workers, initiating structure behaviors are unnecessary to clarify expectancies and instrumentalities and to create alternative task behaviors. They can possibly result in subordinate dissatisfaction. For uncertain tasks and/or inexperienced workers, initiating structure behaviors are necessary to clarify expectancies and develop behavior alternatives. High initiating structure is associated with satisfaction, reduced role ambiguity, and higher performance in this latter case.

### Outside Influence

The amount of influence outside of the work group accounts for the fact that the behaviors of interest occur in an organizational context. Thus, some of the research on small groups must be qualified when generalizing to groups in organizations. The basic premise is that the leader must be influential outside of the immediate work group in order to be influential within it. The supervisor may be highly considerate and willing to grant rewards to subordinates but may be unable to do so because of a lack of influence with the personnel function. Therefore, the ability of a considerate supervisor to create satisfaction within the group will depend on the amount of influence outside of that group. The greater the outside influence, the greater the subordinate satisfaction *if* the supervisor chooses to be considerate.

The evidence is sparse but supports the reasoning above. Pelz reported that when supervisors with high upward influence engaged in considerate behaviors, they had more satisfied subordinates than supervisors with low upward influence who engaged in the same considerate behaviors.[16] These results were replicated in another study but were qualified.[17] The effect of upward influence decreased with the organizational status of the subordinate. To some degree, the influence of a considerate supervisor is a substitute for the lack of influence of the subordinate. The lack of significant results in a study of Research and Development workers supports the substitution hypothesis.[18] Thus, for tasks that are intrinsically satisfying and have some organizational status, consideration and outside influence diminish in importance. On the other hand, the more hierarchical the organization, the less satisfying the task; the lower the status of the subordinate, the greater the importance (and hence valence) of considerate supervisor behaviors and outside influence.

The task remaining is to generalize from this brief review to the subordinate behavior categories in the framework. To some degree, this task has already been done but a review would be useful.

**1. Join and remain.** The leader behaviors exhibited in an organization are not likely to attract people to an organization. The behaviors are primarily related to keeping people with an organization and attending regularly. It can be argued that the greater the degree of consideration (with due regard for outside influence) the greater the satisfaction and therefore the lower the turnover and absenteeism among the subordinates. In addition, the relationship would be stronger for repetitive tasks than for uncertain tasks. For repetitive tasks, the greater the degree of initiating structure, the less the satisfaction and the greater the likelihood of absenteeism and turnover. But for uncertain tasks, greater initiating structure is associated with greater satisfaction and therefore lower absenteeism and turnover. Thus the behaviors of the leader can influence the choice of the subordinate to remain and to attend regularly.

**2. Dependable role behaviors.** The role of the supervisor in rule compliance has already been mentioned. Direct supervision was one method of implementing this form of influence. Since dependable behaviors are the necessary behaviors associated with predictable and lower-level tasks, we would predict that consideration and outside influence are the critical dimensions of leader behavior. However, it is hypothesized that the probability that the subordinate will choose to perform dependably or not is somewhat independent of the style in which the direct supervision is administered. The difference is the basis on which the influence is exercised.

The considerate supervisor can increase the probability that the required dependable behaviors are performed. The reason is that directives from a considerate supervisor are more likely to be perceived as legitimate and nonalienating. In addition, if consideration is given on the basis of dependability, the subordinate is more likely to choose to perform dependably. The considerate supervisor with outside influence is likely to be more effective because of the greater reward power and also more legitimacy. To the extent that a leader has enough outside influence to change or modify a rule when an exceptional circumstance arises, the leader's legitimacy and influence base increases.

Initiating structure would be irrelevant and perhaps redundant for tasks requiring dependable behavior. High initiating structure leaders may run the risk of reducing their legitimacy but, if they have outside influence and can use rewards and sanctions, they can still influence the choice of subordinates. However, they rely on reward power rather than on legitimacy as a basis for this influence. It is possible for both a high-structure, high-outside influence, and low-consideration supervisor and a low-structure, high-outside influence, and high-consideration supervisor to motivate dependable behavior. The former will rely on the reward and punishment power of the position and the latter, on legitimacy. The former will have dissatisfied subordinates and higher levels of absenteeism and turnover. Even here some organizations have remained economically effective by limiting absences through rule compliance (requiring doctors' certificates, telephone calls, etc.) and designing jobs to minimize the effects of turnover. Thus, both types of supervision increase the probability that dependable behaviors are performed and can lead to economically effective organizations in the short run. It may not be possible to sustain a dissatisfied or alienated work force.

In summary, direct supervision backed up with sanctions is what is necessary to influence subordinates to behave dependably. Direct supervision can be implemented with or without dissatisfaction and alienation. The degree of consideration and outside influence of the supervisor combine to maintain legitimate authority and satisfaction for people performing routine tasks and minimize such side effects as grievances, absenteeism, turnover and strikes which are likely to be triggered by dissatisfaction with other types of supervision. But direct supervision increases the probability that individuals will choose to perform dependable behaviors.

**3. Effort above minimum levels.** The influence of supervisory behaviors on the choice of levels of effort follows directly from the path–goal model. To the extent that the individual values considerate behavior (valence) and perceives that performance is instrumental to the attainment of consideration, the greater degree of consideration should increase the probability to choose to perform above minimal levels. To the extent that consideration is independent of performance, it should have no direct influence on the choice of performance levels.[19] The effect of consideration will be augmented or decreased depending on the amount of outside influence.

For tasks involving choices of levels of effort, initiating structure behaviors begin to assume greater importance. In a man-paced, work flow system, initiating structure primarily influences expectancies and instrumentalities. The leader keeps work moving, keeps workers supplied with material and tools, prevents machine breakdowns, etc. Thus, the greater the initiating structure, the greater the probability that individuals will choose to perform above minimally acceptable levels. For tasks requiring choices of levels of effort, both considerate and initiating structure behaviors can be important sources of influence and motivation.

**4. Cooperative and spontaneous behaviors.** As in the discussion of monetary incentives, it must be said that cooperative and spontaneous behaviors are no different from any other behaviors and therefore the normal path–goal predictions should apply. However, some additions and qualifications should be made in order to account for the need for spontaneous behaviors.

First, the satisfying effects of considerate behaviors may be reduced. The type of tasks which require spontaneous and cooperative behaviors usually possess sufficient challenge, variety, and responsibility that they may very well be intrinsically motivating. If the same behavior cannot be motivated by two factors at one and the same time or if there are diminishing returns to increased motivation, one would predict that greater consideration would have little or no effect on satisfaction and anticipated satisfaction. Therefore, leader consideration effects decrease with increase in task uncertainty.

On the other hand, the impact of initiating structure can increase in importance. House and his colleagues report findings which suggest that on uncertain tasks greater leader initiation structure leads to lessened role ambiguity, greater satisfaction, and higher performance.[20] According to our model, these results could originate from two sources. First, on ambiguous tasks, there is a greater need for supervisors to clarify expectancies, instrumentalities, and role perceptions. The clarification of role perceptions and expectancies would lead to increased performance and satisfaction, independent of whether the individual is extrinsically or intrinsically motivated. Thus, there should be larger differences in satisfaction and performance among subordinates of high and low initiating structure superiors on uncertain tasks requiring only effort above the minimum.

The second effect of initiating structure is that it can expand the evoked set of alternatives. The leader can create alternatives, help create alternatives, make suggestions, or help define the situation in such a way that the subordinate can be effective in an unpredictable situation. It seems the greater the uncertainty of the task, relative to the task performer, the greater the importance of evoking forms of influence. Alternative suggestion, information provision, and cueing become the important leader behaviors. Thus, both clarification of expectancies and role perceptions and the evoking of new alternatives result from leader behaviors which can be classified as initiating structure. Those behaviors should increase the probability that subordinates will perform the required behaviors.

In summary, it appears that consideration and outside influence decrease in motivational importance as the uncertainty of the task increases. They are both motivating and satisfying for predictable tasks and diminish to having little effect. Initiating structure increases in importance. From little influence on motivation and a negative influence on satisfaction, initiating structure increases to where it is positively related to motivation and satisfaction.[21]

The implementation of these concepts would be accomplished primarily by selection and/or training of the appropriate leaders. However, the current research on leader training contains the same problems of leader effectiveness.[22]

## GROUPS

There has been a great deal of research and theorizing about groups and organizations. Much of this research has been directed towards group processes,[23] or group problem solving.[24] The interest here is the effect of the immediate work group on the individual's choice of job behaviors.

The research on groups in organizations began with the Hawthorne studies. It was during these studies that psychologists discovered that the group's productivity was not limited by physiological or technological factors but by group norms as to what constituted a fair day's work. Thus the individual's choice of job-related behaviors was believed to be influenced by the nature of the group norms and how strongly these norms were shared (cohesiveness) among the members. The research generally supports the assertion.[25]

First, there are two laboratory studies in which groups with high and low cohesiveness were given tasks to perform.[26] Since the experimenter controlled the communication among group members, the experimenter presumably controlled the norms of the group. To one set communiqués were given indicating that members wanted high performance and to the other set communiqués were given indicating that low performance was desirable. The results were that the most and least productive groups were the highly cohesive groups. The difference was the communications or norms of the groups. The high productivity groups were given the communiqué indicating a desire among the members for high production and the low groups were given the communiqué for low production. The groups with low cohesiveness were in the middle. Similar results were obtained in a field study by Seashore.[27] The groups measured as highly cohesive were among the most and least productive groups. The cohesive groups also exhibited less performance variance within the group. The conclusions from these studies are that groups with high cohesiveness can exert greater influence over their members than low cohesive groups can. However, the direction in which this influence is exercised depends on the norms of the group and these norms can be either supportive or nonsupportive of high production.

Vroom has interpreted these results in terms of the path–goal model. If we can assume that the valence of group acceptance and rewards is related to cohesiveness and that norms are related to perceived instrumentality, these results support the model. Those individuals who desire group acceptance and perceive high production to be instrumental to receiving acceptance will choose to perform at a high level. If the same individual perceives low performance as instrumental to acceptance, low performance will be chosen. On the other hand, the individual for whom group acceptance is not important or the individual in a group where performance behaviors are neither rewarded nor penalized will be unaffected by the group in the choice of performance behaviors. Let us now analyze the effects by the type of behavior and then discuss the implementation of this type of motivation in an organization.

**1. Join and remain.** It is necessary first to separate decisions on joining from decisions on leaving. An individual is probably not attracted to an organization by the anticipation of satisfactions to be provided by the work group. The exception to this may be the professions where an individual chooses an organization because it contains an interesting group of colleagues. But for most people, the organization is chosen for other reasons. If the organization was experiencing difficulties in attracting members, it would not attempt to increase cohesiveness to solve the problem.

On the other hand, increasing cohesiveness and work group acceptance can influence the individuals to remain in the organization. There is some evidence which can be interpreted as saying that those individuals perceiving greater acceptance by the work group also report higher job satisfaction and therefore are less likely to leave the organization.[28] One study reports that individuals experiencing higher status, and therefore acceptance, are less likely to voluntarily leave the group.[29] Thus, if individuals find the group instrumental in satisfying some of their needs, they will not choose to leave it.

**2. Dependable role behaviors.** The acceptance or nonacceptance of an individual is an effective way of increasing the likelihood that the individual will choose those dependable behaviors which are instrumental to group acceptance. Indeed, group norms are legalistic shared perceptions of what behaviors are necessary to maintain the welfare of the group. Norms are the equivalent of rules for the organization, and acceptance is one mechanism for enforcing those norms.

The question for the organization is whether the norms are in concert with or contrary to the dependable behaviors which are needed for effective task execution. Certainly some of the behaviors needed by the group for its maintenance are irrelevant to the organization and some necessary task behaviors are perceived as irrelevant for the group. Another set of behaviors is seen as necessary for both the organization and the group. In this case, the group reinforces the organization's attempts to increase the probability that individuals will choose those behaviors.

A problem arises when the necessary task behaviors are seen to be contrary to the best interests of the group. This case would arise if management introduced an individual reward system into a situation where group members saw themselves as interdependent. This could arise in a factory with a man-paced work flow but in which groups of people perform the same task. From management's point of view, the task requires effort above minimum levels. Therefore it implements a wage incentive to increase the probability that people will choose to perform above minimum levels. The work group, however, sees the problem differently. Since everyone performs nearly the same task, high performance by one member will make the performance of the others look bad. Or worse, if one member produces at 150 percent of standard, the group may believe that the management will increase the standard. Since the new standard applies not just to the high producer but to all who perform the same task, the group may adopt a norm that no one produces over 120 percent. The group sees interdependence and a task requiring dependable behavior. They implement a reward system which increases the probability that the individual will perform at or near 120 percent. The individuals are subjected to two forces. Which behavior will be chosen depends on the valence the individual assigns to money and group acceptance. Those for whom group acceptance is important may form cohesive groups in which everyone performs around 120 percent. This would be consistent with the Seashore finding. Alternatively, those individuals for whom money is important and group acceptance less important will choose to perform at higher levels. These individuals are best characterized in Dalton's study.[30]

In summary, acceptance by the work group can increase the likelihood that dependable behaviors are chosen by employees. However, whether these behaviors are those necessary for effective task execution depends on the norms of the group. The norms can be contrary to or consistent with the necessary task behaviors. We will come back to the subject of norms in the section on implementation.

**3. Effort above minimum levels.** The evidence from the laboratory experiments quoted earlier bears directly on this type of behavior. As in choosing dependable behaviors, the key is in the individual's desire for acceptance and the direction of the groups norms. When the norms of the group support high production and the members desire acceptance, members are more likely to choose to perform above minimum levels. When the norms do not support or are contrary to high production, there is less likely to be high production.

**4. Cooperative and spontaneous behaviors.** The same qualification applies with respect to group acceptance as applied to other extrinsic rewards. That is, there is nothing about a spontaneous behavior that makes it different from a motivational view. The question is a practical one as to whether cooperative and spontaneous behaviors can be made instrumental to the receipt of an extrinsic reward. From this point of view, group acceptance is potentially a more powerful motivator. Since spontaneous and cooperative behaviors are difficult to specify in advance, have effects that are difficult to measure, and are quite often difficult to observe, the extrinsic rewards provided by the organization are less effective. However, since the immediate work group is more likely to observe behaviors and can potentially reward the behaviors immediately after they are executed, group acceptance is more likely to create the perception of instrumentalities close to 1.0. Therefore, if the individual desires group acceptance and the group's norms are consistent with organizational goals, group acceptance can significantly increase the likelihood that individuals will choose to perform spontaneous and cooperative behaviors.

Another previous qualification may apply here as well. It may be hypothesized that there are two effects of group cohesiveness. One is that there will be greater cooperation within the group among its members. The other is that the group may be less likely to cooperate with people or groups who are not members. The organization may create cooperation within groups at the expense of cooperation between groups.

## IMPLEMENTATION

In order to employ groups or group acceptance as a source of motivation for task behaviors, it is necessary to create a situation in which the group norms and organizational goals are congruent. The early inquiry into this subject was motivated by the widespread observance of restriction of output by operative workers even in the presence of wage incentives. The conclusion resulting from these studies was that workers did not believe that higher wages would result from higher output but that higher output would lead to rate cuts, unemployment, and undesirable economic consequences.[31] In order to protect themselves, workers created and enforced quotas.

The next question is why do these perceptions exist and become shared to the extent that they are considered norms. An obvious reason is that management does cut rates following high production. These cuts could occur directly or through the mechanism of redesigning the job because of a change in process. In either case, the worker develops a distrust of management and does not believe that high performance will be rewarded.

This same attitude appears in organizations which have explicit policies stating that they will not cut a rate and which have no history of cutting rates. However, the determinants of the norms are not necessarily management policies but the beliefs of the employees and particularly the beliefs that are shared and reinforced among group members. These beliefs are established when the individual first joins the organization and is the most receptive or unfrozen to new beliefs. Then through the process of recruitment, interview, selection, training, assignment, and on-the-job supervision, the employee establishes an image of the organization and a set of expectations as to how he or she is going to be treated.[32] If the individual develops beliefs that management treats employees like any other raw material or economic good and that he or she is dependent on management's choices, a distrust is created and the groundwork laid for some kind of action for the protection of the individual. If also there are a number of individuals who share the same perceptions of management's likely behavior and of their own dependency on that behavior, collective action such as output restriction is likely to result in order to maintain the group's self-interest. Assuming the characterization above to be true, the design problem is to eliminate incongruity between group norms and organization goals by reducing perception of mistrust and/or dependency.

The first strategy involves increasing the degree of consideration of the organization and communicating this genuine interest to the individuals as they enter and work in the organization. The implementation of this policy first involves an examination and possible changes to the "joining-up" process by which the psychological contract between the individual and the organization is created.[33] Second, the style of supervision must fit the expectations that are created in the joining-up process. There is some evidence to suggest that considerate styles of supervision, in addition to being rewarding themselves, lead to favorable group norms.[34] Thus, through supervisory training the organization may increase its influence directly through the supervisor's effects on the individual's choice of behaviors and indirectly through the establishment of favorable group norms (i.e., norms that are consistent with organization goals). However, it is more likely that consideration prevents the formation of unfavorable norms but by itself will not create favorable norms. Kahn's discussion suggests that consideration and the use of consideration to reward high performance can in combination create favorable norms. Thus by creating a compatible system of selection, training, and supervision and a system that is high in consideration, the organization can create a climate in which employees may believe that high performance leads to rewards rather than layoffs and rate cuts.

The second method of eliminating unfavorable group norms and of creating favorable group norms is to reduce the dependency of the individuals by allowing them to participate in decisions that affect them. By having some influence in decisions which affect them, employees are not likely to feel dependent upon a capricious organization. Under these conditions, unfavorable group norms are less likely to form. In addition, it is even suggested that favorable group norms are created if the influence is implemented through some form of group decision making. The hypothesis is that if a group collectively reaches a decision about a work-related matter, the process also creates group norms which are supportive of the successful execution of that decision. Indeed, Vroom offers this as a possible explanation for why participation can increase motivation.[35] Thus, by implementing forms of group decision making on significant decisions, the organization can create norms which support organization goals.

In summary, the discussion of design decisions to implement group acceptance as a source of job motivation started with an historical perspective on the interest in the subject. It was suggested that unfavorable group norms among subordinates formed when there were shared perceptions of dependence and of distrust of the power structure on which the subordinates were dependent. It was further suggested that these unfavorable norms were less likely to occur if the organization reduced perceptions of dependence by creating devices to give more influence in decisions to subordinates and by increasing trust through employee policies and supervisory styles which could be described as considerate. If, in addition, the influence in decisions takes place in work groups and if the reward power of consideration is used to reward high performance, there is more evidence that these conditions create favorable norms. If there are favorable norms, then work-related behaviors are more likely to become instrumental to group acceptance. This type of motivation could be further increased by selecting individuals for whom group acceptance is important and allowing forms of work group selection.

The observance of restriction of output and unfavorable group norms are less frequently observed in the managerial structure. To some degree managers reduce their dependence through individual initiatives rather than collective action. These managers either conform to the power structure and/or increase their own power through high performance and the maintenance of external visibility and mobility. This individual action, however, not only prevents the establishment of unfavorable norms but also prevents favorable ones from influencing behavior. Thus organizations implementing group processes in the managerial structure are now undertaking team-building activities of various kinds to explicitly negotiate, among other things, those behaviors which are necessary for the group and which are likely to be rewarded by the group.

## SUMMARY

This chapter has presented a discussion of the effects of the behaviors of others in the individual's work place. These others were the official leader of the group and the individual's peers. While entire books have been written on each topic, the purpose here was to identify the major design variables, discuss what is known about them, and relate them to the framework being developed in the book. The strategy was to be selective rather than exhaustive. As before, a paradigm was selected which has some empirical support and which is consistent with the other theories being used.

This chapter ends the section on extrinsic rewards and therefore requires a few words concerning the choice of reward systems in general and extrinsic rewards in particular. On one hand, the choice is determined by the relationship between a policy alternative and the behaviors and attitudes which result from it. The text has been concerned with these relations. On the other hand, the choice is determined by values and priorities assigned to productivity, individual satisfaction, etc., and also by values concerning the use of power and influence relations in organizations. There are a number of ethical questions involved when artificially influencing the behavior of people in low-power positions. Ideally one should present an objective, neutral value view. This is impossible. An author's choice of descriptive words alone gives a value position. In this book there is an attempt to be objective but there is also a distinct organizational bias.

In this particular chapter there are statements saying that consideration and upward influence may increase satisfaction for people performing repetitive tasks and having low influence themselves. Another description of that leadership style implemented on an organizationwide basis is paternalism. Consideration and upward influence could be viewed as a means for maintaining boring jobs and the current power structure. They represent a sugarcoating on a bad situation, and real satisfaction and the elimination of alienation can be attained only by creating more interesting jobs and giving some self-control to the currently powerless. Thus, given the lack of a valid theory, ideology plays a significant role in the choice of reward system despite the fact that it is not discussed in this book. The reader should be well aware of different value positions which are masked somewhat in the reporting of research data.

### NOTES

1. R. Likert 1961. *New patterns of management.* New York: McGraw-Hill.

2. J. March and H. Simon 1958. *Organizations.* New York: Wiley.

3. A. Filley and R. House 1969. *Managerial process and organizational behavior.* Glenview, Ill.: Scott Foresman, Chapter 16.

4. E. A. Fleishman, E. Harris, and H. E. Burt 1955. *Leadership and supervision in industry.* Bureau of Educational Research, The Ohio State University.

5. For a review see A. Korman 1966. Consideration, initiating structure, and organizational criteria—a review. *Personnel Psychology* 19: 349–361.

6. D. C. Pelz 1952. Influence: a key to effective leadership in the first-line supervisor. *Personnel* 29: 3–11.

7. V. Vroom 1964. *Work and motivation.* New York: Wiley, pp. 105–119 and 211–220. J. Campbell, M. Dunnette, E. Lawler III, and K. Weick 1970. *Managerial behavior, performance, and effectiveness.* New York: McGraw-Hill, Chapter 17. R. House 1971. A path–goal theory of leader effectiveness. *Administrative Science Quarterly,* (September): 321–338.

8. Vroom, pp. 219–220.

9. A. Lowin and J. R. Craig 1968. The influence of level of performance on managerial style: an experimental object lesson in the ambiguity of correlational data. *Organizational Behavior and Human Performance* 3: 440–458.

10. J. R. Galbraith and L. L. Cummings 1967. An empirical investigation of the motivational determinants of job performance: interactive effects between instrumentality–valence and motivation–ability. *Organizational Behavior and Human Performance* 2: 237–257.

11. R. House, p. 324.

12. E. Deci 1972. The effects of contingent and noncontingent rewards and controls on intrinsic motivation. *Organization Behavior and Human Performance* 8: 217–229.

13. E. A. Fleishman and E. Harris 1962. Patterns of leader behavior related to grievances and turnover. *Personnel Psychology* 15: 43–56.

14. House, pp. 321–322.

15. House, pp. 321–322. J. March and H. Simon 1958. *Organizations.* New York: Wiley, pp. 53–55.

16. Pelz, pp. 3–11.

17. L. W. Wager 1965. Leadership style, influence, and supervisory role obligations. *Administrative Science Quarterly* 9: 391–420.

18. R. House, A. Filley and D. Gujarati 1971. Leadership style, hierarchical influence, and the satisfaction of subordinate role expectations. *Journal of Applied Psychology,* (October): 422–432.

19. Galbraith and Cummings, pp. 237–257.

20. R. J. House, A. Filley, and S. Ken 1971. Relation of leader consideration and initiating structure to R and D subordinate satisfaction. *Administrative Science Quarterly* 16: 19–30. J. Rizzo, R. House, and S. Lirtzman 1970. Role conflict and ambiguity in complex organizations. *Administrative Science Quarterly* 15: 150–153.

21. This interpretation may be at variance with Fiedler's findings of a U-shaped relation between leader behavior and situation favorableness. The measures of the situation and leader behavior are both different, however. The reader should consult F. Fiedler 1967. *A theory of leadership effectiveness.* New York: McGraw-Hill.

22. Campbell *et al.,* Chapter 13.

23. D. Cartwright and A. Zander 1968. *Group dynamics.* (Third ed.) New York: Harper & Row.

24. B. E. Collins and H. A. Guetzkow 1964. *Social psychology of group processes for decision making.* New York: Wiley.

25. See the review in Vroom, pp. 229–236.

26. S. Schachter, N. Ellertson, D. McBride, and D. Gregory 1951. An experimental study of cohesiveness and productivity. *Human Relations* 4: 229–238. L. Berkowitz 1954. Group standards, cohesiveness, and productivity. *Human Relations* 7: 509–519.

27. S. Seashore 1954. *Group cohesiveness in the industrial work group.* Ann Arbor, Michigan: University of Michigan, Institute for Social Research, Survey Research Center.

28. Vroom, pp. 123–4.

29. P. C. Sagi, O. W. Olmstead, and F. Atelsek 1955. Predicting maintenance of membership in small groups. *Journal of Abnormal and Social Psychology* 51: 308–311.

30. M. Dalton 1948. The industrial rate-buster: a characterization. *Applied Anthropology* 7: 5–18.

31. See the summary in E. Lawler III 1971. *Pay and organizational effectiveness: a psychological view.* New York: McGraw-Hill, pp. 124–128.

32. E. Schein 1972. *Organizational psychology.* Second Edition. Englewood Cliffs, N.J.: Prentice-Hall, Chapter 3.

33. Schein, pp. 50–55.

34. R. Kahn 1958. Human relations on the shop floor. In E. M. Hugh-Jones (ed.), *Human relations and modern management*. Amsterdam: North Holland. M. Patchen 1958. Supervisory styles and group norms. *Administrative Science Quarterly*, (June): 240–251.

35. Vroom, p. 228.

## QUESTIONS

1. This chapter classified leader behaviors into categories of consideration and initiating structure. Identify and discuss five behaviors which you classify as (a) consideration and as (b) initiating structure.

2. How does consideration behavior affect employee motivation? Use the model of previous chapters to illustrate.

3. How do initiating behaviors affect employee motivation?

4. Discuss the behaviors identified in question 1 by predicting their effects in the presence of and without the presence of outside influence.

5. Discuss the impact of the dimensions of leadership on:
   a) dependable role behaviors,
   b) effort above minimum levels, and
   c) cooperative and spontaneous behaviors.

6. How does group cohesiveness affect employee motivation?

7. How does group acceptance affect employee motivation?

8. Discuss the impact of group acceptance on the following behaviors:
   a) dependable role behaviors,
   b) effort above minimum levels,
   c) spontaneous behaviors, and
   d) cooperative behaviors.

9. How can you create situations where group norms are consistent with organizational goals?

# INTRINSIC REWARDS

This chapter completes the analysis of motivational bases of job behavior by focusing on those rewards which are intrinsic to the task itself. Intrinsic rewards are rewards which are a natural consequence of the behavior itself and are independent of any externally mediated rewards. The policy variables and the behavioral consequences of this type of motivation are different from those of extrinsic rewards. First the subject of intrinsic motivation will be discussed. Next the two types of motivational bases—task involvement, and goal identification—will be identified and their behavioral consequences analyzed. And finally the problems and evidence concerning implementation will be presented.

## INTRINSIC MOTIVATION

When one undertakes the task of explaining intrinsic motivation, one faces the problem of which theory to use. As usual, the problem is not the lack of a theory but that there are several theories, each with some claim to validity. There is Herzberg's dual-factor theory[1] which has been discredited by further research[2] but which nonetheless serves as the basis for the apparently successful programs at AT&T and Texas Instruments.[3] There is also the theory of achievement motivation[4] which served as the basis for Patchen's evaluation of the TVA program in participation.[5] Vroom has operationalized a type of cognitive consistency theory.[6] And finally there is the interpretation within the context of the path–goal theory.[7]

As before we shall follow the path–goal model. This choice does not necessarily cause problems because the explanations and predictions emanating from the different theories are quite consistent. Thus, the choice is not as serious as it appeared to be at first glance.

Our point of departure will continue to be the individual in a role situation who is faced with a choice among a set of physically possible behaviors. A subset of these possible behaviors is evoked in the mind of the individual. From among these perceived alternatives (or alternative) the individual selects and acts out that alternative which is most likely to lead to the attainment of the most valued outcome. The perceived outcomes have value to the extent that they are believed to lead or have led to the satisfaction of individual needs. The interest in intrinsic motivation arose partly because extrinsic outcomes were believed to lead to the satisfaction of lower order needs which were reasonably well satisfied in modern society. Thus, if individuals were to be motivated to perform and achieve personal satisfaction, a way had to be discovered to make performance outcomes instrumental to the satisfaction of higher order needs. The focus of attention shifted to the design of jobs in organizations. If jobs could be designed such that individuals, as a result of their own efforts, could meet their aspiration levels, then work would become intrinsically rewarding and instrumental to the satisfaction of higher order needs. The factor which limited motivation and satisfaction was therefore believed to be the available jobs in organizations. The jobs were hypothesized to prevent aspiration levels from rising and therefore to disallow intrinsic rewards and to prevent people from perceiving work outcomes as being instrumental to higher order needs.

When the research on such subjects as job enlargement, job enrichment, and participation carried out by means of field studies, field experiments, and laboratory experiments is reviewed, the results are mixed.[8] There are indeed individuals who respond to challenging jobs with increasing performance and satisfaction, but others do not. Thus, even when jobs apparently permit, some individuals are not intrinsically motivated. It is suggested that some individuals are not yet capable of higher order needs satisfactions. Their lower order needs not being met, they do not respond in the predicted manner to the possible satisfaction of higher order needs. It is further suggested that another group is capable of higher order needs satisfaction but those needs are either not evoked in the work place or high performance is not perceived to be instrumental to their satisfaction. These individuals may have self-concepts, for example, which do not include high job performance as a source of self-esteem. The first group, those that respond favorably to enriched jobs, apparently are those individuals who are capable of higher order needs satisfaction and for whom high performance is instrumental to self-esteem or other higher order needs. These latter individuals are intrinsically motivated while the others are not.

Thus, the intrinsic motivation of interest here will occur when (1) there is a task which allows individuals to attribute to their own efforts their achieved performance outcomes; (2) there is a task the performance of which requires skills and abilities which the individual believes he or she has and values (otherwise performance will not be instrumental to self-esteem) and (3) there are individuals who are capable of higher order need satisfaction. More will be said about these factors in the discussion of implementation.

## TASK INVOLVEMENT AND GOAL IDENTIFICATION

Two types of intrinsic motivation have been identified—task involvement and goal identification. Job involvement has been defined to exist to:

> ...the degree to which a person is identified psychologically with his work, or the importance of work in his total self-image.[9]

That concept is further qualified here to include the identification with some external, occupational reference group. The task-involved individual can usually identify a well-defined group with whom this identity can be shared, such as the professions and crafts. These occupational groups usually have professional associations, training institutions, etc. which socialize and train individuals prior to their entrance into an organization and which reinforce the identity in the organization and in society as a whole. Individuals can conceive of themselves as physicists, physicians, electricians, etc.

Task involvement, however, is not necessarily the same as intrinsic motivation to achieve high performance.[10] The individual may find that the behavior leading to the highest level of performance is not intrinsically satisfying even though the individual is involved in the job. The reason is that performance is defined from the point of view of the organization rather than from the point of view of the group or profession with which the individual is identified. If the organization is to use motivation based on task involvement, then jobs must be defined, tasks undertaken, and individuals selected so that conflict between organizational goals and professional norms is minimized.

Goal identification occurs to the extent that individuals have internalized into their own value systems the goals or subgoals that the organization is pursuing. The goals have value because the individuals acquired them in the process of growing up or because they participated in the determination of the goals for the organization. The achievement of these goals, then, is instrumental to satisfying the needs for self-esteem, growth, or other types regarded as higher level needs. In turn, behaviors perceived to be instrumental to the attainment of these goals acquire an instrumental value and become intrinsically rewarding.

Two types of intrinsic motivation have been defined because it is possible that different behaviors are instrumental to these different intrinsic rewards. To the extent that the organization has different roles requiring different behaviors for effective performance, there may be occasions when one of the types of motivation may be more effective than the other. The design task is to identify those occasions and behaviors where a choice between the two types is necessary. Before analyzing the types of behaviors, however, the two types of intrinsic motivation need to be further clarified.

The two different types of motivation, which were suggested by Katz, a psychologist, are quite similar to the concepts of cosmopolitan and local roles suggested by Gouldner, a sociologist.[11] A cosmopolitan role or identity was "... low on loyalty to the employing organization, high on commitment to specialized role skill, and likely to use an outer reference group orientation." A local role or identity was "... high on loyalty to the employing organization, low on commitment to specialized role skill and likely to use an inner reference group."[12] There has also been a great deal of interest in the hypothesized conflict between the professions and organizations.[13] The conflict was seen to result in part from the conflict between the profession's definition of performance and the organization's definition as perhaps exemplified by the saying, "The operation was a success but the patient died." Therefore, when a professional entered an organization he or she was forced to choose between the norms of the profession and the goals of the organization. These concepts of professional and cosmopolitan roles are almost identical to task involvement while local and organizational identification are similarly related to goal identification.

In this book, however, we will follow the position taken in current research studies that the conflict between profession and organization is not inherent in the relationship. One can find that, within the same organizational context, there is a group of individuals which is measured as cosmopolitans, a group which is local, but also a group that is both cosmopolitan and local and another which is neither.[14] This result may be due not only to role variation within the same organizational context but also to the fact that some individuals find ways to eliminate conflict rather than choosing between the conflicting alternatives. Schein has called these individuals "role innovators." Some roles, such as the role of integrator, require such an individual. The project manager in a research organization needs to follow professional norms to hold the respect of the professionals on the project and needs also to pursue organizational goals in order to complete the project within time and budget constraints. The conclusion to be drawn from this research is that task involvement and goal identification are not on the ends of a continuum, are not even mutually exclusive, and a single individual can be motivated by both at the same time (but not necessarily motivated to display the same specific behaviors).

Another reason why the apparent incompatibility between organizations and professions is not inherent is that there is considerable variation in organizational contexts. On the one hand, the performance criteria of the scientist may be quite different from the performance criteria of an industrial organization. On the other hand, there are professional organizations which are run by and for professionals in which there is no more conflict than that which naturally results between any individual and any organization. Even in some nonprofessional organizations, conflict is minimized by creating a professional department.[15] (This design solves one problem but creates another—that of linking the professional department with the rest of the organization. It seems that this problem can be solved by staffing the leadership position with an individual who can be identified with both the profession and the organization.) Thus, as organizational contexts vary, the compatibility between the professional definition of performance and organizational definition of performance also varies.

In summary, there are two types of intrinsic motivation which differ in the types of behaviors that are perceived to be instrumental to the attainment of intrinsic rewards. These instrumentalities are different to the extent that behaviors and outcomes constituting high professional performance are different from the behaviors and outcomes constituting high organizational performance. For the professional organization, task involvement and goal identification are nearly identical. The nonprofessional organization with the professional department found a way to factor its goals into a set of subgoals some of which can be assigned to professionals and which cause little conflict. Therefore, the professional can feel committed to the organization because there is little conflict for him or her. For other roles the professional must either acquire both professional and organization goals or subordinate professional goals for the pursuit of organizational goals. Given this variation in organizations and variation in roles in organization, it is necessary to analyze each role with respect to the necessary behaviors and outcomes for effective performance and compare them to those considered appropriate by the profession or by the individual's reference group. While a particular individual can be motivated by both task involvement and goal identification, the following analyses will assume only one type in order to contrast the differences.

## TYPES OF BEHAVIOR

The analysis of behavior types and motivation bases will be presented as before. We will consider each type of behavior and then contrast the two types of motivation with respect to the likelihood of influencing that type of behavior.

**1. Join and remain.** The likelihood that an individual will join and remain in an organization is one of the behaviors that is hypothesized to differ between task-involved and goal-identified motivation. The pure type of task involvement does not increase the probability that the individual will choose a particular organization or choose to remain in it. The individual motivated solely by task involvement is indifferent concerning organizations as long as he or she has resources to support his or her work and an interesting group of colleagues with whom to discuss professional problems. If, as is suggested, individuals fail to find stimulation from the same group after a few years, this type of motivation may increase the likelihood that people will leave. But by the same reasoning, professional organizations may not regard high levels of turnover as being a problem.

The statements above need to be qualified based on variation in organizational contexts which affect the availability of outside alternatives. The predictions apply to the profession of physical chemistry. Members of this profession, with due regard for supply and demand, have a wide choice of jobs in governmental, educational, and industrial organizations. On the other hand, the foreign service officer and the priest have very few choices. The United States Department of State and the Catholic Church are about the only choices available for members of these particular professions. Therefore, the interpretation of empirical studies relating to turnover and cosmopolitanism should consider the relative availability of other organizations in which the professional can practice the craft or skill. When there is only one organization in which the professional can practice, the difference between the professional norms and organizational goals is minimal.

On the other hand, goal identification is hypothesized to increase the probability that individuals will choose to join a particular organization and remain with that organization even when there are other available alternatives. To the extent that identification occurs while working in the organization, goal identification is more highly related to the decision to stay or leave rather than to rejoin. To the extent that the organization pursues goals with which the individual is identified or pursues attractive goals, goal identification is also highly related with the decision to join.

**2. Dependable role behaviors.** Intrinsic motivation is, theoretically, the most effective means to increase the probability that individuals will choose to perform the dependable role behaviors necessary to sustain the organization if the behaviors are perceived to lead to outcomes that the individual values. The behaviors are chosen with or without direct supervision because the individual values the outcome. The behaviors must be perceived as valuable and necessary to attain organizational goals. Dependable behaviors perceived as illegitimate or as red tape will not be chosen even though they lead to the accomplishment of organizational goals.

Task involvement is less likely to increase the probability that the individual will perform dependably. For those behaviors which lie within the role with which the individual is identified, task involvement will intrinsically motivate those behaviors. But even in purely professional organizations, there are behaviors which lie outside the professional definition of the role and are usually those that are necessary for organizational maintenance. There are requisitions to be filled out, time cards to be completed, etc. All these tasks are necessary to account for limited funds, estimate costs and budgets, set prices for services, etc. The fact that professional behavior occurs in an organization necessitates nonprofessional behavior in order to maintain the organization. Something other than task involvement is required to motivate all of those behaviors which lie outside the professionally defined role.

**3. Effort above minimum levels.** In similar fashion, intrinsic motivation is hypothesized to be the most effective means to increase the probability that individuals will choose to perform above minimum levels of performance. The hypothesis is based on two assumptions. The first is that intrinsic motivation is instrumental to the satisfaction of higher order needs. Therefore, for individuals whose lower level needs are reasonably well satisfied, performance outcomes can acquire a higher valence than when they are instrumental to extrinsic rewards. Also, since it is believed that higher order needs (self-actualization in particular), increase in importance when they are satisfied, intrinsic rewards are believed to be a sustaining source of motivation and satisfaction.

The second assumption is that the instrumentality of performance for the attainment of intrinsic rewards can be very close to 1.0. First, the individual controls the reward and is not dependent on some other agent to perceive and reward the performance. Second, the attainment of the reward also occurs immediately after the outcome is achieved and recognized. This closer association of outcome and reward and control of reward increases perceived instrumentality. Both of these assumptions and the hypothesis were discussed earlier. It should be stressed that there is a lack of research directly relevant to the hypothesis.

It seems that there should be little difference between task involvement and goal identification with respect to behaviors above minimum levels. As long as the effort is perceived as instrumental to outcomes valued by the individual, there is little reason to distinguish between them. From an operational point of view, however, task involvement may be the more effective. If there is a well-defined task to be performed and individuals are trained to perform that task in educational institutions, task involvement can be implemented by selection and an on-the-job apprenticeship. Organizations lacking goals with which individuals have already become identified must build identification into their administrative processes, perhaps through various forms of participation. Thus, task involvement comes to the organization through prior socialization in other institutions, while goal identification must be established within the organization. This assertion applies to the extent that task involvement and goal identification are different for the role in question and to the extent that individuals are not socialized to identify with the goals to be pursued in the role.

A second reason for preferring task involvement for a specific task is that individuals are probably very skilled at performing the task. Unless they are capable of significant perceptual distortion, those individuals who conceive of themselves as computer programmers are probably good computer programmers. Recall the earlier discussion on aspiration levels. The aspiration level is a function of individuals' past performances and of the performances of others around them. If, after a reasonable period of time, individuals' performances are significantly below those of others, those individuals will probably not incorporate that activity into their self-conceptions. In addition, well-defined tasks are likely to have well-defined performance criteria. The better defined the criteria, the less the likelihood of perceptual distortions which could lead to mistaken self-conceptions. Thus, the self-conceptions leading to task involvement probably rest on a factual basis. Therefore, when a task-involved individual is selected, the organization also selects the individual with the best abilities and skills to perform that specific task. It is the combination of intrinsic motivation and developed abilities that increases the probability of high performance in a well-defined task. Summarizing, there should be little difference between task involvement and goal identification from a purely motivational point of view but, from a performance point of view, task involvement would be the preferred strategy for some well-defined tasks due to the combined effects of motivation, ability, and role perceptions.

**4. Spontaneous and cooperative behaviors.** The same generalization applies here as for the other behaviors. Other things being equal, intrinsic motivation will increase the likelihood that spontaneous and cooperative behaviors are chosen by the individual. The reason is, as before, that the valences and instrumentalities can be higher for intrinsic rewards than for extrinsic rewards. This potentially higher level of motivation is particularly important for spontaneous and cooperative behaviors because there is a difference between them and the other three behaviors. The first three behaviors involve a situation in which there exists, in the evoked set of the individual, a set of alternatives one or several of which will produce, from the point of view of the organization, the desired effect on the environment. The problem is to design a situation in which the individual chooses to perform one of the behaviors which will produce the desired effect. For spontaneous and cooperative behaviors, the individual usually faces a situation for which there is no behavior in the evoked set which will produce the desired effect. Therefore the individual must engage in search behavior to discover an alternative which will produce the desired effect. It is this search behavior which provides the difference. It is a significant difference because search behavior is hypothesized to be very difficult to motivate.

There is not a great deal of evidence directly relevant to search behavior. March and Simon have suggested a Gresham's Law of planning that states that the routine and structured activities drive out the nonroutine and unstructured activities (i.e., those requiring search behavior).[16] March reports a laboratory study in which subjects were asked to equally divide their time between routine and nonroutine activities.[17] The subjects however spent the majority of their time on routine matters, and the routine portion increased as the work load increased. These results when combined with some introspection and observation of colleagues are enough to suggest that search behavior is difficult to motivate. It is difficult because search requires greater effort on the part of the individual and greater risk to execute the newly discovered action. In turn, greater effort requires greater motivation or a higher force to engage in it. Thus, the higher valences and instrumentalities potentially available in intrinsic motivation, increase the probability that search behavior will be chosen by the individual when faced with an uncertain, nonroutine situation.

In general, there should be no difference between task involvement and goal identification from a motivational point of view. Both should be equally likely to motivate search behavior. However, in terms of role performance, differences will appear depending on the type of role behaviors which are required. If the role is one for which individuals are professionally trained, task involvement may be preferable. The reason is that the search behavior has a higher probability of being successful. As before, task-involved individuals are more likely to have the ability to discover alternatives which fit the situation. These abilities are also further developed by training in search processes. If immediate search is unsuccessful, there exists a literature and possibly a network of colleagues to aid the search process. Thus, if the situation requires behaviors which lie within the professional definition of the role, task involvement will be the motivational basis which will generate the highest level of performance.

On the other hand, if the task to be performed requires spontaneous and particularly cooperative behaviors which do not lie within the professional definition of the role, those behaviors will not be perceived as instrumental to intrinsic rewards for the task-involved individual. These behaviors require goal identification. Individuals motivated by goal identification will adopt any legitimate behavior which is perceived as instrumental to the attainment of the desired goals.

The situation is particularly acute for cooperative behaviors. Indeed, one would hypothesize that the greater the degree of task involvement, the less the likelihood of cooperative behavior between unlike roles. If the task requires a team approach or a joint problem-solving effort among specialists of the same profession, the hypothesis is probably not true. Common language, background, and knowledge facilitate joint research. But when cooperation is required between unlike roles or between groups of specialists, cooperation is more difficult to attain in the presence of task involvement.

Cooperative behaviors are not likely to be perceived as instrumental to the need satisfaction of professionals. These behaviors are likely to lie outside the professional definition of the role. In addition, cooperation may be seen as professionally compromising. In order to cooperate with other departments, the professional department may have to pursue a less professionally interesting approach to a problem. Thus, the same motivation that leads to high effort, self-responsibility, and search behavior within a role leads also to resistance to cooperate and differences of opinion between roles. Task involvement can be a two-sided coin.

The bulk of the evidence for these assertions exists in journalistic or anecdotal form. Events comprising jurisdictional disputes among crafts, professional jealousies, etc. are commonplace. In research institutions, successful examples of interdisciplinary research are rare. Those few successes, however, are usually attestations to the post hoc rationalization skills of the report writer who discovered a theme by which he or she could weave together the completed, independent efforts of the "team" members. Equally rare are successful curriculum reforms in prestigious universities. In all these cases there is a need for cooperative behaviors between specialists and specialist groups. Part of the problem is that any change which diminishes the importance of a group is seen as a loss for that group. One could say that the greater the task involvement, the greater the likelihood to see conflicts as win–lose or as zero sum games.

The studies of Lawrence and Lorsch support the proposition put forth here if one assumes that employing different professional groups (task-involved) and also nonprofessional groups in a common undertaking increases differentiation.[18] Their data show that the greater the degree of differentiation, the greater the difficulty in obtaining integration (cooperative behavior) between the differentiated groups.[19] Similarly Dalton's work supports the proposition.[20] If one assumes that staff people are task-involved, then the data on conflicts among staff and line (perhaps goal-identified people) show the difficulty (but not the impossibility) of obtaining cooperative behaviors in the presence of unlike roles that are staffed by task-involved people.

In summary, task involvement is a two-edged sword. It can be the most effective source of motivation for behaviors within a well-defined role and also among the least effective for cooperative behaviors between roles.

On the other hand, the greater the degree of goal identification, the greater the likelihood of cooperative behavior. Individuals will choose to perform those cooperative behaviors which are perceived as instrumental to the attainment of goals with which they are identified. Given the potentially greater valences and instrumentalities of goal identification, it appears to be the most effective method of motivating cooperative behaviors.

In summary, intrinsic rewards are potentially the most effective means of motivation. They lead to both a productive organization and satisfied individuals. This greater motivation can be achieved because intrinsic rewards satisfy higher order needs, are under the control of the individual, and occur immediately after the behavior. Goal identification was the most flexible type and was hypothesized to motivate any behavior, whether it be reliable or spontaneous, which was perceived as instrumental to the achievement of the goals with which the individual is identified. Task involvement varied considerably in its effects. It was hypothesized to have little effect on decisions to join and remain. For the other behaviors, it was either more or less effective than goal identification. If the behaviors were within the definition of the role with which the individual is identified, task involvement is more effective because of abilities to perform the behavior. If the behaviors lie outside the role, they are not likely to be perceived as instrumental and some cooperative behaviors may be negatively related to need satisfactions. In order to choose between these types of motivation one needs to analyze each role and the functioning of the whole group. Let us now turn to the implementation of these types of motivation.

## IMPLEMENTATION AND EVIDENCE

If an organization chooses to base its reward system on intrinsic rewards, how does it go about implementing such a system? What are the policy variables? And what do we know about them? Very simply, intrinsic motivation is implemented by matching a job with an individual who derives satisfaction from performing it. Therefore, the design of the jobs in the organization and the recruiting and selection efforts are the primary policy variables. However, this deceptively simple implementation becomes more difficult as more specific statements are attempted. First, let us look at the design of jobs and then briefly discuss the role of selection.

## The Design of Job Content

The inquiry into the design of jobs has come from a number of sources. There are industrial engineers who believe in some of the industrial engineering principles of job design but believe that these can be taught to individuals in order to design their own jobs. There are psychologists who are interested in the effect of jobs on the satisfaction and mental health of the work force. Others have been interested in the impact of automation, resistance to change, industrial democracy, etc. Most of the interest centered on the powerless worker whose job was being continually simplified in the interest of efficiency. The belief was that the increasing division of labor deprived the individual of any personal satisfaction from the work. In addition, it was hypothesized that it also failed to produce the increase in performance that management desired. In the language developed earlier, the limiting factors were no longer physical or cognitive factors, but motivational ones. Therefore while work simplification still had a positive effect on the physical and cognitive job factors, productivity would decline because simplification negatively affected motivation which was the determining factor. By enlarging jobs the organization could increase the satisfaction of the work force and productivity at the same time.

The next problem was how to enlarge the jobs. One school of thought suggested an approach of adding job elements to a task. Instead of assembling 3 or 4 parts, the job should be expanded to allow the worker to assemble all 15 parts into a completed subassembly. This increase in variety of elements should decrease the monotony of the job. A second school of thought suggested that adding work elements or horizontal job enlargement would have little impact. It was pointed out that a whole job consisted of cycles of planning and organizing the work, doing the work, and the evaluating and replanning of the work. Horizontal job enlargement was concerned only with the doing portion of the job. The worker performing 12 or 15 meaningless elements is no more satisfied than the one performing 2 or 3 meaningless elements. Real motivation results from giving individuals the whole task or from vertical job enlargement (job enrichment).

A similar point of view was developed by those who advocated greater participation in the decision-making process as a means of increasing motivation. In addition to increasing motivation, participation was to allow a reduction in the possibly alienating power differences in organizations. Let us look at the evidence for job design and participation.

The research on job design has been reviewed several times. (See Note 8.) We will only summarize here and draw out the conclusions on which we can build. First, there are a number of case studies in which a job-enlargement program increased productivity or decreased turnover and absenteeism. However, when research designs included a number of plants and jobs, utilized acceptable methodology, and performed multivariate analyses, the generalized support disappeared. Turner and Lawrence developed a scale measuring the degree of complexity, responsibility, variety, etc.[21] When it was administered to 470 workers from 11 industries and 47 jobs, the hypothesized positive relation between satisfaction and the index did not appear. A relationship did appear when the location of the factory was controlled. For workers in factories located in small, rural towns, there was a positive relation between more responsibility and satisfaction with the job. But for workers from cities, there was a negative relationship. These results were supported by Blood and Hulin in their analysis of 1300 blue collar workers from 21 plants.[22] In trying to explain their results, Blood and Hulin suggest that, in general, workers from urban locations are alienated from middle-class work norms and do not value more responsible jobs, have no positive affect for occupational achievement, do not believe in the value of hard work, are not striving for more responsible positions, etc. Thus, there are individual differences in the response to more complex tasks.

As the authors above suggest, the aggregate measure of rural–urban is too simple to have other than suggestive value. The measure suggests that the place of residence or of growing up is an indicator of different socialization processes which have endowed the individual with different values and attitudes and which, in turn, determine what the individual expects from a job and how the individual perceives the job and reacts to it. The simplicity of the urban–rural dimension is called into question in a more recent study.[23] The authors found that people from large communities measured higher in job involvement and responded more positively to participation than their colleagues in smaller towns. The study is not directly comparable because the relation concerns job involvement, not job satisfaction which is a different and independent factor. However, it does question the simple rural–urban dimension and confirms the view that there are individual differences in responses to job characteristics.

There are two sociological studies which have looked in more detail at actual differences between individuals with respect to work expectations and desires.[24] These studies report that there are workers for whom the job provides and is expected to provide extrinsic satisfactions only. These people do not accept the intrinsic value of hard work and receive no satisfaction from occupational achievement. Work-related matters are not central to their self-concepts and self-esteem. The conclusion drawn from these studies is that there are workers who do not respond positively in terms of satisfaction and productivity to jobs with more interest and responsibility.

Hackman and Lawler have combined the perspective above in a more psychological approach.[25] The authors measured the perceived and actual characteristics of jobs and the importance of work for various levels of needs. They found a positive relation between job complexity and satisfaction, motivation, etc. However, the relation was stronger for individuals for whom higher order needs were important than for individuals for whom they were less important. In addition, people with rural backgrounds tended to rate higher order needs as more important. Again, there are individual differences in the response to complex jobs.

The research concerning participation has followed an almost identical history of inquiry. There were the initial studies reporting positive results, the most notable of which was the one by Coch and French.[26] Subsequent research sometimes supports the hypothesis that increased participation increases satisfaction and performance, sometimes not, and sometimes produces mixed results.[27] One of the reasons for the lack of clear results is the effect of individual differences.

Subsequent research has examined some of these individual differences. Vroom reported variations in satisfaction and performance based on personality differences of those participating.[28] Workers with low authoritarian personalities and high needs for independence were more satisfied and performed at higher levels when participation was high. For workers with high authoritarianism and low needs for independence, there was no relation. However, a recent study has failed to reproduce those results.[29] Argyris reports that individuals who are dependent, submissive, and have short time horizons will not respond positively to a challenging job.[30] The Vroom and Argyris results suggest that personality differences will moderate the effects of participation in decision making.

A series of laboratory studies have tested the effects of possessed and valued abilities.[31] After summarizing 11 experiments, Vroom concludes:

> We can tentatively conclude that creditable instructions to experimental subjects to the effect that a task they are about to perform requires an attribute which they believe themselves to possess *or* which they value and would like to possess increases the amount of effort which they will direct toward effective task performance.[32]

Although Vroom offers a different theoretical explanation, these results are consistent with the path–goal model. Tasks requiring abilities that individuals possess or would like to possess are instrumental to the satisfaction of self-esteem needs and more likely to provide intrinsic rewards. On the other hand, giving individuals the opportunity to participate in decisions for which they have no skills and/or which they do not value will not result in increased motivation, satisfaction, and performance. A field study by Patchen reports that the effects of participation at TVA were greater in departments where individuals had skills for the decisions and considered participation legitimate.[33] Thus, as individuals vary in their self-concepts with respect to skills they believe they possess and want to possess, their response to opportunities to use those skill will vary likewise.

Finally, a study of school teachers developed a participation scale.[34] Opportunities to participate were measured relative to the amount of participation desired. Thus, it was possible to find on one end of the scale people who were deprived of having enough opportunity and also those on the other end of the scale who were overloaded and had more opportunity than they desired. Variation in the participative scale was correlated with school district, age, and sex. Older women tended to be overloaded while young men tended to be deprived. Teachers in the rural school district tended to be deprived while teachers in the urban district were either at equilibrium or saturated. The urban–rural dimension appears again but the authors suggest that the decision-making structure in the district is the cause of the reappearance of the urban–rural dimension rather than individual differences between rural and urban teachers. Deprivation in opportunities to participate was correlated with union activity and militancy. Again, there is individual variation in the response to participation in decisions.

This very brief review of job design and participation has a distinctly skeptical tone. The author believes skepticism is an appropriate attitude given the amount and quality of relevant research that is available, particularly with respect to causation. The predictive ability of the research is quite small ($R^2$ rarely exceeds 0.20–0.25 and is usually around 0.11). This prediction ability is increased when different moderating factors are introduced such as individual differences. However, there is not as yet a definitive set of factors which have been replicated over a number of contexts and individuals. However, the job itself, whether measured by perceived challenge or complexity or by participation, remains the best predictor of task involvement and goal identification in a variety of organizational contexts.[35] Even for individuals with low-need strengths, Hackman and Lawler report significant and positive correlations between job complexity and satisfaction and job involvement.[36] Since the Hackman–Lawler work brings together the most specific ways of talking about jobs, about people, and about the interactions of these two in producing intrinsic motivation, job satisfaction, and job performance, let us try to extend their hypotheses so as to specify the means by which one can employ intrinsic motivation.

The increased specificity can be obtained by identifying the attributes of jobs that are important to intrinsic motivation and how they affect the choice of behavior. This purpose is well served with the four task dimensions identified by Turner and Lawrence and employed by Hackman and Lawler. Tasks vary in the amount of:

> ... a) variety, the degree to which a job requires employees to perform a wide range of operations in their work and/or the degree to which employees must use a variety of equipment and procedures in their work; b) autonomy, the extent to which employees have a major say in scheduling their work, selecting the equipment they will use, and deciding on procedures to be followed; c) task identity, the extent to which employees do an entire or whole piece of work and can clearly identify the results of their efforts; d) feedback, the degree to which employees receive information as they are working which reveals how well they are performing on the job.[37]

The four dimensions are not an independent, mutually exclusive set. Sometimes they can be varied independently, sometimes not. For example, assume that the variety of task, which is the opposite of the division of labor, was increased by adding elements to an assembly task where the individual now assembles an entire carburetor. In addition the autonomy may increase. Before the addition of elements, individuals had to coordinate their movements with prior and subsequent operations. The reduced interdependence increases autonomy and permits individuals to choose their own methods and sequences of assembly. However, the supervisor may keep these decisions in which case variety increases and autonomy does not. In this example, the increase in variety or decrease in division of labor also permits an increase in task identity. The individual now assembles the entire carburetor and can take pride in identifying with and establishing ownership in a whole task. Since it is a whole task and the individual can see the results of his or her efforts, increased feedback is provided. Thus, a decrease in the division of labor results in an increase in each of the other three dimensions. However, it was also shown in the case of autonomy that these increases need not take place automatically and can be changed independently. A last example of independent changes would be with feedback. The individual can see the results of his or her efforts at assembly but could also receive test results when carburetors are tested to see if they work and how long they last on the road. It is necessary to evaluate each task independently to see the changes in the four dimensions.

The motivational impact of the dimensions appears, at first glance, to be a monotonically increasing one. That is, more variety (i.e., less division of labor), more autonomy, more identity, and more feedback result in higher motivation, higher performance, and higher satisfaction. However, like most generalizations, this one needs qualification. In order to qualify the generalization, let us look at the connections between effort and needs satisfaction, translate them into expectancies and instrumentalities, and then predict how the task dimensions will affect these path–goal relations. Figure 20.1 is a sequence of relations between effort and need satisfaction.

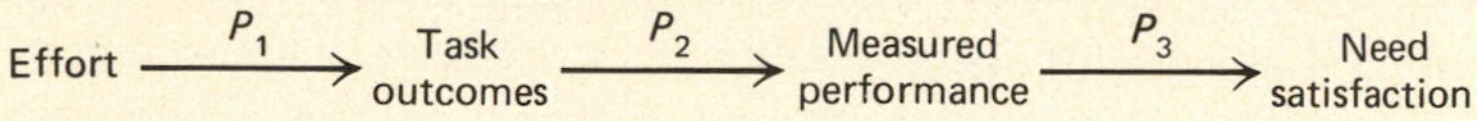

Effort $\xrightarrow{P_1}$ Task outcomes $\xrightarrow{P_2}$ Measured performance $\xrightarrow{P_3}$ Need satisfaction

**Fig. 20.1   Effort-satisfaction sequence.**

The level of effort chosen by the individual leads to the accomplishment of particular task outcomes such as quantity, quality, and timeliness of performance, number of new ideas, etc. In turn, these outcomes lead to measured performance which puts different weights of importance on these outcomes. Finally, performance leads to needs satisfaction. Now if we concentrate only on individuals who are capable of higher order needs satisfaction, variations in performance and satisfaction should be explainable in terms of the impact of the job on $P_1$, $P_2$, and $P_3$ which are perceived probability connections which the individual has learned and are evoked in the job situation. The connections are probabilistic because effort may not lead to higher quantity, higher quantity may not result in higher measured performance, and higher performance may not result in greater needs satisfaction. Whether these probabilities are important or not and whether they vary depend on the individual and the job. (Three probabilities are used to illustrate the arbitrariness and flexibility of the path–goal model. Usually $P_1 \times P_2$ is expectancy and $P_3$ is instrumentality.) Let us look at the impact of the four job factors and hypothesize about their immediate effects.

A decrease in the division of labor is regarded as a necessary but insufficient condition to make performance instrumental to higher order need satisfaction ($P_3 > 0$). That is, by itself, the adding of additional elements to a job, particularly if they are only physical elements, has very little impact on $P_3$. There may be exceptions in the case in which a task requires rare and valued skills. But even in physical activities such as golf, individuals would not derive as much satisfaction if they could not decide themselves to "cut a dogleg" or carry a water hazard. It is the decision concerning one's abilities *and* the execution that provides the satisfaction or dissatisfaction when the results are realized.

The impact of the division of labor on the other probabilities depends on several other factors. If the decrease in division of labor also decreases task interdependence, then it becomes easier to measure individual performance. Outcomes achieved depend increasingly on individual efforts. In that case, $P_1$ and $P_2$ increase. Individuals can perceive more easily the effects of their choices toward performance. Alternatively, decreases in the division of labor which increase interdependence will decrease $P_1$ and $P_2$. In other words, decreases in the division of labor which expand a task in order to assemble an entire carburetor create a relatively independent subtask and permit increases in $P_1$ and $P_2$ and hence an increase in motivation. Further decreases in the division of labor, for example to the point where the individual assembles 1/20 of the entire motor, increase interdependence and decrease $P_1$ and $P_2$. Thus, the division of labor does not have a linear monotonically increasing effect on expectancies and instrumentalities. The effect depends also on the task structure or technology (which should also be regarded as a variable).

A second effect of a decrease in the division of labor depends on the relation between skills required by the task and those possessed by the individual. An increase in the number of elements usually increases skill requirements. If skills required are greater than skills possessed, then $P_1$ will decrease in the short run until the individual acquires the skills necessary.[38] Therefore, in general, increasing the challenge of the job will decrease expectancies or $P_1$ in the hope that $P_2$ and/or $P_3$ will increase.

It was stated above that the division of labor could be decreased without significantly increasing autonomy if the additional elements added to the task involved doing or execution functions only. The reverse appears not to be true. Autonomy is increased only when additional elements are added and usually these elements are of the planning and evaluating types. Therefore the statements made above concerning the reduced division of labor apply here as well. The effects on $P_1$ and $P_2$, however, would be expected to be more pronounced. First, since the planning tasks are more difficult to do well, one would expect a larger immediate reduction in $P_1$. Second, larger reductions and increases in interdependence are possible for planning and evaluating tasks. Thus, when the quality control function is added to a worker's tasks, one would expect an increase in $P_1$ and $P_2$ with respect to measured quality. The worker can more easily perceive and control the translation of effort into measured quality. But, in addition, autonomy is hypothesized to have some effects of its own.

First, if no compensation is made, an increase in autonomy will increase ambiguity, particularly with respect as to what constitutes good performance. If a worker's job is enlarged to include the scheduling function, the maintenance function, the quality control function, etc., there is an increase in the number of dimensions along which performance is measured, which creates a problem of weights of importance. If quality increases and costs decrease while machine breakdowns increase and quantity stays the same, does that constitute improved performance? If no information is provided concerning trade-offs among the dimensions, the perceived connection, $P_2$, between task outcomes and measured performance will decrease and motivation will decrease. Again the leadership role in providing information is important. This paragraph assumes that there is no inherent value attached to any of the task outcomes. The individual may not inherently prefer lower cost to fewer machine breakdowns. But the professional may prefer quality of output to scheduled performance. Therefore, the individual's previous socialization may make unnecessary the passing of information and/or may make the response less flexible if quality should be diminished in the best interest of the customer. Again, professional socialization is a two-sided coin.

The second effect of autonomy is to increase $P_3$. By being able to attribute to themselves the accomplishment of their own performance, individuals make performance instrumental to the satisfaction of self-esteem and other higher order needs. This generalization, too, requires some qualification. First, autonomy is a necessary but insufficient condition to make performance instrumental to the satisfaction of higher order needs. Task must also be high on identity. Second, for some people there is a chance that there can be too much autonomy. Even in the presence of additional information, increased autonomy increases ambiguity. Therefore, those individuals who possess low tolerances for ambiguity will not find these autonomous tasks instrumental to their needs. For each of us at any point there may be an optimal amount of autonomy from which increases or decreases would both result in decreased instrumentality, $P_3$.[39] Thus, autonomy does not have a simple monotonically increasing relationship with expectancies and instrumentalities.

Another factor that must be present in order for performance to be instrumental to higher order needs satisfactions is identity. That is, not only must the task provide several functions to be performed and permit the individual to attribute the outcome to his or her own efforts but it also must be meaningful in some way. Whether a job has meaning or not depends somewhat on the task and somewhat on the individual. The task itself must provide a reasonably whole or complete piece of work. But what is considered to be a complete piece of work depends on the individual. Some engineers are interested in the design, manufacture, and testing of a whole object while others consider the electronics to be a meaningful whole with which they can identify. The identity depends on the skills the individual believes he or she possesses and values. The identity results from the opportunity to use these skills. In addition, the prerequisite is that the individual have a value system which values hard work, work skills, career, and occupational achievement. If the individual does not have these values, a challenging job and the autonomy to perform it will have little meaning for the individual and will not provide for the satisfaction of higher order needs.

Finally, to establish the perceived probabilities at values above zero, the individual must receive performance feedback. Feedback relates positively to all three probabilities. Together the job dimensions determine

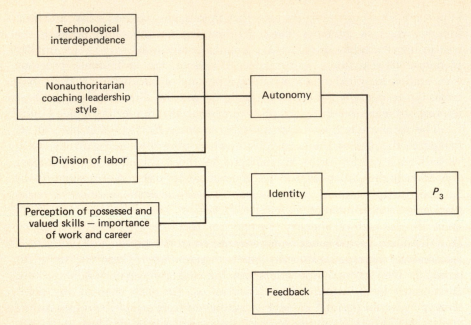

**Fig. 20.2  Relation of job design factors on perceived instrumentality $P_3$.**

instrumentality of performance for higher needs satisfaction. Figure 20.2 summarizes the position taken here. Division of labor is considered as a facilitating factor for identity and autonomy. Whether autonomy results from reduced division of labor depends on the interdependence of the technology. When the technology permits semi-independent activity, it is also necessary to have a leadership style which permits and, indeed, helps the autonomous functioning of the workers. The matching of the task with the value system and self-concept of the worker establishes the identity or meaningfulness of the work. And finally, when feedback, in addition to autonomy and identity, is present, only then is work performance instrumental to higher order needs satisfaction for those who are capable of higher needs satisfaction. Thus, in order to affect intrinsic motivation, the organization must *simultaneously* make design choices for five policy variables. Three of them are relatively easy (but not necessarily inexpensive) to change and control. The *division of labor* and *technological interdependence* result from engineering decisions concerning work flows, parallel or sequential tasks, location of inventories, and number of operations per task.[40] At the same time, the organization *selects* and the individuals *select* themselves to match the division of labor. The information system can usually accommodate the *feedback of information* concerning performance, schedules, etc. However, the implementation of styles of *leadership* which permit autonomous action by subordinates may be the most difficult. It is difficult to change attitudes concerning appropriate leader behavior. In addition, the jobs of middle management are usually not enriched when the jobs of lower levels are enriched. The middle managers are still responsible but feel they lose control when workers become autonomous. But the important point is that intrinsic motivation results from coordinated choices concerning all five variables.

## Selection

The second method for implementing intrinsic motivation is to select individuals capable of receiving intrinsic rewards. While it was suggested in the previous section that it is necessary both to have jobs which permit intrinsic satisfaction and people capable of achieving it, there is a question of emphasis and therefore a question of allocating organization resources. The brief review of the research presented above suggested that not everyone will respond favorably to an enriched job. People who do not have middle-class values, who have authoritarian personalities, who are not capable of higher order needs satisfaction, who have low tolerances for ambiguity, or who perceive that they do not possess the required abilities will not achieve higher satisfaction from enriched jobs. Therefore, one could conclude that it is necessary to select people with the opposite type of personality and attitudes. But one could equally well arrive at another conclusion.

It is possible that favorable personalities and value systems result from enriched jobs rather than determine a worker's response to an enriched job. This position does not refute the previous research findings but makes a different causal argument. The argument would state that people with low needs for independence, low tolerance for ambiguity, etc. would not react favorably to enriched jobs *initially*. But after a period of time these individual traits would change and people would desire more independence, learn to tolerate ambiguity, develop higher order needs, learn that they do possess required abilities, etc., and would begin to respond favorably to enriched jobs. The job opportunity would cause the job attitudes.

That the job is the primary factor is the position taken by Argyris.[41] He argues that the unfavorable attitudes towards work indicate the realism and adaptability of human beings. Realizing that job and career satisfactions are not available to them, workers adopt other values and sources of satisfaction and adapt to their lot in life. But when jobs are changed and workers believe interesting and challenging work is available, their attitudes and sources of satisfaction change also. If this is true, then selection is less necessary. However, the question requires causal evidence which is not yet available.

Whether selection is emphasized or not also depends on the goals and values of the organization. If the organization has the usual goals of efficiency in resource utilization, selection would be necessary. However, one could equally well advocate designing organizations to develop human resources. In that case, selection is less critical. This position identifies greater independence, tolerance for ambiguity, etc. as representing psychological growth and maturity. And if these human traits result from changed jobs, organizations ought to attempt to develop people. Thus, the criticality of selection depends on the values the organization has concerning human resources.

At the moment, the choice of effort level devoted to selection cannot be resolved on the basis of evidence. However, most organizations currently employing new forms of organization and job design devote a good deal of effort to selection. An example is a Procter and Gamble plant in which workers make many management decisions in addition to doing the work.[42] The management interviewed over 1000 workers from which 36 were selected on the basis of being capable of experiencing intrinsic rewards, and after four years 32 still remained. This is a substantial selection effort. The specific selection criteria were not discussed but the workers tended to be former farmers. Again the rural influence appears. However, it was stated that these people were selected because they had experience in performing a whole task rather than because they possessed Protestant ethic values. Farmers make their own investment, purchasing, and resource allocation decisions. They design their own information system and maintain their own equipment. Thus, they already had experience in enriched jobs.

Another example of selection takes place in the Israeli kibbutzim. These are very egalitarian, participative organizations. While the policy varies among the many types, most organizations use a year probation period to allow the individuals and the kibbutz to decide on membership. This process allows self-selection as well and may be the best means of selection if theory cannot provide a valid set of criteria. Thus, some organizations are successfully implementing forms of selection in order to match people with jobs which can provide them with intrinsic satisfactions.

## SUMMARY

This chapter presented the final types of motivational bases of organizational behavior—task involvement and goal identification. These were intrinsic rewards which occurred as natural consequences of effectively performing a task. These rewards could be achieved if the jobs were sufficiently challenging to be instrumental to the attainment of higher order needs, if the individuals possessed values consistent with career advancement, hard work, etc., if the individuals believed they had the skills required by the task, and if they are capable of higher order needs satisfaction. Intrinsic rewards are implemented by designing jobs and matching people with them. The two different types of intrinsic rewards depended upon the source of the identification. For one, the individual identified with a group of people possessing a particular skill (task involvement) and for the other, the individual identified with particular outcomes independent of the skill necessary (goal identification). This difference was significant for some behaviors and for some roles which required well-defined skills.

The task remaining is to summarize the section on motivation, give an example of a reward system and then a case where the reward system is a critical design variable. This is the task of Chapters 21 and 22.

## NOTES

1. F. Herzberg 1966. Work and the nature of man. Cleveland: World.

2. M. Dunette, J. P. Campbell, and M. D. Hakel 1967. Factors contributing to job satisfaction and job dissatisfaction in six occupational groups. *Organizational Behavior and Human Performance* 2: 143–174. R. House and L. A. Wigdor 1967. Herzberg's dual-factor theory of job satisfaction and motivation. *Personnel Psychology* 20: 369–389.

3. R. N. Ford 1969. *Motivation through the work itself.* New York: American Management Association. M. S. Myers 1971. *Every employee as manager.* New York: McGraw-Hill.

4. J. W. Atkinson and N. T. Feather (eds.) 1966. *A theory of achievement motivation.* New York: Wiley.

5. M. Patchen 1970. *Participation achievement and involvement on the job.* Englewood Cliffs, N.J.: Prentice-Hall.

6. V. Vroom 1964. *Work and motivation.* New York: Wiley, pp. 247–250 and 264–266.

7. J. R. Hackman and E. Lawler III 1971. Employee reactions to job characteristics. *Journal of Applied Psychology,* (June): 259–286.

8. Vroom, pp. 220–229 and 236–252. C. L. Hulin and M. R. Blood 1968. Job enlargement, individual differences, and worker responses. *Psychological Bulletin* 69: 41–55. Hackman and Lawler, pp. 259–286.

9. T. M. Lodahl and M. Kejner 1965. The definition and measurement of job involvement. *Journal of Applied Psychology* 49: 24.

10. E. Lawler III and D. Hall 1970. Relationship of job characteristics to job involvement, satisfaction, and intrinsic motivation. *Journal of Applied Psychology* 54, (4): 305–312.

11. A. Gouldner 1957. Cosmopolitans and locals: toward an analysis of social roles. *Administrative Science Quarterly* 2: 281–306.

12. *Ibid.,* p. 290.

13. W. Kornhauser 1962. *Scientists in industry.* Berkeley: University of California Press.

14. A. Grimes and P. Berger 1970. Cosmopolitan–local: evaluation of the construct. *Administrative Science Quarterly,* (December): 407–417. R. Thornton 1970. Organizational involvement and commitment to organization and profession. *Administrative Science Quarterly,* (December): 417–426. D. Luecke 1973. The professional as organization leader. *Administrative Science Quarterly,* (March): 86–94.

15. R. Hall 1967. Some organizational considerations in the professional-organization relationship. *Administrative Science Quarterly,* (December): 461–478.

16. J. March and H. Simon 1958. *Organizations.* New York: Wiley, pp. 185–186.

17. J. March 1964. Business decision making. In H. J. Leavitt and L. R. Pondy (eds.), *Readings in managerial psychology.* Chicago: University of Chicago Press, pp. 447–456.

18. P. Lawrence and J. Lorsch 1967. *Organization and Environment.* Boston: Division of Research, Harvard Business School.

19. *Ibid.*

20. M. Dalton 1950. Conflicts between staff and line managerial officers. *American Sociological Review* 15: 342–351.

21. A. N. Turner and P. R. Lawrence 1965. *Industrial jobs and the worker: an investigation of response to task attributes.* Boston: Division of Research, Harvard Business School.

22. M. R. Blood and C. L. Hulin 1967. Alienation, environmental characteristics, and worker responses. *Journal of Applied Psychology* 51: 284–290.

23. A. L. Siegel and R. A. Ruh 1973. Job involvement participative in decision making, personal background, and job behavior. *Organizational Behavior and Human Performance* 9: 318–327.

24. J. H. Goldthorpe, D. L. Lockwood, F. Bechofer, and J. Platt 1968. *The affluent worker: industrial attitudes and behavior.* Cambridge: Cambridge University Press. R. Dubin and D. R. Goldman 1972. Central life interests of American middle managers and specialists. *Journal of Vocational Behavior* 2: 133–141. R. Centers and D. Bugental 1966. Intrinsic and extrinsic job motivations among different segments of the working population. *Journal of Applied Psychology* 50: 193–197.

25. Hackman and Lawler, *ibid.*

26. L. Coch and J. R. P. French 1948. Overcoming resistance to change. *Human Relations* 54: 512–532.

27. Vroom, pp. 115–119 and 220–229. V. Vroom 1970. Industrial social psychology. In G. Lindzey and E. Aronson (eds.), *The handbook of social psychology.* (Second edition.) Reading, Mass.: Addison-Wesley, Vol. 5, pp. 227–240.

28. V. Vroom 1960. *Some personality determinants of the effects of participation.* Englewood Cliffs, N.J.: Prentice-Hall.

29. H. Tosi 1970. A reevaluation of personality as a determinant of the effects of participation. *Personnel Psychology* 23: 91–100.

30. C. Argyris 1964. *Integrating the individual and the organization.* New York: Wiley.

31. Vroom, Industrial social psychology, pp. 221–222.

32. *Ibid.,* p. 222.

33. M. Patchen 1965. Labor–management consulation at TVA: its impact on employees. *Administrative Science Quarterly,* (September): 149–174.

34. J. A. Alutto and J. Belasco 1972. A typology for participation in organizational decision making. *Administrative Science Quarterly,* (March): 117–125.

35. Patchen, pp. 149–174. D. Hall and B. Schneider 1972. Correlates of organizational identification as a function of career pattern and organization. *Administrative Science Quarterly,* (September): 340–350.

36. Hackman and Lawler, p. 279.

37. *Ibid.*, p. 265.

38. D. Schwab and L. Cummings 1973. Impact of task scope on employee productivity: an evaluation using expectancy theory. Paper delivered at The Academy of Management Meetings, Boston, August.

39. J. J. Morse and D. F. Young, 1973. Personality development and task choices: a systems view. *Human Relations,* (March): 79–92.

40. E. Trist, G. W. Higgin, H. Murray, and A. B. Pollack 1963. *Organizational choice.* London: Tavistock.

41. C. Argyris 1973. Personality and organization theory revisited. *Administrative Science Quarterly,* (June): 141–167.

42. The remarks are taken from an unpublished seminar given by C. Krone at the Sloan School of Management, M.I.T., spring, 1971.

## QUESTIONS

1. What are the differences and similarities between task involvement and goal identification?

2. Discuss a job situation in which first task involvement and then goal identification is the primary determinant of job behavior.

3. What is the impact of task involvement and goal identification on the five task behaviors?

4. Explain and illustrate by example what is meant by the four dimensions (suggested by Hackman and Lawler) of a job,—variety, autonomy, identity, and feedback.

5. Discuss the impact of these four dimensions on the motivational model.

6. Present a comprehensive program for employing task involvement and goal identification as the bases for motivating the job behavior of a specific task.

| | CHAPTER |
|---|---|
| REWARD SYSTEMS— A RECAPITULATION | **21** |

In this chapter we wish to summarize the discussion concerning reward systems, take an overview so as to be able to choose among different kinds of systems and finally to present a sample reward system. The previous chapters introduced the policy variables, the types of behavior, and some evidence and speculation concerning the matching of behaviors and policy variables. This chapter will present a case in which a substantial portion of the problem is the design of the reward system. Later we will deal with the overall design problem and the matching of reward system with structure, task, and information system.

## ANALYSIS AND CHOICE OF REWARD SYSTEMS

The analysis of reward systems was based on the premise that there is an imperfect matching of organizational roles and human personalities. This imperfect matching means that most people do not voluntarily perform the task behaviors that are required to produce the desired effects on the environment without further effort by the organization. This additional organizational effort is devoted to attracting, selecting, and holding the right individuals and/or modifying the roles to accommodate the available individuals. In either case, the effort consumes organizational resources and the effectiveness of the organization depends on the choice of reward system.

The choice of reward system depends not only upon the resources required to implement and maintain it but also on the effects it produces. Thus, a second premise on which the analysis was based is that reward systems vary in the degree to which they increase or decrease the probability that a particular behavior would be adopted. Further, the variation depends upon the type of behavior in question. Since the type of behavior varies with the task, a means is discovered for relating task variation to reward system. The previous chapters analyzed this matching of reward system with behavior. The results are summarized in Fig. 21.1.

The summary is simply the matrix shown in Fig. 16.2 but the blanks have been filled in. Two representations have been used. First pluses (+) and minuses (−) are used to designate whether a policy increases or decreases the probability that a particular behavior will be adopted. The larger the number of pluses, the greater the probability. Second, some of the boxes are divided and contain two different symbols. This is because for some behaviors it is difficult to summarize several pages of discussion with a single symbol. For example, group incentives increase the probability of cooperative behaviors within groups (+) but decrease the probability of cooperative behaviors between groups (−). Let us summarize the earlier discussion by going down the columns instead of across the rows as in the previous chapters.

| Reward system \ Behavior | Join and remain | Reliable role behavior | Effort above minimum | Spontaneous behavior | Cooperative behavior |
|---|---|---|---|---|---|
| Rule compliance | + | +++ | − | − | − |
| System reward | ++ | | | | |
| Group reward | ++ | + | ++ | ++ / − | ++ / − |
| Individual rewards | +++ | + | +++ | + / − | + / − |
| Leadership behavior | + | ++ | ++ | ++ | ++ |
| Group acceptance | + | + / − | + / − | + / − | + / − |
| Task involvement | − | +++ / − − | +++ | +++ / − − | +++ / − − |
| Goal identification | +++ | +++ | +++ | +++ | +++ |

**Fig. 21.1   Summary of reward systems and behaviors.**

## Join and Remain

Every organization must attract people to it and have them remain long enough to contribute something of value to the organization. It can be seen that the different reward systems vary in the degree to which they increase the probability that people will choose to join and remain in the organization. First, two of the reward factors, task involvement and leader behavior (signifying a high initiating structure by a leader on a repetitive task), increase the probability that people will choose to leave. These are designated by minuses. Also task involvement and rule compliance have very little to do with decisions to join an organization. These phenomena are represented by the blank portions of the respective squares for join-and-remain behaviors.

The remaining reward factors increase to various degrees the probability of joining or remaining. Leader behavior and group acceptance can, under appropriate conditions, lead to job satisfaction which in turn reduces the probability of one's leaving. They have only one plus because they have little to do with joining an organization. An individual cannot know enough about local groups and leaders to have them influence his or her choice of joining. Rule compliance, it was stated earlier, can lead to a reduction in absences by enforcing absence rules.

The extrinsic rewards concerning the total wage package (system, group, and individual rewards) have a stronger impact on choices to join and remain. To the extent that these rewards compare favorably in other organizations, they increase the probability that individuals will join and remain. These extrinsic rewards, along with goal identification, play a more important role generally speaking, in the decision to join and remain than the previously mentioned factors. Thus, they carry at least two pluses. In addition, individual wage rewards and goal identification carry three pluses to indicate that these rewards are capable of being instrumental to higher level needs.

System rewards, individual rewards, and goal identification are used by organizations to attract and hold employees. Individual rewards and goal identification are the most effective but system rewards distributed on the basis of seniority are the easiest to administer.

## Dependable Role Behaviors

In every organization, a large portion of the activity consists of the repetitive day-to-day behaviors which are necessary to maintain the organization as an organization. As with the other behaviors, the motivational bases of these behaviors vary considerably. First, it is possible that two factors can reduce the probability that people will choose to perform dependable behaviors. If the behaviors lie outside the role with which the task-involved individual is identified, task involvement reduces the likelihood that these dependable behaviors will be performed. On a similarly contingent basis, group acceptance can increase or decrease the probability. If group norms are contrary to organizational goals, group acceptance will reduce the probability that individuals will adopt those dependable behaviors which are important to the group. System rewards, as is the case with all the remaining behaviors, have little direct effect. System rewards are received as long as the individual is a member of the organization.

The extrinsic rewards of wage incentives and group acceptance (when norms support organizational goals) generally increase the probability of adoption of dependable actions. These factors have only one symbol because of the difficulty of implementing such a system. It is quite expensive to set up a program to measure these behaviors and relate them to a contingent wage payment system.

The remaining four factors represent the principal means of providing for dependable behaviors. The extrinsic factors of leader behavior and rule compliance are not really independent ones. Both rely on the observation and enforcement of dependable behaviors when the situation requires. Rule compliance is a more powerful means to the extent that legitimate authority can be drawn upon by people in observatory positions.

Finally, the other means of increasing the probability that dependable behaviors will be performed is to employ people who have already internalized them. This form eliminates the need for the external observation. Task involvement can be used for dependable behaviors which lie within professional roles and goal identification for all dependable behaviors perceived to lead to the goals. Again, those factors which have been internalized and/or lead to higher order needs satisfaction are given the highest weights.

### Effort above Minimum Levels

Many roles in organizations require more than just dependable behaviors. The organization is dependent on the individuals to exercise effort above minimally acceptable levels. The greater the effort, the better the performance. Again the various rewards are not equally effective. As before, some of the rewards decrease the probability that people will choose to perform above minimal levels. If work groups adopt norms which support the restriction of output, individuals are less likely to perform above the level decided upon by the work group. Similarly, if supervisors attempt to enforce rules to increase output, the probability of high performance within a role is also decreased. Otherwise rule compliance has no direct effect upon the choice of effort levels.

The probability that individuals will choose to perform above minimal levels is increased by the appropriate implementation of the four remaining extrinsic rewards. Leader behavior and group rewards carry two pluses because they are more easily implemented by an organization. Individual rewards have three because they can be instrumental to higher order needs and can also carry higher instrumentalities than group rewards.

Finally, both intrinsic rewards can significantly increase the probability that individuals perform above minimal levels. They carry three pluses because they are instrumental to higher order needs. It should be recalled that task involvement is probably the most effective for professional roles since professionals are also most likely to possess highly developed task-related abilities.

All of these motivational bases are in use in modern organizations. The extrinsic rewards tend to be implemented on lower level tasks, task involvement on profession or staff activities, and goal identification for higher level managers.

## Spontaneous and Cooperative Behaviors

While the majority of the activity that takes place in organizations constitutes behavior within defined roles, perhaps the most important behaviors are those that cannot be predicted in advance. In particular, as tasks increase in uncertainty, the need for spontaneous and cooperative behavior increases. The different reward systems, in addition to having varying effects, produce the largest number of negative effects. Many of the reward systems which have strengths for dependable and within role behaviors are weak for extra and between role behaviors. Task involvement is the best example of these reward systems. If the behaviors lie outside the defined role, the probability that the task-involved individual will choose to perform them is greatly reduced. Similarly, wage incentives measure simultaneously what is to be rewarded and what is not to be rewarded. For many systems the spontaneous and cooperative behaviors are not rewarded, and the probability that they will be chosen is reduced. As before, if one attempts to use rule compliance, one reduces the likelihood of spontaneous behaviors. Otherwise rule compliance, and again system rewards, have no direct effect.

Several of the systems can be effective if properly designed. Individual rewards can increase the probability of acceptance but the more ambiguous and/or more global criteria create lower instrumentalities. If group norms are positive, group acceptance can increase the probability that one will adopt these extra role behaviors. However, for behaviors within the group, the group incentive is judged to be more effective and therefore carries two pluses. Similarly, the flexibility of supervisory rewards makes it easier to make them instrumental for spontaneous behaviors. These extrinsic rewards and particularly supervisory behaviors are used for most of the spontaneous behaviors required from lower level employees.

As before, the intrinsic rewards are the most effective type of reward system with the usual qualification for task involvement. In addition for cooperative behaviors, it is judged that task involvement is less effective even under favorable conditions than goal identification is. Thus, goal identification is the reward system most likely to lead to the performance of spontaneous and cooperative behaviors.

The analysis above of reward systems eliminates some of the alternatives of choice but does not uniquely determine a preferred alternative. For example, if one were performing a task requiring effort above minimum levels, one would not choose a reward system based on rule compliance. However, choice still remains for at least three reasons. First, the analysis says only that there needs to be a match between reward system and task, and specifies which matches are viable. If there is no match, one has the choice of either changing the task to fit the reward system or changing the reward system to fit the task. Which alternative does one choose? The analysis does not tell us. However, the discussion of this problem is postponed to Chapter 22. For to change the task means to change structure and information technology as well. For the present, let us take the task as given and analyze the choice of reward system.

Second, the appropriate reward system for a given task and behavior is not uniquely determined. For tasks requiring effort above minimum levels, there exist three alternative reward systems, with an edge to task involvment, with three pluses signifying about equal effectiveness. How does one choose?

Third, the effects shown in Fig. 21.1 and the costs used to choose between different reward systems are arguments from the point of view of the organization. Indeed, the criteria used throughout this book and which are implicit in Fig. 21.1 are those of organizational effectiveness and efficiency, however vaguely conceived. It is equally legitimate, if possible, to employ other criteria when choosing reward systems and in particular criteria which indicate effectiveness, growth, and development of the individual. Also the impact on these criteria depends on the model of humankind that one employs. Thus, the design choice can vary, as we will see, with the criteria employed and model of humankind that is adopted.

Let us look first at the choice of a reward system for a given, required behavior. The question then becomes, "Is there a reward system which can increase the probability that the given behavior will be chosen to be executed?" The problem is that for most behaviors there are at least two cells which carry three pluses and a few others which carry two. On what other bases can one choose? One basis is the one referred to several times before and that is that the systems vary in their costs of implementation and administration. The hypothesis, more fully stated, is that, other things equal, rule compliance is the least expensive and goal identification the most expensive system to employ. The others fall in between as they are listed in Fig. 21.1. If the organization performs routine tasks and needs only join-and-remain and dependable behaviors, the least costly system that the organization can employ is rule compliance and system rewards. Rule compliance is the least expensive system since the organization can accept almost anyone in the population, train them quickly, and employ them at reasonable wages. The primary means of implementation is through direct supervision. Here again repetitive tasks and hence rule compliance require the fewest number of supervisors. One of the most consistent findings among sociologists is that the more complex and uncertain the task, the smaller the span of control at the first level of the organization.[1] Thus, other things being equal, rule compliance consumes fewer organizational resources.

System rewards are next in the progression. These rewards require the expenditure of organizational resources, in the form of wages, fringes, etc., and a group of people, usually in personnel, to administer them. The administration is usually based on objective criteria such as seniority. Together, rule compliance and system rewards represent the minimum efforts toward motivating organizational behavior.

The individual extrinsic rewards represent ways to increase the probability that other behaviors are performed but also represent increased resources devoted to measuring output so as to be able to distribute rewards on a contingency basis. For example, wage incentives may pay the same total amount to employees as a system reward but will consume more organizational resources in the administration of the incentive. One would also expect that the number of supervisors will increase to the degree that leader behaviors become a major component of the reward system. Thus, one gets increased motivation but at an increased cost.

Finally, the most effective rewards and also most expensive to administer are the intrinsic rewards. They require that organizations select those individuals capable of receiving intrinsic rewards. Thus, the organization must devote some of its resources to recruitment and selection. Also, in order to implement these systems, jobs must permit individuals to exercise discretion and responsibility. These skills may be scarce requiring selection but in some societies the exercise of discretion also consumes time that would have been devoted to doing the task. The individual takes on more of the planning and control activities in addition to performing the task. The processes of recruitment, selection, maintenance of commitment, and high salaries all increase both motivation and costs. Thus, the costs of implementing and administering a reward system are hypothesized to increase as one goes from rule compliance to extrinsic rewards to intrinsic rewards.

A second reason for the expensiveness of intrinsic rewards and of uncertain tasks is the cumulative nature of behaviors and rewards. Recall that if a task requires spontaneous behaviors, it also requires effort above the minimum levels and dependable and join-and-remain behaviors. With the exception of goal identification, the reward systems are not equally effective at increasing the probability of execution for all behaviors. Thus, if one chooses task involvement for the spontaneous behaviors and effort above minimum levels, one would have to choose rule compliance for dependable behaviors lying outside the role and system rewards for join and remain. The organization would incur the costs of administering and implementing three types of reward systems. On the other hand, a task requiring dependable behaviors would require only rule compliance and system rewards for the join-and-remain behaviors. Thus, predictable tasks require fewer resources for motivating the choice of behavior.

On the other hand, goal identification can be used for all behaviors. However, it is still expensive for the reasons listed above. In addition, an organization cannot exist on goal identification alone. It must at least employ systems rewards in the form of wages, vacations, and pensions. It is also likely to have to employ some kind of supervision, although some organizations are now finding ways to eliminate at least first-line supervision. One should also state that another reason for the expensiveness of goal identification is our ignorance concerning how to design organizations where goal identification is the source of motivation for employees other than the very top-management group which is the seat of power.

In summary, if an organization has routine, repetitive tasks, it is cheaper to employ rule compliance and system rewards than any other rewards. As organizations perform more uncertain tasks, they require effort above minimum levels and spontaneous and cooperative behaviors. Then, in addition to rule compliance and system rewards, the organization must employ other extrinsic and/or intrinsic rewards. Since these rewards are used in addition to rule compliance and system rewards and are more expensive, the organizational resources consumed in motivating behavior are increased. Thus, in choosing a reward system one must examine whether the reward system is effective, that is, does it increase the probability that the behavior will be executed? One must also ask whether it is cost-effective, that is, is there a cheaper way to produce the same probability?

The line of reasoning above is based on some assumptions about the relative availability in the population of people capable of experiencing intrinsic work rewards and of people who are willing to work without them. For example, the high costs of intrinsic rewards is based on the assumption that the organization must search for these people. Recall that Procter and Gamble interviewed well over 1000 workers in order to find 36 of whom 32 have remained. If these individuals cannot be found, then a good deal of effort must go into developing the skills and capabilities in other individuals in the organization's employ. In either case, a large amount of resources are consumed for which someone must pay. And as long as the average person grows up in a family, goes to a public school, and attends a university the structures of which are not participative or democratic, work organizations must bear the costs of teaching people to be self-responsible or compete for those who have learned how to be. To the extent that the composition of society shifts, the hypotheses concerning organizational costs must be modified.

To some degree, a shift is taking place in economically developed cultures. This shift highlights another assumption. The assumption is that the efficacy of rule compliance is based on the availability of persons who accept authority, segmented jobs, and low influence. These individuals are increasingly difficult to find in the United States and in Western Europe. For example, the assembly lines of the midwest have had to rely upon the economically depressed. First, it was the people of Appalachia, then the blacks. Events such as Lordstown suggest that even the young and the blacks are no longer willing to accept these jobs. In Cologne and Frankfurt, one does not find Germans on the assembly line but Turks and Yugoslavs. The demands for more wages from the Union of Automobile Workers also questions the long-run economy of rule compliance in developed societies. These assumptions concerning the makeup of the population suggest that the choice of reward system is not just a simple match between task and reward system but a three-way equilibrium between task, people, and reward system as illustrated in Fig. 21.2. Each is dependent on the others.

If people change in their psychological makeup, the organization must change the task and reward system if it is to attract people to perform the work and remain viable. There is an equilibrium when a fit is obtained. If the task or the people change, ineffectiveness results until another equilibrium is attained. Thus, auto companies must either change their tasks

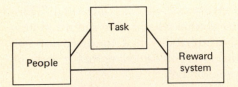

**Fig. 21.2  Equilibrium between task, people, and reward system.**

and perhaps incur costs other than those of strikes, sabotage, turnover, and wages, or move the work to societies where people are still willing to perform assembly line tasks. More will be said later about this concept of equilibrium. At the moment, it suffices to say that the previous statements concerning costs were based on assumptions about the relative ease of obtaining a fit between people, task, and reward system. It was assumed that it is easy to find a fit for rule compliance and repetitive tasks. That assumption can be challenged now in Western societies for the extremely repetitive assembly tasks but perhaps not yet for other routine types of work. It was also assumed that a fit was difficult to attain for goal identification. Even in Western societies, goal identification on a large scale basis is difficult due to the scarcity of qualified people and our ignorance concerning appropriate organization forms.

The second reason for a deeper analysis of the choice of reward system was that one could employ other criteria and/or use other models of humankind. The criteria employed in the analysis of reward systems was whether the reward system increased the probability that an individual would choose to perform a given behavior. It is perfectly legitimate, though not always feasible, to use other criteria for choice. Specifically critics could say the individual and the individual's satisfaction, psychological growth, and development should be the center of focus rather than the effectiveness of the organization.

One line of reasoning could state that this is a false issue. The purpose of the reward system is to bridge the gap between the exigencies of the organization and individual goals. If the choice of reward system does not result in individual satisfaction, search behavior results. If there is a full-employment economy, adequately working labor markets, and dissent-handling mechanisms such as grievance procedures, search behavior should successfully resolve the problem. The organization must provide satisfactions to attract and hold its members. Thus, there may be short-run dissatisfactions but in the long run search behavior will eliminate these discrepancies. The "invisible hand" of the market and dissent mechanisms achieve an equilibrium devoid of dissatisfaction.

The invisible-hand view can be criticized. One line of argument reasons that satisfaction results from a comparison of outcomes received and outcomes expected. Therefore, satisfaction can be achieved either by increasing rewarding outcomes or by maintaining expected equitable rewards at low levels. In this way, poor, uneducated individuals with average wages, considerate supervisors, and uninteresting jobs can be satisfied because they never expected anything more and a search of the environment reveals nothing better. While some would regard this situation as a satisfactory, equitable situation, the critics would not. The critics would begin by identifying two ways of viewing satisfaction.[2] One is external. It starts with the job environment and measures the individual's satisfaction with pay, supervisor, job, and organization. The other starts with the individual and his or her needs and measures the degree to which the job satisfies those needs. This point of view is significant when an additional assumption is made that these needs are hierarchically arranged and that the satisfaction of higher order needs constitutes personal growth and development. Therefore, their criteria for choice is the probability that the reward system will lead to the satisfaction of higher order needs. Since this is the case with intrinsic rewards, goal identification and task involvement will be chosen. Tasks must then be undertaken and structures and information systems adopted that fit with intrinsic reward systems. Thus, by employing a different definition of satisfaction derived from a different model of humankind and employing a psychological growth criterion, one may make other choices of desirable reward systems.

Another set of conclusions can be drawn from another model of humankind.[3] By employing a psychosexual model of personality development, Morse and Young suggest that some people emerge from the oral, anal, and phallic stages of development requiring external approval for their behavior, wanting immediate results from their performance, desiring to be told what to do, and having low tolerance for uncertainty and ambiguity. These people then seek repetitive tasks and authoritarian organizations to satisfy their self-ideal. Without going so far as to suggest that the assembly line is satisfying, the authors do suggest that these people find repetitive, structured, and routine tasks to be intrinsically satisfying. Another group of people would be just the opposite and prefer uncertain, nonrepetitive, and unstructured tasks. These results are compatible with the equilibrium model, illustrated in Fig. 21.2. The simultaneous satisfaction of individual and organizational criteria occurs when there is a fit between the task, people, and reward system.

The two different models lead to different choices and are based on different values. For example, the psychological growth people would describe the individual who needs external evaluation, to be told what to do, immediate feedback, etc. as being basically a child with no mind of its own. Organizations should be designed, they would continue, to provide this person with an opportunity to grow and become a self-sufficient adult. The second group could respond by saying that the personality is formed during childhood and when one finds a 40-year-old man with the attributes described above the best approach is to provide a task which will satisfy the needs he already has. The discussion could go on and on. But the point is that choice depends on the model of humankind that one adopts and the values with which one interprets that model.

It should be mentioned, before turning to an example of reward system, that the choice of criteria is constrained. If the costs of implementing a psychological growth criterion are not paid for by customers, clients, and financiers, the organization is not viable. The criteria must be consistent with the environmental context in which the organization exists.

In summary, the organization must choose a reward system which will provide the behavior it needs, at a cost the environment will support and which will provide satisfaction to the individuals who perform the work. What remains is to illustrate an actual reward system. First, let us describe a reward system in an actual organization. Then let us consider a case in which we must design the reward system. The case will be discussed in Chapter 22.

## AN EXAMPLE OF A REWARD SYSTEM

In this section an analysis of a reward system in an actual organization is presented. Its purpose is to illustrate in a concrete example some of the concepts presented in the previous chapters. The strategy employed here is to choose an extreme case. That is, choose an organization for which the reward system is the central problem around which the administrative organization is designed. This strategy permits us to view the full range of problems and concepts employed in the design of reward systems. To this end, the Forest Service was selected. In the text which follows we will paraphrase in the language of this book the analysis of Kaufmann[4] and add some of the more recent empirical studies.[5]

### Task and Organization of the Forest Service

The general task of the United States Forest Service is the management of the forest resources in the United States, either directly or through cooperation with state and local governments. This management consists of (1) controlling fire, disease and insect problems, the cutting of timber by private users, the use of lands for animal grazing; (2) providing water controls against flood and erosion, water power and irrigation, and recreation, and (3) providing and controlling areas for recreation, camping, and hunting. In addition to the management tasks, the service has an extensive program which supports these tasks. However, our interest is in the performance of the management task which takes place in the local communities and forests. This management task consumes hundreds of millions of dollars and around 1960 required the efforts of some 11,000 full-time and 16,000 part-time (usually summer) people.

In order to perform this task, the forest service has adopted a geographical organization with various integrating or staff departments to coordinate or advise in specialist areas common to all geographical locations. The chart of the organization is shown in Fig. 21.3. Each of these local forest areas is somewhat independent of the others. Each locality shares the same pools of resources but there is not the need to coordinate day-to-day activities as would be the case between sales and production departments. Instead the problem is to see that the forest resources are managed under an equitable national policy. This means that paper companies in Maine operate under the same rules as those in Georgia and farmers in North Carolina have the same advantages as those in Colorado. However, most of the work of implementation and enforcement of these

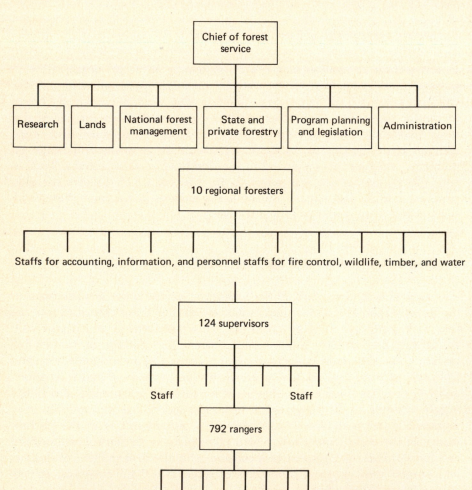

Fig. 21.3   Organization of the United States Forest Service highlighting the forest management activities.

policies and of stewardship of the resources falls to the individual rangers. With rangers located in geographically separated and inaccessible regions, what is to prevent the United States from having 792 forest policies with all the consequent injustices and inequities? Basically what prevents the fragmentation into 792 forest services is the reward system. Let us follow Kaufmann's analysis which identifies the behaviors needed by the organization, the forces on the individual which encourage fragmentation, and the forces (reward system) which encourage integrated policies.

### Behaviors

The Forest Service, like any other organization, requires a range of different kinds of behaviors in order to accomplish its goals. At a minimum, the Service requires individuals to join and remain in the organization and adopt certain dependable behaviors. For example, there are laws passed by Congress regulating the amount of timber to be cut, there are rules concerning fire prevention and detection, there are laws concerning the timing of hunting seasons, etc. It is expected that rangers will adopt these rules and laws as determinants of their behavior. But these behaviors are not sufficient for the attainment of the goals of the Service. The Service is dependent upon the rangers to choose to perform other behaviors.

The Service is dependent, first, upon the rangers to perform above minimal acceptable levels. For example, in the area of fire protection, there are rules of good practice taught to the rangers and large advertising campaigns conducted by headquarters personnel for the public at large, but great emphasis is also placed upon locally conducted campaigns directed toward those people who are in closer contact with the forests. For example, rangers speak to Kiwanis Clubs, the Rotary, high school audiences, women's clubs, etc. They visit local industry located near to the forest. Clearly the greater the number of talks, visits, etc., the greater the awareness of fire prevention and the lower the probability of fire. Thus the Service is dependent upon the rangers to choose to perform these talks and visits and to choose to perform many of them.

The Service is also dependent upon the rangers to perform many behaviors that cannot be predicted. Therefore, there is a need for many spontaneous behaviors. Continuing with the fire prevention example, some rangers have discovered other more innovative ways to reach the public. These innovations occur because a large number of talks and visits takes time away from activities of equal importance. Thus, some rangers have discovered ways to reach the public and conserve some of their time. This involves establishing contact with local newspapers, writing articles and editorials, securing prime space, etc. Similarly, another ranger found he could work through the radio by reporting events from the scene to news broadcasts. Such spontaneous behaviors decrease the likelihood of fires and simultaneously conserve the rangers' time. In another area of activity, the ranger discovers that not all trees are equally valuable to loggers. Some rangers have discovered ways to persuade loggers to remove less desirable species along with desirable ones. If loggers don't remove the trash trees, crews may have to remove them. These examples could be multiplied many times but the facts are the same. Each example requires performance of behaviors outside prescribed roles in the sense that it is unlikely that anyone would notice their absence and each is the result of search behavior. The organization is dependent on these individuals to search for alternatives, exercise judgment in choosing among alternatives, and to perform these alternatives. Let us now turn to the forces operating on the rangers and analyze the factors which will determine their choice of behaviors.

### Forces toward Fragmentation

The previous section demonstrated that the Forest Service is quite dependent on the rangers to choose to perform those behaviors which lead to goal accomplishment. In making the choices, there are several forces acting on these individuals which are viewed as obstacles for the organization. That is, there are forces which tend to decrease the probability that individuals will choose to perform the acts required by the organization.

Most of the forces about to be described are characteristic of those encountered by most organizations. The distinguishing features of the Forest Service are its wide geographical dispersion and the relative inaccessibility of many ranger districts. These features magnify the normal forces acting in all organizations. The same problems arise in all organizations with far-flung operations such as multinational business firms.

The first force toward fragmentation is the fact that rangers bring with them varied backgrounds, values outlooks, and frames of reference. This variance creates difficulties in achieving an integrated forest policy. For example, while rangers may share (and probably do, as we shall see) a common outlook concerning conservation of wildlife and forests, they may have quite different outlooks concerning the government's role in commercial activities. Thus, because the individual's job experiences are only a part of the ranger's total experiences, individual variations create a centrifugal tendency at the action level of the Service.

The second major force toward fragmentation manifests itself in different forms of what is referred to as "local capture." The assumption is that the ranger will have more contacts and closer, more intimate contacts with local groups than with other members of the organization. Therefore, the individual can be subject to greater local influences than to organizational influences. The first form of influence can take place in the ranger's work group. This group usually consists of permanent people with long experience in the district in contrast to the rangers who move often. Thus, the permanent employees know the district well and the ranger becomes dependent on them. Since these work groups develop norms of their own which may be contrary to Service goals, rangers may find themselves in conflict situations.

The second form can take place within the local communities. Rangers are encouraged to take an active part in community affairs. They can easily begin to adopt the point of view of their friends and neighbors. In addition, it becomes difficult to refuse grazing requests or to bargain hard for timber prices with one's firends. Thus, local capture can create many different forest policies.

Finally, many local interest groups can bring pressure to bear on the rangers to influence their decisions. Members of interest groups can visit with rangers at their homes or offices or bring pressure through debates at civic meetings or through local newspapers and radio. It may be easier for rangers to yield at times than to enforce Forest Service policy. If not successful directly, the interest groups can go to the rangers' headquarters or to members of Congress. There is a well-defined procedure of appeals for ranger decisions. Yet the appeals are annoying for rangers. They are distractions from productive work, a cause of more paperwork, and a possible trigger for inspections and inquiries from headquarters. If there are frequent complaints about a ranger, the ranger's judgment may be doubted. So the ranger would like to avoid complaints and, as a consequence, may yield rather than fight another appeal. In summary, Kaufmann states:

> Were the Forest Service not as large and complex as it is, had its massive responsibilities not been imposed on it all at once, did it not depend so heavily on its officers in the field to make the kinds of decisions that translate its enunciations of policy into tangible actions and accomplishments, it would still have to contend with powerful forces drawing the Rangers along many different paths. For there are many influences besides the top policy pronouncements shaping their behavior. The customs and standards of the groups they work with, the values and attitudes and pressures of the communities in which they reside, and the preferences and prejudices they bring with them from their extra-organizational experiences and associations may lead them in a variety of directions. And the problems of internal communication makes the task of directing them a complicated and difficult operation, leaving them vulnerable to the fragmentative influences. Unchecked, these influences could produce such diverse Ranger dis-

trict programs as to dissolve the Forest Service into an aggregate of separate entities, destroying it as an integrated, functioning organization.[6]

For all these reasons, the Forest Service must devote some of its resources to removing these obstacles to choice if the policies voted by Congress are to be implemented in the field. The next section describes the programs by which the Service attempts to influence the ranger choices.

## Reward System

The rangers have their behavior influenced by many mechanisms, some of which are not limited to removal of goal limitations. The rangers also face cognitive limits of lack of knowledge and information. It is impossible to be an expert in wildlife, water management, forestry, fire prevention, recreation, etc. Therefore, there are many guidelines, policy programs, and rules that are designed by experts to guide the rangers' decision making. For difficult decisions, the rangers refer the problems up into the hierarchy. There is also a planning and goal-setting process around the budget which determines the relative emphasis of fire protection, tree planting, etc. However, the problems of the different localities are so diverse that considerable discretion must be exercised by the rangers in self-contained geographical groupings. This discretion is largely a choice of means to meet Service policies. The reward system is designed to increase the probability that this discretion is exercised so as to support organization goals.

The reward system of the Forest Service has two features in common with most reward systems. First, there is not one but several bases of motivation. Although the motivational bases were discussed one at a time and are considered to be alternatives, most organizations employ several systems, even for the same group of individuals. The second feature is that there are elements of the system which were not intended to be elements of the reward system but which influence behavior just the same.

The Forest Service's reward system consists of rule compliance and, to a lesser extent, system rewards, individual rewards, and goal identification. Each of these elements will be discussed individually. One of the distinguishing features of the Forest Service is the use of rule compliance in the face of its apparent denial. That is, the geographical dispersion and inaccessibility of ranger districts renders impossible the direct supervision of daily work, the usual means of implementing rule compliance. However, there are other sources of information which compensate for the difficulty of direct supervision. The problem of implementation of rule compliance is the inability to detect deviation from rules. The Service has directives and sanctions but appears to lack a detection capability for rule enforcement. This apparent lack is compensated for by several mechanisms.

**1. Provision of overhead services.**  The ranger districts are often too small to have their own capacities for heavy equipment, computers, etc. Thus, these services are centralized and shared and this is their primary purpose. However, significant deviations from policy can be detected during the use of these services.

**2. Rotation of personnel.**  The Forest Service moves its personnel frequently. Again, the purpose is not to detect deviation from practice but the fact that if there is deviation it will be noticed eventually.

**3. Inspections and audits.**  The use of inspections and audits is directly aimed at discovering deviations, correcting them, and in educating the rangers to prevent them from occurring again. It should be pointed out that the auditors are more than just a traveling group of policemen, although in one sense they are. Auditors are also educators of the rangers in that they bring new policies, techniques, and practices. They act as an upward communication channel by carrying messages to headquarters. And finally, they serve a function of informing the socially isolated rangers about their friends in the service. But they do reduce the probability of deviation from accepted practice.

**4. Reports and diaries.**  A source of information concerning deviation can come from the rangers themselves through their reports and daily diaries that must be maintained. These self-reports tend to be reliable because of the other redundant channels, the willingness of the ranger to report actual figures and the difficulty of falsifying data for a long enough period of time. Again, these reports are for information collection, legislation preparation, cost estimation, etc. But they have as an unintended effect the reporting of deviations from policies and plans.

**5. Complaints from the public.**  The last source of influence to be discussed is an influence that lies outside the Service. Private individuals who write to their representatives or senators always get a reaction. While most cases arise because a ranger is adhering to policy, this mechanism can be embarrassing if there is a deviation. The mechanism can significantly reduce deviation because of its randomness. It can occur at any time and can concern any policy bringing to light deviations from practice in tangentially related areas.

Collectively these five mechanisms make up the rule compliance system. They significantly increase the probability that rangers perform the dependable behaviors necessary for goal accomplishment. Indeed, the problem may be that rule compliance is so successful that it inhibits innovation and risk taking in order to adjust to changing local situations. But adhering to policy has a higher value in government organizations which conduct their activities in a fishbowl.

The Service also offers system rewards. These are not discussed specifically but there are outside opportunities for professional foresters in industrial positions. Thus, the Forest Service must offer a wage package which at least prevents people from leaving. It is assumed that individuals join for other reasons and that industry uses salary and fringe benefits as its attraction. The Service must however keep its benefits above dissatisfying levels.

The Service employs individual rewards based on performance and conformance with policy for promotions to higher positions. Indeed, the promise of a career in an organization dominated by professional foresters is an attraction and motivating force. All promotions are from within and the Chief of the Service has always been a forester rather than a political appointee. The rangers' performance is determined by measured results in reports and inspections. Making performance instrumental to promotion increases the likelihood of high performance for those rangers who desire a promotion.

The last and principal source of motivation for the rangers is goal identification. It is impossible to rely on rule compliance and extrinsic rewards exclusively. Individual rewards are difficult to administer and one cannot legislate spontaneous behaviors. In addition leadership and various group incentives and acceptance are impossible due to the isolated nature of the work. Thus the Forest Service has turned to goal identification as the primary means of influence decisions of the rangers. (Given the professional dominance of the organization, there is little difference between task involvement and goal identification.) The identification is implemented through selection, then reinforced by postentry training, and maintained on the job through a number of mechanisms. Let us look at each of these briefly.

**Selection.** The Service relies heavily on recruiting, self-selection, and selection to find individuals who already have internalized the goals of the Forest Service. The recruiting efforts are directed at young men in high school and early years of college to influence their choice of career. The Service devotes a substantial amount of budget for this function. In addition, Kaufmann describes the promotional material as "strikingly candid" in that it paints no idealized picture of working in isolation in the woods. Thus, those who choose the Service are those who value the work and those for whom the agency is attractive.

Actually anyone can become a member of the Service but the overwhelming majority of rangers come from the 30 or so schools of forestry. Thus, the rangers have received some additional socialization through university training. The Service works closely with these schools.

Finally, there is a year's probation period before the individual is given full status and protection under civil service laws. During this time if there are any value conflicts, inabilities to accept Forest Service policies, etc., they should be discovered and the individual either changes his values or leaves the organization. Some 10 percent leave during the first three years. This is the percentage that would account for most of the deviance in most social systems.

Thus, through the resources devoted to recruiting, selection, and probation period, the Forest Service attracts an individual who wants to do voluntarily that which the Forest Service wants done. Thus, the Service is successful in obviating the need for direct supervision which is difficult to implement in the circumstances.

**Training.** The Service does not rely solely on selection to match the goals of the Service with the goals of the individuals. The Service also adds new values and reinforces the old ones by postentry training. As in most cases, there is a trade-off between selection and training in that the more effective the selection, the less the need for training. Much of the training is to teach substantive content. However, when individuals first enter a situation, they are most receptive to new values and ideas. The Service, like many organizations, puts the probationary individuals into groups, initially for instruction about the Service.[7] Thus they are removed from previous social supports and presumably "unfrozen." Then they are placed in the field under a ranger's guidance. The ranger is to serve as the model around which the "refreezing" is to take place. In this way, individuals either acquire new values and attitudes that are needed to be able to work in the organization or they discover that they should leave.

**Maintaining identification on the job.** In addition to selecting, training, and advancing individuals receptive to the Service's programs, the Service maintains an environment which continually reinforces the values and attitudes of the rangers. The rangers tend to associate their own welfare and future with that of the Service. The Service encourages this with a number of practices, some of which have already been mentioned.

A primary method of increasing identification is promotion and transfer which are far more than methods of staffing. The long, slow promotion process and promotion from within constitute a career system. The data collected by Hall and others show that identification with the Forest Service increases with length of tenure in the system.[8] In addition, transfers foster identification. In younger years, rangers are transferred quite often. As soon as they learn one place, they are transferred to another. The only source of continuity, structure, and support is that of the Service. Individuals cannot establish roots in a local community nor identify with a local work group for any length of time. The Service becomes their community and source of identification.

Another method of implementing goal identification is to pursue goals that are desired by the rangers themselves. Thus, the Service has implemented a decision-making process which accords a high level of influence to the rangers. The rangers are more likely to identify with and be motivated by goals that they have some influence in setting. There are numerous channels through which information and opinions are gathered. There are formal polling and surveying, the inspections, the normal contacts through the hierarchy, and the budgeting procedure. In all these cases the rangers' advice and opinion are sought *and* acted upon. The rangers have, in fact, an influence on decisions made within the Service. They are regarded as individuals who possess a good deal of the information and knowledge relevant to questions facing the Service. This is probably the reason that participation was started in the first place but it has as a consequence the maintenance of identification and the provision of intrinsic rewards.

Rangers are also continually reminded that they are rangers by the use of uniforms and badges and by reactions toward them from the community. Certainly the purpose of a uniform is to distinguish the wearer from others and tie him or her to others with the same dress. Almost all organizations whose members work in isolated ways—some delivery truck drivers, guards, police, service personnel, etc.—furnish uniforms. The uniform signals others about how to relate to the wearer.

In addition, we all come to regard ourselves partly as others regard us. In the communities where the rangers work, they are regarded as rangers and expected to behave in particular ways. These cues and expectations tie them to the Service and reinforce their identification.

Thus, through selection, training, promotion, transfer, and on-the-job experience, rangers identify with the Service and come to make choices in terms of consequences and criteria of the Service. They voluntarily make choices in the best interest of the Service. These internal forces are selected and reinforced by the experiences within the Service. These internal forces are not left to chance, although some may develop incidentally, but they are usually the result of the reward system of the Service. This reward system has successfully overcome the forces toward fragmentation.

This case illustrates a reward system utilized by an actual organization. It was shown to employ several bases of rewards (rule compliance, individual rewards, and system rewards) but to be based primarily on goal identification. The goal identification was implemented primarily by selecting individuals who had already acquired values that the organization needed. The Forest Service had a mission and employed activities with which individuals were already identified. The problem of implementing goal identification in circumstances in which it cannot be selected will be taken up in the next chapter.

## SUMMARY

This chapter has summarized the previous chapters around the subject of choosing reward systems. It was shown that some alternatives were eliminated by considering the fact that different tasks require different behaviors and different behaviors require different reward systems. Thus, if an organization has an uncertain task requiring spontaneous behaviors, it would not choose a reward system based primarily on rule compliance. It would not work. The fact that choice remained even after this matching of task and reward system necessitated a discussion of costs of administering and implementing reward systems. It was suggested that rule compliance was the least expensive to use and goal identification the most expensive with other extrinsic rewards falling in between. Other criteria for choosing reward systems were discussed based on other values and other models of humankind. The section also introduced the concept of an equilibrium fit between able people, task, and reward system. Finally, an example of reward system based on goal identification for the entire organization was discussed. We move now to an analysis of an organization which will use goal identification but cannot select it.

## NOTES

1. J. Woodward 1965. *Industrial organization: theory and practice.* London: Oxford University Press, Chapter 4.
2. R. H. Roberts, G. A. Walter, and R. E. Miles 1971. A factor analytic study of job satisfaction items designed to measure Maslow need categories. *Personnel Psychology* 24: 205–220.
3. J. J. Morse and D. F. Young 1973. Personality development and task choices: a systems view. *Human Relations* 26, (3): 307–324.
4. H. Kaufmann 1960. *The forest ranger: a study in administrative behavior.* Baltimore: Johns Hopkins Press.
5. D. T. Hall, B. Schneider, and H. T. Nygen 1970. Personal factors in organization identification. *Administrative Science Quarterly,* (June): 176–191.
6. Kaufman, pp. 86–87.
7. E. Schein 1961. Management development as a process of influence. *Industrial Management Review* 2, (May).
8. Hall *et al., ibid.*

## QUESTIONS

1. Discuss the following behaviors by moving down the respective columns in Fig. 21.1, and discuss the entries. Explain why there are minuses or pluses.
   - a) join and remain
   - b) dependable role behaviors
   - c) effort above minimum levels
   - d) spontaneous behaviors
   - e) cooperative behaviors

2. Why is goal identification expensive?

| AN INTEGRATING CASE STUDY | CHAPTER<br>**22** |
|---|---|

In this chapter, a case study is analyzed in order to integrate some of the concepts that have been discussed and particularly to illustrate the problem of creating coherence between strategy organizing mode and integrating scheme. The vehicle chosen for this task is an organization faced with the problem of designing a new factory. The chapter proceeds from a description of the situation facing the firm in question, through the history of the events which took place in the design task force, and finally, to a description and rationale of the chosen design.

## A NEW FACTORY

The Standard Products Company found itself with the task of designing and building a new factory for a new product line. The decision to build a new factory was made after a new product idea was suggested by one of the engineering groups in the Instrument Division and it appeared to have both a good future and a bad fit with the established product lines. We enter the situation following the appointment of a task force consisting of some of the managers who will subsequently serve on the management of the factory, some technical people from headquarters, a representative from personnel, and an outside consultant with expertise in organization design.

Standard Products was an established, successful company. It had grown over the years, diversified its product lines, and assumed a multinational structure. One of the major divisions was the Instrument Division which designed, manufactured, and sold measuring and testing instruments. The technology was basically electrical and electrochemical. The instruments were sold to manufacturers for inclusion in production processes, to laboratories of many types, and to medical labs and clinics. It is this division that generated the new idea.

Several years before, an engineer was testing a design modification of an instrument when she realized that the instrument produced electrical signals which moved a dial so that a human could read them. She then converted the numbers which registered on the dial back into electrical signals by punching some buttons on an electric pocket calculator in order to determine the significance of the test results. She reasoned that a better idea might be to attach the calculator or even a minicomputer to the instrument itself and avoid the intermediate step. The idea became a project, received support from the R&D budget and, indeed, several applications were eventually found in which either increased accuracy, reduced time, or on-line computation were important. Several test models were built with the collaboration of a customer and the effort resulted in an order. Then slowly over the next couple of years, more orders were obtained and a market began to develop.

The new product line generated more than its share of problems, however. Most of the problems were described as organizational problems, as people problems, or as resistance-to-change problems. The first problems appeared in marketing or, more specifically, in the sales department. After a few successful sales to customers with whom the engineers had collaborated during the design phase, the sales department attempted sales to other clients having the same application. To their dismay, the applications were never the same. The client was initially enthusiastic but always required significant modifications of the apparatus. Selling now required a technical dialogue whereas in the past standardized instruments were sold from catalogues. Sales were fairly predictable and quotas and commissions could be established. Many items were carried in stock. The new products, however, needed to be custom designed. The sales personnel needed to negotiate over technical matters, lead time, and price. The uncertainty of the new products made the quota system difficult, and members of the sales force preferred to spend their time on the established products from which they could more easily obtain immediate sales orders and therefore commissions. The sales department could respond, and still not satisfactorily, only after adding new sales personnel.

Another set of problems arose in manufacturing. Production personnel were accustomed to working on large batches of standard products. Foremen concentrated on keeping costs down and meeting schedules. However, with the new product, cost and schedule performance were less important. It was more important to discover problems, call in engineers, work to resolve the issues, etc. But the production people were annoyed because the technical problems affected their schedules. They went over their cost standards, the productivity figures fell, and there were forever engineers on the shop floor. The superintendent accused the engineers of turning the factory into a hobby shop.

These problems and others came to the attention of top management. After a little study, they chose the alternative of building a new factory. The demand projections were favorable. It appeared that a factory housing between 600–1000 people would be needed in five to ten years. In addition, there were now two announced competitors. It would be some time before the market would stabilize to the point where the product line could be made consistent with other product lines and the current organization practices and systems. Thus, the task force was created.

## Task Force—Initial Discussions

The task force began to meet regularly soon after its inception. At first, members devoted some time to getting to know one another, working out a schedule of meeting days, and reviewing the history of the product line. They then began to address the question of the design of the new plant. Initially, there was an unexpected level of enthusiasm as everyone shared the belief that something new had to be done. The old forms of organization and management practice would not be effective. One member suggested that they rely heavily on the new concepts in the behavioral sciences. A need for new practices arose because of the close cooperation required between salesmen and engineers, and engineers and production people. A second apparent need for behavioral science knowledge was in the assembly operation. It was pointed out that the organization would be extremely dependent on the women working on assembly to identify potential problems, report them quickly, work with other personnel to resolve them, and work under intense conditions.

However, one of the members interrupted to say that what he was hearing was not new and that the discussion implied that several decisions had already been made with which he did not agree. Specifically, the discussion had assumed the existence of a certain amount of role differentiation to the degree that there were salespersonnel, engineers, production managers, and (the group who performed the work) assemblers. Many of the problems would disappear if one person would design, produce, and sell the instruments. What had happened was that the task force had assumed the current role structure as given and was looking to the behavioral sciences to find ways to make it work.

The interruption had an unsettling effect on the group. One member suggested that they had to be realistic. There would always be managers and workers. Another added that there would always be managers and workers if people like themselves assumed there would always be workers and managers. After some more discussion, they agreed that the underlying issues would not be resolved at this meeting but that a good point had been made. They had assumed as given something that was in fact a design variable—the division of labor.

The interruption served to open up the discussion and to begin a search for what the design variables were and *what could be assumed as given*. The group wanted to find something that could be taken as given. It seemed that everything could vary including the division of labor, the technology, the structure, the people, and the decision processes. Finally, they decided that a good part of the basic task was given and that they could start with that to define the constraints to which the organization design must adhere and then generate feasible alternative designs.

## Task

The task force recognized that the given element was the product line. The product line was associated, in the short run, with a market and clients, it was made up of particular materials, and some operations in the technology and the sequence of operations were given. From this starting point some of the activities to be performed could be determined and the analyses concerning division of labor, etc., could be made.

The analysis of the market suggested several things. It was generally concluded that the market would be very dynamic for some time to come. The dynamism was believed to come from three sources. (1) The *customers* likely to use the products were still being discovered and so were the possible applications of the products. (2) The technical configuration and underlying *technology* of the product was constantly changing. This was particularly true for the computing technology. (3) The likely *competition* was uncertain as well.

What appeared to *be* certain was that the key to success and basis of competition would be the generation of new designs, discovery of new customers and applications, rapid adaptation to discoveries by others and, in general, staying up to date with the changes in the market and the technology as they occurred.

Certain elements of the production technology could be taken as given. Some investment constraints by headquarters further delimited some of the feasible production processes. The products consisted of particular materials some of which could be purchased and others of which had to be fabricated. Although there were some alternatives remaining, there was a given sequence of operations consisting of receipt of materials, fabrication, subassembly, final assembly, testing, and, finally, distribution to customers. In addition, headquarters advised that it preferred a minimum level of investment; the implication being that the new factory should buy as many parts as possible rather than invest in capital equipment and produce parts itself. In addition, for those parts that were critical to the performance of the instrument or those that could not be purchased, the investment must be in versatile equipment which is inexpensive and easily adaptable to different purposes.

From these given attributes of the technology, market, and financial constraints, the task force could draw some conclusions concerning the types of activity that were necessary. First, there must be a good deal of searching for new applications in the marketplace with existing and new customers. This search, however, could be successful only if the customer had sufficient trust and confidence in the new factory to permit it to enter their organization, to allow it to work with their production and/or laboratory personnel, to give to it information concerning their internal processes and, if necessary, to modify some of their own processes to fit the new technology. The potential applications that result from the search must then be modified to fit what is technically feasible and/or the technology augmented to fit what is commercially feasible. Thus, a second conclusion was that the organization had to maintain its technical capability with respect to changes in miniature computing technology in general and the combination of computing with electrical and chemical analyses in particular; the latter being the distinctive competence of the unit.

The commercially and technically feasible application also had to be modified in order to be producible and economically feasible. The decisions concerning the design of the product had to be taken in full cognizance of the capability of the organization and the equipment. Every time the design of the instrument was changed, the process for producing it was changed also. The flexible, general purpose equipment permitted this possibility but it also increased the number of variables to be considered when conceiving of a new product design. Thus, the first portion of the organization's task consisted of discovering a potential application and conceiving of a device which was commercially, technically, and economically feasible. Once the design was conceived, the task became one of translating a paper conception into a physical reality.

The physical realization of the instrument would take place in a sequence of steps. An analysis revealed that 85 to 90 percent of the parts could be purchased from outside vendors or be supplied by other units within the Instrument Division. However, two fabricating steps could not be subcontracted nor did the task force believe they should be subcontracted. The fabrication steps produced the units which married the analysis portion of the instrument to the computing portion. These parts changed with each application. Sometimes there was considerable interaction between the two portions to the extent that initial results were fed back to the analysis portion which would determine which of a sequence of tests would be performed next. Thus, these parts were critical to the performance of the instrument and were to be under the control of the new factory. In addition, some machines had already been purchased in order to produce the initial orders.

The task force recognized that considerable choice remained in the subassembly, final assembly, and testing operations. It is here in the labor-intensive portion of the tasks that considerable choice was possible concerning the division of labor, both on a horizontal and a vertical basis. To be sure, there were technical constraints in that some operations had to be performed before others. But there were choices of whether to have buffer inventories or not and where to locate them. There were also choices concerning whether there should be one long assembly operation through which orders and small batches could be sequenced, or whether there should be many small, self-contained assembly units. If the choice was to have many small, self-contained units, on what basis were they to be self-contained. By products, by customers, etc.?

The critical attribute of the doing portion of the work was its intimate connection with the conceptual work. This attribute is critical because of the uncertainty surrounding the design. Since the organization had to continually conceive of new designs utilizing new technology, serving new customers, aimed at new applications, and requiring different combinations of flexible equipment, there was a high probability of error. Each of the many components might be optimally conceived but when combined might not function together as a finely tuned instrument. Awareness could come after these components had been created and assembled. The task force realized that the designs would never be 100 percent complete but that there would be times when the organization would think that they would be only to have the question reopened by the discovery of a new problem. The problems had to be recognized as problems and acted upon quickly before considerable labor and materials were invested in the instrument. Many of the components were such that, if faulty they could not be repaired but must be rejected. Therefore, it appeared that quality-control testing to discover rejects would be costly. What was needed was someone who could recognize when something was going wrong and make appropriate changes to remedy the situation before a reject was created. But often these changes would again call into question the problem of modifying the process, the technology, or the end application. It appeared to be quite difficult to separate the doing and conceiving portions of the organization's task.

## Behaviors and Reward System

On the basis of the analysis of the task and those elements of the environment which could be taken as given, the task force tried to reject as many alternative designs as possible so as to be able to concentrate more deeply on those that remained. In particular, the task force concentrated on the kinds of behaviors that would be needed to effectively perform the task that had been described. It was assumed first that, like all organizations, they would need people to join and remain in the organization and to perform the reliable role behaviors associated with their positions. These behaviors were not considered to be critical to the design of the new organization largely because the organization felt that it knew how to deal with turnover, recruitment, absenteeism, and reliability. It was assumed in the second place, however, that the new organization would be different from most other organizations in that almost all major roles would require effort above minimum levels and spontaneous, individually responsible behaviors. That is, because of the intense concentration required of the doing roles, the uncertainty of the task, and the inseparability of the doing and conceptual portions of the task, the vast majority of roles would have to possess a substantial amount of spontaneous behavior in order to be performed effectively. In addition, even a minimum degree of division of labor would create a need for spontaneous cooperative behaviors among these same roles. Thus, because of the task, the new organization would require spontaneous cooperative behaviors from almost all roles rather than from a few roles which would make up the in-group or the "dominant coalition."

Members of the task force then addressed themselves to the alternative ways to motivate the spontaneous cooperative behaviors. It appeared that the likelihood of the spontaneous kinds of behaviors could be increased in general by using either group incentives, individual incentives, appropriate styles of leadership or, in some cases, task involvement or goal identification. In particular there appeared to be some operational problems connected with each of these alternatives. For individual incentives, there was the problem of arriving at a clear, understandable standard of individual performance under the conditions of interdependence. Members of the task force believed that incentives would increase performance on the dimensions measured but were not convinced that what was individually measurable would be collectively desirable. Individual performances that would be collectively desirable could only be agreed upon by making them ambiguous. Thus, particularly at low levels, individual incentives could be made operational only by reducing their motivational impact through reductions in expectancies and instrumentalities.

Some of the skepticism disappeared when group incentives were discussed and, indeed, a couple of advocates for them were found who argued that clear output measures could be found for groups, and groups would incorporate the kind of cooperative behaviors that would be needed. In addition, the advocates believed that motivation would be high because the people would value money (have high valences for money). The reasoning was based on the assumption that most workers would be women. These women, it was argued, would not be interested in participation and influence. The reason they would want to work was to increase family income. An incentive would permit them to earn more and to satisfy the need that caused them to work.

The majority of the task force disagreed with the position above for various reasons. One member stated that first it would be impossible to find a group structure which would not still require a good deal of cooperative behavior between groups as well as within them. And even if a group incentive increased the likelihood of cooperative behaviors within groups, it would, at best, be neutral or, most probably, reduce the likelihood of cooperation between groups. The only group structure that would encompass all the cooperative behaviors would be the organization as a whole, and a factorywide profit-sharing plan would have little or no motivational impact.

A second line of reasoning was based on the assumption that the measurements would cause too many dysfunctional behaviors. Groups prefer stable products (on which they can make incentive earnings) over new products (which may have many quality problems). Instead of reporting quality problems, groups would be encouraged to ignore them and to put pressure on quality-control inspectors to let marginal work pass. Advocates of this line of reasoning pointed out that in ambiguous and changing situations there are many ways to increase measured performance which do not involve increases in actual performance.

Some also suggested that it would not be useful to create a performance measure which included quality and other factors. The reason is that any incentive, group or individual, requires a comparison between actual performance and a standard. In the situation that was going to exist, it would be almost impossible to maintain standards that would not cause dysfunctional behaviors because they would be inequitable and incorrect.

The majority of the task force, instead, favored an approach using intrinsic rewards. They thought intrinsic motivation was going to be necessary in order to provide the commitment and strength of motivation necessary to generate spontaneous and cooperative behaviors. Intrinsic motivation is the strongest source of motivation for these behaviors and is also associated with the other required behaviors. In addition, it avoids some of the operational problems associated with extrinsic rewards. Another group argued that the organization should acquire some competence in the design and operation of intrinsic systems of motivation. That group believed that in the future the individuals in the work force would demand those kinds of jobs, and that the organization would have to know how to provide them.

The use of intrinsic rewards carried some operational problems of its own, however. First, if there was going to be extensive use of task involvement, some problems of cooperation would arise. Second, there would have to be a considerable effort directed toward selection and/or training in order to find people to work in such a system or to give them the capability to do so, respectively. Some members of the task force pointed out that they could not rely on selection as the Forest Service did in order to generate identification. People are not socialized in the greater society to value the design and production of measuring instruments in the way that people acquire the values of public service and conservation on which the Forest Service relies. Therefore, the sources of intrinsic motivation must be generated within the organization.

A third problem was pointed out by one of the advocates of the group-incentive alternative. He said that if the new factory was to generate identification from within, the task force would face the same problem of finding a small-group structure—a problem that had plagued the group-incentive approach. That is, the organization must be designed to permit the exercise of discretion and influence in small groups. Therefore, what structure will the group take which would permit the local autonomy necessary for local discretion? How could the large, complex, interdependent task be broken into semiautonomous pieces each manageable by a small group so as to permit local discretion and influence? Or could a system be designed in which 500–600 people could participate and identify with the factory as a whole?

The task force members addressed the problem as to whether, from a motivational standpoint, they needed to worry about breaking up the staff into semiautonomous groups. Their assumption appeared to be that only through a process taking place in small groups could individuals identify with a set of goals the subsequent realization of which would provide the intrinsic motivation and satisfaction associated with spontaneous behaviors. Upon examination, the assumption appeared to be reasonable. Since employees would arrive at the organization without having already identified with its goals, they must have some influence in establishing the goals, have some part in the realization of the goals, receive information concerning the attainment of the goals, and have some stake in the outcome concerning whether the goals were achieved or not. In a large group, the influence of the average individual declines, his or her part in the realization declines, and hence his or her identification is reduced. Similarly, the larger the group, the more global the goals and the more ambiguous the connections between an individual's behavior and the realization of the goals. This year's profit cannot guide the choice of behaviors for individuals deciding to accept or reject a subassembly or to cooperate or not with a colleague. Profit is simply too distant. Profit performance will not significantly affect the self-esteem of most employees and therefore cannot be a basis of intrinsic motivation. Thus, the task force members' working hypothesis was that the larger the group, the less the participation and influence of the average individual and, due to increasing remoteness, the lower the instrumentality of group-goal accomplishment for the satisfaction of self-esteem needs of the individual.

Therefore, the task force members decided that if they were going to implement intrinsic rewards, they must break the organization into semiautonomous groups. Since it was not possible to determine an optimal size, the numbers of between 10 and 25 were used as rough guides. In these groups, individuals would have the opportunity to influence the goals, help in the realization of the sales, and comprehend their part in the group. The problem then was to determine the basis for creating 30 to 50 groups such that the individuals within them would identify with the goals of the group, would be able to exercise influence, and would receive intrinsic satisfaction from the realization of the goals, while at the same time the collective goal realization of the groups would add up to the goal realization of the factory as a whole.

After some additional discussion, members of the task force chose to pursue the alternative of intrinsic rewards for the whole organization. Their reasoning was that intrinsic rewards would provide stronger motivation for the needed behaviors, would provide sustained motivation and satisfaction for the employees, would permit the organization to acquire a competence in organization design for future factories, would avoid many of the operational problems connected with extrinsic rewards and measurable standards. They also reasoned that some of the operational problems of group design would be encountered in any case with group acceptance rewards or group incentives. In addition, many of the design choices necessary to implement leadership behaviors, group acceptance, and group incentives are the same choices one needs to make for goal identification. It was also believed that the additional cost would pay off either in short-run performance or in long-run investment in organization design competence and organizational capacity to adapt to unforeseen events. With that choice made, the task force concentrated on the design of the group structure for local influence and overall system performance.

## COMPARISON OF EIGHT ALTERNATIVES OF ORGANIZATION DESIGN

### Design of Semiautonomous Groups—Alternative 1

In addressing the design problem, task force members faced the usual problem of where to start. They knew of the alternative bases of group structures such as those built around common products, processes, functions, and geographical areas. However, they wanted some way to come to grips with their specific problems. What they needed was an approach which would systematically generate the alternative group structures from which they could select one which they preferred. In addition, they wanted to generate several alternative structures, analyze differences among them, and then evaluate and choose among them. Finally they started with the most independent structure and analyzed the reasons why they should deviate from it. That is, they started with 25 groups of 20–25 persons with each group designing, producing, and selling a product. This structure would minimize interdependence and coordination between groups and permit the greatest amount of local autonomy. The groups would share only the physical facilities and the financial resources which would be allocated through a budgeting process. Internally, the groups would have only a temporary division of labor. That is, some division of labor would be necessary to facilitate the simultaneous performance of tasks, to achieve a higher output, and to perform tasks that must be done in different locations. But by rotating people through these roles, there would be no permanent division of labor. The temporary division of labor would prevent the formation of specialties with private languages and different statuses and therefore would minimize the barriers to communication within groups. In addition the elimination of barriers to communication would maximize the likelihood that people would participate in and understand the decision-making processes of the group and therefore identify with the group. Thus, this strategy would achieve the identification and spontaneous behaviors and also the global integration by reducing the need for coordination between roles and groups. The strategy would eliminate the interdependence and need for communication between groups and eliminate barriers to communication to maximize communication between roles within groups.

The task force accepted this design as a starting point and recognized it as an extreme form. That is, they saw the design as a viable one that could achieve group identification and, in total, achieve factory goals but that would achieve these goals by minimizing differentiation and specialization. They realized that every role is like every other role and, with due regard for product differences, every group is like every other group. But the task force members now had a basis on which they could assess increases in role differentiation within groups and the creation of separate and different groups.

## Division of Labor within Groups: Alternative 2

The task force members began to create the other alternatives by increasing the amount of permanent role differentiation. However, they realized that given the variety of applications, customers, and products, and the level of performance necessary to remain competitive, each increase in the division of labor or role differentiation would increase, depending on the basis of the division and on the amount of information and communication that had to take place. Each would also increase the likelihood of a barrier to communication. Thus, there had to be some benefit associated with increases in the division of labor in order to offset the added amount of organizational resources that would be consumed in the communication processes.

In general, task force members felt that increases in specialization would increase the performance of various subtasks. The starting-point strategy minimized the likelihood that there would be excellence in the performance of any subtask. A task force member suggested that on some subtasks in particular a permanent division of labor would significantly increase subtask performance by matching skills with the subtask requirements, increasing subtask skills, and increasing motivation to perform the subtask.

Attention was then focused on which particular functions were critical and/or would benefit significantly from permanent role specialization. First, the sales–marketing function appeared to be critical in making contacts with users, and some permanence in the contact also appeared to be beneficial. These factors might be worth the additional communication efforts. Second, it appeared that the technical function could also benefit from permanent specialization. The depth of knowledge and skills needed for the technology would be worthy of full-time attention. In addition, the reduction of the wholeness of the task was believed not to reduce motivation. That is, the resulting tasks were still believed to have enough interest, challenge, and meaning to be able to maintain intrinsic satisfactions. Thus, the second alternative would have a three-way role specialization of marketing, manufacturing, and technical functions.

The permanent role specialization would create three different functional subgroups within each product group and thereby increase the amount of time and difficulty of communication across the three interdependent functions. However, the size of group, the number of specialties, and the limitation of focus to a common product or product line suggested that the coordination could take place within the 20–25 person groups.

## Division of Labor between Groups—Alternative 3

The second design of the factory recognized a permanent division of work within the product groups whereby technical, marketing, and production people would be permanently responsible for different portions of the task for their product. The specialization would present communication problems but, by working within 20–25 person autonomous groups, the problems could be addressed easily. Now, the next step was to raise the question as to whether some functional groups could split off from the product groups. That is, should the technical people be considered as members of a product group or placed in a group of their own to work on a consulting basis with each of the product groups By addressing the question concerning whether or not specialists should have their own group, the task force was moving still further away from the minimum specialization model of Alternative 1 and toward design Alternative 3.

The task force addressed the easiest question first and decided that sales representatives should stay within the product groups. They would permanently specialize within the group in order to maintain continuity of contact with the buyers of the group's product over time. However, the factory would rely on Standard Product's Instrument Division sales force to make the initial contact, make routine calls, handle formal correspondence, etc. Then the sales representatives from the new factory would handle subsequent contacts in order to negotiate prices, delivery, and technical specifications of the products in which they specialized. Sales representatives would then represent the customer in the conception and doing phases by following the order through design, production, and delivery. They would also be the customer's permanent point of contact. Sales representatives would bring customer information to bear on the continuous trade-off decisions concerning technical, economic, and marketing feasibility. Thus, the representatives would be based at the factory and travel to the customer. This would permit the continual contacts to be handled by the Instrument Division's larger sales force and permit the representatives to participate as members of their respective product group. The cost would be the travel necessary for the representatives to have contact both with the customer and the product group.

Constructing the manufacturing function, however, proved to be a little more difficult. First, there were two fabricating operations which produce output for all products. The performance of these operations required both expensive equipment and skilled operators. The task force could think of no way to distribute these operations over the product groups which would not involve significant investment in duplicate equipment and the use of less skilled operators. The second problem was that several activities were common to all product lines, three of which required a high quality of performance. Since there was to be a high volume of purchased parts, the performance of the material purchase and control activity might benefit from some specialization. There were common parts for products and opportunities to pool orders to negotiate lower prices and faster delivery. The quality-control and testing activity was also quite critical due to the priority given to the quality of the product, the necessity to discover problems early, and the sophistication of the testing equipment. Thus, this activity would be in need of some special attention. Finally, the maintenance of the equipment, especially in fabrication, would be critical and require skilled attention.

The technical function also presented some difficulties on closer examination. Many of the technical activities were common to all products and, by bringing them together in a technical group, a greater degree of specialization could be achieved than by scattering technical people throughout the product groups. The technical representatives felt that a finer degree of specialization would permit the specialists to keep up to date with the continual changes in the underlying technology. In addition, they felt that there should be a number of projects which were not connected with any particular product but which might eventually either become a product or affect the design of a number of different products. Thus the creation of a technical group would permit greater specialization around the needs of the development of the underlying technology.

The task force then began to create the third alternative so that the product groups could maintain a level of influence and autonomy sufficient to maintain motivation and yet permit some additional functional specialization to permit a higher quality of performance in some of the work judged to be critical to the factory's survival. In manufacturing, task force members judged that the two fabricating units could be set up separately and treated simply as another supplier. The work flow indicated in Fig. 22.1 shows that all the groups could still function autonomously because of the parallel

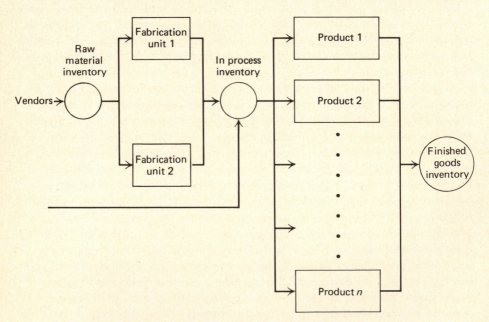

**Fig. 22.1   Work flow of the factory under Alternative 3.**

nature of the work groups and the existence of an in-process inventory between the fabricating and product groups. In addition, most of the maintenance could be placed in the two fabricating groups which used most of the equipment. For the other activities of quality control and material control, the task force decided not to set up separate departments for this alternative but to use teams which would meet periodically to manage the commonalities across products. The team members would be the individuals in the group currently responsible for the activity in the product group.

The technical function was also separated from the product groups but presented its own problem of grouping. The technical function was estimated to consist of about 150 people. Thus, having one large functional group would not permit the local influence desired for intrinsic motivation. On the other hand, having a group for each product and fabricating unit would not permit an increase in specialization since each group would have 5–8 persons who would provide all the necessary technical support. However, the task force recognized that each move away from this form would create a barrier to communication and identification with common problems. The task force then looked for technical activities which were common to all or some product groups. The only activity which was common to all groups and which could benefit from specialization was the activity concerned with computing technology. The process design activity was common also, but the task force felt that, except for the two fabricating units, the activity would not benefit significantly from specialization to justify the creation of a separate group. For the remainder of the activities, the task force thought that there would be commonalities around the nature of the customers who used the product. That is, the industrial customers would have common features as would the laboratory and medical users. In addition, each product group would be associated with one of these three customer categories. This matching would facilitate technical-product group contracts. Thus, the technical function would consist of five groups, as shown schematically in Fig. 22.2. The first group would be one which served all three products and would be dedicated to computing technology. This group would also be concerned with future changes in the technology, would maintain the state of the art in the factory, and would generate new products outside the three product categories. The next group would be one devoted to process design activities within the two technically sophisticated fabricating units shown in Fig. 22.1. The last three technical groups would be based on the three different types of customers—industrial, laboratory, and medical. It would be their task to maintain technical excellence in areas peculiar to their product category, to create new products, and to work with the sales representatives and other people from the product groups in the constant design–redesign decisions which were made from order receipt to delivery.

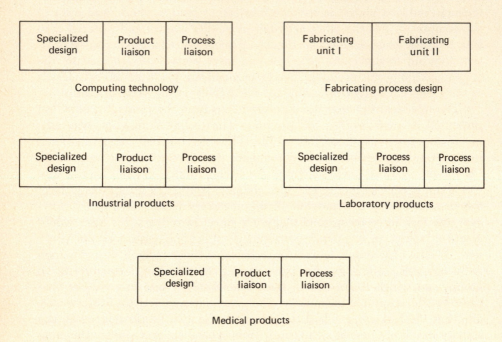

Fig. 22.2 Technical groups in Alternative 3.

Internally each group would be further divided between specialized design activities in which the true technical specialists would be found and technical personnel performing liaison roles. The liaison activities would be for both product and process design decisions. These liaison people would be permanent members of their technical group but would attend product meetings and thereby link the technical function with the manufacturing and marketing functions. In this way, the specialization of the design function necessitates the use of design resources to coordinate and communicate with the other groups. With the specialization of the technical function, the task force completed the preliminary design of Alternative 3.

### Integrating Roles—Alternative 4

The task force began to consider the next alternative which would logically follow. As a consequence, they searched for additional ways to continue to increase the quality of performance of the critical functions while maintaining the overall integration of the functions. Two ways were discovered. First, the task force noticed that for several activities which remained within the product groups there were decisions that were made in every group. By combining these decisions into a single role, which would be occupied by a specialist, the total decision time spent by the organization could be reduced and the quality of the decisions made would be improved. In this way, the design could take advantage of expertise in a decision area and of economies of scale in decision making, and could also eliminate a duplication of effort. Second, a member of the task force suggested that there were decisions in each activity which were not directly related to any product on a day-to-day basis. There were the planning decisions and decisions on new techniques which would be ignored due to the pressure of daily routine. In addition, there were some interdependencies with the technical function which was now separate. For example, there would be testing techniques and equipment that needed to be developed along with the new products and processes. For these reasons, additional specialization would provide a benefit.

The task force was also anxious to avoid a significant reduction in the autonomy and/or influence which would be exercised by the product groups and to avoid more permanent role differentiation within the groups. They wanted to find a way to increase the amount of expertise that could be brought to bear but did not want to pay the price of more division of labor in groups nor to reduce the autonomy of the groups by creating separate functions. Instead, the task force chose to create several integrating roles. That is, for the marketing, quality and testing, material control, information (accounting and information systems), and personnel functions, they created an integrator. Several integrators would be created in quality control due to the volume of work. The bulk of the work still would take place in the product groups by the individual currently performing the activity. The integrator would perform the work common to many products and the longer range planning functions. However, the integrator would always work through the functional team composed of integrators and members of product teams. In this way, the factory could bring some additional expertise to bear, avoid changing the division of labor within the groups, and maintain group influence as long as the teams functioned effectively. The cost of the design is the creation of the new roles to be added to the structure.

In summary, this design was intended to provide further increases in the quality of the performance of critical activities without significantly reducing the autonomy of the product groups. The solution was the creation of integrating roles for these activities and the linking of these roles to the product groups by the use of teams consisting of representatives who currently perform that activity in the product groups. The addition of the five integrating roles and three more activity teams to Alternative 3 resulted in Alternative 4.

### Product Line Groups and Managers—Alternative 5

The task force, in attempting to create Alternative 5, became concerned about specialist integration during the conceptual phase of new products and applications. In Alternatives 1 and 2, both the conceiving and producing activities were performed within the product groups. But Alternative 3 split off the technical work and Alternative 4 provided for some independent contact between some functions like testing and technical. Thus, the task force thought it might be possible to split the conceiving and producing activities to some degree. The split would leave the previously called product groups as the vehicles for producing the product. Now the question was how would one provide for coordination in the conceiving phase and still provide for the apparent inseparability of the conceiving and producing activities.

It appeared that some benefit could be achieved by splitting the two phases. The conception phase would involve decisions which are more unstructured, require longer time horizons, and confront issues not immediately concerning any particular product line. In the press of day-to-day activities, these are the decisions that would be slighted. By creating another vehicle for the conception phase, the factory could ensure that the longer range, less structured decisions were adequately handled so that they would not cause more day-to-day problems.

In choosing the coordination vehicle, the task force also faced another problem. The products which would determine the product groups were not very stable. That is, products would come and go. The product structure might not have enough stability to permit the conceptual process to operate effectively. Thus, the task force thought that the customer or end-user structure employed by the technical function would be preferable to the structure used in Alternative 4. They therefore chose to provide a means of coordination for the industrial, laboratory, and medical customer markets. They then chose a team structure to provide the coordination.

The establishment of the teams then created the problem of who would be the team members. In general, each team should be composed of those functions which would do the work and which could provide information for the choice of product design. In the technical function, a portion of the work was already divided on the same basis, so one representative from each of three product groups would participate on the respective team. From the computing function, there was no permanent representative. But at the initiation of a design project, a member of the design project group would participate in the team and represent the computing design group. Similarly, the technical people working in the fabricating area would participate when they were needed rather than being assigned permanently to the team.

In order to choose the representatives from marketing, the task force needed to separate marketing from the product groups and place it into a group of its own. Marketing and sales function would be involved more in the conceptual than in the producing phases. Therefore, three marketing groups were created, one for each customer market. One representative from each marketing group would participate in the customer market teams. Contact individuals for each product group were also designed and would participate in product producing teams on an as-needed basis. In this way, the marketing groups could maintain the coordination with interdependent functions during the conceptual and production phases and adopt their own internal organization for conducting the sales and other marketing activities.

Some difficulties arose when the task force considered selective representatives from the manufacturing activities. One proposal was to expand the integrating activities of each function such as manufacturing to include three integrators, that is, one for each customer market team. These integrators would represent their functions during the conceptual phase and would keep themselves and the producing teams informed through the functional teams. Several people felt, however, that this structure would divorce the producing teams from the product design phase in the customer market teams. And given the interdependence between the conceiving and doing activities, this structure would give so much power to the integrators, because of their access to information and knowledge of prior decisions, that the power would reduce the influence of the product groups. The structure would compromise the motivational bases needed to perform the work. The feeling led to a discussion of the integrating role and the following design decisions. First, it was agreed that the integrating role was to provide training, consultation, and advice for the teams and that there would probably be enough work for three integrators per function. Thus, the number of integrators in the manufacturing, quality control, material control, and information functions was increased to three, one for each customer market team.

The second division, which concerned representation on the new customer market teams, was that the integrator from each function would represent that function in the respective market teams, except for manufacturing. Manufacturing would be represented by a representative from each of the product-producing groups supplying that particular market. Thus, each customer market team would be composed of representatives from sales, the market technical function, computing technology, quality control, material control, information, and five or six people from the product producing groups. This pattern of representation included every function and activity that would either do the work or could provide expertise relevant to the design decisions except the fabricating operations.

The fabricating operations presented a little difficulty because there were two of them. Also there were two design groups to be matched to the three customer market teams. For the time being, they chose to have one representative from one of the two fabricating units in each team along with a technical representative from the opposite unit. The representatives were considered to be of equal status. These additions then completed the composition of the teams for product design.

Before leaving this alternative, several members of the task force voiced some uneasiness concerning the functioning of the team, especially in resolving conflicts. They said that they knew that there were decisions yet to be made concerning the functioning of the product groups, also. However, they felt that they could find people and processes to generate effective performance and intrinsic satisfactions for the product groups. But for the customer market teams, they thought it would be more difficult. Specifically, they felt each change in permanent role differentiation and the formation of specialist groups would increase the performance of the specialization in question. However, at the same time, the changes determined and channeled the flow of information. They also increased the selective access to information, the likelihood of different perceptions of reality, and the development of separate languages. The result might cause great difficulty in communicating and integrating the dispersed information to solve abstract design problems. There might also be differences in power due to the selective access to information. The marketing and technical expertise and information would be contained in a single role while the manufacturing information would be dispersed among five or six representatives and some specialists. This power might not be exercised in the best interest of the market group. The subsequent discussion led to the creation of market integrators for each market group. These individuals would be technically competent and have experience in manufacturing and marketing. They would represent an overall point of view and would be independent of the other groups. When agreement was achieved on this addition, the fifth design was completed.

In summary, the fifth alternative added to the fourth alternative larger integrating functions and customer market teams for product development. It also split off the marketing function and created customer market integrating roles. The group structure consisted of five technical groups of about 30 persons each, fifteen manufacturing groups (product-producing groups) of 20–25 persons each, two fabricating units of 20 people each, three marketing groups of 25 each, three customer market integrators, four integrating functions of 3–5 persons each, three customer market teams across functions and activities, and four activity teams across the product producing groups within manufacturing. Thus the number of different kinds of groups and roles and, necessarily, intergroup coordinating processes had increased substantially from the first alternative of 20–25 identical groups with all coordination being intragroup.

### Division of Labor in Manufacturing Groups—Alternative 6

The next step in the alternative creation process is to change the division of labor within the manufacturing function as had been done in the technical and marketing functions in prior alternatives. The first and minimal step in that direction was allow a permanent division of labor within the existing product groups. That is, the 15 product groups and two fabricating units were to remain as before but internally there would be a permanent assignment of tasks as indicated by Fig. 22.3. This change would permit

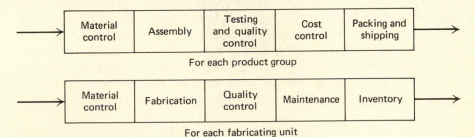

Fig. 22.3   Division of labor within manufacturing units.

greater skill development within the specialties but would also increase the need for a coordinating function within the groups. The permanent division of work and establishment of functional careers was the change which created Alternative 6.

### Groupings for the Manufacturing Function—Alternatives 7 and 8

The next step toward greater specialization requires the combination of product groups. That is, instead of forming fifteen groups of 20–25 people in manufacturing, one could form three groups based on customer markets of 100–125 each. Then, instead of four people per subgroup for quality control, one would have 20 people. With 20 people there could be a greater division of work and greater skill specialization. Thus, by pooling the product groups together, one would pool the skills within them. The resulting group structure would be one fabricating group with functional specialization within and three manufacturing groups (one each for industrial, medical, and laboratory markets) with permanent activity specialization within.

The permanent specialization, the grouping of specialists and functional careers reduces the need for functional teams. The intrafunctional coordination and learning processes which were to take place in the functional teams now would take place in the permanent groups. However, the interfunctional coordination which was to take place within product groups now should take place across groups in order to maintain the rate of new application introduction. For this reason, three product teams within each market team were created to coordinate across the manufacturing functions, the technical functions, and the marketing functions during the producing phase. Some of the representatives would attend both the market and product team meetings in order to coordinate the conception and doing phases. These nine product teams would replace the previously planned functional teams in order to maintain coordination and local discretion.

The creation of Alternative 8 is simply to carry the pooling and division of labor one step further in manufacturing. That is, the task force could create groups around the activities of assembly, material control, etc., without regard to products and create one long assembly operation. In addition, specialists could be removed from the floor and be physically collocated. For example, the 25 or so people working in material control would be placed in a single group, further specialized by material control activity, and physically collocated to facilitate the coordination of material control activities.

This change would further increase the quality of the performance of the individual manufacturing activities but also increase the amount of effort needed to maintain interfunctional and interactivity coordination. The need would be particularly acute in the producing areas. Thus, the addition of a full-time integrator for each product line and the liaison function in material control were believed to be adequate to solve the problem.

The task force could have continued in this manner by looking for additional changes. However, it seemed quite clear that any further change in the direction of more role specialization would cost more in resources for coordination than it would produce in benefits of higher quality role performance. Indeed, several people thought the last change also reduced the likelihood of achieving the motivational climate they were seeking. So they stopped at this point to take an overview and eliminate whatever alternatives they could before designing the system of governance and other processes. Table 22.1 illustrates the eight alternatives and their primary differences in group structure, division of labor, integrating roles, and integrating processes.

## COMPARISONS AND CHOICE OF ALTERNATIVES

At the completion of the alternative creation exercise, the task force members believed, in general, that each of the eight alternatives would generate the appropriate level of intrinsic motivation by permitting local discretion and influence within groups and yet maintain overall coordination between groups. They now wanted to take an overview of the alternatives and see how each scored on other criteria such as efficiency and profitability in order to eliminate some of them.

In reviewing the alternatives shown in Table 22.1, it was clear that as one moves from Alternative 1 to Alternative 8, the primary change is in the amount of permanent role specialization. The level of intrinsic motivation, however, would be unchanged. The jobs continually would permit the individual to exercise influence and perform a task that he or she would think was meaningful. The type of intrinsic motivation would change, however. As role specialization increases, the proportion of jobs in which task involvement, rather than goal identification, becomes the source of intrinsic motivation increases. This type of motivation is reinforced by the group structure change. The successive grouping of specialists in homogeneous groups increases the amount of colleague contact and the amount of identification with a peer group, and also allows careers in a specialty. The immediate effect of increased permanent role specialization is an increase in the quality of performance of the subtasks receiving the specialized treatment due to an increase of time devoted to it and a sharpening of skills applied to it.

The second effect of role specialization can be seen in the two bottom rows of Table 22.1. The price of increased role specialization is increased resources devoted to coordination of specialized roles and groups of specialists so that the right hand knows what the left hand is doing. In this case, increased role specialization results in increased role interdependence and consequently in a need for interrole coordination. The additional coordination and communication is purchased in the form of intergroup coordinating teams and full-time integrators. The benefits of increased quality of subtask performance are purchased at the price of more management time to replace the coordination that took place in the minds of single individuals and through spontaneous processes of face-to-face work groups at lower levels of specialization.

After some deliberation, the task force members settled on Alternative 5 as the design they would continue to work with and modify as needed. They felt that Alternative 5 provided the motivation, coordination, and quality of subtask performance that would be required by the new factory's environment in both the conceptual and doing phases. The increased costs

**Table 22.1 Comparison of eight alternatives.**

| Differences \ Alternatives | 1 | 2 | 3 | 4 | 5 | 6 | 7 | 8 |
|---|---|---|---|---|---|---|---|---|
| Group structure | 25 identical product groups of 20–25 | 25 identical product groups | 18–20 product groups for manufacturing and marketing | 18–20 product groups 5 technical groups 2 fabrication groups | 15 product groups 5 technical groups 2 fabrication groups 3 marketing groups 4 support activities | 15 product groups 5 technical groups 2 fabrication groups 3 marketing groups 4 support activities | 3 customer market groups in manufacturing 5 technical groups 2 fabrication groups 3 marketing groups 2 support activities | 5 activity groups in manufacturing 6 activity groups in fabrication 3 marketing groups 2 support activities |
| Division of labor | Within each group everyone performs same role—no permanent role specialization | Specialization within groups by technical, manufacturing, and sales-marketing functions | 3 specialties in each technical group; specialization by manufacturing and marketing in product groups | 3 specialties in each technical group; specialization by manufacturing and marketing within product groups | None in product groups 3 technical specialties 4 activity specialties 3 customer market specialties within marketing | 5 specialties in manufacturing 3 specialties in technical groups 3 specialties in marketing 6 specialties in fabrication | 5 specialties in manufacturing 3 specialties in technical groups 3 specialties in marketing 6 specialties in fabrication | 5 specialties with greater specialization within each in manufacturing 6 specialties in fabrication 3 specialties in technical groups 3 specialties in marketing |

| | | | Liaison roles between technical and product groups | Technical liaison between technical and product groups 5 activity integrators | Technical liaison between technical and product groups 20 activity integrators in manufacturing 3 customer market integrators | Technical liaison between technical and product groups 20 activity integrators 3 customer market integrators Marketing liaison between marketing and product groups | Technical liaison with manufacturing 3 customer market integrators 5 activity integrators | Technical liaison with manufacturing 3 customer market integrators 9 product integrators |
|---|---|---|---|---|---|---|---|---|
| Integrating roles between groups | None | None | | | | | | |
| Intergroup integrating processes | None | None | 2 teams material control team quality control team | 5 teams material control quality control information personnel marketing | 4 activity teams 3 customer market teams | 4 activity teams 3 customer market teams | 9 product teams in manufacturing 3 customer market teams | 9 product teams 3 customer market teams |

of coordination were judged as necessary to support the continual flow of new designs to the market.

## DETAILED DESIGN OF GROUPS—MANUFACTURING

The next phase of the design process focused on a more detailed design of jobs, rewards, and processes within the various groups. To accomplish the work, the task force expanded to include 12 employees currently working on the new product line. Then they split into three subgroups to consider the organization of marketing, manufacturing, and of the technical function. We shall follow the process within the manufacturing subgroup.

The subgroup concerning itself with manufacturing consisted of three members of the original task force plus two operators, two supervisors (from maintenance and production) and one each from personnel and production control. Their first task was to review the previous decisions and set some goals and time limits for their deliberations. They tentatively decided to consider the tasks and responsibilities of the 15 manufacturing teams, the remainder of the reward system and the information support system.

### Team Responsibilities

The basic responsibility for each manufacturing team would be to assemble and test a product line or class of products within one of the three market sectors. The team consisting of about 20 people would take components from the stock area after their purchase or fabrication, create subassemblies, perform intermediate tests, call in technical help if a component or subassembly performed improperly, create final assembly, perform final testing, and finally pack and prepare for shipment. In addition, team members would perform the support functions as well. All these activities would be performed with the maximum amount of autonomy consistent with overall coordination between the functions and the conceptual phase. Thus the team task would be a whole task and one with which the team members could identify, see the fruits of their labors, and have end-to-end responsibility. The team would control most of the factors necessary for the assembling and testing and would be party to influential groups controlling the other factors. This situation was believed to be sufficient to create the autonomy and identity necessary to make job performance instrumental to higher order needs satisfaction.

The division of team responsibilities within each group would be shared. There would be a division of labor but it would be temporary. The team would allocate tasks to its members and allow for a rotation in order that each member have a chance to perform each task. Each task itself would have a great deal of variety built into it. For example, the assembly operators, in addition to assembling an entire instrument with two to five other operators, would maintain their equipment, and design their work places. They would also take responsibility for improvements in the design of new methods, jointly schedule work to be done with others assembling the instruments, participate on the design team for a new instrument, review costs and suggest ideas to reduce them, perform standard tests on the instrument, respond to customer complaints about their instruments, train and help new employees, as well as perform less desirable portions of the work such as housekeeping. Thus, each task would include "managerial" as well as doing activities. The placement and coordination of these discretionary or managerial activities were made possible through the overall group structure.

The team members also would perform the support activities necessary for their product line and participate in the establishment of support activity policy through participation in support functional teams. Thus, a member or two would be temporarily responsible for quality, cost and information, maintenance, personnel or material control. Another representative would participate in the conceptual phases of new designs. It was also anticipated that many other temporary assignments and liaison activities would arise continuously as new products were introduced and problems surfaced. In this way, the tasks of the team members had the support activities, interdepartmental activities, and planning/controlling activities built into them in addition to the performing or doing activities. These jobs had sufficient challenge and gave sufficient control to team members to create the desired intrinsic motivation.

## Information System

The next step was to provide the information necessary to support the decisions that were to be made in the groups.

In order to support local discretion in the presence of interdependence, the decision makers, i.e., team members, would require access to global data to supplement the continuously available local data. The data would have to be updated continuously as design changes were made in the technical function or as the customer changed a delivery date, batch size, or product specification.

It was also recognized that the channeling of, filtering of, and selective access to crucial information would be a major determinant of the distribution of power. In situations of high uncertainty and change, individuals who played linking roles between the organization and the sources of the change could filter information which they fed into the decision process and thereby exercise considerable influence on the decision outcomes.[1] This lack of essential information could prevent the exercise of influence even when the organization structure and political ideology support it.[2] Therefore, in order that the group's autonomy be preserved, it would have to be given direct access to critical data.

Finally, as mentioned in Chapter 20 on intrinsic rewards, the team members would need feedback information on how well they were doing relative to the goals that had been set. When these data are not normally or easily available to the group, they must be acquired, transmitted, and displayed to the members. Thus, the information system design was to be examined from the point of view of its effect on the cognitive limits (providing global data base), on the power distribution, and on intrinsic motivation. The subgroup faced two problems—first, the acquisition of information lying outside the teams and then, the dissemination of that information within the team.

The first source of external data would be verbal contacts with other groups, teams, integrators, etc. Verbal contacts would provide the very current, "hot" information about events, changes, and priorities. Thus, data could be obtained through the team members' links with other activities and support teams and through liaison personnel from other functions working in the team's area. The second type was the formally collected information about costs, productivity, schedules, parts in stock, quality, etc. All of these data were to be made directly available to the teams. From the cognitive viewpoint, major classes of decisions would be identified as well as sources of information to support those decisions. Then media to transmit the data were suggested. For example, groups of two to five team members would make their own daily scheduling and work assignment decisions. In order to make these decisions effectively, this small group would need to know the delivery dates promised to customers, availability of parts, the suggested technically preferred sequence of operations, and whether deviations were possible, the design and configuration of the instrument and recent changes to it, etc. Some of the data, such as part availability, could be ascertained from routinely provided listings, in this case, of the inventory. Such listings would provide global status information necessary for rational local decision making. The rest of the information would be provided by individuals playing linking roles, in this case, the team's material control liaison. In between updatings, they would provide current information about the inventory in order to reflect quality rejects, engineering changes, and part usage since the previous update. Thus, the mechanisms would exist to provide global current data to support the local discretion. The exact details of the categories of information, frequency of reporting, computerization, etc. were left to the information function and the team's information liaison who would work on the functional team to design that system.

The manufacturing subgroup of the task force also analyzed the information system from a power perspective. Their purpose was to share power and essential information between and within groups. For example, groups would be given direct access to data not normally shared, such as correspondence from customers containing compliments and complaints about instruments. With both sales and manufacturing having the same information, a salesperson would be less likely to overemphasize some part of a letter in order to get his or her way. This would equalize the power derived from selective access to information. Indeed, team members would be expected to accompany sales people and technical representatives on occasional customer calls in order to get a firsthand impression or appreciation of customer problems and feelings.

This same power perspective would be applied to the internal workings of the groups as well. In the normal work group, the supervisor is the sole source of contact for all types of information and is therefore the most powerful member of the group.[3] However, with support functions included in the group, there would be a single source of contact for each type of decision but several people would perform the linking task. In addition the rotation of tasks would prevent the monopolization of key linking roles. These two features of the work design would spread the information and power, and increase the likelihood of an egalitarian decision process.

The analysis of information from a motivational point of view was simply to see that the group had access to performance data on goals they had set. This data could be provided and posted from the formal recording of data on cost, quality, and productivity and from other critical evaluations of the team's work such as customer letters. This historical information was believed to be adequate feedback so that the group could learn how well or poorly it was doing.

The second information problem faced by the task force subgroup was to provide for the within-group dissemination of information. The sharing of points of contacts would share power but would make it difficult to keep everyone informed. Therefore, every effort was made to collocate the team and its liaisons in a section of the factory along with a chart room in which information about cost, schedules, quality, etc. could be displayed for everyone to see. A sense of territory might develop as well. In addition, a comfortable place would be provided to encourage the many informal interactions needed to "get the word around." The factory itself would be designed physically to facilitate informal interaction.

It was felt that the verbal links with other functions and teams, the formal provision of cost and schedule data, access to correspondence, the chart room, and the architecture which facilitated interaction would prevent the manufacturing teams from becoming dependent on any information-rich group and allow them to exercise the discretion needed for intrinsic motivation.

### Reward System

The job design was the primary component of the reward system but the subgroup also had to consider the other human system policies so that they could enhance the motivation potential of the job design or at least not be detrimental to it. There were two broad categories of compensation and of person-job matching processes that were addressed.

**1. Compensation.** The compensation system was decided upon first. After a review of previous discussions, the newer members of the task force asked a series of questions of their own but eventually arrived at the conclusion that, due to the interdependence with a number of different groups and the continuous change of products and processes, the dysfunctional effects would outweigh the benefits of using any individual or group incentive scheme. They therefore chose to have a salary for each employee. The task force then focused on the basis for adding increments to that salary. Several alternatives were feasible.

The use of individual or group incentives was rejected because of the task force's inability to determine a valid standard, but the use of merit raises based on subjective assessments was still feasible. However, the task force's evaluation of this alternative was almost entirely negative. First, it was thought to be redundant. The choice of effort levels, of spontaneous behaviors, etc. was already encouraged by the job design. The added benefit of money incentives would be small. And second, there would still be side effects. In situations characterized by ambiguous standards, individual evaluations tend to be made by comparisons. This type of judgment would introduce competition. Finally, the subjective evaluation would be made by a boss and the reward power might reduce the egalitarian climate that was desired. Therefore, subjective merit increases were rejected.

A reasonable case could be made for seniority increases. If the intrinsic satisfactions provided by the task would influence most of the job-related behavior choices, the purpose of the salary and increments to it would be to attract people to the organization and reward their continued membership. A salary of sufficient amount will attract and hold people, and increments based on seniority will reward those who remain. This system is objective and relatively easy to administer. In addition, it reduces turnover and encourages long careers in the manufacturing function thereby reinforcing goal identification as the motivational basis.

The alternative to the seniority program is one which has been adopted in a number of new plants and which grants increments to salary based on the number of jobs learned.[4] This system rewards the learning, growing, and changing which would be necessary in the new factory. It was suggested that the number of jobs learned would be positively correlated with seniority. Therefore, the learning incentive would have the same benefits as the seniority program plus the benefit of reinforcing learning. The disadvantages would derive from the subjectivity of the decision as to when a job was learned and from possible variation in job difficulty. When rewards are given on the basis of a subjective judgment, some power goes to the party making the judgment, and the likelihood of disagreement and conflict increase. The likely parties in this case would be either a team leader, the integrator in the specialty being learned, or a group of peers, including the team leader and integrator, who have already learned the job. In addition, if some jobs were easier to learn or had more relaxed standards, team members would want access to the easy jobs. The possibilities for perceived inequities were far greater under any system which attempts to reward individual behaviors in uncertain, ambiguous situations. Thus, the leading incentive was more likely to generate disputes over fairness and is more expensive to administer.

The choice of the basis of salary increments distribution hinged on whether or not the team members would "naturally" rotate tasks and prevent a permanent form of division of labor from creeping in. After members of the subgroup reaffirm their preference for not having a permanent division of labor with manufacturing, they pondered whether the incentive was necessary to maintain homogeneous groups. Would people learn one or two tasks and then try to keep them, thereby creating a permanent division of labor? Could rules or group norms be established to support task rotation? Or must an incentive be established to guarantee rotation and occasionally unpleasant learning? Finally the subgroup chose the incentive with peer group evaluation. The others were rejected because some incentive was believed to be necessary and higher level coercion might have been necessary to force it. While final details were left to the personnel team, the recommendation of a 4 percent increase for rotation and 10 percent for qualification was agreed upon by the subgroup.

The last part of the compensation package was a recommendation for a plantwide profit-sharing plan. It was recognized that such a plan would have little motivational effect on day-to-day behavior choices because of the number of people and a once-a-year distribution. On the other hand, the job design would provide that source of motivation. Profit sharing was intended to provide an explicit, shared higher level goal and to suggest that the factory as a whole was the unit with which to identify. In addition, profit was an absolute and not dependent upon a comparison with a standard which could be disputed in ambiguous situations. Thus, all employees would be salaried, would receive increments to that salary based primarily upon the number of jobs they would learn to perform and secondarily upon seniority within any number classification. They would receive an annual distribution based on that year's profit.

**2. Person-job matching processes.** The other part of the human system to be determined was the process of recruitment, selection, assignment, training, transfer, and promotion. Again, the primary concern of the task force was to adopt processes which would support, or at least which would not contradict, the motivational bases of the work teams.[5] The organization design subgroup started with recruitment and worked through to transfer and promotion.

It was decided to place heavy emphasis on recruiting and selection. On one hand, the organization could not use specific tests for selection because jobs were not well defined and, indeed, were to be largely determined by the employees themselves. On the other hand, the organization needed to find people who would be willing to design their own jobs, who would participate in many work group decisions, who would be capable of higher order needs satisfaction, and who could satisfy their needs by means of job performance. To find these people, heavy emphasis was placed on recruiting at local vocational schools and technical colleges where electronics was taught. The approach was to use the team members themselves to call on the prospective employees and then to "lay it on the line"; that is, explain exactly how it was going to be. By explaining the advantages of autonomy and growth, the constant group interaction, the significant amounts of responsibility, and the disadvantages of acting as janitor, too, the prospects could choose themselves. The other choice was to be made by the group members themselves. Upon entry, the new member would work with another employee who would introduce him or her to the group, teach the immediate job, and generally show the newcomer how things were done. Thus, the work group itself would play the major role in recruiting, selecting, and training the new employee. All these processes were believed to be consistent with giving the individual some freedom of choice and keeping responsibility within the work group.

The assignment and rotation of jobs was a decision made by the teams themselves. New team members could be obtained from the other teams or the outside. An open position was to be posted and first preference given to employees on other teams who might be temporarily blocked in attempts to learn new positions. The team would do the choosing of new members. Some members would move out and start new teams during the growth phase. This new team start-up would provide the experienced employee an opportunity to exercise some leadership and a type of promotion. Particularly, qualified personnel would be able to move into the manufacturing or other integrating roles.

Thus, the task force felt this type of system would be consistent with the autonomous group structure determined by the previous organization design decisions. The people could make informed choices about the significant questions that impacted their work. They could influence resource allocations, select new members, and choose to move to new groups.


## THE GOVERNANCE SYSTEM

The entire task force reconvened after the subgroups completed their work on the detailed reward system. The final step in the design process was to agree upon a system of governance for conflict resolution. In essence, they needed to create a hierarchy of positions and analyze the vertical distribution of power. In preparation for this design, the task force reviewed the experiences of a number of the new factories and also the empirical literature on egalitarian organizations.

The group started with the leader function in the manufacturing teams. They chose to follow the example of Procter and Gamble and of Volvo's new Kalmar plant by eliminating the management-appointment supervisor role. This role has always been difficult as the occupant typically tries to play a traditional supervisory role.[6] In addition, there is less need for the position since the parts of the role are spread across a number of workers' roles. Instead, the group will select a group leader to act as a point of contact for problems not handled by liaison roles. The personnel functional team will select temporary group leaders for new groups. The function may very well be rotated like the others.

A second group of roles were designated as higher status roles. These were the functional specialists for information, material, manufacturing, quality, marketing, personnel, and technical areas and the three industry integrators. Each of these were to be staffed with older, more experienced, and higher paid persons. Each of the work groups would report to these people in the marketing and technical areas. In the manufacturing area, these roles would be integrating or consulting roles even though the role occupants would be more powerful. The task force chose to follow a strategy suggested by a similar role change in a grocery store chain.[7] Role occupants were to be selected and trained to play consulting roles.

It was felt that this hierarchy would give the direction necessary, resolve conflicts, and still permit the autonomy necessary for intrinsic motivation.

## SUMMARY

In summary, the structure that was chosen is one of many that could have served the purpose. The intention here was to illustrate one of the newer forms. It also illustrates a comprehensive design in which structure, reward system, people, task, and information system are designed to fit. The case gives an example of the contingency-theory approach to organization design.

## NOTES

1. A. Pettigrew 1972. Information control as a power resource. *Sociology,* (May): 187–204. A. Pettigrew 1973. *The politics of organizational decision making.* London: Tavistock. C. R. Hinings, D. J. Hickson, J. M. Pennings, and R. E. Schneck 1974. Structural conditions of intraorganizational power. *Administrative Science Quarterly,* (March): 22–44.

2. Proceedings of the *First International Conference on Participation and Management* 1972. Dubrovnik, Yugoslavia, December, 13–17, Vols. 1 and 2, especially J. Goricar, workers' self-management: ideal type—social reality. Vol. 1: 18–32, and Josip Obradovic, Distribution of participation in the process of decision making on problems related to the economic activity of the company. Vol. 2: 137–164.

3. H. Mintzberg 1973. *The nature of managerial work.* New York: Harper & Row.

4. R. E. Walton 1972. How to counter alienation in the plant. *Harvard Business Review,* (Nov.-Dec.): 70–81.

5. E. Schein 1972. *Organizational psychology.* (2nd ed.) Englewood Cliffs, N.J.: Prentice-Hall, Chapter 3.

6. Walton, p. 77.

7. R. A. Luke, P. Block, J. Davey, and V. Averch 1973. A structural approach to organization change. *J. Applied Behav. Sci.* 9, (5): 611–635.

# Indexes

# Author Index

# Subject Index

Two-factor theory, 268. *See also* Dual-factor theory

UAW, 227, 366
Uncertainty
  absorbing, 154
  definition, 36–39
  environmental, 50, 101–102, 201–221
  reduction, 75
  task, 35–39, 41–56, 61, 83–85, 87–94, 97–100, 102, 116–117, 148–150, 174–183, 188–189, 252–253.

*See also* Organization design, Task analysis
Unit manager. *See* Integrating roles
Unity of command, 16–18, 28, 167, 293

Valence, 269–288, 299, 302–304, 311, 318, 324, 326, 339–341, 343. *See also* Expectancy theory
Vertical integration, 50, 238. *See also* Strategic maneuvering
Volvo, 107, 217, 414

Zone of acceptance, 246–247, 292, 295. *See also* Area of acceptance